Praise for *Rigoberta Menc* 
the Story of All Poor Guate

"Riveting and masterfully researched ... devastating.... David Stoll's book has rightly caused an uproar."

—*The New Republic*

"Stoll's book is not an attempt to debunk Rigoberta's story, but to serve as a warning that elevating one version of history to cult status inevitably silences a multitude of others."

—*Kirkus Reviews*

"[Stoll's] generally supportive attitude toward the peasants' cause and his denunciation of the army's terror makes his book all the more convincing. This is provocative reading that's sure to shake up assumptions—and rile tempers—across the political spectrum."

—*Publishers Weekly*

"More than an exposé or refutation, Stoll's account presents an increasingly complex—and I think ultimately sympathetic—portrait of an exceptional, eloquent individual caught up in personal and historical tragedies doing her best to maintain her integrity. The strength of this book lies, not in its refutation of Rigoberta Menchú's story but in its inquiry into what the instant worldwide appeal of her autobiography tells us about how we choose to understand recent Guatemalan history, rural Guatemalan society, and more generally, revolutionary struggle and authenticity in the voices of others. This is a well-written, engaging (for some, enraging) book."

—John Watanabe
Dartmouth College

"The rule of all sociological study should be a simple one: no icons. Not Karl Marx; not Max Weber (sigh); not Michel Foucault; not anyone. Rigoberta Menchú should not be an exception. This book is going to explode over Guatemalan and Latin American studies."

—Timothy Wickham-Crowley
Georgetown University

"Stoll's frank examination of Rigoberta Menchu's life is the best biography to date of the indigenous leader.... The book is an important contribution to the truth."

—***Christian Century***

"If books such as Menchú's are going to be required reading, then Stoll's is more necessary still—as a corrective."

—***Atlanta Journal-Constitution***

"Based on ten years of research by Stoll, ... this book questions the veracity of Menchú's autobiography, specifically aspects of her family background, her childhood, land questions, and violent acts against her family. This volume will be important for Stoll's analysis of how the academic and political Left functions and uses symbols to idealize victims of oppression. A landmark publication that most academic and large public libraries should acquire."

—***Library Journal*** (starred review)

"*I, Rigoberta Menchú* is a widely used college text, and Stoll's book makes a pedagogically important complement to the issues raised by that text."

—Edward F. Fischer

Vanderbilt University

Rigoberta Menchú and the Story of All Poor Guatemalans

Rigoberta Menchú and the Story of All Poor Guatemalans

David Stoll

Westview
PRESS
A Member of the Perseus Books Group

Published in 1999 in the United States of America by Westview Press, 5500 Central Avenue, Boulder, Colorado 80301-2877, and in the United Kingdom by Westview Press, 12 Hid's Copse Road, Cumnor Hill, Oxford OX2 9JJ

Library of Congress Cataloging-in-Publication Data
Stoll, David, 1952–
Rigoberta Menchú and the story of all poor Guatemalans / David Stoll.
p. cm.
Includes bibliographical references and index.
ISBN 0-8133-3574-4 (hc).—0-8133-3694-5 (pbk.)
1. Menchú, Rigoberta. 2. Quiché women—Biography. 3. Human rights workers—Guatemala—Biography. 4. Mayas—Civil rights. 5. Mayas—Government relations. 6. Guatemala—Politics and government. 7. Guatemala—Ethnic relations. I. Title.
F1465.2.Q5M3885 1999
972.81'00497415—dc21
[b] 98-42832
CIP

The paper used in this publication meets the requirements of the American National Standard for Permanence of Paper for Printed Library Materials Z39.48-1984.

10 9 8 7 6 5 4 3 2 1

Contents

Preface viii
Acknowledgments xvi
Chronology xviii

1 The Story of All Poor Guatemalans 1

PART 1
Vicente Menchú and His Village

2 Uspantán as an Agricultural Frontier 15

3 The Struggle for Chimel 29

PART 2
Popular Revolutionary War

4 Revolutionary Justice Comes to Uspantán 43

5 The Death of Petrocinio 63

6 The Massacre at the Spanish Embassy 71

7 Vicente Menchú and the Committee for Campesino Unity 89

8 Vicente Menchú and the Guerrilla Army of the Poor 107

9 The Death of Juana Tum and the Destruction of Chimel 125

10 The Death Squads in Uspantán 141

PART 3

Vicente's Daughter and the Reinvention of Chimel

11 Where Was Rigoberta? 159

12 Rigoberta Joins the Revolutionary Movement 167

13 The Construction of *I, Rigoberta Menchú* 177

14 Rigoberta's Secret 189

PART 4

The Laureate Goes Home

15 The Campaign for the Nobel 203

16 The Lonely Life of a Nobel Laureate 219

17 Rigoberta and Redemption 231

18 The New Chimel 249

19 Rigoberta Leaves the Guerrilla Movement 265

20 Epitaph for an Eyewitness Account 273

Notes 285
Bibliography 311
Index 323

Preface

In 1992 a Guatemalan peasant won the Nobel Peace Prize. Except for people interested in Latin America or indigenous rights, the usual reaction was, "Rigoberta who?" Even for some acquainted with her name, Rigoberta Menchú was an unlikely peace laureate. Neither she nor anyone else had been able to end the civil war afflicting Guatemala since she was a child. Her public career had begun only a decade before, when she told an anthropologist in Paris the story of her life to the age of twenty-three. Born in a K'iche' Maya village, Rigoberta never went to school and had learned to speak Spanish only recently. She told of working on plantations as a child, being evicted by landlords, and learning how to organize. Then she told what soldiers and police had done to her family, terrible stories of death by torture and fire. The book created from the tape-recorded interviews, *I, Rigoberta Menchú* (1983), propelled her into a position of astonishing prominence for a person of her background. She became the best-known representative of the indigenous peoples of the Americas, a figure who could call on the pope, presidents of important countries, and the UN secretary-general.

What if much of Rigoberta's story is not true? This is an awkward question, especially for someone like myself who thinks the Nobel award was a good idea. Still, I decided that it must be asked. While interviewing survivors of political violence in the late 1980s, I began to come across significant problems in the life story she told at the start of her career. There is no doubt about the most important points: that a dictatorship massacred thousands of indigenous peasants, that the victims included half of Rigoberta's immediate family, that she fled to Mexico to save her life, and that she joined a revolutionary movement to liberate her country. On these points, Rigoberta's account is beyond challenge and deserves the attention it receives. But in other respects, such as the situation of her family and village before the war, other survivors gave me a rather different picture, which is borne out by the available records.

If part of the laureate's famous story is not true, does it matter? Perhaps not. Rigoberta won the peace prize on the five hundredth anniversary of the European colonization of the Americas. She has been the first to acknowledge that she received it, not for her own accomplishments but because she stands for a wider group of people who deserve international support. Whatever the facts of her particular life, the prize was intended to dramatize the historical debt owed to the native people of the Western Hemisphere. The prize was also intended to encourage peace talks in her homeland of Guatemala. Although Rigoberta's village background is an interesting issue, it is not the most important one.

Despite Rigoberta's merits as a Nobel laureate, I decided that the problems with her 1982 account should be brought to wider attention. To some readers, a critical examination of *I, Rigoberta Menchú* will not be welcome. It sounds like giving ammunition to the enemy—in this case the army that has dominated Guatemala's political life for decades and still has much for which to answer. If Rigoberta is fundamentally right about what the army did, why dissect a personal account that is inevitably selective, like any human memory of anything? If her story expresses a larger truth, surely a sympathetic anthropologist should not challenge its credibility. As a colleague reasoned with me: "Maybe it's the fault of the French anthropologist who edited her testimony. Maybe the accuracy of her memory was impaired by trauma. Maybe Mayan oral tradition is not grounded in the same definition of fact as a Western journalist's. It's not like she lied in court. She spent a week talking to someone in Paris! Maybe she was tired, maybe there were communications problems, maybe she was just doing what advocates always do—exaggerating a little."

I agree that it would be naive to challenge Rigoberta's account just because it is not a model of exactitude. Obviously, stories can be true even if they are selective in what they report. Indicting a Nobel laureate for inaccuracy is not the point of what follows. Even though Rigoberta is a genuine survivor of human rights violations, even though this makes her a symbol for victims of such abuses, the question remains: Why did such a catastrophe befall her family and village?

This is an issue meriting close examination, especially now that the war has ended, exhumation teams are digging up massacre victims, and truth commissions are publishing their findings. Where the contradictions between Rigoberta's version of events, that of neighbors, and the documentary record put her story into a different light is the problem of why the killing began locally. The most obvious answer—the well-attested brutality of the Guatemalan security forces—does not suffice as the only one. An underlying issue is far from settled. Was the guerrilla movement defeated in the early 1980s a popular struggle expressing the deepest aspirations of Rigoberta's people? Was it an inevitable reaction to grinding oppression, by people who felt they had no other choice?

On this question *I, Rigoberta Menchú* carries great authority, more than it deserves in my judgment. Although the laureate's views have changed over the years, in 1982 she presented herself as an eyewitness to the mobilization of her people. There is no stronger claim to authority, and most readers have taken her at her word in a way that matters beyond the confines of her own country. For some of my colleagues, dissecting the legacy of guerrilla warfare is like beating a dead horse. It is indeed a strategy that much of the Latin American left would appear to have repudiated. But it continues to be romanticized, as illustrated by the aura surrounding Che Guevara, and it has hardly disappeared, as demonstrated by news reports from Colombia, Peru, and Mexico.

What I discovered in Rigoberta's hometown is not very surprising in view of how celebrities and movements mythologize themselves. When the future Nobel laureate told her story in 1982, she drastically revised the prewar experience of her village to suit the needs of the revolutionary organization she had joined. In her telling, a tragic convergence of military moves and local vendettas became a popular movement that, at least in her area, probably never existed. Rigoberta told her story well enough that it became invested with all the authority that a story of terrible suffering can assume. From the unquestionable atrocities of the Guatemalan army, her credibility stretched farther than it should have, into the murkier background question of why the violence occurred. The result was to mystify the conditions facing peasants, what they thought their problems were, how the killing started, and how they reacted to it.

That a valuable symbol can also be misleading is the paradox that obliged me to write this book. The problem does not exist simply on the level of what did and did not happen in one corner of Guatemala. It also extends into the international apparatus for reporting human rights violations, reacting to them, and interpreting their implications for the future—the world of human rights activism, journalism, and scholarship. In a world swayed by the mass media, in which nations and peoples live or die by their ability to catch international attention, how do the gatekeepers of communication deal with the mixture of truth and falsehood in any movement's portrayal of itself, including those we feel morally obliged to support? Must we resign ourselves to be apologists for one side or the other?

In Guatemala I learned that it was impossible to discuss political violence without trespassing upon powerful symbols that assume what needs to be discussed, cloaking the debatable with the mantle of unquestionability. Like any symbol of sacrificial commitment, Rigoberta's image commands loyalty by fusing together a great deal of experience, feeling, and conviction. The destruction of her family stands for the deaths of thousands of others for whom justice could never be done. This was Rigoberta's purpose in telling her story the way that she did: It enabled her to focus international condemnation on an institution that deserved it, the Guatemalan army. But the condensing power of such a symbol comes at a cost.

When a person becomes a symbol for a cause, the complexity of a particular life is concealed in order to turn it into a representative life. So is the complexity of the situation being represented. Sooner or later, in one form or another, what the legend conceals will force its way back to our attention. The contradictions glossed over by a heroic figure will not go away because we wish to ignore them. In Guatemala much of what needs to be debated about the last half century of revolution and counterrevolution, bloodshed and peacemaking, is still wrapped up in symbols that prevent frank discussion. What was filtered out of *I, Rigoberta Menchú,* and what often gets filtered out of discussions about Guatemala, is the subject of this book.

Not at issue is Rigoberta's choice as a Nobel laureate or the larger truth she told about the violence. Unfortunately, such distinctions do not mean much to Rigoberta and some of her supporters, who regard challenges to her version of events as racist. In 1997 she produced a new book about her life, especially the fifteen years since the last one. *Crossing Borders* was, according to rumor, going to correct factual problems with the previous account. As it turns out, the new book is revealing but not revelatory. Although Rigoberta diverges from her earlier story in interesting ways, she makes no retractions.

Earlier in 1997, I sent the laureate an outline of my findings, asked for an interview, and offered to send her a copy of the manuscript for this book. There was no reply. To a second letter by certified mail, the head of Rigoberta's New York office responded that Rigoberta was too busy for an interview. But he did ask for a copy of my manuscript, which I sent in June, again by certified mail. Half a year later, Rigoberta attacked the editor of *I, Rigoberta Menchú,* the anthropologist Elisabeth Burgos. "That is not my book," she said of her first life story. "It is a book by Elisabeth Burgos. It is not my work; it is a work that does not belong to me morally, politically, or economically." She accused Elisabeth of excluding her from the editorial process, depriving her of the royalties, and despoiling her of her testimony. "Anyone who has doubts about the work should go to Ms. Burgos," she said.[1] Fortunately, I already had.

What follows is not a biography of the Nobel laureate. Instead, I compare her 1982 life story with local testimony and documentary sources. Then I suggest why the story took the shape it did, as well as why it appealed to an international audience before being transmitted back home, where Guatemalans have made it part of a national debate about who they are. The first chapter describes how my interviewing in northern Quiché Department called into question the most widely read account of the Guatemalan violence. Published in 1983, *I, Rigoberta Menchú* used the compelling story of one family to personify the moral dualisms of a society at war with itself. With its noble Indians and evil landlords, ancestral ethnic hatred and revolutionary martyrdom, Rigoberta's story became a deeply influential portrait of the violence in Guatemala.

Vicente Menchú and His Village

The tragedies that befell families like the Menchús are undeniable. How these were understood by the revolutionary movement, its foreign supporters, and human rights activists is another matter. What guerrilla strategists wished to find among Mayan peasants were cohesive communities, in subjection to landlords and eager to take up arms. What they stepped into was rather different, as can be seen from the case of Rigoberta's father, Vicente; his struggle for land; and who he had to fight to get it. Chapters 2 and 3 put the supposed imperative of guerrilla warfare into the context of one locality that, in Rigoberta's retelling, would become archetypal. *I, Rigoberta Menchú* encouraged the Guatemalan left and its foreign supporters to continue viewing the countryside as a contest among social classes, ethnic blocs, and structural forces. Meanwhile, the dramas played out in peasant villages burlesqued the grand paradigms.

Popular Revolutionary War

In the second part of the book, I look at how Rigoberta's father and neighbors responded to the Guerrilla Army of the Poor (EGP), an organization led by a friend and admirer of Che Guevara. Chapter 4 introduces army rule in Guatemala and the armed opposition, then tells how the two sides descended on Uspantán to commit the first political killings there in August 1979. The discrepancies between *I, Rigoberta Menchú* and local accounts raise a host of issues, among them: Why did the guerrillas want to make connections with men like Vicente Menchú? Did he and other Uspantán peasants have any idea of the sacrifices that the EGP expected them to make? Did they join for any reason but to defend themselves from the army's reprisals?

A recurring question is, Whom to believe? How do we weigh the reliability of Rigoberta's account against the versions I collected and documentary sources? Chapter 5 compares various accounts of the murder of Rigoberta's brother Petrocinio, the emotional climax of *I, Rigoberta Menchú*. Although the laureate's version of what happened is true in important ways, I show that it cannot be the eyewitness account it purports to be. Chapter 6 describes the death of Rigoberta's father during a protest at the Spanish embassy in Guatemala City, in a conflagration that took the lives of thirty-six people. A careful look at how the fire started will suggest the revolutionary movement's ability to turn an unfounded version of events into an internationally accepted fact.

The next two chapters explore Vicente Menchú's relation to two revolutionary organizations, the Committee for Campesino Unity (CUC) and the EGP, and how the war's arrival further divided his community. The key question in Chapter 7 is whether CUC was a grassroots response by an increasingly oppressed peasantry, or whether the EGP invented it as a way to lure peasants into confronting the state. Chapter 8 explores the implications of EGP strategy for Uspantán peasants, specifically, the idea that they could be organized to defeat an army with a well-deserved reputation for brutality. Chapters 9 and 10 describe the climax of army repression in Uspantán, including the death of Rigoberta's mother and her brother Victor. Although no single source on such a terror-filled situation can be taken as authoritative, I hope to convince readers that the EGP never developed the strong social base in Uspantán that Rigoberta would have us believe.

Vicente's Daughter and the Reinvention of Chimel

Whose war, then, was this? Until now, our main subject has been Vicente Menchú, the peasant patriarch eulogized in his daughter's story, and contradictory interpretations of his life. Chapters 11 and 12 return to Rigoberta, her whereabouts as her family was hunted down, and how she found a new home in the political apparatus of the Guerrilla Army of the Poor. Chapters 13 and 14 explore the question of whether *I, Rigoberta Menchú* was really her story. As soon as the book appeared, skeptics wondered how an unschooled peasant, illiterate and monolingual until a few years before, could be so fluent with concepts like class, ethnicity, culture, identity, and revolution.

Suspicion was quick to fall on the anthropologist who tape-recorded Rigoberta in Paris and turned her stories into a book. Elisabeth Burgos was the wife of Régis Debray, the French Marxist who theorized that the rest of Latin America could follow the guerrilla road to revolution pioneered by Fidel Castro and Che Guevara in Cuba. Cuban promotion of Rigoberta and Elisabeth's book suggested that it might be speaking for the guerrillas more than for peasants. The internecine disputes dividing Rigoberta's neighbors dropped out of the story, making armed struggle sound like an inevitable reaction to oppression, at a time when Mayas were desperate to escape the violence. *I, Rigoberta Menchú* became a way to mobilize foreign support for a wounded, retreating insurgency.

The Laureate Goes Home

Rigoberta was not well known in Guatemala until the campaign to give her the Nobel Peace Prize. Yet by 1992 her story had translated right-wing terror in a small, obscure country into international symbolism that could be used to oppose it. Even though the army had won militarily and politically, the guerrillas fought on from the margins to maintain their claim to be a national bargaining partner. The more important war was fought abroad, through images, and it is the international propaganda war that the guerrillas won with the help of *I, Rigoberta Menchú* as a testimonial linchpin for their claims.

Chapters 15 and 16 follow Rigoberta's path to the Nobel Prize and the challenges she faced in the Guatemalan peace process, which did not halt the fighting for another four years, until 1996. As foreign activists focused on the army's abuses, peasant survivors complained that they were "caught in the crossfire"—from the guerrillas as well as soldiers. Rigoberta had to deal with metaphorical crossfire from four directions: the army, the EGP, the international community, and her own people. Although foreigners presumed that she was a leader, few Mayan peasants supported the armed struggle to which she was mortgaged.

Chapter 17 addresses the question of why so many foreign activists and scholars have attributed such authority to her story. The larger-than-life Rigoberta I will explain as an icon, a quasi-sacred symbol that resolves contradictions for the people who believe in it in a way that is not to be questioned. Chapter 18 returns to Uspantán to look at how Chimel's survivors overcame countless obstacles to resettle their land and how the Menchús are remembered locally. Chapter 19 describes how Rigoberta's efforts to represent her people have led her away from the guerrilla movement that launched her career.

To show how misleading it is to take Rigoberta's story at face value, I will have to distinguish between what can be corroborated and what cannot, what is probable and what is highly improbable. However, identifying factual shortcomings is only a means to an end. The underlying problem is not how Rigoberta told her story, but how well-intentioned foreigners have chosen to interpret it. Especially now that many academics are eager to deconstruct any claim to settled truth, Rigoberta's story should have been compared with others. If she wanted to blame the violence entirely on the army and support the guerrillas, she had the right to a hearing. So did the many Mayas who also blamed the guerrillas for the violence and did not feel represented by them. Such differences begged for comparison. Yet Rigoberta's version was so attractive to so many foreigners that Mayas who repudiated the guerrillas were often ignored or discounted. This bolstered the claim that the guerrillas represented the mass of Mayan peasants, long after there was good reason to doubt this.

The air of sacrilege about questioning the reliability of *I, Rigoberta Menchú* gives us at least three reasons to do so. The first is what it can tell us about the Guatemalan violence, its popular roots, and how these were mythologized to meet the needs of the revolutionary movement and its supporters. The second is to challenge underlying romantic assumptions about indigenous people and guerrilla warfare, for which Rigoberta's people will not be the last to pay dearly. The third is to raise questions about a new standard of truth gaining ground in the humanities and social sciences.

The premise of the new orthodoxy is that Western forms of knowledge, such as the empirical approach adopted here, are fatally compromised by racism and other forms of domination. Responsible scholars must therefore identify with the oppressed, relegating much of what we think we know about them to the dustbin of colonialism. The new basis of authority consists of letting subalterns speak for themselves, agonizing over any hint of complicity with the system that oppresses them, and situating oneself in relation to fashionable theorists. Certainly there is much to be said for listening, but which voices are we supposed to listen to? What I will show in the case of *I, Rigoberta Menchú* is that critical theory can end up revolving around romantic conceptions of indigenous people, mythologies that can be used to sacrifice them for larger causes.

David Stoll

Acknowledgments

In keeping with ethical norms in anthropology, particularly where sources could be subject to reprisal, I have avoided identifying them by name. For the sake of coherence, I have identified certain families, particularly those involved in land feuds, but usually not individuals if they are still living. One of the few exceptions is Rigoberta's only surviving brother, who played a heroic role in recovering his father's land and could not remain unidentified without suppressing an important part of the story. I have also named various individuals, none currently living in the area or interviewed by me, who many Uspantanos identify as assassins for the Guatemalan army. Unattributed quotations come from my interviews between 1988 and 1997, mainly in the *municipio* (district) of Uspantán.

The interviewing was done primarily in Spanish, a language in which many K'iche' Mayas are proficient. From 1994 to 1996, I was often accompanied by Barbara Bocek, an archeologist from Stanford University working as a Peace Corps volunteer. Once I began to work with Barb, it became hard to understand how I accomplished much without her. Fluent in K'iche' Maya, she took the lead in dozens of interviews, especially with widows who spoke little Spanish. Not everything we heard supports my argument, and what is incongruent I have reported as well, so that readers can draw different conclusions if they wish. Despite the limitations of what follows, I hope it will encourage more survivors of these events to speak out, which could lead to a better interpretation in the future.

This book was written as part of a larger study of the impact of human rights symbolism on the peace process in northern Quiché Department. I am indebted to the Harry Frank Guggenheim Foundation for two years of generous support; to the Woodrow Wilson International Center for Scholars for a year's fellowship; and to the Bellagio Center for a month's residency at Lake Como. Over the past year, my colleagues at Middlebury College have provided encouragement on a number of occasions when it was needed. I would also like to thank my colleagues elsewhere, many of whom had doubts about the wisdom of this project or advised me to proceed differently than I did. I appreciate their disagreements as much as their suggestions. They include Jeffrey Ehrenreich, Stener Ekern, Henrik Hovland, Susan Burgerman, Abigail Adams, Antonella Fabri, Diane Nelson, Daniel H. Levine, Mitchell Seligson, Paul Kobrak, Pascual Huwart, Pietro and Kate Venezia, Betty Adams, Lynn Roberts, Jan Lundius, David Holiday, Tania Palencia, Jan Rus, Joseph Gaughan, Michael Brown, Mick and Tico Taussig, Rachel Moore, Kamala Visweswaran, Elizabeth and Jacqueline Sutton, Sharon Stancliff, Robert Carlsen, Duncan Earle, Erica Verrillo, Richard Wilson, Manuela Canton Delgado, Daniel Rothenberg, Victoria Sanford, Kathy Dill, Norman Stolzoff, Terri Shaw, Robert Packenham, Dave Thomas, Steve Tullberg, Elaine and Stephen Elliott, Mary Jo McConahay, Joel Simon, Colum Lynch, Victor Perera, Michael Shawcross, and Paul Goepfert.

I am also indebted to Timothy Wickham-Crowley, Richard N. Adams, Ted Fischer, and John Watanabe for their comments to Westview Press, with apologies that I was not able to follow more of their suggestions. Without Karl Yambert of Westview Press, this book would still be unpublished. Of the many people I interviewed, I am able to thank by name only two: Elisabeth Burgos and Ambassador Máximo Cajal y López. My gratitude to them is profound, but no more than to the many people of Uspantán who were so courageous in sharing their experiences with myself and Barbara Bocek. This book is dedicated to the memory of their loved ones.

D. S.

Chronology

1530	Spaniards conquer the Mayan kingdom of Uspantán in what is now the Department of El Quiché.
1821	Guatemala becomes independent from Spain.
1920	Vicente Menchú is born.
1944	A democratic revolution overthrows the last of the Liberal dictators, General Jorge Ubico.
Late 1940s	Vicente Menchú marries Juana Tum Cotojá and starts farming at the future site of Chimel.
1954	The CIA overthrows President Jacobo Arbenz and installs Colonel Carlos Castillo Armas as the new president.
1959	Rigoberta Menchú Tum is born in the hamlet of Chimel, fifteen kilometers northeast of the town of Uspantán, administrative seat of the *municipio* of that name.
1966–1967	The Guatemalan army defeats a Marxist guerrilla movement in eastern Guatemala. In Uspantán a dispute over 151 hectares escalates between Vicente Menchú and his in-laws, the Tums of Laguna Danta.
1972	The future Guerrilla Army of the Poor (EGP) starts organizing in the Ixcán rain forest northwest of Uspantán.
1978	The Committee for Campesino Unity makes its first public declaration.
1979	EGP columns hold a rally in the town of Uspantán (April 29), visit Chimel for the first time (possibly May 3), and kill two ladino neighbors, Honorio García and Eliu Martínez (August 12). The army kidnaps Rigoberta's younger brother, Petrocinio Menchú (September 9). Vicente Menchú leads a protest at the Guatemalan congress (September 26). The army murders Petrocinio and six other prisoners at the town of Chajul (December 6). The National Institute for Agrarian Transformation gives Chimel provisional title to 2,753 hectares of land (December 28).
1980	Vicente Menchú and thirty-five others die during a protest at the Spanish embassy in Guatemala City (January 31). The army kidnaps Rigoberta's mother, Juana Tum Cotojá (April 19). Chimel is attacked for the first time (December 24).

1982	From exile in Mexico, Rigoberta visits Paris and tells her life story to the anthropologist Elisabeth Burgos-Debray. Four guerrilla organizations, including the Guerrilla Army of the Poor, form the Guatemalan National Revolutionary Union (URNG).
1983	*I, Rigoberta Menchú* is published in Spanish. Rigoberta's brothers Victor and Nicolás surrender to the army; Victor is killed trying to escape.
1986	Nicolás Menchú begins petitioning to recover Chimel.
1991	The Guatemalan government and the URNG start peace negotiations.
1992	Rigoberta receives the Nobel Peace Prize.
1996	The Guatemalan government and the URNG sign a UN-sponsored agreement ending more than three decades of civil war.
1998	Rigoberta publishes a new account of her life, *Crossing Borders*. UN- and Catholic-sponsored truth commissions prepare their reports.

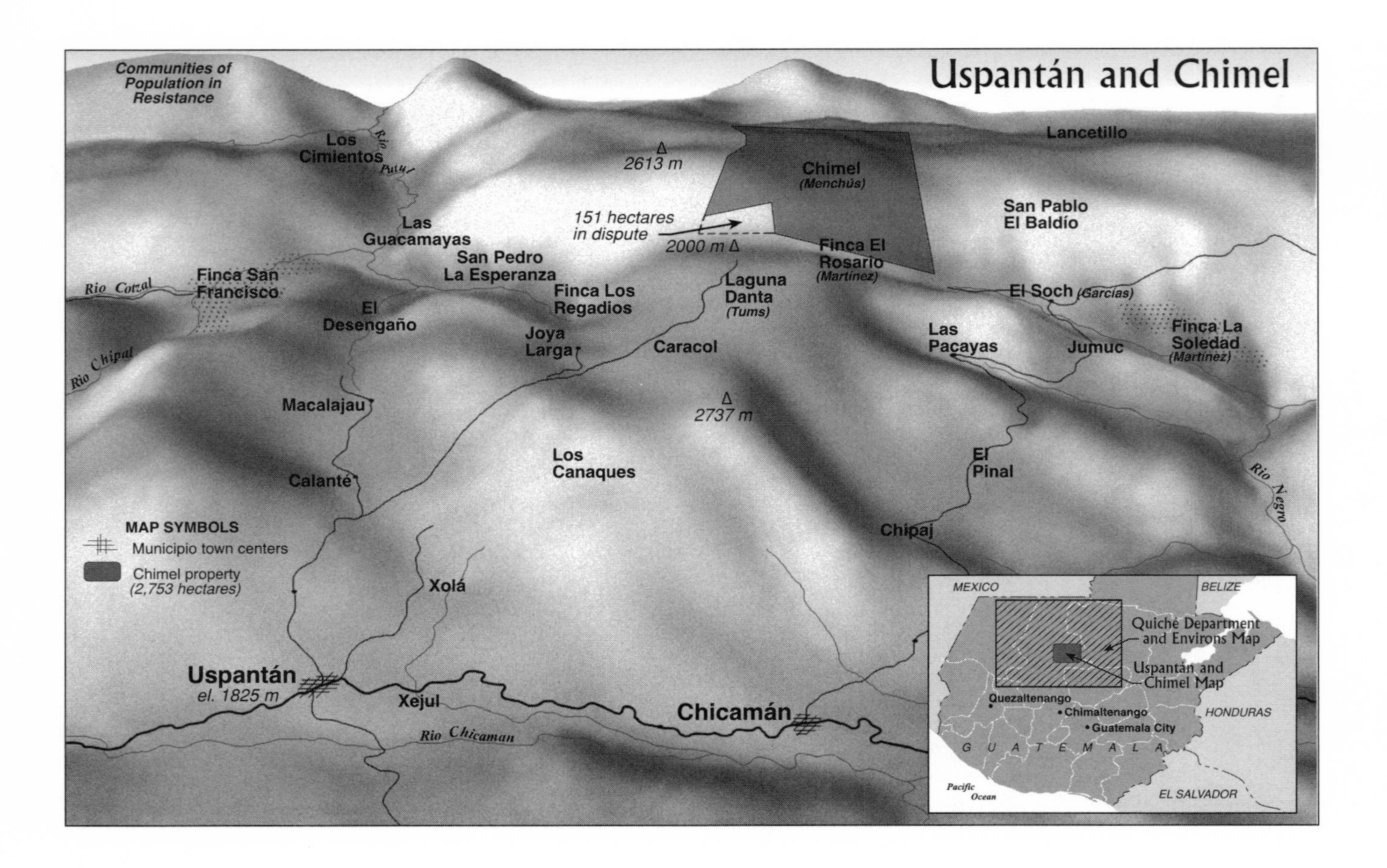
Uspantán and Chimel
Communities of Population in Resistance
Los Cimientos
Rio Putul
2613 m
Chimel (Menchús)
Lancetillo
San Pablo El Baldío
151 hectares in dispute
2000 m
Las Guacamayas
San Pedro La Esperanza
Finca El Rosario (Martínez)
Rio Cotzal
Finca San Francisco
Finca Los Regadios
Laguna Danta (Tums)
El Soch (Garcías)
El Desengaño
Joya Larga
Caracol
Las Pacayas
Jumuc
Finca La Soledad (Martínez)
Rio Chipal
Macalajau
2737 m
Los Canaques
El Pinal
Calanté
Rio Negro
Chipaj
MAP SYMBOLS
Municipio town centers
Chimel property (2,753 hectares)
Xolá
Uspantán
el. 1825 m
Xejul
Chicamán
Rio Chicaman
MEXICO
BELIZE
Quiché Department and Environs Map
Uspantán and Chimel Map
Quezaltenango
Chimaltenango
Guatemala City
HONDURAS
G U A T E M A L A
Pacific Ocean
EL SALVADOR

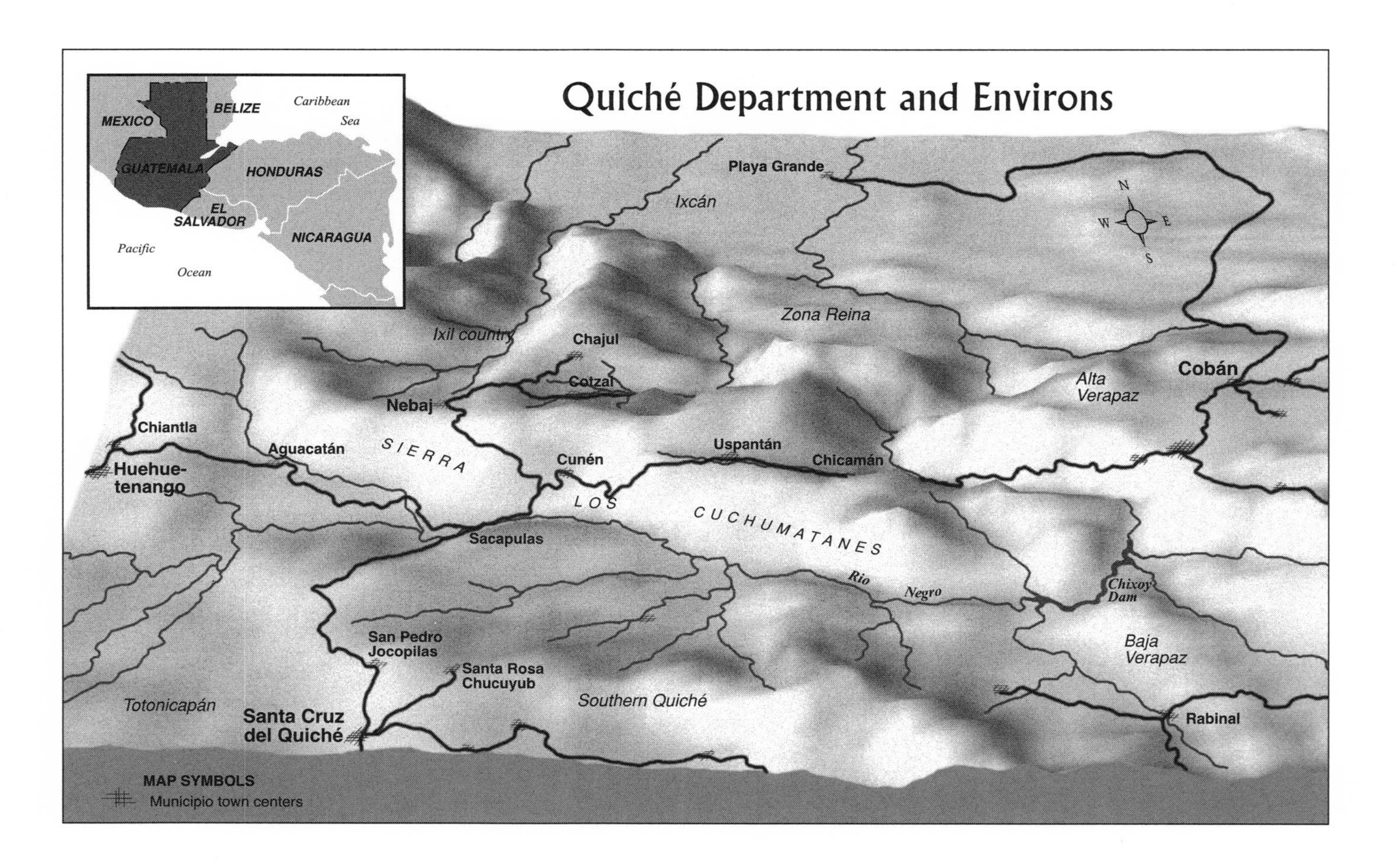
Quiché Department and Environs
MEXICO
BELIZE
Caribbean
Sea
GUATEMALA
HONDURAS
EL
SALVADOR
NICARAGUA
Pacific
Ocean
Playa Grande
Ixcán
N
W
E
S
Zona Reina
Ixil country
Chajul
Cotzal
Cobán
Alta
Verapaz
Nebaj
Chiantla
Aguacatán
SIERRA
Uspantán
Cunén
Chicamán
Huehue-
tenango
LOS
CUCHUMATANES
Sacapulas
Rio
Negro
Chixoy
Dam
Baja
Verapaz
San Pedro
Jocopilas
Santa Rosa
Chucuyub
Southern Quiché
Totonicapán
Santa Cruz
del Quiché
Rabinal
MAP SYMBOLS
Municipio town centers

Rigoberta Menchú and the Story of All Poor Guatemalans

1

The Story of All Poor Guatemalans

> *My name is Rigoberta Menchú. I am twenty three years old. This is my testimony. I didn't learn it from a book and I didn't learn it alone. I'd like to stress that it's not only* my *life, it's also the testimony of my people. . . . The important thing is that what has happened to me has happened to many other people too: My story is the story of all poor Guatemalans. My personal experience is the reality of a whole people.*
>
> **—*I, Rigoberta Menchú,* p. 1**

Gingerly, I was feeling my way into the Ixil Maya town of Chajul, in the western highlands of Guatemala. Except for the occasional fiesta, it was a quiet place of white-washed adobe and red-tiled roofs, where children played ingenious games with pieces of junk and adults were more polite than friendly. The majority spoke a bit of Spanish, but their own language was Ixil (pronounced ee-sheel), one of the twenty forms of Maya spoken by Guatemalans descended from the pre-Columbian civilization. In the early 1980s, the Guatemalan army burned down all the surrounding villages in order to defeat a Marxist-led guerrilla movement. Occasionally the army still brought in prisoners from the surrounding mountains, to be trucked off to an unknown fate. Or it flung down a corpse in the plaza as a warning of what happened to subversives. Under the circumstances, I had no right to expect that anyone would be willing to talk about what had happened—not while peasant guerrillas continued to fight, certain villages remained under their control, and the rest of the population was under the army's suspicious eye.

Fortunately, some Chajules were willing to help me. Among them was an elder named Domingo. Now that he had related the town's sufferings, I was asking about other incidents in human rights reports, to see if he could corroborate them. Suddenly Domingo was giving me a puzzled look. One of my questions had caught him off guard. The army burned prisoners alive in the town plaza? Not here, he said. Yet this is what I had read in *I, Rigoberta Menchú*, the life story of the young K'iche' Maya woman who, a few years later, won the Nobel Peace Prize.[1]

Domingo and I were on the main street, looking toward the old colonial church that towers over the plaza. It was the plaza where, according to the book that made Rigoberta famous, soldiers lined up twenty-three prisoners including her younger brother Petrocinio. The captives were disfigured from weeks of torture, their bodies were swollen like bladders, and pus oozed from their wounds. Methodically, the soldiers scissored off the prisoners' clothes, to show their families how each injury had been inflicted by a different instrument of torture. Following an anticommunist harangue, the soldiers soaked the captives in gasoline and set them afire. With her own eyes, Rigoberta had watched her brother writhe to death.[2] This was the climactic passage of her book, reprinted in magazines and read aloud at conferences, with the hall darkened except for a spotlight on the narrator. Yet the army had never burned prisoners alive in the town plaza, Domingo said, and he was the first of seven townsmen who told me the same.

Quiché Department, where Chajul is located and Rigoberta was born, is inhabited by peasants with a seemingly unshakable dedication to growing maize. There is an epic quality to its mountains and valleys, and Quiché strikes many visitors as beautiful. But up close the mountainsides are scarred by deforestation and erosion. Many of the corn patches are steep enough to lose your footing. They would not be worth cultivating unless you were short of land, which most of the population is. The terrain is so unpromising that after the Spanish conquered it in the sixteenth century, they turned elsewhere in their search for wealth. Instead of seizing estates for themselves, they handed the region over to Catholic missionaries. Only a century ago did boondock capitalism come to Quiché, in the form of outsiders who used liquor to lure Indians into debt and march them off to plantations. By the 1970s the descendants of several heavily exploited generations were defending their rights more effectively than before. But if the worst had ended, there were still plenty of accumulated grievances.

Arguably this is why a group called the Guerrilla Army of the Poor (EGP) suddenly became a popular movement at the end of the 1970s. The brief liberation it effected was followed by a crushing military occupation. Like other guerrilla strongholds of the 1980s—such as Chalatenango and Morazán Departments in El Salvador and Ayacucho Province in Peru—Quiché became a burned-over district. In 1981–1982 the war here and in other parts of the Guatemalan highlands killed an estimated 35,000 people and displaced hundreds of thousands of others. Afterward, one item not in short supply was the horror story. In Chajul, for alleged contacts with guerrillas, soldiers hung dozens of civilians from the balcony of the town hall. Others had their throats cut and were left to be eaten by dogs.

Still others died inside houses that soldiers turned into funeral pyres. And this is not to mention the widows (645) and orphans (1,425). To defeat an invisible enemy, the army killed thousands of civilians in Chajul and the two other Ixil municipios. Hundreds more were killed by the guerrillas to keep their wavering followers in line.[3]

The most widely read account of the Guatemalan violence came from a twenty-three-year-old woman who grew up in the nearby municipio of Uspantán. Rigoberta Menchú was born in a peasant village where Spanish was a foreign language and nearly everyone was illiterate. Instead of reciting massacres and death counts at numbing length, Rigoberta told the story of her life into a tape recorder, in Spanish rather than her native language of K'iche' Maya, for a week in Paris in 1982. The interviewer, an anthropologist named Elisabeth Burgos-Debray, transcribed the results, put them into chronological order, and published them as a *testimonio*, or oral autobiography, running 247 pages in English.

Rigoberta's story includes warm memories of her childhood in an indigenous village living in harmony with itself and nature. But her parents are so poor that every year they and their children go to Guatemala's South Coast, to work for miserable wages harvesting coffee and cotton. Conditions are so appalling on the *fincas* (plantations) that two of her brothers die there. Back in the highlands Rigoberta's father, Vicente Menchú, starts a settlement called Chimel at the edge of the forest north of Uspantán. The hero of his daughter's account, Vicente faces two enemies in his struggle for land. The first consists of nearby plantation owners, nonindigenous *ladinos*, who claim the land for themselves. On two occasions plantation thugs throw the Menchús and their neighbors out of their houses. Vicente is also thrown into prison twice and beaten so badly that he requires nearly a year of hospitalization.[4]

Vicente's other enemy is the government's National Institute for Agrarian Transformation (INTA). In theory INTA helps peasants obtain title to public land, but according to Rigoberta what it really does is help landlords expand their estates. There ensues a purgatory of threats from surveyors, summons to the capital, and pressure to sign mysterious documents. To pay for the lawyers, secretaries, and witnesses needed to free Vicente from prison, the entire family submits to further wage exploitation. Rigoberta goes to Guatemala City to work for a wealthy family who feed their dog better than her.[5] Her father becomes involved in peasant unions and, after 1977, is away much of the time, living in clandestinity and organizing other peasants facing the same threats. After years of persecution, he helps start the legendary Committee for Campesino Unity (CUC), a peasant organization that joins the guerrilla movement.

In the course of these events, the adolescent Rigoberta acquires a profound revolutionary consciousness. Like her father, she becomes a catechist (lay leader) for the Catholic Church. When the army raids villages, she teaches them to defend themselves by digging stake pits, manufacturing Molotov cocktails, even capturing stray soldiers. But self-defense fails to protect her family from being devoured by atrocities. First there is the kidnapping of her younger brother Petrocinio, who after weeks of torture is burned to death at Chajul. Then her father goes to the capital to lead protesters who, in a desperate bid for attention, occupy the Spanish embassy on January 31, 1980.

In a crime reported around the world, riot police assault the embassy. Vicente Menchú and thirty-five other people die in the ensuing fire, which is widely blamed on an incendiary device launched by the police. International opinion is outraged. But that is no protection for Rigoberta's family. Next the army kidnaps her mother, who is raped and tortured to death. In homage to her martyred parents, Rigoberta becomes an organizer for the Committee for Campesino Unity. Never having had the chance to attend school, she learns to speak Spanish with the help of priests and nuns. As she becomes a leader in her own right, the security forces pick up her trail, and she escapes to Mexico.

Ten years after telling her story to Elisabeth Burgos, Rigoberta received the Nobel Peace Prize, as a representative of indigenous peoples on the 500th anniversary of the European colonization of the Americas. The Nobel Committee also wanted to encourage the stalled peace talks between the Guatemalan government and its guerrilla adversaries in the Guatemalan National Revolutionary Union (URNG). In theory Rigoberta's homeland had returned to democracy, but the army still imposed narrow parameters on what could be said and done. Perhaps international recognition for one of its victims would encourage the army to make concessions.

An International Symbol for Human Rights

We won the Nobel for literature for a country that is illiterate, and now we win the Nobel for peace for a war that never ends.

—Old man in the street, 1993[6]

When *I, Rigoberta Menchú* appeared in 1983, no one imagined that the narrator would become a Nobel laureate. Soon it was clear that this was one of the most powerful narratives to come out of Latin America in recent times. The book had quite an impact on readers, including many who know Guatemala well. Because it was effectively banned from Rigoberta's country during the 1980s, most readers were foreigners, who could pick up the book in any of eleven languages into which the original Spanish was translated. Rigoberta became a well-known figure on the human rights circuit in Europe and North America, served on UN commissions, and was showered with honorary doctorates. A few months before the Nobel, she was sorting through 260 international invitations, including one from the prime minister of Austria and another from the queen of England. Two years later she said there were more than seven thousand.[7]

One reason Rigoberta's story achieved such credibility is that, to anyone familiar with how native people have been dispossessed by colonialism, it sounded all too familiar. Her experiences were an amazing microcosm of the wider processes that over the past five hundred years have taken the land of indigenous people, exploited their labor, and reduced them to second-class citizens in their own countries. Standing in for European colonizers were their contemporary heirs, the Spanish-speaking whites and mestizos known as ladinos.

As the chronicle of a woman belonging to an oppressed racial group, *I, Rigoberta Menchú* spoke to wider concerns in intellectual life. In North American universities, it became part of a hotly debated new canon at the intersection of feminism, ethnic studies, and literature known as multiculturalism. For conservatives, the book exemplified the displacement of Western classics by Marxist diatribes.[8] To their ears, Rigoberta's references to cultural resistance, liberation theology, and armed struggle sounded like an improbable pastiche of politically correct jargon. Even well-wishers could find her sanctimonious, a fountain of hard-to-swallow ideology whose virtuous peasants and villainous landlords were all too reminiscent of several centuries of the Western literary imagination. In Rigoberta's own country, the upper classes regarded her as a dupe for the *comandantes,* the URNG's exiled ladino leaders in Mexico. Many ordinary Guatemalans were uneasy, too, over her ties to a guerrilla movement that, even after she received the peace prize, rejected calls for a cease-fire.

But for the Guatemalan left, its allies in the rest of Latin America, and their North American and European sympathizers, *I, Rigoberta Menchú* was a stirring example of resistance to oppression. They regarded it as an authoritative text on the social roots of political violence, indigenous attitudes toward colonialism, and debates about ethnicity, class, and identity. That it took place in Guatemala was no coincidence, because this is a country that has long attracted foreigners out of proportion to its size. What they find is a rich culture and a political tragedy, the latter of which many date to 1954, the year the United States overthrew an elected government and replaced it with an anticommunist dictatorship. When Rigoberta told her story, a credible presidential election had not been held for thirty years. At the start of 1982, nonetheless, a coalition of Marxist guerrilla organizations seemed on the verge of changing everything. Victory was within reach because the army officers running Guatemala had gone berserk, to the point of alienating their own upper-class allies. Indignant over government kidnappings and massacres, more Guatemalans were looking to the guerrillas for liberation, especially in the indigenous-populated highlands northwest of the capital.

Taped in Paris, Rigoberta's testimony captured the terror and hope of the revolutionary apogee in Central America. Like the guerrillas in neighboring El Salvador, the Guatemalan rebels wanted to repeat the 1979 Sandinista victory in Nicaragua. They wanted to dismantle a repressive military apparatus, distribute landed estates, and turn a capitalist society into a socialist one. But the rebels expanded too quickly, beyond their capacity to organize supporters. Weapons failed to arrive from revolutionary Cuba, leaving villagers at the mercy of an army on the rampage. Just as the various guerrilla organizations coalesced into the Guatemalan National Revolutionary Union, the tide turned against them. Their civilian infrastructure failed to hold up under the army's slaughters. By mid-1982 they were in headlong retreat. To all but their staunchest supporters, it was clear that the army had won the war.

A decade later the guerrillas were still a nuisance, but they never recovered the support they had in the early 1980s. Without hope of seizing power, the URNG kept up a bush war to obtain "peace with justice"—major concessions in negotiations that dragged on for six years. Guatemala returned to civilian rule in 1986, but it was still dominated by the army, which saw no reason to be generous with an enemy that was only a shadow of its former strength. This was the stalemate behind one of the longest internal conflicts in Latin America. As international pressure mounted on the belligerents, debates over human rights became a more decisive arena than the battlefield.

When Rigoberta told her story in 1982, she was straightforward about her relation to the guerrillas. Unlike her two younger sisters, she was not a combatant in the Guerrilla Army of the Poor. But she did belong to two organizing fronts, the Vicente Menchú Revolutionary Christians and the Committee for Campesino Unity, which were openly committed to the EGP. Although cadres like herself usually did not carry weapons, they were as good as dead if caught by the security forces. At the time, Rigoberta's candor about her revolutionary affiliations was not a liability because the enemy was a dictatorship that had lost all legitimacy. The guerrillas seemed to have a good chance of winning and enjoyed wide sympathy abroad. Within a few years, however, it was clear that armed struggle was going nowhere. The guerrillas lost credibility with most Guatemalans; the army transferred power to civilians in a supposed return to democracy. Around this time Rigoberta's relation to the URNG and the EGP became murky. It turned into a delicate subject that could not be raised without counteraccusations of red-baiting.

Still, Rigoberta remained an obvious asset for the guerrillas because she focused all the blame for the violence on government forces. Never did she criticize her old comrades. Her story was so compelling that she became the revolutionary movement's most appealing symbol, pulling together images of resistance from the previous decade. She put a human face on an opposition that still had to operate in secret. She was also a Mayan Indian, validating the revolutionary movement's claim to represent Guatemala's indigenous people, who comprise roughly half the country's population of ten million. Although they were not free to speak their minds, she was, and she clearly supported the revolutionary movement even if it was led by non-Indians.

Rigoberta also became the most widely recognized voice for another movement that was distinct from the insurgents. By the early 1990s, Pan-Mayanists were starting dozens of new organizations to overcome the barriers between Indians from different language groups, defend their culture, and achieve equality with ladinos. Unlike fellow Mayas who were already in URNG-aligned "popular organizations," the new wave of activists was critical of the guerrillas as well as the army. On the subject of Rigoberta, they had doubts about her apparent career with the URNG. But they could identify with her story of persecution, even if they did not know who she was until the revolutionary movement began publicizing her as a Nobel candidate. For this large audience, Rigoberta and her story represented what they had suffered.

Following the peace prize, one of my colleagues came across a man who told him: "All those things that happened to Rigoberta, they happened to me. I even wrote everything down, just like she did. And then I buried what I'd written. I buried it in the ground. But Rigoberta didn't bury what she wrote. She actually published it in a book, and now everybody can read what happened!"[9] "She is working for our people," a relative told me. "She is our representative for the indigenous people, who are somewhat backward, not for people with power. What a miracle that someone like us who eats tortillas and chili arrived at the Nobel Prize. How I would like to know how that happened! She is speaking out for all of our people, not just for herself. I wish the blessings of God upon her."

Until the Nobel nomination allowed Rigoberta to tour Guatemala, her main audience was international. That was where she began to tell her story and where it vouched for the revolutionary movement's claim to represent Guatemalan Indians. Once the guerrillas had been defeated in most respects, their military activities declined to the level needed to maintain their claim as a national bargaining partner. The more important war became the international one, of images, and that is the war the guerrillas won with the help of *I, Rigoberta Menchú*. By telling the story of her life, Rigoberta translated easily ignored crimes into powerful international symbols that could be used against the army.

Most of the pressure that forced the army and the government to negotiate came from abroad, and it was generated by human rights imagery. In a recurring chain of events, the Guatemalan army would be accused of an atrocity, which human rights groups would then broadcast abroad. Obliged to respond, foreign governments and international bodies would then demand accountability from the Guatemalan government, on pain of withholding the next human rights certification or trade package. The country's elites learned that the only way to normalize relations with the rest of the world was to accept UN-sponsored peace talks. Without that transmission belt, which turned often complicated local situations into dramatic international symbols, a peace agreement probably would not have been signed at the end of 1996 between a civilian government, the still powerful army, and a rather vestigial guerrilla movement.

Taking Another Look at *I, Rigoberta Menchú*

When I began visiting northern Quiché in 1987, to interview peasants about the violence and reconstruction, I had no reason to doubt the veracity of *I, Rigoberta Menchú.* Nor did anyone else as far as I knew. What Rigoberta said about the Guatemalan army, the most important point of the book for most readers, rang true to other testimony. I recall being surprised when a routine atrocity check, described at the start of this chapter, failed to corroborate the immolation of her brother and other captives in the Chajul plaza. Since I was able to corroborate that the brother had died at Chajul, if not in the precise manner described, I did not feel obliged to call a press conference. My interviews were confirming so many of the accusations against the Guatemalan army that the problem seemed minor.

Only after becoming very familiar with what peasants had to say did I realize that their testimony was not backing up Rigoberta's in two significant ways. Not at issue was the record of the Guatemalan army—in that respect her picture of the violence was true enough. Nor were the feelings of peasants toward the army. Most seemed just as bitter toward it as she was, even if they spoke in low tones because they were still under military occupation. What most peasants did not share with Rigoberta was, in the first place, her definition of the enemy. Unlike *I, Rigoberta Menchú,* which describes the guerrillas as liberation fighters, my Ixil sources tended to lump soldiers and guerrillas together as threats to their lives. Instead of being popular heroes, the guerrillas were, like soldiers, people with guns who brought suffering in their wake.

"They look for trouble, not the needs of the family," an ex-combatant told me, explaining why he accepted a government amnesty. "Both the guerrillas and the army like trouble. But we're a civilian population; we just want to cultivate our maize." An Ixil civil servant said, "It's not a problem between the people and the guerrillas, nor between the army and the people, but between [the army and the guerrillas]. . . . They're using us as a shield because, when there are confrontations, the army sends patrollers [Ixil militiamen] to fight. And when the guerrillas attack, they bring civilians to fight with other civilians."

Obviously, the contrast with Rigoberta's testimony could be one of time. She was telling her story in 1982, at the height of revolutionary mobilization, when more peasants supported the guerrillas. Back then, many more peasants might have echoed her statements. Perhaps I was simply arriving too late to hear how they felt, and how they might express themselves in the future. Yet my interviews with Ixils also raised a second, more troubling contrast with Rigoberta's portrait of the violence that could not be explained as the result of disillusion with once popular guerrillas.

The peasants of *I, Rigoberta Menchú* have been pushed to the wall by plantation owners and soldiers hunting down dissidents. Her village has little choice but to organize for self-defense and look to the guerrillas for help. The insurgency therefore springs from the most basic need of peasants, for their land. This is the socioeconomic explanation for insurgency, the immiseration or oppression thesis, which is how guerrilla organizations and their supporters customarily justify the cost of armed struggle. If the people face ever worsening conditions, then they have no choice but to confront the system, whereupon the guerrillas show up to provide leadership.

These were not the prewar conditions I heard about in my interviews with nearby Ixils. Certainly they were living under a military dictatorship, some ladinos had evil reputations, and at least a few Ixils were eager to become guerrillas at an early date. But this was not a population that could defend itself only by force. Instead, Ixils were learning to use local elections and the courts. The 1960s and 1970s were for them, as for many Guatemalan peasants, an era of modest gains. The first armed groups in their accounts were usually guerrillas, whom many blamed for the subsequent arrival of soldiers. Army kidnappings began not in reaction to peaceful efforts by Ixils to improve their lot but to guerrilla organizing and ambushes. If anyone ignited political violence in Ixil country, it was the Guerrilla Army of the Poor. Only then had the security forces militarized the area and turned it into a killing ground.

Had nearby Uspantán been different? Or was *I, Rigoberta Menchú* voicing a rationale for insurgency that did not really come from peasants, that instead came from someone claiming to speak for them? No one had ever interviewed Rigoberta's old neighbors to compare their stories with hers. In June 1989 I went to Uspantán for the first time. My visit confirmed the basic outline of *I, Rigoberta Menchú*—that she came from the village of Chimel and that her father, mother, and younger brother died early in the violence. Yet a single day in Uspantán raised other problems with Rigoberta's account. At this point I did what any sensible graduate student does with a controversial discovery. I dropped the subject and scuttled back to my doctoral dissertation. It was only later, back in the United States, that I realized that I would have to face the authority of Rigoberta's story. An unimportant discrepancy, over how her brother died in Chajul, was the first sign of a more significant one: the considerable gap between the voice of revolutionary commitment incarnated by Rigoberta and the peasant voices I was listening to.

My findings in Ixil country raised broader issues, debated wherever men with guns claim popular support. Did armed struggle begin as a defensive response by oppressed peasants? Or was it a strategy launched by some outside group? Does the rapid spread of a guerrilla movement demonstrate that it has wide backing? Or could it thrive on the basis of a small vanguard, with repression and polarization forcing inhabitants to choose sides? When peasants provide food, shelter, and fighters to rebels, do they want to accomplish more or less what the rebels want to accomplish? Finally, do guerrilla strategists achieve what they claim to? Does armed struggle protect peasants from repression and empower them, or is it a high-risk strategy that usually ends in defeat and disillusion, after sacrificing peasants to romantic images of resistance?

Judging from Ixil stories about the violence, I decided that debates in sociology and political science about why peasants join insurgencies were not taking into account the elementary facts of life in such situations. According to Ixils, once the EGP moved into the area and started holding village rallies, they were on the horns of a dilemma. If on the one hand they cooperated with the guerrillas, the army would kill them. If on the other hand they cooperated with the army, the guerrillas would kill them. "Estamos entre dos fuegos," they told me—"we're between two fires" or "we're caught in the crossfire." Since the guerrillas were less homicidal and more appealing than the soldiers, for a time many Ixils looked to them for protection against an enraged army. But most had not joined the guerrillas as a way of meeting their own needs. Instead, they did so to survive the repercussions of the EGP's own strategy. What resulted was not a deeply rooted popular movement, which helps explain why most peasants soon became disillusioned with it.[10]

By the time my dissertation turned into a book, in 1993, the title had become *Between Two Armies in the Ixil Towns of Guatemala*. It was not well received by many of my peers in the overlapping solidarity movement (which organizes support for the Central American left), the human rights movement (which is supposed to operate on principles of international law rather than political loyalties), and the scholarly community (many of whose members are activists or defer to them).[11] The prevailing view was that the Ixils, and by extension the Guatemalan people, were not "between two armies." That was to draw a false equation between two forces with very different levels of credibility, one of whom the majority of Guatemalans saw as liberators and the other of whom they saw as oppressors. If fifteen percent of the population had died in the area where I was interviewing, how on earth did I know that survivors were telling me how they really felt?

Another objection was, "That's not what we read in *I, Rigoberta Menchú*." Rigoberta's 1982 story, produced while she was on tour for the revolutionary movement in Europe, had become the most accepted perspective on the relation between Guatemalan guerrillas and peasants. In the late 1980s and early 1990s, the aura around Rigoberta's version of events extended far beyond her hometown, to encompass the entire war in the western highlands. Any analysis that contradicted her claims and those of the revolutionary movement that she validated was sure to raise hackles. In the solidarity and human rights milieu, as well as in much of the scholarly community, many still felt that Rigoberta's account deserved to be interpreted literally, as a monument to the popular roots of the guerrilla movement in its northern Quiché heartland. Or if the story had to be taken with a grain of salt, it was not the business of a North American anthropologist to confront it.

Actually, there were two arguments against challenging Rigoberta's 1982 account. One was pragmatic. Since her testimony had generated international pressure, which was finally forcing the government to negotiate with the guerrillas, it might not be the best time to question its credibility. This was an argument I could not dismiss. It was one of the reasons I decided to withhold my findings, in the hope that a peace agreement would be signed. I was less impressed with the second argument—that an anthropologist did not have the right to contradict Rigoberta's story because that would violate the right of a native person to tell her story in her own way.

Anthropologists have long collected life histories from people. Ordinarily we do not dwell on whether the results are true or not. The very idea of refuting a life story sounds journalistic. More important is the narrator's perspective and what this tells us about the culture. Aside from being a life story, however, *I, Rigoberta Menchú* was a version of events with specific political objectives. It was also the most widely hailed example of testimonio, the Latin American genre that has brought the lives of the poor into scholarship in their own powerful words. Everyone concedes that testimonios reflect personal viewpoints. But advocates also regard them as testimony—reliable sources of information and representative voices for entire social classes. "My story is the story of all poor Guatemalans," Rigoberta said, and her claim has been taken very seriously, by everyone from supporters of guerrilla movements to the Nobel Committee.[12]

Although the laureate's reliability is a legitimate issue, the nature of my findings is inopportune for many scholars. Sociocultural anthropologists like myself are classified as social scientists, but much of our research belongs in the humanities. Recently we have been much affected by literary theory and postmodern skepticism about the very possibility of knowledge. Like other scholars influenced by these trends, we increasingly doubt our authority to make definitive statements about subordinate groups. Recoiling from the contribution of Western thought to colonialism, worried about our right to "represent" or depict the victims of this process, we wish to relegitimize ourselves by deferring to the perspective of the people we study and broadcasting their usually unheard voices.

As a believer in this project myself, I was trying to do just that, by complementing one indigenous voice with others that were not being heard. But not all such voices have been created equal. Some, like Rigoberta with her attractive politics, have been more welcome than others. Mayan peasants who reject the left tend to be dismissed as sellouts. Or perhaps they have been too repressed to say what is really on their minds, therefore what they say does not reflect their true feelings. In any case, identifying with certain kinds of marginalized voices has become a powerful new standard of legitimacy in scholarship, and Rigoberta Menchú is an obvious symbol of it. Sometimes she is invoked as if she were a patron saint, authorizing an otherwise illegitimate excursion into the affairs of her people. To some scholars, therefore, challenging the reliability of *I, Rigoberta Menchú* is little short of outrageous. It casts doubt on the entire project of bestowing authority on the voices of the oppressed—and on the authority that they themselves derive from it.

In Europe and the United States, *I, Rigoberta Menchú* has been one of the touchstones for widespread assumptions about Guatemala. If Rigoberta's portrait of how the violence started in Uspantán is true, then my interpretation of events in Ixil country could not be extended to a nearby area. It could mean that I was wrong about Ixil country. But if Rigoberta's version of events was misleading, then the acclaim for her 1982 story was encouraging misapprehensions about the problems facing peasants. It could also prop up a dubious standard of responsibility for outsiders—that it is enough to identify some person or group as representing the oppressed, then refrain from contradicting them.

PART ONE

Vicente Menchú and His Village

2

Uspantán as an Agricultural Frontier

What happens between Indians is worse.
—Member of Menchú family to author, 1991

From the south, the Sierra of the Cuchumatanes is a long blue ridge wrapped in clouds. Beyond the department capital of Santa Cruz del Quiché, the road winds through eroded valleys and pine-forested ridges. There is little but grass and brush that is yellow most of the year, punctuated by scraggly maize patches and sad-looking hamlets that draw their life from the road rather than the land. After Sacapulas, a tidy town of whitewashed adobe, the road switchbacks up the mile-high wall of the Cuchumatanes, which is equally unpromising most of the way. Then a rare sign of fertility—the green valley surrounding the town of Cunén. The road turns east; negotiates a stony gorge, then a long narrow valley offering certain agricultural hopes; and finally reaches the town of Uspantán. With some 3,000 inhabitants, this is the urban center for the surrounding municipio of the same name.

Unlike the outlying villages where most of the population lives, the town of Uspantán has basic comforts—tables at which to eat, mattresses on which to sleep, electricity, plumbing, and telephones. But it never has become a mecca for seekers of the indigenous, even now that it can claim a Nobel laureate. Few foreigners stay longer than the evening required to board the next bus heading east or west. The outsiders that Uspantán has attracted are instead seekers after land, mainly Guatemalans. North of town rises the crest of the Cuchumatanes, around which the clouds gather every afternoon. On the way up, pine trees and pasture give way to tropical cloud forest—or what is left of one. Only fringes of this moist, fragrant biotype still cling to the steepest slopes, above what peasants have cleared for grazing and agriculture.

Farther north, a second ridge is still covered with a rich damp forest that stretches for miles. The narrow valley between the two ridges, the first deforested and the second still luxuriant, is the cradle of our story. It is here that Rigoberta's father started a new settlement called Chimel in the 1950s. This is where the agricultural frontier, of men cutting into the trunks of trees so much larger than they, was halted by the violence. It is where rain still abounds, unlike around the town of Uspantán, where it no longer falls as before, and where forest clearing has now resumed.

The Uspantán landscape is not a simple one, ecologically or ethnically. Rigoberta was not formulating a scholarly monograph when she told her story in 1982, so the milieu is more complicated than readers might infer. This includes its ethnic makeup, the progression of indigenous and non-indigenous groups that have moved into the area over the years. *I, Rigoberta Menchú* presents a titanic struggle between two opposed groups: her own indigenous K'iche' people and the ladinos (of European or mixed descent) who have subjugated them. These are the oppressed and the oppressors, clearly defined by ancestral hatreds that parents carefully impart to their children. Eventually Rigoberta learns that not all ladinos are bad, that many are poverty-stricken peasants like herself, and that some are comrades in the revolutionary movement. But what remains is a bipolar model of ethnic relations, the same one that appears in virtually every description of Guatemala.

The ladino-indígena distinction is not wrong. Most Guatemalans are willing to identify themselves as one or the other, which they understand in terms of *raza* (biological race). You can walk into a crowd and pick out individuals who look like they stepped off the stelae left by ancient Mayas. You can also see European descent in the majority of ladinos. But many ladinos acknowledge that they are mestizos—of mixed descent, mainly European and Mayan—and so are numerous indígenas. It does not take long to find ladinos who look like indígenas and indígenas who look like ladinos because the distinction is ultimately cultural rather than biological. Indígenas can redefine themselves or their children as ladinos by some combination of moving away from home, getting a good education, disclaiming their natal language, marrying into the ladino raza, or acquiring wealth.

Another limitation of the bipolar model is that it downplays the differences among Indians. Not only are there twenty different Mayan language groups in Guatemala, but one of them is conspicuously missing from Rigoberta's portrait of Uspantán. I am referring to the Uspanteko Mayas, who used to be the municipio's principal inhabitants. That they are no longer is due to the K'iche's and ladinos who have moved into the region. It would be misleading to equate the K'iche' and ladino migration streams in all respects, but both have been attracted by the same thing:

open land in what used to be a sparsely populated municipio. Ladinos and K'iche's are both also, to different degrees, dominant ethnic groups. Ladinos have a monopoly of power at the national level, where they run the state, the army, the Catholic Church, and every other national institution. The Spanish they command is the language of power and status, and no one without it is able to get very far.

In the western highlands, however, K'iche's carry a certain weight of their own. Just south of the small Uspanteko homeland, K'iche' speakers ruled a wide region before the Spanish conquest; have remained the bulk of the population (hence the name of Quiché Department, spelled an older way); and are finally making a comeback. This is obvious in the regional economy, where K'iche's figure prominently in a new indigenous bourgeoisie; in municipal governments; and in the Pan-Mayan movement, in which speakers of K'iche' play a major role.

Since the late 1980s, the Mayan movement has brought together K'iche's and other language groups in ways that could transform Guatemalan politics. But the term "Maya" is so new in Guatemalan discourse that Rigoberta barely mentioned it in her 1982 account. Until recently, it was used mainly by anthropologists to designate five or six million speakers of thirty related languages in southeastern Mexico, Guatemala, and Honduras. Even now it is not necessarily a common form of identification for the people themselves. Instead, many still identify themselves in terms of their village and municipio, or as indígenas or *naturales* ("naturals" as opposed to "people of reason"), or in terms of the particular language they speak.

All but the most detailed linguistic maps give the impression that speakers of each Mayan language live together in a contiguous territory. Closer inspection shows that this is not the case, especially in the Sierra of the Cuchumatanes. Kanjobals, Q'eqchi's, and Poqomchi's have been on the move, as have ladinos and Rigoberta's people, the K'iche's, whose villages dot the front range and have become a political factor in several municipios. Although the native populations of Sacapulas and Cunén have held up demographically and linguistically against the K'iche' migration, this is not the case with the Uspantekos, who are now a small minority in the municipio that carries their name.[1]

Aside from the bipolar model of ethnicity, a second issue on which *I, Rigoberta Menchú* requires comment is land. Peasant farmers in Guatemala have become chronically short of it, pushing many up mountainsides that might better be left in forest. One of the reasons for the shortage is detailed in Rigoberta's 1982 story, as it is in most accounts of Guatemala: unequal land tenure. The most fertile land is controlled by plantations producing coffee, sugar, cotton, and cattle for export, especially on the Pacific coast, whereas most indigenous farmers (and many ladino peasants) are confined to small subsistence holdings in the highlands. In the mountain valleys around Uspantán, there are a few estates that could be broken up for smallholders, but the extent to which the latter would benefit should not be overestimated. Most land is already owned by peasants. Even much of the estate land has already been loaned out to the peasants who reside on it.

The other reason for land scarcity is missing from *I, Rigoberta Menchú*. It is often downplayed in accounts of Guatemala because any but a passing reference sets off political, cultural, and religious objections. It would not be an insurmountable problem if agricultural productivity could keep pace with it, nor would it be as urgent if land were distributed more equally, but nothing can really diminish its importance, which looms larger with every passing year. I am referring to rapid population growth.

Mayan farmers are said to be rooted to their land, but the primordial imagery is almost a denial of how their relationship to it requires periodic uprooting. Like so many other farmers, Mayas have regularly worn out their land and gone in search of new. Cycles of settlement, population growth, overexploitation, and migration date back to the Classic Maya and their spectacular collapse around 800 A.D., to the northeast in what is now Petén Department. Over the past century, another great cycle has been under way, in which the Guatemalan population has quintupled.[2] In Quiché Department the densely settled municipios of the south have sent landless peasants north, into the mountains of Uspantán and neighboring municipios. There they deforest steep slopes and rob the soil of fertility by growing maize year after year by traditional methods. "Now it's tired out; all the good land is gone," a Chimel settler told me of his former location. From land that has become "tired," "dry," or "weak," men look for fresh terrain, still in forest, that can be slashed and burned to grow maize. Eventually they take their families to settle at a new location, in a movement repeated every few generations.

In Uspantán the quest for agricultural productivity is apparent most days of the week, as men and women range over hill and dale to cultivate the small patches of land they have inherited or purchased, often at different altitudes and in different ecozones. A friend in Caracol, a village on the road to Chimel, had a fairly typical schedule: On Thursday he would hike two hours over a ridge to cultivate a patch of carrots, then return the same day. On Friday he planned to walk two and a half hours downhill in another direction to cultivate a bean patch, then trudge back uphill that same day. Saturday would require walking only an hour and a half along a ridge to cultivate beans and maize. On Sunday he would walk three hours downhill to the weekly market in Uspantán, then four hours uphill to come home. None of the journeys was long by local standards, but over four days he would spend twenty hours walking up and down mountainsides, often carrying heavy loads because, like most peasants, he was too poor to own a pack animal.

This chapter delves into the ecology behind such exertions, a degenerative process of population growth, slash-and-burn agriculture, and migration that is complicated, but not necessarily altered in any fundamental sense, by the ladino-indígena conflict and inequitable land tenure to which Rigoberta gives so much attention. Romanticizing peasants is a hoary tradition that has the virtue of dramatizing their right to their land. But romanticism can also be used to ignore the damage that peasants do, how they compete for fresh land, and the feuds that result—as exemplified by the story of one pioneer on Guatemala's agricultural frontier, Rigoberta's father, Vicente Menchú.

The Rise and Fall of Ladino Hegemony

What is left of the Mayan fortress of Uspantán sits on a ridge forty minutes' walk from the contemporary town. Not much is visible from afar. Then low stone foundations emerge between maize stalks. There are also mounds with traces of stone wall. Unlike the town founded by the Spanish in the 1500s, lower down on a plain, the pre-European Uspantán was sited for defense against attack. On either side the ridge drops off steeply. To the west the exit is blocked by a steep earthen bank, then a deep ditch the size of a railroad cut. According to Spanish chronicles, there was a small kingdom ruled from this fortress, which held out after conquistadores destroyed the K'iche' kingdom to the south. In 1529 the Uspantekos repulsed a Spanish expedition, only to succumb to another the following year.

Since the area was unattractive to Spanish settlers, Dominican friars were placed in charge of the surviving population. Under the Pax Dominicana, in Jean Piel's phrase, indígenas were forced to live together in new towns. Gradually, church haciendas became a door for ladino settlement through the ladino servants who managed them.[3] But indígenas escaped some of the most destructive forms of colonialism. Around the town of Uspantán, property and population remained almost entirely Uspanteko. The town's oldest ladino families trace their local forebears only to the late nineteenth and early twentieth centuries, when they arrived as cattle-grazers from southern Quiché. Although most ladinos settled in the dry southernmost outcrops of the Cuchumatanes, the K'iche's who began to arrive during the same period settled close to the town of Uspantán, then began to clear the humid forest on the ridge to the north.

Out of the east came the most exotic immigrants of all—Germans from Alta Verapaz Department. Until they were deported during the two world wars by dictators under pressure from Washington, German entrepreneurs set the pace in the coffee economy. They dominated Alta Verapaz and turned it into one of the most prosperous corners of the country. They also moved into the lowland tropical valleys of northern Uspantán, the fabled Zona Reina, which is cut off from the municipal seat by daunting ridges and dense forests. But the Zona's remoteness defeated even the Germans. The children they sired "lost themselves among the people," according to a local saying. Their descendants are not much better off than the rest of the population, mainly Q'eqchi' Mayas who also arrived from Alta Verapaz in search of land.

By the second half of the twentieth century, K'iche's were in the majority around the town of Uspantán, but they did not control it. In ethnic terms, political power had passed from a diminishing Uspanteko population to a small but growing ladino element. At first sight Uspantán looks like a ladino town, but this is partly the result of a 1985 earthquake that destroyed much of the old adobe construction. As late as the 1950s, there were few ladinos in town, and they are still probably outnumbered by indígenas. Just how outnumbered is as unclear as the total population. According to the 1981 census (an undercount), twenty-six percent of the municipio's 42,685 inhabitants were ladinos. There is, however, a clear pattern to how ladinos have settled into the landscape. Outside the municipal seat, they tend to live in a ring of villages to the south, where there are few indígenas. North of town, in higher and wetter valleys, ladino peasants predominate in only a few villages, and a large majority speak K'iche' as their first language.

Contrary to *I, Rigoberta Menchú*, ladinos in Uspantán do not stand apart as a wealthy upper class. Instead, they work mainly in commercial and service occupations, as skilled laborers, teachers, and nurses. Many are poorer than the more prosperous indígenas, and a ladino owning more than a *caballería* of land, the local measure equivalent to forty-five hectares, is hard to find.[4] One ladino owns a bus line, and a few have stores, but other stores are owned by indígenas, who also claim part of the town's vehicle fleet and own some of the real estate near the plaza. The bars dispensing liquor to the vulnerable are owned mainly by indígenas. There used to be a few ladino labor contractors, but they have been replaced by indígenas.

Ladinos indeed dominated town affairs from the late 1800s to the 1970s, and they still exercise authority beyond their numbers. The lack of an economic power base suggests that their political advantages have instead been cultural and social, based on their command of Spanish and superior connections to the national system. Why were there no indigenous mayors until recently? I asked elders. "Because the ladinos gave a lot of advice and we said yes," explained one. "There's lots of confidence in ladinos," said another, an old friend of the Menchús who helped win a major legal victory against a plantation. "They know how to express themselves when there are delegations. So people were content."[5]

As is often the case where Hispanic politeness reigns, more than a few inhabitants, indigenous as well as ladino, deny that ethnic tension is a serious problem. However, the right question elicits stories about a more oppressive time. "The discrimination was without end," a K'iche' human rights activist told me. "When people visited the town hall to conduct their affairs, they were not attended to. They were told to wait two or three days. And also the unpaid labor obligations. Indígenas would work for a week without being paid." "As far as I'm concerned," one of Rigoberta's relatives declared, "my grandfather was treated like a slave because he was sent to Guatemala carrying a burden of 125 pounds, plus his own food, which he had to carry on top of that. Ladinos always had the people under their command because the indígena allowed himself to be ordered around."

The worst abuses became less common under the labor reforms of the 1930s and 1940s. Over the next thirty years, the K'iche's of Uspantán gradually loosened the ladino grip on the town hall, just as indígenas did in many towns during this period. In Uspantán ethnic subordination began to crumble with a revolt against the institution of the *alcalde indígena,* or "Indian mayor." This was a system dating to the Spanish colony, in which indigenous towns maintained hierarchies of communal duties known as *cargos* (burdens). Although some cargos involved service to the town hall, others revolved around worship of the saints—Catholic saints in the form of wooden statuary, for whom it was customary to hold fiestas in which the population drank itself into a stupor.

When ladinos replaced indígenas in the office of mayor, cargo obligations were placed under the authority of a second, indigenous mayor. He was appointed by an assembly of elders, who also named younger men to serve under him. The Indian mayor dealt with problems among his people in their own language. Unfortunately, a concession to indigenous sovereignty also became a way for ladinos to exploit indigenous labor. Men serving under the Indian mayor were at the beck and call of ladino authorities, as messenger boys and burden-bearers, and they were not paid for their work.

The Uspantán system collapsed in the late 1960s because of opposition from catechists. These were indígenas (including Rigoberta's family) whom a new generation of Spanish clergy organized to spread church doctrine, discourage drunkenness, and modernize their communities. Because catechists refused to attend the annual assembly to appoint the next year's cargo holders, the duties weighed more heavily on a dwindling number of traditionalists. Once some villages were no longer participating, others refused to as well, until the Indian mayoralty and its labor obligations were abolished. Catechists were key players in such dramas of change and empowerment in many towns.

In Uspantán the catechist movement was responsible for electing the first indigenous town mayor in living memory. He won in 1978 as a member of the Christian Democrats, a reformist party associated with the Catholic Church. As a paralegal scribe, the new mayor was well prepared for his duties and ended his four-year term without being accused of graft, a distinction in Guatemalan public life. But his administration was not to the liking of the more conservative ladinos, who felt that an indígena in the mayor's chair detracted from their town's image of modernity. One result was the secession of Chicamán, the municipio's second largest population center, as a jurisdiction in its own right. Ladinos are the majority in the town of Chicamán, and they also abound in many of the villages that joined the new municipio. There were other complaints, too, but the new municipio was a ladino breakaway from indígenas' winning their share of political representation.

Uspantekos, K'iche's, and Land Titles

Only a small minority of Uspantán's population still speaks Uspanteko. Unlike the Sacapulteco and Cunense spoken in nearby municipios, Uspanteko is not a local version of K'iche' Maya. Instead, it is a closely related but separate language whose intelligibility with K'iche' is sixty percent. According to the Summer Institute of Linguistics, an evangelical mission specializing in Bible translation, three thousand people still speak Uspanteko. But of these, only one thousand use it as their main form of communication, and they are concentrated in two villages. Where other Uspantekos live, the dominant languages are K'iche' and Spanish. The most obvious reason for the decline is that Uspantekos have intermarried heavily with outsiders, especially K'iche's. Language loss is common when one such group is demographically stronger than the other. Since K'iche' is the largest Mayan language group in the country, with an estimated million speakers, it can be used far more widely than Uspanteko, so it is what children of mixed couples tend to learn.

As Uspanteko speakers diminish, more than a few have become disinterested in identifying themselves as indígenas, especially in the town center. "Practically, the majority no longer want to speak Uspanteko; they speak K'iche' and Spanish. They want to be ladinos, but it's impossible because of their surnames and also because of the color of their skin," one elder said. "Many deprecate our dialect. We feel very close to being ladinos, but we're not ladinos," an Uspanteko hoping to revitalize the language told me. "Many of us speak lots of Spanish with our children, and this is why they don't learn Uspanteko." Their decline as a distinct group has been rapid. Two elders recalled that when they were children in the 1920s and 1930s, there were few ladinos and K'iche's in town. Another claimed that as late as the 1940s Uspantekos still outnumbered K'iche's. Now they are a remnant, surpassed by ladinos as well. Even visually, Uspanteko women have become difficult to distinguish from K'iche's on the basis of dress.

Until a recent flurry of ethnic organizing, the significance of which remains to be seen, Uspantekos put up little resistance to the ethnic transformation of their homeland. Instead, many sold their property around town and retreated into the mountains. When I asked elders why, their answers always had to do with ecology. Accompanying the influx of ladinos and K'iche's were disturbing changes, including the loss of open land, deforestation, and the diminution of rainfall. Among Uspantekos, the more traditional felt obliged to pull up stakes. "Nearly everyone had cattle; even the poor had two or three," an elder told me. "But now the town is bigger, and there is no vacant land without an owner." Another elder said, "When I was young, there was more rain, and it started April 20. Now sometimes in May and sometimes in June. Maybe because the people are so abundant, they've cut down many trees and don't plant new ones. Or perhaps because this is what God wants."

Fresh land has become very hard to find in this milieu. Serious hostilities can be the result, and not just between indígenas and ladinos. Although Uspantekos have generally managed to avoid becoming mired in interminable conflicts, this is not the case with the K'iche's. In the nearby municipio of Nebaj, Ixils refer to K'iche's as *ulá*—people from somewhere else. The term implies a competitive edge to personal conduct, at odds with ideals of communal harmony. In the words of one Ixil detractor: "They like to grab land. They buy a piece and then grab more." To be fair, some K'iche's manage to live in harmony with their neighbors. If they have a reputation for litigious ways, it is because of the manner in which many of them came into Ixil country, through the system of national land titles that Liberal dictators set up in the late nineteenth century.

The Liberals wanted to develop land in indigenous municipios. The intended beneficiaries were ladinos, but K'iche's were able to take advantage of the new laws, too. Some were members of militias who had gone to war for Liberal dictators. Others simply knew more about national titling legislation than the backward Ixils did. Unfortunately, this was a strategy at odds with the local conception of land rights, which dates to the Spanish colony when indígenas held their land through communal titles. Even today, few Ixil peasants have obtained private titles because they cost too much. Instead, they swear out property documents at the town hall, which usually suffices among neighbors but has little validity in court.

Generations of conflict, with no end in sight, grew out of the turn-of-the-century land grants by Liberal presidents. In theory the recipients of these grants could not receive title to land that was already occupied. In practice they could bribe surveyors, registrars, and judges to overlook indígenas who were already there. Even where land was vacant, it tended to be the hinterland of an Indian town that, based on colonial law, viewed it as a territorial reserve for its own growing population. Or absentee landlords obtained titles at the national level without manifesting their rights locally, until after homesteaders had invested decades of effort under the mistaken impression that the land was unclaimed.

Confusion was common in the dense forests north of Uspantán. Survey maps show that most of it was titled during the Liberal land rush, but some of the new owners were slow to occupy their property, leaving what seemed like open land for homesteaders. Boundaries were so vague that it was not uncommon to mistakenly settle on someone else's property. There were poorly surveyed titles dating to the nineteenth century; squatter rights for homesteaders who improved unoccupied land; and the fractious legacy of surveyors, notaries, and judges who stamped their seal on anything for which they were paid.

In charge of sorting out all the problems is the National Institute for Agrarian Transformation (INTA), which was set up to alleviate pressure for land reform. In theory and sometimes in practice, INTA can use a tax on idle property to force plantation owners to transfer it to peasants. The agency's more important function has been to parcel out public land. Both require mediating between rival claimants who are often indigenous. It would be hard to exaggerate the dimensions of the task for a budget-strapped institution. Year after year, hundreds of conflicts must be managed by a handful of INTA investigators who usually lack any practical way of resolving them, with the result that they never end.

Not surprisingly, INTA has been the subject of harsh criticism by virtually everyone who has dealt with it. Exhausted and bankrupted by countless trips to its offices, petitioners accuse it of indifference, ineptitude, and corruption. There is no question that INTA has tested the stamina of thousands of peasants. But when you take a case like the one that we are about to examine—more conflictual than most but by no means rare—a disturbing possibility emerges. The petitioners themselves could be making a solution impossible.

The Land Claim of Vicente Menchú

One question raised by Rigoberta's 1982 account is why she and her family would spend so much of the year away from the new land they were homesteading, to work for low pay on distant plantations. It is true that it takes years to turn tropical forest into a good maize crop, as Rigoberta mentions (the tree trunks have to be burned, the roots must rot, and the earth dry out before yields reach their maximum). Yet maize will grow from the start. Spending the majority of the year away on a plantation sounds like too much for peasants clearing new land of their own.[6] Judging from Uspantán sources, the reason for the incongruency is that Rigoberta never worked on plantations. Some neighbors did go to the Pacific coast, but mainly between October and December, while waiting for their maize crop to ripen.

As for Rigoberta's father, Vicente, he worked on plantations early in life but stopped long before she was born in 1959. The reason is that he was not poor by local standards. True to Rigoberta's account, he did grow up in poverty, fatherless and therefore landless, after being born in the southern Quiché town of Santa Rosa Chucuyub in 1920. His father died when he was small, according to Rigoberta, whereupon his mother took him and two younger brothers to Uspantán, where they made their living as servants.[7] According to her granddaughter, Rosa Menchú worked for a wealthy ladino *patrón* who exploited her sexually and forced her to give Vicente to another family. When I tracked down the patrón's family, they turned out to be Uspantekos rather than ladinos, as did a previous family for whom Rosa worked.[8] "Everyone lived and worked together with a hoe," claimed a son who grew up with Vicente.

Socially and ethnically, Uspantán was a more fluid society than conveyed by Rigoberta's 1982 story. Because she was from a village dedicated to farming and was narrating a history of oppression, she provides a sense of her people that is more conservative than what would emerge from, say, a sociological survey. During her youth, elders told of excruciating experiences from earlier in the century. Although indígenas were still second-class citizens, forced labor was a thing of the past except for military conscription, from which Chimel was conveniently remote. Meanwhile, indígenas were learning better ways to make a living. They were not working for plantations as much as before.[9] Instead, they were going to school in record numbers. Some were prospering in business. One symptom of these developments is the vestigial folk Catholicism of Rigoberta's 1982 account. She was from a village that had rejected it, along with the heavy fiesta drinking that contributed to poverty.

Indígenas were also starting to emigrate to the United States. A first cousin of Rigoberta's mother, just as indigenous as she, moved to the city of Quezaltenango, married a ladino, and for decades has lived with her two sons in Los Angeles, California. Her grandchildren (Rigoberta's second cousins, once removed) are U.S. citizens. The Uspanteko with whom Rigoberta's father grew up is an indigenous farmer, but he has a son who lives in Maryland and a daughter who lives in Switzerland, plus two granddaughters working in Italy. "We have never been discriminated against for being indígenas," claimed a daughter who knew Rigoberta as a girl. "[My family has] always had good relations with ladinos. The majority of our neighbors are ladinos. The indígena is half to blame for discrimination. Sometimes discrimination gets worse if one deprecates oneself, if one doesn't feel equal. If someone says, 'Because I'm an *indio,* I'm not equal,' then [that person] is discriminated against. But if one feels equal, no."

Vicente and his two younger brothers were among the many in their generation who moved up in the world. This is attested not just by their own independent lives but by those of most of their descendants. One way Vicente established himself was through service to ladinos, first in the army and then in the town hall as a deliverer of summons. He also became a Catholic catechist. Still another way Vicente improved his situation was by marrying into a well-off peasant clan. An earlier and less fortunate marriage is not mentioned in *I, Rigoberta Menchú*. It lasted long enough to produce four children, two of whom survived. The union fell apart after Vicente returned from military service around 1943, renewed his interest in agriculture, and fell in love with a girl still in her teens. Her name was Juana Tum Cotojá. Two of their first children died while still small, but one born in 1949 survived, as did six others.[10] The fourth of the seven to reach adulthood was the future laureate, born on January 9, 1959.

Vicente's first father-in-law had given him land to farm, but his second had a good deal more. Juana Tum Cotojá was from the prosperous K'iche' community of Xolá. Located in a fertile bowl in the mountains, a short walk northeast of town, Xolá was colonizing new land to the north. In Rigoberta's 1982 story, her mother's family is just as poor as her father's, but she corrected this portrait herself a decade later.[11] According to the later account, the family of Juana's mother (the Cotojás) hailed originally from Lemoa, a village near the departmental capital of Santa Cruz del Quiché. The family of Juana's father (the Tums) were Chiquimulas—natives of Santa María Chiquimula, in the Department of Totonicapán—who were known as the "gypsies" of Guatemala because they left their overcrowded municipio to become itinerant merchants.

The Tums and Cotojás may have been poor when they arrived in Uspantán. But by 1928 both families were part of a group that bought more than eight hundred hectares of forest a day's walk to the north, at a place called Laguna La Danta.[12] With good land at Xolá, more at Laguna Danta, and even more uninhabited land stretching north of the new location, the Tums and the Cotojás had the requisites for an independent life for their children and grandchildren. What lies just north of Laguna Danta is a dramatic trench valley running east and west. The drop to the bottom is long and steep—three hundred meters—and the northern wall of the valley rises even higher, more than five hundred meters, to an altitude of 2,613. This is the ridge of old-growth forest that cuts off the southern part of the municipio, around the town of Uspantán, from its northern reaches in the

Zona Reina. It was also public land that never had been successfully titled during the Liberal land rush, making it among the last unclaimed tracts in the region.

A slice of the ridge, almost twenty-eight square kilometers, was the land claimed by Vicente Menchú and his group of homesteaders. The only disputed boundary was at the southeast corner, where a ladino family claimed a narrow wedge of forty-five hectares that INTA subsequently adjudicated to Vicente. If he could have been satisfied with this small kingdom, he would have received his title a decade earlier than he did. Unfortunately, he had already situated his house and settlement just beyond its southwestern corner. The new hamlet of Chimel sat between the 2,753 hectares recognized by INTA and the older village of Laguna Danta, where Vicente had arrived as son-in-law. The Tums of Laguna Danta considered the additional 151 hectares on which he was sitting to be their own.[13]

From that seemingly small disagreement was to pour a river of tragedy. Vicente's father-in-law had begun clearing the forest there in the late 1930s, with his new son-in-law arriving a decade later to farm next to him. Trouble seems to have begun soon after Vicente appeared, not with his father-in-law, Nicolás Tum Castro, but with the latter's brother Antonio and his sons. With a gesture of helplessness, one of Vicente's older daughters recalled that when she went to live with her father at Chimel in 1949–1950, he and Antonio Tum "already were fighting for the holy earth . . . for questions of land, of boundaries." The 151 hectares in dispute was the most accessible land in Vicente's claim. It was also well watered, with streams running down the hillside where Vicente built his house. As a Tum son-in-law, moreover, he had already invested years of labor in clearing it. In comparison, the 2,753 hectares must have seemed like a howling wilderness.

The quest for a title began before Rigoberta was born. Toward the end of the CIA-installed regime of Colonel Carlos Castillo Armas (1954–1957), another K'iche' homesteader recalls accompanying Vicente to the national land office. After the office turned down the petition, Vicente and his partner went to a retired colonel and lawyer in the department capital, Francisco López, who told them to "gather more people." To obtain the title they wanted, the colonel advised, they would have to invite other homesteaders to join their claim. Unfortunately, recruiting outsiders increased the ire of Vicente's in-laws. "As a son-in-law," a Tum elder told me four decades later, "Vicente was a member of the Laguna Danta community, for having asked for a woman from there. But he never asked us for permission to bring in outsiders, and he never asked us to join. . . . We already had our title, and we already had our land. Maybe our children would want the land, but not yet. . . . It was *municipal* land: Vicente didn't have the right to bring together people from other places."

3

The Struggle for Chimel

My father fought for twenty-two years, waging a heroic struggle against the landowners who wanted to take our land and our neighbors' land. After many years of hard work, when our small bit of land began yielding harvests and our people had a large area under cultivation, the big landowners appeared: the Brols. It's said there that they were even more renowned criminals than the Martínez and García families, who owned a finca there before the Brols arrived.

—*I, Rigoberta Menchú*, p. 103

Breaking through Rigoberta's descriptions of exploitation are childhood memories of her village as a bucolic place. This I heard from others as well. "Here in Chimel there was a chapel, a school, medical clinics, a soccer team that played with other villages," one of her relatives told me. "There were little stores. Hardly anyone went to the coast. They grew the maize they needed—no one had to buy maize. And the people had their little fiestas; they got together to kill a sheep, a pig, and everyone ate together. In their fiestas there was no *kuxa* [homemade cane liquor]; the people didn't want it. Everyone belonged to one religion—the Catholic—but they did not permit these makers of *kuxa*. In Laguna Danta nearly everyone had his still, but here no one. If there was a hoe or ax left around, no one took it. Nearly everyone had respect."

An abrupt ridge dominated the skyline above Chimel, with the houses nestled among hillocks and hollows at its foot. Vicente's house stood in a pasture watered by a small stream. Even after the valley was cleared of trees, the lush forest on surrounding heights guaranteed rain throughout the year. The rainfall was so abundant that Chimel was too wet to dry mud bricks into adobe, the preferred building material, so houses were built of wooden planks and covered with roofs of thatch or tin. Every afternoon clouds billowed up from the valley that drops away to the west. It was a desirable place that was cherished long before it was lost.

One of the most appealing features of Rigoberta's story is her father's defense of Chimel against the large landowners who want to take it away from him. Vicente Menchú's struggle to defend his land from the Garcías, Martínezes, and Brols echoes popular images of indigenous resistance. *I, Rigoberta Menchú* dramatizes the most basic demand of Native Americans, for land, and it also lays the blame squarely on the colonizers who took so much of it. Not only are the people of Chimel thrown out of their houses twice by finca owners, but Vicente is thrown into prison twice, on the first occasion for fourteen months and on the second with a sentence for life. In between, he is beaten so badly by landlord thugs that he never fully recovers, and all this before going to his death at the Spanish embassy.[1]

Rigoberta's indictment of the National Institute for Agrarian Transformation, the government land office, sums up centuries of indigenous experience with imposed legal systems. Although INTA claims to help peasants obtain land titles, *I, Rigoberta Menchú* describes a two-faced institution that steals their land in league with plantation owners. Hence the repeated occasions on which INTA surveyors remeasure Chimel at community expense, not to mention others in which the villagers are threatened by plantation surveyors, and the countless summons to the capital by INTA authorities for Vicente to sign another mysterious paper that will be used against him.

In Uspantán today Vicente Menchú is indeed remembered for his struggle for land. I heard how the people of Chimel were evicted from their houses on two occasions; how Vicente made countless trips to INTA; how he was dragged off to jail twice and beaten badly enough to be hospitalized. But what emerged from my interviews was rather different from Rigoberta's account, so different that it casts her entire story in another light. When I asked after Vicente's land conflicts, the answer that came back can be summarized in a name that goes virtually unmentioned in *I, Rigoberta Menchú*—the Tums.[2] A prewar boundary dispute with the Martínez family also comes up, as does a dispute with the García brothers following Vicente's death, but everyone seems to agree that his most serious land dispute was not with ladino plantation owners. Instead, it was with K'iche smallholders like himself: his in-laws, the Tums of Laguna Danta.

The same conclusion can be derived from a visit to an archive in Guatemala City. True to the spirit of *I, Rigoberta Menchú*, the INTA building to which Vicente recurred so many times is down the street from the grim, turreted headquarters of the national police. Amid the warren of offices, crowded with functionaries and petitioners, is a small room stacked with bundles of documents from floor to ceiling. They include two thick folders of petitions, counterpetitions, appeals, and counterappeals submitted by Vicente Menchú, his adversaries, and their heirs. The documents span four decades, from 1961 to the present, in a case that may never end as long as there is a government to which the feuding parties can appeal.

The War of Petitions at INTA

Rigoberta's 1982 testimony weaves together many threads of the indigenous experience in Guatemala, but one that is missing is land conflict between peasants. In view of how common such disputes are, even more so than conflicts with plantation owners, this is a significant omission. But it reflects a view of indigenous peasants that is widely held on the left and sometimes voiced by indígenas themselves. Two of the corresponding assumptions are well represented in *I, Rigoberta Menchú*, that (1) indigenous communities are more cohesive than nonindigenous ones and (2) peasants' most important conflicts are vertical, with external oppressors such as plantation owners and state authorities, which explains their proclivity for rebellion. But is this the usual state of affairs? And do peasants usually view outsiders as the main problem they face? Unfortunately, a heroic view of peasants blinds us to the possibility that they consider their main problem to be one another. It also blinds us to the possibility that instead of resisting the state, peasants are using it against other members of their own social class.[3]

The finca-owning ladino families damned in *I, Rigoberta Menchú* exist, but they are only peripheral actors in the many petitions filed by Vicente Menchú and other homesteaders. The content of the petitions is suggested by a tally of who presented them. Fifteen from 1961 to 1978 were from Vicente Menchú; four others were from his companions in Chimel. The majority of the petitions were asking INTA to please hurry up, but five made complaints against other K'iche smallholders, chiefly the Tums of Laguna Danta. Only one of the nineteen petitions was directed against a ladino (see Chapter 4). Meanwhile, the Tums were equally active. From 1966 to 1979, they filed seventeen counterpetitions, mainly against Vicente Menchú and his supporters. This is not to mention another twenty-five petitions from four other groups of smallholders. The four include two dissident factions within Chimel, who petitioned against Vicente, plus two newly arrived groups of claimants, who petitioned against the Tums, Vicente, and each other. Because most of the people involved were K'iche' Mayas, nearly all the complaints were aimed against each other rather than ladinos.

The first petition mentioned in the archive is from Vicente and dates to 1961, followed by his appeals to each new administration.[4] The documents were typed out by a lawyer or scribe, then affixed with the thumbprint of Vicente and any associates who happened to be with him.

Early on he learned that to wait quietly for an answer was to be ignored—the authorities did not respond to one petition for three and a half years. His appeals were always polite, but they often lost the supplicatory tone of a peasant appealing to authority as he pointed out the time and expense to which he had been put.

It is not hard to see why his many trips to the capital made him bitter, a classic peasant experience that is seconded by men who knew him. "Vicente's struggle was always for the land," a ladino told me. "INTA deceived him many times. It would say that his petition had been lost, that his lands had to be surveyed again. It said that it would deliver his titles and not do it. Trip after trip to the capital. Those people, that man, they went through hardships. Here in the town hall we did what we could." "INTA is completely impossible," another ladino sympathizer said of his own struggle with the agency. "It leaves you without money. There turns out to be a landlord with more money, and it leaves you with nothing." Another claimant remembered Vicente saying, "The government is a bandit because it always takes our money. The land belongs to us, not the government."

Yet INTA was not the main impediment to his claim. His K'iche' in-laws were, to the unending distress of his wife, Juana Tum Cotojá. Her uncle Antonio and his sons challenged each of Vicente's petitions, made trouble after every INTA inspection, and took their protests to the town hall, the department governor, and the courts. Until the 1960s the disagreement had not been carried outside the valley to national institutions. But as Vicente became a steady petitioner, the Tums shored up their position by purchasing a land title from a ladino named Angel Martínez, for 360 hectares of land including the 151 they were disputing with Vicente.[5] Unfortunately, the document never impressed INTA because it failed to specify boundaries. This put the Tums on the defensive at the land titling agency, with which they had more reason to be bitter than Vicente.

The Tums were more successful with the judicial system. It was they—not ladino finca owners, as reported in *I, Rigoberta Menchú*—who were responsible for evicting the inhabitants of Chimel on two occasions and putting Vicente in jail on two other occasions. The first eviction was ordered by the district court in the department capital on September 18, 1967.[6] According to local accounts, some ten *judiciales* (judicial police or plainclothesmen) showed up, ordered the people out of their houses, removed their possessions, and nailed shut the doors. Vicente spent a month at INTA persuading it to intervene. The rest of the village spent the month camped outside their houses, wet and miserable. Finally INTA sent a commission, which decided in Vicente's favor and enabled his community to reoccupy their homes—until another court-ordered eviction forced them to repeat the process.

In 1970 the Tums managed to put Rigoberta's father in jail. On September 29 he was arrested for *hurto,* or theft, and taken to Santa Cruz del

Quiché.[7] Vicente was accused of dismantling a dwelling in Chimel belonging to one of the Tums, then carting off the materials to improve his own abode. Four of my sources believe he was guilty; a lone defender thinks it was a setup. He was convicted of the charge, sentenced, and spent as much as fifteen months in the departmental prison in Santa Cruz del Quiché. Seven years later two of Vicente's fellow homesteaders who would die in the violence, Pedro Jax and Manuel Tiquiram Tum, were in jail because the Tums of Laguna Danta accused them of invading their property. Finally, on November 7, 1978, as Chimel was making the down payment on its land to INTA, national police arrested Vicente because of another complaint by the Tums. This time he spent only a week or two in jail before the community bailed him out, and the case never went to trial.[8]

The Tums were not the only ones to recur to the national police and the courts. Vicente did, too, as when he succeeded in having two men jailed in Santa Cruz on February 22, 1974, for assaulting and injuring him. The two were part of a dissident faction in his own village, and this could be the incident that led to his being hospitalized in Santa Cruz del Quiché.[9] According to one of Vicente's kinsmen, the Tums had paid the two to attack him. But three other relatives say that the beating that sent Vicente to the hospital was administered directly by the Tums, so it is possible that there was a second such incident. "The Tums spent a lot of money and sold many of their animals to pay lawyers, but they could not [dislodge Vicente]," one of the three told me. "So they waited for him in the road and beat him with sticks, and he spent six weeks in the hospital."

My evidence on the assaults and litigation is fragmentary. One reason is that someone burned the judicial archive in Santa Cruz del Quiché (for reasons unconnected to the Menchús) just before I went looking for it. Another is that many of the principals died in the violence, with others tending to reticence. "What is he looking for?" an ex-litigant turned evangelical pastor asked about me when Barbara Bocek and I showed up at his house. "He's a writer; he writes books about history and people,"Barb explained in K'iche'. "I only want to talk about things of heaven," Vicente's old adversary responded. "I no longer talk about things of this world. . . . Does he write the word of God?" "No, he writes about the history, the land, the people," my companion explained. "Least of all do I want to talk about political things and land," concluded the pastor.

Still another reason these incidents are difficult to recover is that bystanders were confused about exactly who was doing what to whom. By 1972–1973 Vicente was confronting not just the brothers of his Tum father-in-law but a group of opponents within his own village. There were also two new groups of claimants, each of which wanted the 210 hectares in Laguna Danta's defective title that Vicente did not claim. The tract in question ran along the cleared valley bottom between Laguna Danta and Chimel—

"Chimel Chiquito" as opposed to Vicente's "Chimel Grande." The first group was led by a ladino from the village of Los Canaques, but it consisted mainly of K'iche's, including Vicente's son Victor Menchú, and staked its claim with Vicente's help. The second group consisted of K'iche's from another nearby village, Macalajau. Soon both groups were adding to the sad history of physical confrontations and anguished appeals to INTA. What never emerged from the accounts I heard was identification of Vicente as a political prisoner. In this, his daughter's account is unique.

A Factionalized Village

> *The moment I learned to identify our enemies was very important for me. For me now the landowner was a big enemy, an evil one. The soldier too was a criminal enemy. And so were all the rich. We began using the term "enemies," because we didn't have the notion of enemy in our culture, until those people arrived to exploit us, oppress us and discriminate against us. In our community we are all equal. We all have to help one another and share the little we have between us. There is no superior and inferior.*
>
> **—*I, Rigoberta Menchú*, pp. 122–123**

Any speaker of K'iche' can confirm that the language has a word for enemy—*k'ulel*—which surfaces quickly in hostilities with other K'iche's and was doubtless in use around Chimel. Far from being peaceful, Rigoberta's village was known for being more conflictual than most. The homesteaders of Chimel were from various ethnic groups and locales; what they had in common was above all their desire for land. Whatever sense of community they were able to build was repeatedly fractured by the problem of boundaries. Rigoberta is not the only person who remembers Chimel as a warm, cohesive community, but it was also the transitory home of a shifting population, the majority of whom left because of the feuding.

Any homesteading community tends to be unstable because of the hardships involved. "There is always coming and going," one veteran told me. This was certainly the case in Chimel, as suggested by a comparison of five lists of household heads over the years.[10] By 1978, just before the start of the violence, Vicente Menchú and four other household heads were the only men left from the first census sixteen years before. Eighty-eight others had disappeared from the list, for a total attrition approaching ninety-five percent.

In the 1960s Vicente fleshed out his community with "Cobaneros," Q'eqchi' Mayas trying to become independent from finca patróns. Many of them were intimidated into leaving by the Tums, particularly after the latter's success in evicting them from their houses, if only temporarily, then jailing Vicente in the departmental capital. The next wave of arrivals in Chimel were K'iche's like the Menchús themselves. Some were from nearby villages of Uspantán, but more—twenty-four families—were from Parraxtut, a K'iche' colony in the municipio of Sacapulas, to the west along the front range of the Cuchumatanes. The Parraxtut homesteaders originally wanted public land far to the north in the Ixcán region. But there were so many obstacles that INTA sent them to Chimel, to build up the number of families needed to settle twenty-eight square kilometers. Men from Parraxtut began accompanying Vicente on his visits to INTA and filing petitions in his absence. But within a few years, they were in revolt against his leadership.

According to the first complaint, by two Parraxtut men in 1972, Vicente had given them house lots that were only half the size of those allocated to others. Then Vicente threatened to take the lots back, claiming to do so with INTA's authority.[11] By the end of 1973, twenty-three more household heads added their thumbprints to a letter blasting Vicente for pursuing his interests at their expense.[12] The letter asked INTA to recognize two of the Parraxtut leaders as Chimel's representatives. Now the dissidents included K'iche's from Uspantán.

In 1976 Vicente acknowledged that *la comunidad* was divided into two factions. Although forty-one family heads were willing to help with community tasks, such as paying INTA for their titles, he claimed that the other fifteen were not, having rebelled against the group's leadership.[13] According to the dissidents, Vicente was threatening to throw them off their land, and they no longer recognized him as their representative.[14] The result was a second exodus of households. Because INTA continued to insist on more people for such a large claim, in the late 1970s Vicente recruited a third wave of homesteaders to serve as replacements—twenty-four families who were again K'iche's, but this time from Uspantán. The newcomers arrived just in time for the violence.

Refusing to Compromise

> *I've been spending some more time in the hospital, and moose-hunting to rebuild my spirits, and of course feuding with my neighbors over land. The time we waste quarreling is worth more than the land itself. But to farmers where I live, to give an inch of land in a dispute is like giving up everything we're supposed to believe in. Pigheadedness in land disputes is also a great way to bond with your forefathers, and you become instantly popular with your older relatives. I guess Norway and Guatemala are not so far removed from each other as one might think.*
>
> **—Henrik Hovland, 1994[15]**

To summarize a complicated situation, five groups of Mayan peasants were competing for land in and around Chimel. First there was Vicente Menchú and the homesteaders of Chimel; then the Tums of Laguna Danta, who never stopped insisting on the validity of the defective title they had purchased; then a dissident faction within Vicente's group, led by homesteaders from Parraxtut; then two other groups from the villages of Los Canaques and Macalajau. Except for a few individuals from Los Canaques, all the claimants were indigenous.

In dispute was a tract of 360 hectares, lying between the village of Laguna Danta and the 2,753 uncontested hectares that INTA was willing to title to Vicente Menchú. Within the 360 hectares was the land that Vicente had first farmed via his in-laws, where he had built his home, and where he had established the hamlet of Chimel. But of the 360 hectares, he claimed only 151, leaving the remainder to be disputed in a three-way contest between the colonists from Los Canaques (who were joined by one of his own sons), the colonists from Macalajau, and the Tums of Laguna Danta.

All parties appealed regularly to INTA functionaries, but these had no legal authority to impose a solution, let alone the muscle to enforce one. All they could do was mediate, repeatedly and unsuccessfully. Eventually INTA officials tried to end the controversy by titling Vicente and his companions to the 2,753 hectares that were not in dispute. Perhaps they could be persuaded to move from the disputed 151 hectares, on which their village sat, to the 2,753 where no one would bother them. The Parraxtut homesteaders were willing to do so, but not Vicente.

One of his earliest partners, who left Chimel because "we don't like to fight with neighbors," told me about an INTA meeting in the early 1970s at which Vicente refused to compromise. "Who is fighting for the land in dispute?" an INTA functionary asks. The leader of the Parraxtut contingent at Chimel, Diego De Leon Imul, says he doesn't want to fight, but Vicente raises his hand and says, "I'm the one who's fighting." "Now that it's been surveyed, are you going to continue fighting?" asks the INTA official. "Yes, I'm going to continue fighting," Vicente responds. "You are Guatemalans," the INTA official pleads, "the two of you, Antonio Tum and Vicente Menchú as well. If one of you was from another country, fine, but that is not how it is; both of you are sons of the same father, of the same country. So it's better if you do not continue fighting." Then to Vicente: "Now that you have the land [the 2,753 hectares] surveyed, you can pass over to live in it." "But he didn't want to," Vicente's partner recalled. Only Diego De Leon of Parraxtut signed the survey, according to this source; Vicente refused.

The refusal to stop fighting for the 151 hectares, thereby delaying the INTA title for the 2,753, became the basic grievance against Vicente within

Chimel. Hence the 1978 complaint by five men who asked (unsuccessfully) to rejoin the forty-five household heads who were about to get a provisional land title. The reason they had left Chimel, according to the petition, was their realization that Vicente's legal battles were "his personal caprice, and that it was not convenient for us to support his attitude."[16] Now they had been left out of INTA's final census, and only because they refused to give him more money for his struggle against the Tums. "He always names himself the leader and wants to give orders as if he were the patrón of a finca."[17]

"That is why Vicente Menchú turned against us, because we did not want to fight for the land in dispute," one of the men told me recently. "That is why [the titling of the 2,753 hectares] was delayed for so long. . . . For not wanting to let go this sliver [of land], he went to jail, and it's still in dispute." Another member of old Chimel said, "If you were willing to fight for the three caballerías [the local measure for the 151 hectares], then you had rights to the sixty-one caballerías as well. Anyone who didn't want to fight for the three could take himself elsewhere. People really got tired of making contributions." The least charitable explanation for Vicente's behavior, the one offered by opponents, is that he was fattening off the collections for legal expenses. If village households did not have cash, as was often the case, they paid him with turkeys, ducks, or chickens. "People say that self-interest was part of it, to pay for his days, his travel expenses, and something to maintain his family," explained a defender who doubts the truth of the charge.

Why did Vicente not recruit the extra colonists that INTA required from Laguna Danta, thereby avoiding blame for importing outsiders? One of his Tum antagonists claimed that he never invited them—and that if he had invited them, they would have said no. Various Tums did join Chimel, so perhaps Vicente tried. But he may have needed more households than Laguna Danta's kin networks could provide, especially since men with sufficient land would not want to go to all the expense and trouble of petitioning for more. Then, too, Vicente's leadership drives were probably too strong for the deference that his adversaries expected from a son-in-law who had married into their land. In any case, only the most intense animosity, all too common in peasant land disputes, can explain a self-destructive feud that cost the adversaries more than they could ever hope to obtain from the hectares in question. Of Vicente's opponent Nicolás Tum Castro, who would also die in the violence, an elder recalled that he "had good oxen, a mill for grinding sugar cane, and cattle, but he sold it all to fight Vicente Menchú. The lawyer took advantage of him."[18]

The Vicente Menchú who emerges from recollections of the land feud may seem hard to reconcile with the figure portrayed by Rigoberta. But once we weigh the nostalgia of an orphaned daughter against the bitterness of opponents, there is less distance than might appear. According to *I, Rigoberta Menchú,* Vicente was a strong father figure in his community.[19] "He gave us lots of counsel," a nephew agreed. "'You have to get along with people; there's no need to rob; you have to be a good person.' He talked a lot about God. He advised me well that we have to be good with people, also about work, using well what you inherit from your father. He was a señor who spoke carefully. He had a good mind. He helped us when they wanted to take our land; he helped us get it back. He had lots of ideas; he knew how to demand his rights."

This is the wise, vigilant patriarch of his daughter's book. In contrast to the hostile assessments quoted above, it is not hard to find men who speak of Vicente in the highest terms. "He was modest, tranquil, peaceful," an old friend recalled. "He was without education but shrewd." Still, patriarchal authority can always be experienced as tyranny. "He was a bit authoritarian and strict, like the father of a family," a Chimel survivor told me. "If someone didn't obey, he could leave for another community." According to INTA regulations, every household in Chimel had equal rights to the land that the community was titling. But until just before the violence, Chimel was not recognized as a village by the town hall, therefore did not elect an auxiliary mayor like others did. Even after authorities were elected, they consisted of Vicente's sons or allies. In Mayan society fathers have the right to withhold recognition and property from disobedient sons. As the founder of an independent settlement, Vicente apparently saw himself as the community's father and felt he had the right to punish members who disobeyed him. That would give him the right to judge whether other men were in good standing with the community or not, as defined by their willingness to support his struggle for the fatal 151 hectares.

There are two noteworthy differences between Rigoberta's portrait of her father and the man who emerges from other recollections. One is his attitude toward ladinos, as dramatized by his daughter's considerable emphasis on ethnic hatred. In *I, Rigoberta Menchú,* Vicente and his father-in-law have come to hate ladinos and teach their young to hate them, too. Were the Menchús to have suffered from ladinos as severely as Rigoberta claims, this would be understandable. Yet it is not the picture that emerges from local recollections. Any wrongs that Vicente suffered as a child servant would have been at the hands of Uspanteko patróns, not ladinos; and his main land dispute was with his K'iche' in-laws, whom he could thank for legal expeditions to the capital, at least one beating, a trip to the hospital, and two stretches in jail.

Instead of going into Vicente's problems with his K'iche' in-laws, *I, Rigoberta Menchú* plays up his conflicts with ladino finca owners. As a capable man facing the ethnic subordination that all indígenas did, Vicente probably harbored feelings about ladinos that he did not express to them.

Certainly there was distrust between the two ethnic groups—but also restraint, reliable overtures through everyday rituals, and friendships. What Rigoberta's testimony virtually denies is that ladinos coexisted peacefully with indígenas around Chimel. Both groups consisted of peasants who made do with little but their land and ingenuity and, in many respects, shared the same way of life. As for Rigoberta's father, he was especially known for his good relations with ladinos. Although his own settlement of Chimel Grande did not include any nonindigenous families, he invited a mixed group led by a ladino from Los Canaques to homestead the nearby Chimel Chiquito.

A second difference between Rigoberta's portrait of her father and the man who can be reconstructed from local memories is his relation to the state. Much of Vicente's stature as a leader can be attributed to his success in dealing with ladino or foreign-controlled institutions, including the army, the Catholic Church, INTA, and the urban left. There was nothing reprehensible about this in the view of fellow K'iche's. It was a virtue, a requirement for successful village leadership, as was Vicente's command of Spanish. What does arouse comment—criticism from some and bafflement from others—is Vicente's inability to make peace with his in-laws. With land at stake, in a pattern that is very common among peasants, the two sides became accustomed to appealing against each other to the state.

In lieu of this history, Rigoberta provided her father with a long and personal genealogy of oppression by Guatemala's dictatorships. At the age of eighteen, he is rounded up for military service. During the 1954 invasion of Guatemala by a CIA-organized army of right-wing exiles, he is taken prisoner along with many other men and hauled off to a barracks, from which he barely escapes with his life. By the early 1970s, after repeated betrayals by INTA, the Vicente of *I, Rigoberta Menchú* is a radicalized peasant who expects nothing from the system. Twice a political prisoner, he is ready to take up arms to avenge his son.[20]

Generations of indigenous boys have indeed been hauled away to the barracks. But according to a member of Vicente's family, he joined the army as a volunteer. An elder recalled that, after his first year and a half of duty, he liked the army well enough to reenlist. As for being captured during the 1954 CIA invasion, one of his children denied any knowledge of the episode: "Here we are very isolated; there is not that kind of conflict."

Judging from local recollections, until Vicente's last year his politics were rather different from those described by his daughter. In relations with ladinos and the state, he employed a cautious style, imbued with the legalistic norms of Hispanic bureaucracy, which village leaders in Guatemala have practiced for centuries.[21] Any dealing with an outside authority, sometimes even a visit by an anthropologist, leads to writing up an *acta*—a record of the occasion, carefully kept in a register—even though most villagers are unable to read it. Certainly, ladinos have long feared the fury of the indigenous *turba* (mob). But because of advances in state firepower and communication, indígenas of Vicente's generation had virtually abandoned confrontation as a method of struggle against the state. Like most peasant leaders schooled in Guatemala's unforgiving definition of the permissible, he instead resorted to ceaseless petition. Even after the army kidnapped his son and he went to the capital to protest, he appealed to the law.

Rigoberta's book does echo faithfully the tendency of Uspantán peasants to blame someone else—government functionaries or ladinos—for their land conflicts with each other. "But the ones who caused the problem are the very Spaniards," an in-law insisted, "by doing bad surveys, by demanding bribes. How many surveyors have shown up there! It took me a long time to figure this out; it cost me a lot to understand, but there is where it began." It is true that an archaic, corrupt land titling system has sown many a conflict. But that does not explain why in-laws with an abundance of land were unable to cooperate with each other. As we shall see in the following chapters, this is far from the only case in which taking a claim to victimhood at face value means accepting a very partial version of the events that produced so many victims.

PART TWO

Popular Revolutionary War

4

Revolutionary Justice Comes to Uspantán

The prime problem for the Guatemalan revolution is to integrate the Indians into the planning, the execution and, this above all, the leadership of the revolutionary war; it is also the most difficult problem to solve. How is this war to become their *war?*

—Régis Debray, with Ricardo Ramírez, 1974[1]

Months of rumors preceded their arrival. Peasants wondered whether they were animal or human. In the case of Uspantán, they had occupied an estate in the far north of the municipio, then ambushed an army truck. But it was only on April 29, 1979, that the Guerrilla Army of the Poor (EGP) suddenly materialized, after filtering into town in civilian dress. Once in uniform, they numbered more than a hundred, mainly Ixil and K'iche' Mayas along with a few ladinos. Because none wore a mask and none was recognized over the several hours they occupied Uspantán, none seems to have been local. "They went through all the town and painted everything red," a K'iche' widow told me. "They went into the market, grabbed the tax collector's money, and threw it into the streets for people to grab. They chopped open the jail and let loose all the prisoners. When they got to the town square, they shouted, 'We're defenders of the poor' for fifteen or twenty minutes."

"They cut off communication, the telegraph," a K'iche' functionary added, "and brought the national police, the ex-mayor and the municipal tax collector to a meeting in the square. They said they were the guerrillas. That they were going to win and that they were defending the poor because the government committed many injustices and there was lots of inequality. That the hospitals lacked medicine, that the rich had the good land, that they paid their workers badly on the plantations of the South Coast, and that the army conscripted Indian boys." There were no shootings and no threats. But there was a multitude present because this was market day.

Some say the crowd applauded the EGP's orators, others that there were few signs of approbation. How did people feel? I asked the widow quoted above, who now helps lead one of the left's popular organizations in Uspantán. "They frightened us," she replied. "Everyone was frightened because lots of them arrived and they were armed. There seemed to be women in the group, but you couldn't see them well because everyone was in uniform. There were some [in the crowd] who said, 'This isn't good because maybe they are going to kill us.' Others said, 'This is good because they're going to help the poor.'"

How Uspantán peasants felt about the arrival of the EGP—broadly, their political consciousness—is a complex issue that we will explore through the next seven chapters. Let us start with the easiest questions: where the guerrillas came from in Guatemalan politics, what they wanted to accomplish, and why they were looking for allies in Uspantán. The answers are to be found in a second and far more powerful institution, the Guatemalan army, which dominated national life into the 1990s. Next, this chapter looks at two locales that attracted the guerrillas in their search for revolutionary kindling. The first is a large coffee plantation west of Chimel called the Finca San Francisco. The second is El Soch, a narrow valley east of Chimel occupied by a string of much smaller coffee fincas. In the 1970s each fit the spirit of Rigoberta's 1982 account better than her own village did. One was the site of the first political killings in Uspantán.

The Democracy That Gave Way

As the campesinos of northern Quiché contemplate their misfortunes, they sometimes refer to soldiers and guerrillas as if they came from the same root. "It is said that the very army set up the guerrillas, that their leaders sowed the seed," one Uspantano told me. This happens to be an apt summary of Guatemalan history. When Central America became independent from Spain in the early nineteenth century, a stable despotism disintegrated into civil war. Once free of the central authority of the Spanish empire, local elites were unable to contain their differences within a republican form of government. Only military caudillos were able to restore order.

Not in question was the subordinate status of the mass of the population, the peasantry, who in Guatemala were still heavily indigenous. After the Spanish vanquished a panoply of small Mayan kingdoms in the sixteenth century, European diseases reduced indígenas to a small fraction of their former numbers. To save the labor supply from extinction, the Spanish monarchy prohibited settlers and their mixed-race offspring from acquiring land around indigenous settlements. A lack of opportunities to export wealth to Spain eventually reduced the demands on indigenous labor. Gradually Indians recovered some of their numbers and built an economy of agriculture, artisanry, and petty commerce that survives to this day.

The position of indígenas deteriorated again in the nineteenth century, after Guatemala became a republic. Following half a century of civil war, Conservatives (who supported the old protectionist legislation for Indians) were vanquished by Liberals (who were fervent believers in modern capitalism). Beginning in the 1870s, Liberal dictators welcomed foreign investment, especially for exporting coffee. Mayan peasants posed two obstacles. First, some of the best land for growing coffee was still in their hands. To allow outsiders to buy it, the Liberals therefore established new titling laws, with the results described in Chapter 2. Second, so many peasants were self-sufficient that they were not very interested in working for plantations. The Liberals therefore made it easier to conscript indígenas for agricultural labor and public works. They also relaxed liquor laws, making it easier to lure indígenas into debt servitude. As a result, modernizing Guatemala meant reinstituting semifeudal conditions for Indians.

Why did they not revolt? Fear of indigenous rebellion has been a constant in Guatemalan history. Although resistance has never been lacking, it tends to be local and directed against specific instances of ill treatment, not against the system as a whole.[2] When blood does flow, it is usually indigenous rather than ladino. Under the Liberal tyranny, increasing demands for Mayan land and labor were accompanied by new telegraph lines and repeating rifles that made it easier to suppress opposition. From the national palace, a *señor presidente* presided over regional oligarchs and foreign investors, who administered their respective domains like private estates. When rebellion finally gathered, it was not in the countryside but in the heavily ladino capital, where agropastoral tyranny left little room for the middle-class professionals—teachers, lawyers, civil servants—needed to keep up with the rest of the world's rush to modernity.

In 1944, urban dissidents persuaded army officers to overthrow the last of the Liberal dictators, a general and plantation owner in the Prussian mold named Jorge Ubico. The subsequent decade of elected government is memorialized by the left as the country's springtime of democracy and by the right as a downward spiral into communism. Under Presidents Juan José Arévalo (1945–1951) and Jacobo Arbenz (1951–1954), forced labor was abolished and unions became legal. The most fateful step was a long-awaited land reform. President Arbenz was a colonel and plantation owner himself, but the predictable opposition from his social class forced him to the left. Prominent among his advisers were intellectuals from Guatemala's communist party, some of whose organizers were encouraging peasants to seize estates. Washington decided to act after Arbenz expropriated (with compensation) the plantations of the United Fruit Company. In the belief that Guatemala had become a Stalinist beachhead, the U.S. government organized an invasion of right-wing exiles to recapture it.[3]

Through displays of airpower and other forms of intimidation, the Central Intelligence Agency paralyzed the Guatemalan army. Its officers were already of two minds on the implications of land reform, especially for their own dreams of retiring to a finca. Although crowds gathered to defend the revolution, rifles were never handed out. Arbenz was intimidated into resigning. His army commanders swallowed their pride. Instead of defending the constitution they had helped establish, they accepted the new president chosen by the North Americans, a colonel named Carlos Castillo Armas. The land distributed to peasants was returned to its previous owners.

A decade later, even Washington would be urging land reform to stave off other revolutions. If land had been redistributed in Guatemala, it would have helped more peasants become small commercial farmers and encouraged a more equitable distribution of income. By increasing the purchasing power of the lower classes, land reform also would have encouraged Guatemala's elites to invest their capital at home. In another election or two, the opposition would have checked the push to the left, with the political center coming to rest in social or Christian democracy. The country could have evolved in the direction of Costa Rica, which leads Latin America in per capita income and political stability. Instead, the 1954 counterrevolution shut a mainly law-abiding left out of the electoral system and encouraged the Guatemalan elite to consider itself above the law. After Washington restored its idea of democracy, the government became more corrupt, elites refused to pay any but nominal taxes, and capital fled to the United States, crippling the economy's ability to provide jobs for a growing population.

Virulent anticommunism became the response to any challenge to the status quo. To stop ex-president Arévalo from winning reelection, in 1963 the army seized control of the government. When another reformer was elected president in 1966, the army allowed him to take office only if he gave it a free hand to crush a guerrilla movement in the eastern part of the country. This the army did, with a reign of terror that took thousands of lives. One of the masterminds, Colonel Carlos Arana Osorio, won the next presidential election in 1970. Four years later, the regime rearranged electoral results to impose its defense minister as the new president. Four years later, the same thing happened again. The defense minister became the next president, in what promised to be an endless succession of military rulers.

A Revolutionary Generation

If there is a single reason for the guerrilla movement and its premise that Guatemala required armed liberation, it was the CIA's overthrow of an elected government in 1954. For the left, that was the event that forced it to take up arms. But when guerrillas appeared eight years later, the first leaders were not Marxist intellectuals, class-conscious workers, or angry peasants. They were young army officers, Guatemalan patriots indignant over their country's subordination to the United States.[4] During a 1960 military coup, rebel soldiers were mobbed by ladino peasants asking for guns so that they could fight, too. After the coup failed, dozens of officers and soldiers went into hiding, contacted Guatemalan communists, and with their help organized the first guerrilla columns.

The formative experience for the generation that launched the insurgency in the 1960s and led it into the 1990s was the shock of the CIA invasion. The trauma was all the greater because these were young men and women who had grown up in an era of free expression, reform, and boundless possibility that suddenly ended as they reached adulthood. What remained was a powerful sense of patriotic mission, including the belief that their compatriots awaited the right kind of leadership to rise up against the Guatemalan oligarchy and U.S. imperialism.[5]

One of the generation's members was Ricardo Ramírez, the head of the Guerrilla Army of the Poor. He was not from a poor background: His father was in the army during the period when it turned against the Ubico dictatorship. Ramírez himself studied agronomy at the well-known technical school of the United Fruit Company in Zamorano, Honduras. By the time Arbenz fell, he was a student leader in Guatemala City. Taking sanctuary in a foreign embassy, he made friends with a young Argentine who had come to join the revolution, only to have to seek refuge like hundreds of others. It was Che Guevara, who would later invite Ramírez to join his circle of revolutionary exiles in Cuba.[6] Under the nom de guerre of Rolando Morán, Ramírez went on to organize the Guerrilla Army of the Poor, whose flag would bear the famous image of Che gazing skyward.

Another member of Guatemala's revolutionary generation was Mario Payeras. Born in 1940 to a well-off family, he also traced his political awakening to 1954, when he watched antiaircraft guns behind his house shoot at CIA-piloted fighter planes: "Afterward came the frustration, the shame, the tremendous burden that the revolution had been defeated." Joining the revolutionary underground, he went to San Carlos University to study philosophy, then continued his education in Mexico, where he met revolutionary exiles who sent him to study in East Germany. Eventually he joined the expedition that issued in the EGP, rose to the rank of comandante, and went on to write candid accounts of the war.[7]

For Guatemalans who wanted to resurrect the accomplishments of the early 1950s, the example of Che Guevara, Fidel Castro, and the guerrilla war they waged from the Sierra Maestra of Cuba came to seem the only possible road. Like many other Latin Americans, they saw the Cuban revolution as a model for liberating a fettered region. Condemned to poverty and premature death, the Latin American masses were hungry for change, which was being frustrated by national oligarchies and their allies in Washington. Since the United States could be counted upon to crush democratic reform, the masses awaited their liberators.

Just as the Cuban revolution stimulated the hopes of the Guatemalan left, it also aroused the fears of the country's elite. For the Guatemalan right, their country's tragedy began not with liberation from communist rule in 1954 but the initiation of guerrilla warfare in 1962. All over Latin America, attempts to follow Fidel Castro's path to power moved national armies to switch from defending national borders to fighting internal subversion. For counterinsurgency planners in Washington, Cuban-supported guerrillas provided a rationale for modernizing Latin America's semimoribund militaries. One of the institutions that most obviously needed help was the Guatemalan army, whose officer corps had been confused and divided by the events of 1954.

Perhaps because army officers and guerrilla commanders were equally fed up with North American proconsuls, their war with each other began as a contest between gentlemen, who placed old ties at the military academy ahead of the unpleasant task of killing each other. After lieutenant-turned-comandante Luis Turcios Lima died in a car accident, his funeral procession was saluted by military cadets. When Colonel Enrique Peralta Azurdía seized power in 1963, he was sufficiently mindful of his officers' feelings to resist U.S. advice on how to fight the rebels. With the army in a halfhearted state, the guerrillas scored some successes; organized peasants in several areas; and entered into talks with the next civilian president during the 1966 election. But they also let down their guard at a time when their advances were galvanizing the army into working with U.S. advisers. Soon the army drove them out of the areas they had organized and slaughtered their supporters.

The guerrillas of the 1960s operated mainly among ladinos in eastern Guatemala. Although some indígenas joined, others were quick to inform the nearest police post. To avoid further disasters, the guerrillas of the 1960s made no concerted effort to organize Indians, regarding them as incommunicable and reactionary until such time as the revolution could bring them into the twentieth century. The salutary result was that most indígenas escaped the repression that fell upon eastern Guatemala. Instead, many became involved in grassroots organizations sponsored by the Catholic Church. They joined cooperatives and peasant leagues rather than guerrilla networks. Despite occasional threats and illegal arrests, many campesinos remember the 1960s and 1970s as a time of peace and prosperity.

Meanwhile, survivors of the first guerrilla columns were looking for a new social base from which to liberate their country. Returning to burned-over districts was out of the question. Their most enthusiastic supporters were in the grave, others wanted nothing to do with them, and their old haunts were sown with informers. The unintended (but typical) result of guerrilla strategy had been to turn eastern Guatemala into a bastion of reaction. Where to turn next?

One place was the capital. Guerrillas infiltrated popular organizations, robbed banks, and machine-gunned police stations. They also kidnapped oligarchs and ambassadors to exchange them for political prisoners and ransom. This last innovation was disastrous because the ultraright and the army responded in kind and far more effectively, with death squads.[8] The urban cells went down with guns blazing. Instead of building political momentum, their inferior firepower gave the army an excuse for militarizing society. The results of urban guerrilla warfare for the above-ground left, in labor unions and schools, were just as devastating. Interpreting their mandate liberally, the security forces murdered anyone who might be involved.

Another possibility for guerrilla warfare was the southern piedmont and coast, whose coffee fincas, sugar and cotton plantations were the agroexporting engine of the Guatemalan economy. Large owners held virtually all the land, their permanent workers had virtually none, and every year hundreds of thousands of indígenas descended from their homes in the highlands to work for pitifully low wages. Here the proletarian consciousness that Marxists regarded as an essential condition for revolution should abound.

This is where the Organization of the People in Arms (ORPA) established itself, among volcanoes and coffee fincas, and continued to operate until 1996. Yet the southern coast and piedmont did not become the next major theater. One reason may be that knowledge of what the army had done in eastern Guatemala diffused through a Spanish-speaking population. Another may be that rural proletarians were completely dependent on the plantation economy for their livelihood, hence knew they could not survive a strategy that cut off their wages.

Instead, the next major theater became the western highlands, where the country's Mayan-speaking population is concentrated. In the words of the revolutionary journalist Marta Harnecker, "The small minifundista producer disposes . . . of far more flexibility and can be an army's source of supply."[9] In other words, highland peasants had a subsistence economy that could provide food and recruits. They lived in mountains where guerrillas could hide. And judging from my interviewing, they had little idea of what the army could do to them.

But how to overcome indigenous distrust toward outsiders with guns and political agendas? One possibility was to appeal to the relatively sophisticated Mayan population living near the Pan-American Highway, along a corridor running from Chimaltenango, Sololá, and southern

Quiché to Totonicapán and Quezaltenango. Here Mayan entrepreneurs and activists had built an indigenous-controlled regional economy. By the 1990s this was also where the Mayan movement and the left's renascent popular organizations were strongest, with the most advanced political consciousness in the highlands. The guerrillas did have considerable success in southern Quiché and Chimaltenango, as we shall see in Chapter 7. Yet this is not where they started. Even after part of the population joined the insurgents, they were not able to concentrate enough forces to hold the area, and they never became strong in the core of the region, around Totonicapán and Quezaltenango, perhaps because Mayan ethnic consciousness preempted their appeals.

The proto-EGP chose to start instead in the Ixcán, a lowland jungle region near the Mexican border being settled by highland peasants. The geography of the Ixcán was attractive. Logistics could be channeled through Mexico, the area was remote, and guerrilla organizers could hide in the forest for years, connecting with the local population but running less risk of coming to the army's attention than in more populated areas. The Ixcán rain forest was also an agricultural frontier where peasants had moved away from the traditional authorities in their hometowns, where the struggle for survival compelled them to work with strangers from other places, and where they were already organized by the Catholic Church. Here the first fifteen EGP fighters established themselves in 1972, northwest of Uspantán.

The Lucas Terror

If Cuba inspired the Guatemalan insurgents of the 1960s, their model in the late 1970s was Nicaragua. Rising against the dictatorship of Anastasio Somoza were the youth of entire neighborhoods. They built barricades, held off the national guard with revolvers and gasoline bombs, then melted into the countryside to join the Sandinista guerrillas and prepare for the next insurrection. In July 1979 the national guard collapsed and the Somoza family fled. Could Guatemalans do the same thing? The time seemed ripe because, under the military president Kjell Laugerud (1974–1978), the army scaled back repression. After the February 1976 earthquake, which took thirty thousand lives and left a million people homeless, international aid programs stimulated the growth of grassroots organizations. The remaining guerrillas did not seem active and the Laugerud regime talked about reform. In retrospect this was the eye of the storm. Although more labor unions started than at any time since 1944–1954, many owners refused to recognize them. A steady stream of unionists were murdered. In the belief that another wave of repression was inevitable, revolutionary organizations set up clandestine networks for another round of guerrilla warfare.

The Laugerud administration lost the last of its legitimacy in the massacre at Panzós, a fertile district of Alta Verapaz where finca owners called in the army to fend off Q'eqchi' Maya peasants challenging their property lines. On May 29, 1978, landowners and soldiers machine-gunned a crowd of demonstrators in the town square. The army had declared open season on campesinos demanding their rights, or so it appeared. Yet under Laugerud a new generation of opponents had learned to express their anger. As the rebel youth of Nicaragua demonstrated the potential of street warfare, Guatemalans listened on their radios and dreamed of liberating their country.

Just as the Sandinista revolution was an inspiration for the Guatemalan left, it was a clear warning to the Guatemalan right, which was determined to prevent it from being repeated. The general occupying the presidential palace at the time was Romeo Lucas García (1978–1982). "From here in the national palace," he declared, "they are not going to extract me as they did Anastasio Somoza."[10] Judging from the president's doddering performances, he may already have been suffering from the Alzheimer's disease that would destroy his mind. His subordinates blamed the rising tide of political abductions and murders on right-wing extremists, who proved to be coordinated by a military communications center next to the presidential palace.[11]

Under siege in the capital, the left was looking to the countryside for liberation, as was supposed to have happened in Cuba and Nicaragua. The indígenas were finally rising up—so said the Guerrilla Army of the Poor and the Committee for Campesino Unity. Imagery about the countryside often plays an important role in urban-led political movements because it affirms claims to national representivity. Far from alone in idealizing peasant villages, the Guatemalan left supposed that they were cohesive communities whose most significant struggles were vertical (against plantation owners, labor contractors, or the state) rather than horizontal (among themselves or with other peasants).[12] If Indians faced increasing exploitation, as revolutionary strategists also presumed, then they should be receptive to the idea of armed struggle. Certainly, there were communication barriers to overcome. But guerrilla leaders believed that indígenas were on the verge of embracing a revolutionary movement and could become an indestructible bastion of support.

For observers, reports of guerrilla occupations, death squad kidnappings, and army sweeps in the Department of El Quiché seemed to confirm that peasants were casting their lot with the guerrillas. By June 1978 the Catholic diocese counted more than seventy-five government kidnappings in Ixil country, plus dozens more in the Ixcán.[13] Yet other areas seemed untroubled, among them Uspantán.

The Finca Owners of San Francisco and El Soch

Before the violence this was a peaceful town, or so it seemed. There was always discrimination, the indígena was not taken into account, but there were no confrontations.

—Uspantán human rights activist, 1994

That there were no ethnic confrontations in Uspantán prior to the violence is not strictly true. But it is true enough to deserve careful consideration by the many readers of *I, Rigoberta Menchú* who assume that the insurgency grew inexorably out of the everyday violence, structural and otherwise, of the Guatemalan countryside. To recruit rural cadres, the Guerrilla Army of the Poor needed to appeal to grievances against oppressors, whom it supposed would consist of plantation owners, labor contractors, military commissioners, and foreigners, particularly North Americans, whose military advisers had played a major role in the destruction of the 1960s insurgency. Chimel might not seem the most attractive kind of place to start organizing: It was an independent community, unbeholden to finca owners. Its main conflicts were with other K'iche' smallholders. Yet freeholders have more liberty to organize than peasants who depend on a patrón. Chimel was also on the edge of two plantation districts where the kind of grievances for which the EGP was looking were more apparent.

The Finca San Francisco, the largest and most productive coffee plantation in northern Quiché, was one of the places where the Menchús and their neighbors went to market. An Italian named Pedro Brol began amassing the property early in the century, by purchasing national-level land titles, which he passed to his sons. Eventually they claimed sixty-eight hundred hectares and, at the height of the harvest season, employed up to thirty-five hundred workers, including K'iche's. Finca headquarters is a half day's walk west of Chimel, in the Ixil municipio of Cotzal, but the Brols used to claim land that was closer. Thus in *I, Rigoberta Menchú*, the Brols survey Chimel in order to seize it.[14] However, not a single person I interviewed could recall a conflict between the two. In the thick INTA files, the only reference to the Brols is a 1971 boundary survey that they did not contest. They did object to the nearby settlement of San Pedro La Esperanza, but the disagreement never degenerated into violence. The land in question was still a wilderness. As San Pedro's ladino and K'iche' homesteaders established themselves, the Brols gave up their claim.

Other K'iche's did have a serious conflict with the Brols on more attractive land, at a place called Guacamayas. Some of the Guacamayas colonists were old friends of Vicente Menchú, including Rigoberta's godfather. In 1976 thirteen of them were hauled off to jail. But they were sufficiently well connected to have lawyers who brought in the press. A court ruled against the Finca San Francisco, and the K'iche's were released. The Brols agreed to give up twelve hundred hectares, then sold the settlers another six hundred or so. When the K'iche's had to defend their Guacamayas property again in the early 1990s, they were on good terms with the Brols. Now they faced Ixils from Cotzal, who claimed Guacamayas and much of the rest of the Finca San Francisco.

The municipal claims of the Ixils of Cotzal made them the Brols' staunchest opponents. During the Liberal land rush around the turn of the century, they lost up to forty-five percent of their small municipio to estate owners. From the Arbenz land reform the Cotzaleños obtained expropriation decrees, only to see these reversed by the CIA-sponsored counterrevolution. Going to jail briefly in 1954 were Cotzal's agrarian leaders, one of whom went on to become the town's cacique by changing sides, becoming an ally of the Finca San Francisco, and stealing elections. His enemies were the first Ixils to welcome the guerrillas. In 1969 finca heir Jorge Brol and his driver were murdered in a payroll robbery. Cotzaleños and a short-lived guerrilla column proved to be responsible. Three years later, members of the same anti-Brol faction contacted a new guerrilla column that became the Guerrilla Army of the Poor.[15]

Meanwhile, owing to financial difficulties, the Finca San Francisco was changing its managerial regime. Until this point, Jorge and his brothers had maintained good relations with their permanent workers by continuing the paternalistic policies of their father. Now impersonal administrators were taking a tougher line. One move was to abolish a privilege long conceded to *quinceneros* ("fifteen-dayers"), who worked for the finca half the month and cultivated parcels of their own the other half. The parcels were on finca land, but quinceneros could plant and sell their own coffee. The arrangement was not without its temptations: Quinceneros could enlarge their own harvest by helping themselves to the finca's. Even before Jorge Brol's death, in 1968, new administrators prohibited the quinceneros from planting more of their own coffee bushes. In 1972 they forced the quinceneros to give up their groves and expelled resisters. A government commission arrived to investigate abuses. A union tried to organize, only to be broken. Hundreds of workers were expelled.

The Guerrilla Army of the Poor found another organizing opportunity in the much smaller fincas of El Soch, a few hours' walk from Chimel in the other direction, to the east. Strung along a narrow, warm valley, this chain of properties was owned by various members of the García and Martínez families. Unlike the Brols of the Finca San Francisco, several Garcías would play a central role in the destruction of Chimel. Because the landholdings of the Garcías and Martínezes were complicated by inheritance, intermarriage, and feuding, outsiders tended to confuse individual members and properties. The Martínez family arrived early in the century—before even the Tums, let alone Vicente Menchú—as administrators for an absentee owner who eventually sold them his holding. The family seat was the Finca La Soledad, a coffee property of 250 hectares down the valley from Chimel. On the edge of Chimel, the Martínezes also owned the Finca El Rosario, a less developed tract of 450 hectares on which they raised cattle, maize, and sugar cane.

The founder of the other clan, Carlos García Fetzer, arrived in the 1930s. The son of a German, he reversed his surnames (from Fetzer García to García Fetzer) during World War II to hispanicize his paternity and avoid being interned in the United States as was the rest of the German community. Carlos also arrived as an administrator for an absentee owner, who subsequently gave him the property—twelve to fifteen hundred hectares (estimates differ) centering on the Finca El Soch. Since local K'iche's and Uspantekos were too independent to give him the labor he needed, he imported Poqomchi's from Alta Verapaz who remember him warmly to this day, as do others who recall numerous good works. At his death in 1965, he left his peons seven hundred hectares on the south wall of the Soch valley, permitting them to organize their own, more autonomous community.

One of Carlos's sons developed a harsher reputation. Honorio García Samayoa was born on the South Coast to a mother who was also half German but left her marriage to Carlos García before he moved to Soch. Honorio joined his father at Soch only in his early twenties, and only after the elder García was raising a second family. Relations between father and son were not very good. When the elder García died, he left most of his property to his second wife, who lost it to the bank—a common fate in the heavily mortgaged coffee sector. Honorio remained with little more than a hundred hectares, which one of his sons may later have complemented with another hundred. Perhaps because Honorio was so much poorer than his father—he had as few as four and no more than ten Poqomchi's working for him, whereas his father's labor force had reached 160—he was known for insisting on his rights and holding a grudge.

I, Rigoberta Menchú gives a misleading impression of solidarity among the ladinos of El Soch, demonstrating that indígenas can have as hard a time appreciating conflicts among ladinos as ladinos among indígenas. By the 1970s, with their patriarchs dead or one foot in the grave, the Garcías and the Martínezes were not the imposing finca owners described by Rigoberta. Instead, they had subdivided their properties among numerous heirs, some of whom the violence would reduce to little more than peasants—the condition of most rural ladinos in Uspantán. The two families also invested more energy in quarreling with each other than with their indigenous neighbors.

But Rigoberta paints the Garcías and Martínezes harshly, accusing them of turning Chimel families out of their houses in 1967 (when in fact the Tums of Laguna Danta were responsible). "Those few days confirmed my hatred for those people," Rigoberta continued. "I saw why we said that ladinos were thieves, criminals and liars." By her account, one of the two "wickedest landowner[s]" was Angel Martínez.[16] Yet according to Angel's family, Vicente Menchú used to visit and trade garden produce for fruit. According to a Menchú, Angel's wife used to stop in Chimel to gossip with Vicente's wife.

The other evil landowner in Rigoberta's account is Honorio García. Yet he and Vicente Menchú also appear to have enjoyed cordial relations. "Honorio and my father were on good terms," one of Rigoberta's siblings told me. "He went there to buy coffee, bananas, and bricks of brown sugar, while we sold them *chilicayotes* and beans." Unlike Angel Martínez, Honorio and his sons did become key figures in the tragedy of Chimel, but the reason is conspicuously missing from *I, Rigoberta Menchú*. Instead, Rigoberta relates one of her most gruesome stories—the murder of Petrona Chona, a young mother working for the Garcías. After spurning the advances of Honorio's son Carlos, according to Rigoberta, her friend Petrona is chopped to pieces by Honorio's bodyguard, who also hacks to death one of Petrona's two infants and cuts off the other's finger. Since no one else dares, to Rigoberta and her father (who happen to work for the Garcías at the time) falls the grim task of picking up the remains.[17]

No one around Soch or Chimel could remember the Petrona Chona named in Rigoberta's account. But they did recall the murder of a nineteen-year-old Pascuala Xoná Chomo, the wife of one of Honorio's Poqomchi' laborers.[18] On June 29, 1973, Pascuala's husband came home from market in a state of inebriation, became angry that his lunch was not ready, and killed her with his machete. He is said to have doubted her fidelity. According to one of Honorio's sons, the husband's drinking companions had been taunting him about what a good woman he had, as if they had been enjoying sex with her. According to another source, Pascuala was one of several indigenous liaisons of her husband's patrón, Honorio García.

Rigoberta's story about Petrona Chona (or Xoná—a different spelling for the same surname) could therefore have a grain of truth. But it is also possible that Honorio's role was invented by the rumor mills of Soch to rationalize an otherwise inexplicable tragedy. Even if concubinage was involved, Pascuala was killed by her own husband, not Honorio's bodyguard. Contrary to Rigoberta's image of a murder that went unpunished, Pascuala's husband served a long prison term. Also of significance, not even harsh critics of the Garcías agree with Rigoberta that they ever employed bodyguards.

The fate of Pascuala Xoná does echo the subordination of the Soch labor force, however. It consisted mainly of Poqomchi's from nearby Alta Verapaz who were considered *sometidos* (dependent and exploited) compared to K'iche's like the Menchús. "Just look at their laborers—they're treated like dogs. They cannot even speak!" exclaimed a ladino critic of the Garcías. Before the war, laborers typically lived on the patrón's land and spent half the month working for him, at lower pay than on a coastal plantation (I heard estimates ranging from Q.30 to Q.80—the equivalent of thirty to eighty cents—a day). For the other half of the month, laborers could cultivate their own maize on the patrón's land if they were not working for someone else. The Menchús were not about to accept terms like this, and no one recalled that they ever did, for the Garcías or any other ladino landowners. Instead, Vicente had his own land and was an employer of laborers himself, including some of the same men who worked for the Martínezes and Garcías.

There were disagreements over land in Soch, but not necessarily along the indigenous-ladino divide that *I, Rigoberta Menchú* so emphasizes. One example pops up in the INTA file for San Pablo El Baldío, a new settlement of indígenas and ladinos perched on the ridge above Soch. In 1964 the community's ladino representative issued a double-barreled complaint against a Martínez and Vicente Menchú. Judging from the wording, the two had joined forces to occupy San Pablo land.[19] According to a member of the Martínez family, one of his kinsmen had paid for a survey of forest, only to learn that Chimel and San Pablo had a prior claim, prompting him to go elsewhere. As for Vicente, he may have ended up in the complaint merely because someone from his group had enthusiastically cleared forest beyond an invisible boundary.

Judging from the INTA archives and local recollections, there were no physical confrontations between Chimel and the ladinos of Soch until after guerrillas and soldiers appeared. There were disagreements, but not of the dimensions of the Tum quarrel, let alone of the epic struggle described in *I, Rigoberta Menchú*. The main issue was the location of the boundary between Chimel to the north and the Finca El Rosario to the south. In 1971 an INTA surveyor decided in Chimel's favor, displeasing the Martínezes, who believed that Chimel was still occupying a narrow strip of their land along a steep hillside.[20] Five years later Vicente complained that the Martínezes had logged eighteen of his community's pine trees, trampled maize (loose cattle?), and occupied a strip of land beyond the correct boundary.[21] This was the only complaint against the Martínez family that I found in the records for Chimel. As for the García family, whose property runs up to Chimel's southeast corner, I could not find a single reference to them in the INTA records.

Whether Vicente's relations with his ladino neighbors were warm or merely formal, the important point is that the Martínezes and the Garcías were never responsible for evicting anyone from Chimel. As we saw in the previous chapter, local testimony and the INTA archives confirm that Vicente's own K'iche' in-laws were responsible. In view of Rigoberta's portrait of the amicability reigning among indígenas and their undying enmities with ladinos, it is ironic that INTA was more successful mediating Chimel's boundary with ladinos than its boundary with other indígenas.

The Dispute with San Pablo El Baldío

> *These señores, Miguel and Angel [Martínez] and Honorio [García], were only half plantation owners. They were campesinos, too. They weren't plantation owners like those on the South Coast. Those really are plantation owners.*
>
> **—Member of the Menchú family, 1995**

Honorio García had a serious problem with a neighboring village, but it was not Chimel. The problem was with San Pablo El Baldío, a village of homesteaders on the ridge looming over his property. Like the upland forests of Chimel, those of San Pablo remained *baldío* (unoccupied) into the 1950s because of a lack of running water. Gradually land was cleared by a mixed group of ladinos, K'iche's, and Poqomchi's, including families from the García and Martínez fincas who wanted a more independent life. San Pablo was not as well organized as Chimel. It lacked the strong leadership of Rigoberta's father, and its petitions for a land title never went far with INTA. Perhaps because more San Pablans had broken away from patróns, ladinos viewed them as more troublesome. "When they started drinking," a Soch ladino told me, "they would fight with anybody. The Tum family of Chimel [*sic*] was not the same as the Tum family of San Pablo. People from Chimel didn't act like that."

Some of these feelings were expended on Honorio García. Once he and his brother-in-law Eliu Martínez were in their graves, the revolutionary movement identified them as military commissioners who mistreated their farmworkers and threatened the San Pablans with guns.[22] As with Rigoberta's story about Petrona Chona, local sources describe a more complex situation. After Honorio's death, his sons would indeed be blamed for dark deeds. But even according to detractors, before the violence none of the family so much as owned a firearm, Honorio being opposed to their use, and neither he nor his fellow victim Eliu were military commissioners.

Local testimony does confirm the left's version of events in one important sense: Honorio indeed closed a path that San Pablans used to descend to the weekly market at El Soch. This forced the villagers to take a longer detour around his property. Significantly, local accounts are so unpolarized that some of Honorio's relatives criticize him for being too brusque with the San Pablans. "He had problems with all the people; he tried to humiliate them," an in-law told me. "Honorio wanted people to work in his own way; he lacked patience and calm. He died because he treated the people badly," another in-law said.

Meanwhile, the three San Pablo survivors I was able to interview said that Honorio had defensible reasons for closing the path. According to them, the problem originated with members of San Pablo who were ladinos like Honorio, not indígenas like themselves. Being more commercially minded than their Mayan neighbors, the ladinos had never settled in San Pablo. Instead, they only farmed there and brought out their harvest on beasts of burden. Because the path was steep, narrow, and muddy, the animals crashed into Honorio's maize with their bulky loads and grabbed at it for fodder. At first Honorio asked San Pablo's committee to please talk with their people, to reserve the trail for foot traffic. "I know that it's outsiders who are causing the problem," a San Pablan quoted him. "It's not you who live there because you don't have the beasts." But the new route that swung around the edge of his property was longer. The ladinos continued to bring their animals down the old trail, prompting Honorio to block it off and antagonize a wider spectrum of San Pablo.

The First Executions and Kidnappings

> *Passing animals were doing damage, so [Honorio García] closed off the path. The people of San Pablo El Baldío went to the governor, who arranged a longer route, but the people were not in agreement. The guerrillas did not know how to make justice. They just took the life of the owner of the finca. Little time passed before the army arrived to shoot things up, kidnap the people, and burn nearly forty houses.*
>
> **—Uspantán human rights activist, 1994**

The Garcías and Martínezes were not the first local targets of the Guerrilla Army of the Poor. That honor went to a North American missionary couple belonging to the Summer Institute of Linguistics (SIL). Stan and Margot McMillen were running a medical clinic in the Uspanteko village of Las Pacayas near Soch. It is possible that someone asked the guerrillas to drive them out—their organization had become controversial in some countries. However, no local grievances were mentioned by the twenty-five or so guerrillas who rousted the McMillens and their children out of bed on the morning of July 16, 1979.

"Gringos are liars," the EGP commander told the villagers in Spanish. "They offer something but only to take other things from people. They hand out old medicine and they treat Guatemalans in the United States like slaves, making them clean toilets." As the guerrillas denounced the missionaries for being imperialists, they burned their house and clinic. They also warned the McMillens that they would be killed if they did not leave the area and showed them a death list. One person on the list was a North American running local health and agricultural projects. Another was Honorio García.

Three weeks later, around dawn on August 12, an EGP column showed up at the house of Eliu Martínez in the Finca El Rosario. There were three adults and about fifteen youth, all in uniform with their faces masked or charcoaled. They dragged the forty-two-year-old Eliu out of his house in his underwear and marched him down the path toward Soch with his arms tied. According to a brother who survived, the only thing the guerrillas said was, "Where are the dead?"—as if they had been told they were avenging earlier killings. Opposite Honorio's house, the guerrillas shot Eliu in the head. They also fractured the skull of his brother and assaulted two of Honorio's sons who were within reach.

Honorio lived in a stone house roofed with metal—larger than what his laborers lived in but unmistakably rustic. He was surprised in his bed around 5:30 A.M. His four-year-old grandson, also named Honorio García, was sleeping in the same room. To defend himself, the elder Honorio thrust the child in front of him before he was shot to death. The guerrillas beat the grandchild to subdue him, then locked him inside the room with the body of his grandfather. Two days later, according to relatives, the boy went into convulsions. When I met him fifteen years later, he was a severely retarded epileptic. Whether trauma could produce such a condition I do not know, but his family thinks it did.

According to conventional wisdom in Soch, the guerrillas targeted Honorio because San Pablo had denounced him for closing the path. But the other man who died was not involved in that dispute, and why the EGP killed him is something of a mystery. Like his brother-in-law Honorio, Eliu Martínez ran a small commercial farm, in his case tending maize, sugar cane, and ten cows. Some of his laborers lived in nearby Chimel. He did not have the brusque personality of Honorio, nor did he have problems with neighbors (except for his own relatives, as noted below), and he was appreciated for his promotion of village soccer, which indígenas and ladinos played side by side.

Perhaps the EGP was looking for a man from each family to kill: Eliu was one of three Martínezes whom the guerrillas sought that morning. There is another possibility, growing out of a conflict between Martínez heirs that is tangled enough to be worthy of the Menchús and Tums. Like Vicente's feud with his in-laws up the valley, the quarrel dividing the Martínez family can be blamed on antiquated legal structures. Two of the first Martínezes in the valley, the brothers Angel (who died in the early 1970s) and Miguel (who died a decade later), began to disagree over property left intestate by their parents. It was the next generation that came to blows, particularly over the Finca El Rosario bordering Chimel.

According to Angel's branch of the family, an irresponsible kinsman sold twenty hectares of El Rosario first to them and then to the other branch. According to Miguel's side of the family, the first sale had never been completed by payment, freeing the parcel for sale to their branch, in particular Miguel's son Eliu, who would be killed by the EGP. The disappointed claimants on Angel's side of the family tried to have Eliu arrested, then lost the court case, leaving him in possession of the twenty hectares. Around 1974 there was a confrontation on the premises, during which Eliu killed his cousin Edgar Martínez.

Eliu's side of the family says that he shot his cousin in self-defense, after Edgar attacked him with a machete. He and the laborers who witnessed the killing were hauled off to jail, and Eliu served three years in prison before being released just two years before he was executed by the guerrillas. To reiterate, Eliu may have been murdered simply because the EGP wanted to target a member of his family for symbolic purposes. But because a localistic population tries to explain such deaths in terms of local causes, not just a guerrilla movement that seemed to come out of nowhere, the assassination of Eliu has also been attributed to the other branch of the Martínez family.

The response to the EGP raid was not long in coming. A week later, on August 19, the army kidnapped two San Pablo elders from the Sunday market at Soch. Since the soldiers were in uniform, "arrested" might seem a more appropriate term. Unfortunately, as was the army's custom during this period, it never acknowledged holding the two men, and they were never seen again, at least by their families. Paulino Morán and Ambrosio Yujá Suc were on the committee administering San Pablo. In their fifties and sixties, they were the first of nine peasants kidnapped over the next month, typically by soldiers accompanied by men from the García family or their in-laws.

A day or two later two brothers from San Pablo, Marcelo and Ramon Tum Gómez, were also captured. They were taken to the army camp at Xejul, just outside the town of Uspantán on the road to Cobán. Unlike so many other prisoners at Xejul, they managed to escape. They reported being kept "in large open holes in the ground, covered by wooden beams."[23] A fifth victim, Domingo Yujá Pacay, was the son of Ambrosio Yujá Suc. Having served in the army until a few months before, he may have gone to the Xejul base to find his father, only to be taken prisoner, too. Another young villager named Gregorio Xoná was returning home from a finca when he was captured. The seventh and eighth victims from

San Pablo were Felipe Morán, son of the aforementioned Paulino Morán, and Juan Yat López. They were arrested by judicial police as they traveled with their families through southern Quiché.

Eventually the best known of the nine victims would be the single one from Chimel, Rigoberta's younger brother Petrocinio. Besides accusing San Pablo, Honorio's sons were also blaming Chimel. The guerrillas were said to have held a meeting there in the months before their raid. Strangely, *I, Rigoberta Menchú* never mentions the meeting in Chimel, the dispute over the path, or the EGP's murder of the two ladinos. If these are the events that triggered the kidnapping of Rigoberta's brother, their omission is notable. Instead of bringing the EGP into the picture, Rigoberta says that the Soch landlords sent the army against Chimel to seize its land.

Some readers may be disturbed by my approach because it is not the usual one to political violence in Guatemala. Since the army committed most of the killing, activists and scholars have been tempted to heap all the blame on it, demurely averting their gaze from what the other side might have been doing. In defense of this approach, solidarity activists argue that the guerrillas were an inevitable reaction to oppression, or that they cannot be singled out for blame when the violence originated in an unjust social order, or that outsiders have no right to criticize the poor when they use violence to defend themselves. There has been an even stronger aversion to specifying how peasants who died in the violence might have contributed to their fate. Not wanting to blame victims and dilute responsibility, human rights activists argue that the most important issue is who killed whom, not what led up to that outcome.

Exonerating the guerrillas may be necessary for solidarity work. Ignoring them may focus human rights campaigns on government abuses. But neither solidarity nor human rights approaches should be confused with sociohistorical analysis. The reason is that the first two require dichotomizing participants into victims and victimizers. On one side is the army and its local allies, on the other hapless victims. Conveniently for the guerrillas, they remain at the margin, along with issues such as how they tried to recruit peasants, how men like Vicente Menchú responded to them, and how survivors assess the blame for what happened. Failing to ask such questions protects the left's assumptions from scrutiny. Among them is the belief, vouched for by *I, Rigoberta Menchú,* that if guerrillas were active, many peasants must have shared their objectives.

5 The Death of Petrocinio

My mother was weeping; she was looking at her son.
—***I, Rigoberta Menchú*, p. 177**

With problems cropping up in Rigoberta's testimony, readers may ask, How reliable are your own sources? Perhaps many of the people I interviewed have some reason to discredit Rigoberta or her father. Or perhaps they did not like being questioned and misled me. In some of the chapters that follow, disagreements among my Uspantán sources will become evident. Whom are we to believe? If there are disagreements, might not the stories I gathered be as unreliable as Rigoberta's? Perhaps they are even less reliable: While Rigoberta was presumably free to tell her story in Paris, peasants in Guatemala must still reckon with the power of the Guatemalan army. Maybe the truth is unknowable, because the milieu is too ambiguous and fraught with repression to have confidence in any particular version.

The hardest question to answer—and the one running through the next five chapters—is to what extent peasants like the Menchús supported the guerrillas. Fortunately, many survivors are not mute on the subject, and their accounts suggest certain conclusions, even if these should remain tentative. Explanations for why peasants collaborate with insurgents can be summarized under three headings. Perhaps peasants are inspired by revolutionary ideology, that is, the idea of transforming society. Or perhaps, without giving much credence to such visions, they think they have something more immediate to gain. Or perhaps they are pressured into cooperating with the guerrillas, after being swept up in a process of provocation, retaliation, and polarization that forces them to choose sides.[1]

Skeptics who doubt guerrillas have the broad support they claim favor the pressure-and-polarization model. This became my preferred theory after interviewing peasants in what was reputed to have been a guerrilla stronghold. Many Ixils told me they had been attracted to the revolutionary vision, of a society where they would be equal with ladinos. But they began joining the guerrillas in numbers only after the army's reprisals forced them to defend themselves.[2] In secret the EGP had launched the process of induction some years earlier, by setting up a network of collaborators who did not reveal themselves to neighbors until guerrilla columns passed through and held a rally. Soon after that, the army's reaction presented fence-sitters with a fait accompli. Certainly some Ixils joined for ideological or pragmatic reasons, but the larger forces at work meant that that they or their neighbors were simultaneously being obliged to join. Once the army started kidnapping suspects, peasants could choose only between cooperating with one of the two sides, at the risk of being murdered by the other, or fleeing their homes.

Scholars who are more sympathetic to guerrillas tend to stress the ideological explanation: that peasants join an insurgency because they see it as a way to fight exploitation and build a better society. This is also how guerrilla movements see themselves, in terms of the immiseration thesis. Peasants face ever worsening oppression, which raises their consciousness and leads them to embrace armed struggle. As it happens, immiseration is not a good description of the conditions that highland peasants faced before the war. Instead, compared with the harsh conditions recalled by elders, they perceived mild improvements and hoped for more in the future.[3] Yet this did not prevent coteries of Ixils—including adventurous youth, students, and political activists—from welcoming the guerrillas at an early date, whether because of specific grievances (such as the theft of an election) or broader frustrations, neither of which was in short supply under a military dictatorship.

The same could be true of Uspantán and Vicente Menchú. Even if he was not the persecuted agrarian radical of his daughter's story, even if he was fairly well-off for a man of his origin, that does not disqualify him as a potential revolutionary. To the contrary, future revolutionaries have often experienced some success before they collide with injustice. Perhaps Vicente supported the guerrillas not because he was among the most oppressed but because he identified with them and thought that armed struggle was the only way to help them. This is a reasonable reinterpretation of *I, Rigoberta Menchú,* minus some of the melodrama, which retains its essential claim of a revolutionary peasantry. But is it true? Alternatively, could Vicente have thought that he had something to gain from the guerrillas, without giving too much credence to their larger vision? Or following the pressure-and-polarization model that I argued in the case of Ixil country, could he have been swept up by forces beyond his control?

In the previous three chapters, we looked at what can be gathered about the situation of Chimel before the violence, its relations with ladino and K'iche' neighbors, and how the first political killings occurred. This is an essential basis for understanding how Vicente and his people responded to the Guerrilla Army of the Poor. Over the next five chapters, I will take up other key episodes and topics that bear on this difficult question. They include the army's murder of one of Vicente's sons and how he responded to it; the death of Vicente himself, along with thirty-five other people, at a protest in Guatemala City; his relation to the Committee for Campesino Unity and to the Guerrilla Army of the Poor; and how the violence destroyed Chimel.

The evidence bearing on these subjects is not slight. It includes other revolutionary accounts as well as Rigoberta's, human rights reports, press stories, and transcripts of interviews with peasant protesters, including Vicente. It also includes my interviews with survivors of these events. Since they do not always agree with each other, it would be best to treat their recollections neither as settled facts nor as unreliable, but as what my colleague Paul Kobrak calls "reconstructions of the violence," expressions of how people situate themselves in relation to a traumatic period. This is a view of history from the village level, through the eyes of peasants, whose very limitations will suggest how they experienced the war.[4] As for the factuality of my conclusions, I do think some issues can be settled by comparing sources, but others lead only to more and less likely scenarios. If what results is more reliable than Rigoberta's account, the reason is that it encompasses a wider range of versions, deals with contradictions that she does not, and acknowledges more of what cannot be established.

To show the advantages of the method, let us compare contradictory versions of how Rigoberta's brother Petrocinio died at the town of Chajul. It is there that Rigoberta places the calvary of her younger brother, in the climactic chapter of *I, Rigoberta Menchú.* By 1979, according to her account, Chimel is fully organized and most of her family is in hiding. Her father has gone underground in the Committee for Campesino Unity, while Rigoberta is doing her own organizing in the Department of Huehuetenango. Remaining behind in Chimel is Petrocinio, a sixteen-year-old serving as the community secretary. He is kidnapped on September 9, while on an organizing trip to another village, after a member of the community betrays him to the army for a small sum of money. With Petrocinio at the time are a girl and her mother; they risk their lives to follow him and his captors to the army camp, where twenty other prisoners are already subject to gruesome tortures.

Immediately the Menchú family reassembles. The army announces that it will carry out a public punishment of the guerrillas it has captured, in Chajul, and it summons the populace to witness the spectacle. Overnight Rigoberta and her family hurry through the mountains. Chajul is twenty-five kilometers from Chimel—on a clear day its huge church can be descried from a nearby ridge—but it is farther over the mountain trails that loop in and out of ravines. The most conservative of the three Ixil towns, with few ladinos and relatively little Spanish spoken, Chajul has hallowed associations for traditional Catholics. Every Lent, from as far away as Mexico and El Salvador, thousands of pilgrims converge on its whitewashed colonial church to worship a larger-than-life statue of Christ staggering under his cross and imploring heaven.

The Menchús join the crowd in the plaza just as soldiers drag Petrocinio and the other prisoners off an army truck. Wearing army uniforms, the captives are ordered to stand in line but can barely hold themselves up, so hideously have they been tortured. Petrocinio's head has been shaved and slashed; he has no fingernails left, nor soles on his feet, and his wounds are suppurating from infection. As an army officer harangues the crowd on the evils of communism, he orders his soldiers to scissors off the prisoners' clothes, to explain how each mark was inflicted on the tortured bodies. Finally, the officer orders each prisoner soaked in gasoline. As they cry for mercy, they are set afire. The horror stirs the crowd to rage; many raise their machetes and rush the soldiers, who fall back shouting slogans to army and fatherland.[5]

The White Flower Protest

In Guatemala City, seeking to rescue his son, Vicente would describe him as Chimel's secretary. "He always has the notes for all that land that we are soliciting, maybe just for that they took him. And as he already knows how to read and everything, sometimes he talks a bit about injustice."[6] A Catholic eulogy refers to him as a literacy worker at a school that he and his father obtained for Chimel.[7] But in Uspantán I heard Petrocinio remembered only as a youth who might have had a bit of schooling, not as a village catechist, secretary, or organizer. He is presumed to have been *agarrado* (grabbed) because he was within reach at a time when his family was being blamed for the EGP raid on Soch. Perhaps with little intimation of danger, as no one from Chimel had been kidnapped, his father asked him to buy sugar at the Sunday market. The date was September 9, 1979. Spotted by informers, he left the plaza and was walking ahead of his girlfriend and her mother, toward their village, when soldiers and vigilantes ran him down near the town's Calvary chapel. Because shots were fired, some think he put up enough resistance to be shot and wounded.

"Yes, it's my son," Vicente told a journalist in the capital four months later, just a few days before he went to the Spanish embassy. "It was November 9 [*sic*] at three in the afternoon, there in the town of Uspantán, it wasn't in [our] house, they grabbed him in the street. . . . When they grabbed him, I wasn't there. . . . As he's already engaged, his girlfriend was with him and the señora, the mother of the girl. In front of them they grabbed him and took him to the garrison of Uspantán."[8]

Petrocinio was last seen being dragged in the direction of the army camp at Xejul, just east of town along the road to Alta Verapaz. When I visited the site, long after the army's departure, I was struck by how indefensible it seemed in military terms. Instead of being on a knoll, the usual location for an army garrison, it was in a woodlot at a low point, as if defense against attack were no concern. The location suggests that it was intended only as a torture camp. So do the stories about mutilated bodies that were trucked out to be dumped elsewhere. Other victims are presumed to be there still, in pits that have been filled but are still visible among the trees. Fourteen years later some of Petrocinio's relatives suspected that he was still there, at the bottom of one of them.

Even though men wearing uniforms had taken Rigoberta's brother and the other victims, army officers denied any knowledge of their whereabouts. The local army commander refused to meet with the families, as did the commander in Santa Cruz del Quiché, the interior minister, and President Lucas García.[9] An army communiqué suggests the level of denial that the villagers faced: "Undoubtedly the false accusations victimizing the Army of Guatemala are nothing but the product of . . . subversive groups that frequently assassinate their own comrades . . . who are no longer useful for their evil-minded purposes. Or these are self-kidnappings, from which they obtain the same . . . lucrative profits. . . . The Army of Guatemala reiterates that it is at the service of the Fatherland and never at the service of particular persons. . . . It will continue zealously fulfilling its constitutional duty, so as not to permit that our democratic system be undermined, much less permit that the nation fall into the hands of international communism."[10]

Because local commanders adopted noms de guerre, their identity is for the most part unknown to Uspantanos. But the occasional officer developed friendships, or years later his face and name appeared in newspapers. Such is the case of Carlos Roberto Ochoa Ruiz, a captain who was apparently second in command at Xejul when Petrocinio died and who left shortly after the fire at the Spanish embassy. Thirteen years later he was a lieutenant colonel under indictment for smuggling half a metric ton of cocaine to Florida.[11]

There were two occasions when Rigoberta's family and neighbors unquestionably lived up to her portrayal, when they went to the capital in September 1979, and again in January 1980, to protest the army's kidnappings. On the first occasion, fifty campesinos arrived in the capital and spent the night at the headquarters of the Guatemalan Workers Federation (FTG). The next morning, carrying white flowers to signify their peaceful intentions, they entered the national congress in small groups and demanded the right to speak. Accompanying them were urban allies from the FTG, the Robin García Revolutionary Student Front (FERG), and the Democratic Front Against Repression, for a total of sixty people. Security guards barred the way to the legislative chamber; hostile deputies upbraided them. Eventually the protesters were ushered upstairs to a committee room, where they were allowed to speak.

The delegation had not been received warmly, but at least it caught the attention of the press. Then the situation turned ominous. Hundreds of soldiers and riot police surrounded the building. After congressmen escorted the protesters back to the FTG's union hall, the security forces surrounded that building as well. Five students and union activists ventured outside to buy food, only to be taken away by heavily armed plainclothesmen.[12] The following evening two hundred more demonstrators broke through the diminished police cordon, loaded the campesinos onto trucks, and brought them to San Carlos University, a stronghold of the left, from which they returned to Uspantán escorted by journalists and student leaders.

The Menchús and their neighbors were not the first peasant delegation to protest army kidnappings, but the press was so muzzled during these years that, thanks to their urban allies and the bold tactic of occupying the congress, this one received unusual attention. The statement for congress suggests that it was written by the delegation's urban allies, not the peasants themselves, most of whom were illiterate. Before listing the victims and relating how pleas for their release have been rejected, the statement blames the repression on the three sons of Honorio García and an in-law who want to rob their land. It makes no reference to the EGP's presence in Uspantán or the assassination of Honorio and Eliu Martínez.[13]

At a press conference just before the peasants returned to Uspantán, several of them voiced complaints in their own words. They talked about the gamut of security forces persecuting them, not just the army and the mobile military police but the treasury guards (who were switching from persecuting moonshiners to kidnapping guerrilla suspects) and even a *guardia forestal,* which was supposed to protect forest cover. Once again, there was no reference to the assassinations of Honorio García and Eliu Martínez, nor to the dispute over the path to San Pablo. One campesino denied having organizational ties with students, and he also denied that they were in opposition to the army or the government. They just wanted to be left in peace, he said—which the never-mentioned guerrillas were guaranteeing would never happen. The generic nature of the complaints suggests that the particularities of Uspantán were already being swallowed by the left's national-level discourse against the army.[14]

How Petrocinio Died at Chajul

From a military truck they threw down the cadavers, one by one, one by one. I think there were seven. They [soldiers] rang the church

> *bells and summoned the people, to say that [the dead] were guerrillas. The army also said that they were from San Miguel Uspantán. To make the people afraid, to make an example [of the victims], but the people only got angrier. Yes, they burned a body. But he was already dead; he wasn't alive.*
>
> **—Testimony from Chajul, 1994**

When I started visiting Chajul regularly in 1987, it was not hard to hear stories about the violence. People told me how the army used to hang accused guerrilla collaborators from the balcony of the town hall. Usually this was done at night, enabling the town's volunteer ambulance brigade to take the bodies down at dawn, but not always. One unfortunate woman was arrested for trading with the enemy after soldiers and civil patrollers fell into an ambush. Brought onto the balcony before a crowd, she asked for mercy, then for a last chance to nurse her infant. After she nursed the baby, it was taken from her, and she was put over the side like dozens of others.

True to Rigoberta's account, it was not rare for the army to humiliate and torture captives before they were killed, even in front of their families. Nor was it unknown for the army to burn people alive—usually when they were trapped inside their houses. But when I brought up Rigoberta's story of prisoners being burned alive in the plaza of Chajul, all I harvested were quizzical looks. Prisoners from Uspantán were killed early in the violence, townspeople confirmed, but what they recalled was rather different. One man remembered seeing five or six cadavers, dressed in military clothes and next to old shotguns, a kilometer out of town toward the army garrison. A helicopter had brought the men before they were killed: The army claimed that they were guerrillas from Uspantán attacking Chajul.[15]

To some readers, an exegesis of exactly how Rigoberta's brother died will seem pointless or naive. Given the vagaries of memory and the translation of eyewitness accounts into secondhand ones, it is hardly surprising that there are conflicting versions. Perhaps my sources in Chajul were still too afraid of the Guatemalan army to acknowledge what they had witnessed. So why is their version of events more credible than Rigoberta's? The reason is that a peasant delegation, including Rigoberta's father, was communicating the Chajules' version of events soon afterward, in a second round of protests in the capital in January 1980.

"On December 6," the delegation announced with the help of the Democratic Front Against Repression (FDCR), ". . . the army brought to Chajul seven campesinos whom it had kidnapped in Chicamán,[16] dressed them all in olive green and forced them to go up the road that leads to town. A few meters away, soldiers were hidden and shot at the seven campesinos until they were all dead. After that, the army threw down a pair of old shotguns without ammunition next to the cadavers and began to say that the dead were guerrillas who had wanted to attack the garrison in Chajul. The cadavers lay there for many hours, until they were put in two holes in the Chajul cemetery, after [the army] burned one of the bodies with gasoline."[17]

The construction of this version of events can be seen in a fascinating interview that Vicente's delegation gave in the capital, five days before the death of many of its members at the Spanish embassy. Vicente had yet to accept that his son was really dead: "I don't know if they are alive or if they [soldiers] already killed them." Then a Chajul campesino interjected the delegation's version of events—except that townspeople are summoned to witness the execution of the seven in front of the church. Other members of the delegation insisted that the seven were killed on the road into town, as my sources described in the late 1980s and early 1990s, then dumped in the plaza to dramatize one of the army's antiguerrilla harangues. The reason the delegation believed that the seven were from Uspantán was that the army said so.[18] The bodies were never positively identified, hence Vicente's uncertainty about whether his son was among them. With only minor variations, this is the same version of events that appeared in human rights reports, with the EGP's Mario Payeras adding that the army was retaliating for a guerrilla ambush.[19]

In and of itself, the contrast between Rigoberta's account and everyone else's is not very significant. Except for sensational details, Rigoberta's version follows the others and can be considered factual. She is correct that the army brought prisoners to Chajul, claimed that they were guerrillas, and murdered them to intimidate the population. As best anyone can determine, they included her younger brother.

The important point is not that what really happened differs somewhat from what Rigoberta says happened. The important point is that her story, here and at other critical junctures, is not the eyewitness account that it purports to be. Although she presents her parents, siblings, and self at the scene, Vicente was professing ignorance about the fate of his son shortly before his own death. The Chajules only supposed that the seven victims were from Uspantán because the army said so. In short, no relatives were on hand to identify them, and Rigoberta was not there either.[20]

6

The Massacre at the Spanish Embassy

Since then, the dead combatants have stretched out in their immense metallic forms and our action has followed new courses.

—Mario Payeras, *El Trueno en la Ciudad,* 1987[1]

Taking hostages at embassies and government ministries is a common form of protest in Latin America. Even repressed or indifferent news media pay attention. In 1978 the Sandinistas captured the entire congress of Nicaragua to dramatize their struggle against the Somoza dictatorship. An archbishop agreed to mediate, Somoza released political prisoners, and the guerrillas departed heroically from the airport to international acclaim. But the tactic can go terribly wrong. When guerrillas seized the Colombian supreme court in 1985, the army responded with tanks. All forty-one militants died, along with twelve justices. Another occupation that ended disastrously was in Guatemala City on January 31, 1980. Masked protesters took over the Spanish embassy to protest government repression, whereupon the police stormed it. Thirty-six people—all but two of the occupiers and hostages—died in a mysterious conflagration.

To this day, it is not agreed who started the fire at the Spanish embassy. But the holocaust was not a defeat for the revolutionary movement. Because the police assaulted the building over the protests of the Spanish ambassador, the Guatemalan government was held responsible for a violation of diplomatic immunity and the deaths of the people inside. Like no other event, the fire captured the brutality of the security forces and played it out in front of television cameras. The violation of international law was so flagrant that it made the Lucas García regime an international pariah. Within Guatemala, the massacre became a powerful symbol for pulling together a broad revolutionary coalition. The dead protesters were remembered as peasants struggling to protect their families from government kidnappers. They became exemplary victims, martyrs whose death presaged victory. Among them were six people from Rigoberta's village, including her father, Vicente Menchú. How and why they died is the subject of this chapter.

Chimel Receives Its Land Title

> *The Alouette helicopter settled in a cloud of dust outside the remote Indian village of Chimel and a small crowd of land reform officials from the capital stepped out to present land titles to 45 Indian families. But the new landowners were nowhere to be found. The mayor of the village approached the officials and showed them a laboriously handwritten note. Because of the "oppression of the government's army," it said, the Indians were afraid to come to town to get the titles.*
>
> —***Washington Post,* February 3, 1980**

At one point in *I, Rigoberta Menchú,* the treacherous National Institute for Agrarian Transformation persuades the peasants of Chimel to sign a document that none can read. Supposedly it is the title to their land. Two years later, when large landowners renew their attacks, INTA reveals that it is an agreement to leave. Following more persecution, the agency offers to sell Chimel its own land for the impossible sum of Q 19,000 (U.S.$19,000)—equivalent to an order to leave.[2] A very different story emerges from the INTA archives, however, and it is fully corroborated by Chimel survivors. Just before Vicente Menchú died at the Spanish embassy, he received the land title for which he had petitioned so many years.

Under agreement number 26–79, dated December 20, 1979, the agency gave forty-five households provisional titles to 2,753 hectares, for a total price of Q 19,270.[3] Two caveats are in order. First, the new titles were to the tract that INTA had long recognized. They did not include the 151 hectares on which the houses of Chimel sat. This disappointed Vicente and his sons, who were not about to leave. Even so, the 2,753 hectares were titled over stiff opposition from the Tums of Laguna Danta, who felt that INTA was strengthening Vicente's grip on the 151 hectares they claimed as their own.

Second, INTA would not grant the final titles until the homesteaders paid the entire price—the usual terms for buying public land. Since Chimel had already made a down payment of Q1,980, the remainder of the debt (Q17,290) was to be paid in twenty annual installments of Q864.50. With the quetzal still at parity with the dollar, this meant an annual burden of US$20 per household. According to a member of the Menchú family, the debt was sufficiently manageable that they hoped to pay it ahead of schedule.

By the time the titles arrived, unfortunately, Chimel was so afraid of the army that it refused to come to the town hall to pick them up. "A message arrived to summon Vicente Menchú and his compañeros to meet the head of INTA and receive their documents," a then town official recalled. "But there was already a military garrison here and the people felt threatened. The violence had begun and they did not come for fear of the army. They were afraid they would be kidnapped." Having helicoptered from the capital to the municipal seat, INTA vice president Rubén Castellanos flew the documents to the village for a tense, unhappy ceremony that can be dated to December 28, 1979. "The people gathered to receive the title but with fear. 'We know that if we come to Uspantán the army will kidnap us,'" Vicente is supposed to have said.

Only days later, on January 9, the army collided with San Pablo El Baldío, the village that had suffered most of the kidnappings in retaliation for the EGP's raid in August. According to the army, one of its patrols was suddenly attacked by rebels. The San Pablans told a different story. According to a communiqué in peasant handwriting and grammar addressed to the Guatemalan Workers Federation, the soldiers accused the people of being guerrillas. They forced the women to feed them, separated the men, and started shooting. The people took up machetes, hoes, firewood, and stones to defend themselves. In the confusion the soldiers shot several of their own number, one of whom was wounded so badly that the commander put him out of his misery.[4] In subsequent versions published by urban supporters, the number of dead soldiers increased to three, with the army wounding two San Pablans and destroying many houses.

According to a San Pablan interviewed recently, the shooting began with an altercation between a soldier demanding food and an outraged householder waving his machete. The soldier fired a shot that nicked one of the man's fingers. This startled the other soldiers, who retreated with guns blazing and mortally wounded one of their own. No houses were destroyed, nor would any be destroyed until the following year. Even after the confrontation, the army returned to San Pablo several times "just to talk," the San Pablan told me. "First the army came to tell the people not to get involved with the guerrillas. Three or four times they arrived. The people said they didn't have anything to do with the guerrillas, but the army didn't believe them. . . . The doubt remained."

Vicente Dies for His Son

Some days after the incident at San Pablo, peasants from there, Chimel, and other villages met at the Catholic church in Uspantán. Then they went to Guatemala City, perhaps in a chartered bus via Alta Verapaz to avoid army checkpoints in southern Quiché. Rendezvousing with delegations from the Ixil towns, the Uspantán campesinos took up residence in classrooms at San Carlos University. Over the next two weeks, guided by San Carlos students, they tried to get media coverage for their grievances by staging occupations. But the press, intimidated by the Lucas García regime, was slow to respond. A few hours after a labor lawyer named Abraham Ixcamparí received the peasants, he was abducted and murdered.

Under the same kind of peril, striking workers had obtained concessions from their employers by occupying foreign embassies. For the peasants from Quiché, the Spanish embassy was an attractive choice because Ambassador Máximo Cajal y López had just visited their department. Besides inspecting an archeological dig, he conferred with the Spanish clergy about the threats they faced. At the embassy the peasants could expect a sympathetic hearing—which would give rise to accusations that the ambassador himself had helped plan the occupation.[5] Adding to the suspicion was an unfortunate coincidence. When the protesters occupied the embassy, among the twelve people they caught inside were an ex–vice president of Guatemala, Eduardo Cáceres Lehnhoff, and an ex–foreign minister, Adolfo Molina Orantes. They were there to ask the Spanish government to sponsor a legal conference. Had the protesters been invited to show up just in time to seize valuable hostages?[6]

The Spanish embassy was in an unguarded residence on a suburban street. Wearing bandannas over their faces, the occupiers came through the front door at 11 A.M. They announced that all those on the premises were now hostages. They also telephoned the media to call a news conference for 1:30. Before the press could enter the embassy, it was surrounded by hundreds of riot police as well as plainclothes *judiciales* (detectives), who often moonlighted in death squads. Inside, Ambassador Cajal and the embassy secretary were anxious to avoid a confrontation. Over the telephone they implored the Guatemalan foreign ministry, the presidential palace, and their own foreign ministry to order the police to withdraw—until the police cut off the connection. The entreaties of the two Spanish diplomats were reinforced by appeals from Molina Orantes and Cáceres Lehnhoff, the two Guatemalan dignitaries, but they were ignored as well, even when they went to the windows with a megaphone.

The police began to break into the embassy around 2 P.M. Television footage shows the violence of the assault, with the security forces smashing through doors and windows. The protesters retreated to the second floor, behind a metal gate blocking the top of the stairs. Nervous but defiant, the protest leaders offered to march to San Carlos University in pairs with their hostages—if the police withdrew beforehand. The police refused. They wanted the occupiers to leave the building one by one—an offer that the latter refused, knowing how many detainees had reappeared as corpses. The occupiers also asked the president of the national Red Cross to mediate. He refused.

As the police broke through the metal gate, the occupiers herded their hostages into the ambassador's office and barricaded the wooden door with furniture. There ensued fifteen minutes of verbal confrontation through a crack in the doorway. Around 3 P.M. the police began to batter through the door. Outside the building, journalists and other spectators heard an explosion inside the room, then saw smoke and fire through the windows. Since the windows were framed in metal and barred with iron security grilles, no one could escape through them. The flames and screams for help lasted several minutes. Because the police were blocking the front door, firefighters could only spray water from the ground. When they finally entered the room, most of the victims were piled on top of each other toward the windows. The majority seemed to have died of smoke inhalation.[7]

There were only two survivors, and soon there was just one. Ambassador Cajal had been at the door of his office trying to negotiate with the police when the fire started. Hair and clothes on fire, he was able to shove through the doorway. The other survivor was Gregorio Yujá Xoná of San Pablo El Baldío. Among the dozens of smoke-blackened corpses, he was at the bottom of the pile and still unaccountably breathing. The following evening Gregorio was kidnapped from his hospital bed by heavily armed men. A few days later, his body was dumped at San Carlos University with a bullet through the forehead. "The ambassador of Spain runs the same risk," said a sign left with him.[8]

By ignoring the ambassador's protests and invading the embassy, the Lucas regime had committed a gross violation of international law. The Spanish government held it responsible for everything that followed and broke diplomatic relations. Three days after the fire, the burial procession for the occupiers drew thousands of supporters. In the grand tradition of political funerals, two students and a policeman died in a shootout, while a police commander was wounded and a protester was kidnapped.

The Embassy Martyrs

Elio was for me a man in every sense of the word: good, caring, respectful, responsible. Although it might appear an exaggeration, never did I hear an insult from him. He always gave me the best of himself and, in this sense, became the beginning of my true life. I don't say the end, although at this moment I don't want to keep living without him, but I will try to hold fast to the duty I have, that his child he loved so much be born.

—Epitaph for one of the students who died at the embassy, 1980[9]

Exactly how many people died inside the embassy was the subject of confusion. The Spanish government blamed the Lucas García regime for the death of thirty-nine people. But the Red Cross reported finding only thirty-six bodies, and only thirty-six names were ever published. According to the list, the dead protesters included six campesinos from Chimel, three from San Pablo El Baldío, two from the nearby village of Macalajau, and another from the village of Los Platanos, for a total of twelve from Uspantán, plus another three from the town of Chajul in Ixil country.

Besides the fifteen occupiers from northern Quiché, there were five activists from the Committee for Campesino Unity, two from urban popular organizations, and four students from San Carlos University, for a total of twenty-six occupiers who died in the fire. Adding the short-lived survivor Gregorio Yujá, sixteen campesinos from northern Quiché and eleven activists from revolutionary organizations entered the embassy, for a total of twenty-seven occupiers. The ten dead hostages included the two Guatemalan dignitaries, seven members of the embassy's staff, and a Spanish citizen who happened to show up at the wrong moment.

I, Rigoberta Menchú says that eight people from Chimel were inside the embassy—"our village's best, most active compañeros."[10] But only six names came up in my interviewing. Aside from Vicente Menchú, there was another catechist named Mateo Sic Pinula. Around thirty-three years old, he worked as a carpenter as well as a farmer, was the secretary of the village Catholic Action chapter, and left behind a widow and three children. Juan Us Chic may have been the treasurer of the Chimel committee. He extracted lumber for a living and was about thirty-seven when he died, leaving behind a widow and five children. Regina Pol Suy was an unmarried woman in her early thirties who left behind two children. Juan Tomás Lux was a youthful in-law of the Menchús, through a sister married to Vicente's son Victor. Maria Pinula Lux was a fourteen-year-old girl.

Four men from San Pablo died. Two of them—José Angel Xoná Gómez and Gavino Morán Xupe—are said to have been sons of the village elder Paulino Morán who was kidnapped in August 1979. Like a third, a peasant farmer in his late twenties named Mateo Sis, they were involved with the Catholic Church and left behind widows and orphans. Gregorio Yujá Xoná, the survivor kidnapped from his hospital bed, seems to have been a middle-aged catechist who faithfully attended Catholic Action meetings in Uspantán. He may have been born on the Martínez property in Soch, grown up as a dependent laborer, then helped lead the move up the ridge to San Pablo.

Two of the dead were from the village of Macalajau. Juan López Yac was a twenty-eight-year-old cooperative member in charge of the village's maize grinder; he left behind a widow and three small children. Juan Chic Hernández was a youth of fourteen who had reached seventh grade in the Uspantán schools. An old schoolmate remembers that, in the last months of his life, "he had problems; he was being investigated and was running in and out of school, always accompanied by friends, as if he was afraid of being kidnapped."

From the village of Los Platanos in Uspantán was a man named Francisco Tum Castro, who may have been a health promoter like Vicente Menchú's two sons. From the Ixil town of Chajul was the catechist Gaspar Vi, to whom we will return, as well as two sisters who shared the name María Ramírez Anay, the older of whom was a catechist.

Of the five activists belonging to the Committee for Campesino Unity, three were K'iche's from the vicinity of Santa Cruz del Quiché, the department capital where CUC originated. According to their organization:

- Victoriano Gómez Zacarias was from the village of Pamesebal. Twenty years old, he had just finished sixth grade—an accomplishment for the time and place—and was learning to be a weaver in the village of La Estancia, a CUC stronghold that would soon be destroyed by the army. Victoriano also worked as a village organizer. He was a cofounder of CUC and belonged to its regional coordinating commission.
- Mateo López Calvo was another young man, from the village of Cucabaj, who worked as an itinerant trader and seasonal plantation worker. Struggling to become literate, he was a village coordinator and member of CUC's national coordinating commission.
- Salomon Tavico Zapeta, a twenty-two-year-old from the village of Chitatul, was also a member of CUC's national coordinating commission. He "still lacked aggressiveness and initiative" but had survived arrest and torture by the security forces.

Two of CUC's dead were older men who had moved farther from the village ambience:

- Francisco Chen Tecu was an Achí Maya from Rabinal in the Department of Baja Verapaz. Thirty-two years old, he had served in the army like Vicente Menchú and Gregorio Yujá Xoná. Since then he had worked on plantations and itinerated as a petty merchant. He left behind a widow and five children.
- Juan José Yos also seems to have been in his thirties, with a family of six children in the CUC hotbed of Santa Lucía Cotzumalguapa on the Pacific coast. His parents were from the Kaqchikel Maya town of San Martín Jilotepeque, in the Department of Chimaltenango. A longtime plantation laborer, he recruited many of

his fellow workers into CUC, was a traveling organizer, and at the time of his death was leading the regional coordinating commission.

Another activist accompanying the peasant delegation was Felipe Antonio García (twenty-seven years old), from a family of indigenous peasants who came to live in the capital. According to an obituary, he started working at the age of twelve. After being fired from a series of factories for union activity, he became an organizer for the Guatemalan Workers Federation and a leader of the National Committee for Labor Unity (CNUS), which coordinated union opposition to the Lucas regime. He also participated in the occupation of the national congress in September 1979.

Of the four students from San Carlos, all were members of the Robin García Revolutionary Student Front. Three were from the law school, while the other was studying economics.

- Sonia Welchez (twenty-six years old) was from a working-class family in the capital and lived a spartan life in solidarity with the poor. Her father was an active union man who two years before had been accused of being a guerrilla. He was kidnapped from his house, tortured, and found dead underneath a bridge. The reality of the indígenas she was accompanying, Sonia said shortly before her own death, had provoked an enormous growth in her revolutionary consciousness. "No one is redeemed without sacrifice," she also said. A hostage who escaped before the final moments thought she was leading the occupiers.[11]
- Rodolfo Negreros Straube was from the coastal town of Retalhuleu and played a notable role in factional struggles at San Carlos University. "He always was inflexible with those who argued that our struggle could not be directed by the firm alliance between workers and peasants. . . . He always made it very clear that our struggle is directed by the worker-peasant alliance." He was also "very anxious when tasks took a long time to accomplish" and "too energetic a compañero, always finishing tasks without caring that these lost the organizational character that they ought to have."
- Leopoldo Pineda Pedroza (twenty-five years old) was active in revolutionary theater. A son of ladino peasants, he grew up in Escuintla on the coast and was still dealing with the sudden death of four members of his family. He was also getting over a wild, drinking youth in which he was accustomed to getting into fights "with finca owners, military commissioners, or other reactionary persons who were not in agreement with his ideology."

The theater group he organized became one of the foundations of the Robin García Front.

- Luis Antonio Ramírez Paz (twenty-six years old) seems to have been from a higher-class background than the other students who died at the embassy. He had done revolutionary theater with Leopoldo but was better known as founder of a radical student newspaper, as well as a leader in the CNUS, the Democratic Front Against Repression, and the Robin García Front. According to a movement obituary, it was he who led the student delegation at the embassy.[12]

The Ambassador's Story

At 1500 hours, the commandos managed to break through the door and throw the first incendiary chemical bomb. At that very instant, Ambassador Máximo Cajal was able to escape with great burns. Then the door was shut.

—Rigoberta Menchú and CUC, 1992[13]

The revolutionary movement invariably memorializes the occupation as a peaceful one. Certainly, the manner in which the protesters seized the embassy was nonviolent compared with how the police stormed it. But the embassy staff offered no resistance, so there was no reason for the occupiers to use force, and what followed was hardly coercion-free. The twenty-seven protesters were armed with machetes, three or four revolvers, and Molotov cocktails. Nor were they play-acting when they took hostages, who were kept under close guard. As confrontation loomed, the occupiers never gave their prisoners—including four Guatemalan women working for the embassy and a fifth woman from Spain—the chance to flee to safety. Instead, the hostages were herded along at gunpoint to be used as shields.

The left accused the security forces of using an incendiary device such as napalm or white phosphorus to incinerate the victims. "Student opposition groups claim to be gathering 'surprising facts' about the massacre at the embassy, contradicting the official version that the deaths were the result of 'self-immolation,'" reported *El País* of Madrid. "A spokesman for the Robin García Revolutionary Student Front said that 'the police probably used napalm.' He also claimed that there exists a recording of a police chief giving the order to 'go in and finish off everyone.' But these proofs were not presented to the press. It was also claimed that the Molotov cocktails that the occupiers brought were simple ones, of gasoline with powder fuses, and incapable of bringing about the massacre that occurred."[14]

Since then, most accounts of the fire have echoed revolutionary sources and blamed the security forces for starting it. Rigoberta's 1982 story is unusual in leaving the question open. But a decade later, she and CUC joined the consensus by blaming the government and arguing that it wanted to "divert attention" from its deteriorating image.[15] How burning alive thirty-seven people inside a foreign embassy would divert attention defies comprehension, yet it is true that the Lucas García regime was bold in its brutality.

Elías Barahona y Barahona, a press officer in the Interior Ministry who defected to the EGP, claimed to have personal knowledge of how the president and his cronies decided to immolate the occupiers. "When the situation dragged on, [President] Lucas called Interior Minister Donaldo Alvarez Ruiz to ask him what was going on, why he had not settled the problem. He told him that the situation was difficult because the embassy's territory, in accordance with international law, was inviolable. Lucas told him to stop saying foolish things, that he had to solve this problem soon. He was told that former vice president Cáceres Lenhoff and former foreign minister Molina Orantes were also inside.

"Then I remember well that Lucas told him: It does not matter. You resolve the problem. Then the minister asked him to define more precisely the order, and he told him: Take them out as you can. At that point, the police broke into the embassy throwing grenades, throwing all kinds of projectiles, but the comrades who were inside the embassy went up to the last office, which was the ambassador's office, and took refuge there. The new situation was discussed and Lucas said: Set them on fire. Then the police put a metal lock on the door of the ambassador's office and launched fire bombs. The spectacle was horrible. . . . From the street, thousands of people could see how thirty-nine human beings writhed and died burning."[16]

Barahona corroborates the left's preferred version of events, but both are contradicted by the fire's sole survivor: Ambassador Máximo Cajal y López. "When the police entered my office," the ambassador told National Radio of Spain within a day of the incident, ". . . one of the campesinos threw a Molotov cocktail. The fire spread rapidly and the office was transformed into a roasting pan."[17] "Police broke down the door to my office. The occupiers, who were desperate, threw a Molotov cocktail and there was a shooting," he told a Bogotá radio station over the telephone. "I was closest to the door, and I managed to shake loose from one of the occupiers, who had a pistol trained on me."[18] "Despite my attempts at dialogue," *El País* of Madrid quoted him from his hospital bed, "the police began to destroy the door with axes. At the moment there was great confusion, some shots rang out, I cannot specify from whom, and one of the occupiers threw a Molotov cocktail against the door. I was very close to the exit and jumped through it with my clothes on fire, like the lions in a circus."[19]

Could Cajal be biased against the protesters? No—his sympathy for them was so evident that he was accused of staging the occupation. He vouched for their peaceful intentions and begged the authorities to stop their assault. From the moment of escaping, he denounced the police as "beasts" and "brutes," and he never wavered in holding the Guatemalan government responsible for the deaths. Yet he repeatedly attributed the start of the fire to the protesters. Still, could he have been misquoted? No—in an official report a week later, the Spanish foreign minister relayed the following conversation with the ambassador from his hospital bed.

"When the police assaulted the embassy, the occupiers and hostages took refuge in the office of the ambassador, upon whom one of the occupiers trained a pistol in those moments. Cajal insisted that [the police] not enter. The police began to break down the door and an occupier threw a gasoline bomb, which did not explode and spilled liquid on the floor. Another [occupier] threw a match, trying to start a fire, and it was Cajal himself who managed to stomp it out with his foot. Later, another occupier threw a second gasoline bomb, which exploded and set everything in the room on fire. Cajal escaped from his guard, jumped through the door and the flames, heard gunshots inside and rolled himself on the floor of a room next door to put out the fire on his clothes. According to the ambassador, he does not believe that the Guatemalan police fired at the moment that the room went up in flames."[20]

When I contacted Ambassador Cajal fifteen years later, he confirmed seeing a masked occupier throw a bottle of gasoline and splash fuel. He also confirmed stamping out a match intended to light it—but this episode occurred well before the explosion and his escape through the door. The most important clarification he wished to make was that, not having eyes in the back of his head, he never saw the fire's actual source, therefore cannot say for sure that the protesters started it.

"All the occupiers were masked, so I couldn't tell who was who," he said. "I have no idea which one was Vicente Menchú. Some were carrying guns, many of them machetes; I know because a machete was held to my neck. At first the occupation was quite civilized, but as the police occupied the embassy, [the occupiers] became ever more nervous, ever more excited. They rejected my suggestion that they leave the embassy and I would publicize their demands; they didn't believe I was in solidarity with them. They were carrying Molotov cocktails; I know because I saw them—Coca-Cola bottles stopped up with rags. I even suggested that they put the Molotovs in my office, so that when they left the embassy the sight of them would not antagonize the police. . . .

"Through the door the police accused me of siding with the occupiers, of being a communist, of being a son of a whore. Police were breaking through the door with axes or machetes, to the point that the hole was very big and there were just a few pieces of furniture piled in front of it, like when you're moving house. Suddenly there was an explosion, a boom, and a fire. I cannot say where it was. I was completely stunned. From behind [inside his office] I heard one, two, three shots. . . . I insist that I don't know who started the fire. I didn't see anyone behind me [start the fire], nor anyone in front of the door, as I couldn't see through it even though it was in shambles. The police were massed in front of it. I can't say honestly whether it was a flamethrower or a Molotov cocktail."

Why wasn't anyone else able to escape through the door? "I do not know why. . . . My only explanation is that the police—who had retreated a few meters below on the stairway . . . perhaps surprised by the fire and the gunshots, which came from the office because I heard them whistle past me—regrouped and returned to the second floor. There they surrounded me (I was in another room, opposite the office) and led me to a patrol car. . . . Everything happened in a matter of seconds. My firm conviction is that the police impeded the departure of all or some of those who found themselves trapped. It appears impossible that no one else could do what I had done, even if I was burned in the process."[21]

Who Started the Fire?

> *Neither we nor any of our compañeros can say what the real truth is, because no one from the Spanish embassy siege survived. All of them, every single one died; the compañeros who coordinated the action and the compañeros who were keeping watch. Some were gunned down in other places after the embassy events.*
>
> **—*I, Rigoberta Menchú*, p. 186**

Absent an official inquiry, I showed newspaper photos of the event to two arson investigators in California. Judging from appearances, they said, the relatively intact corpses and clothing suggest a fire of only medium intensity. White phosphorus burns so intensely that it would have incinerated the bodies and put a hole through the building. Instead, the fire petered out quickly and left the structure intact. Napalm is a more plausible hypothesis. But as a jelly that sticks to skin, it would have damaged the bodies more. What they were looking at, my two long-distance experts surmised, was a flash fire that could easily have been caused by gasoline. Although the left's postmortems ridiculed the idea that a few Molotov cocktails could kill so many people, gasoline is highly volatile and can vaporize quickly, not least in the body heat of a crowded room.

Burn marks on one of the victims—a roasted head but little damage below—suggests that gas fumes could have exploded in the upper part of the room. Those not killed by flames could have died from smoke inhalation, even next to the open windows, as unbreathable air vented outward from the fire. The lethal injuries from inhaling fire or smoke would not have prevented victims from thrashing and screaming for several minutes, as many did.[22]

Attributing the fire to the occupiers was, of course, the government's version of events. That alone was reason to pin responsibility on the Lucas García regime: It had invited disbelief on many occasions. Now it claimed that the embassy secretary had asked the police to intervene (being dead, he could not speak for himself); that the occupiers were mainly armed terrorists accompanied by a few peasants; and that they were a suicide squad planning to immolate themselves to embarrass the government.[23] Not all the official story was outlandish. Even the left concedes that the occupiers were armed with Molotov cocktails. Threatening to use them was not unusual. Three days before, some of the same protesters seized a radio station, brandished gasoline bombs, and threatened to light them.[24] When CUC members occupied the Brazilian embassy in May 1982, they carried Molotov cocktails as well.

This last episode merits attention, as the aim was the same as at the Spanish embassy two years before—to draw attention to army atrocities. The difference was that the seven protesters lived to tell their story, including how they expected to use their weapons. The leader was CUC cofounder Domingo Hernández Ixcoy, who says they agreed they were ready to die. When security forces stormed the building at night, the occupiers packed themselves and their hostages into a small room, just as their predecessors had at the Spanish embassy.

"If you show fear, you change a lot, you cannot make decisions," Hernández said of the crisis atmosphere. "That's why a compañero . . . was about to throw a Molotov when the helicopter started tossing down sacks of sand [on the roof, apparently to sound like assault troops]. So I told him, 'No, compañero, it is still not the moment. The one who has to give the order for anything is I. Everything's OK. Keep it in your bag; maybe we'll use it soon.' If you show too much nervousness in these activities, you can easily commit an error. For example, inside the embassy one compañero let off a shot." Even after the disaster at the Spanish embassy, in short, militants were ready to use gasoline bombs under similar circumstances.[25] They were not brought along merely to wave in the air.

Another window on the events at the Spanish embassy is the occupation plan found by the police. Unfortunately, it lays down only how the embassy was to be seized and the hostages controlled, not how the occupiers would respond to attack, as if they expected to be protected by diplomatic sanctuary. The plan refers to the gasoline bombs only as "self-defense materials," without explaining how they were to be used.[26] How could fire bombs be used inside a building? Presumably they could be tossed out a window, down a hall, or through a door to keep the police at bay, just as they are used in street protests. At best they might dissuade the security forces from attacking, and bringing them along would at least widen the occupiers' options.

Widely credited with having led the occupation were the students from San Carlos University. Three of the four had been active in a 1978 labor confrontation, in which workers dismissed by the Swiss-owned Duralita factory occupied the Swiss embassy for three days. This raises the possibility that the embassy takeover in which they died was not their first.[27] A frank account from the left would be invaluable, but we may never have it owing to the death of all the occupiers, and no small number of their comrades, as the security forces demolished their organizations over the next year.

Students have been the most consistent constituency for revolutionary movements throughout Latin America. In Guatemala they and their teachers led the popular uprising against Ubico in 1944, were a bulwark of resistance to right-wing rule after 1954, and kept the guerrilla movement alive from the late 1960s to the late 1970s. In the very rough world of Guatemalan politics, violent protests by students are expected and even condoned. One of the few platforms for the guerrilla movement in the capital was San Carlos University. Like many other public universities in Latin America, it is administratively autonomous. Students and faculty elect school authorities; campuses are legally off-limits to the security forces. Eventually, the elections for university authorities allowed guerrilla supporters to take over the campus. By January 1980, in reaction to the Lucas terror, San Carlos was boiling with newly organized and poorly disciplined guerrilla cells, particularly in the faculties of psychology, sociology, and law.

The Robin García Revolutionary Student Front (FERG) was a key organization in this milieu. It was named after a high school student kidnapped by the security forces in 1977. Robin García was a leader at a teacher training institute where, underfunded and out of control, the students not infrequently poured into the streets to riot. Whether or not he worked with the Guerrilla Army of the Poor, as many presume, the organization named after him did. By 1980 FERG activists were in rebellion against not just the dictatorship but a university administration controlled by the local communist party. Like other Moscow-line groups in Latin America, the Guatemalan Labor Party (PGT) viewed the radical left as immature and self-destructive. Led by older, middle-class intellectuals, it was holding back from the insurrection into which the EGP was plunging. PGT cadres are said to have objected to the plans for occupying the embassy but been ignored, and the action is debated within the left to this day.

Self-defense is a plausible scenario for using fire bombs, but it is not the one construed by a municipal firefighter who helped recover the bodies. Here is what he says he found at the scene. Contrary to the scenario outlined by my California fire investigator, that gasoline vapor might have exploded at head level, the firefighter said that he did not find a burn mark high on the wall. Instead, he found the burn mark lower down, less than a meter off the floor, indicating a fire that started from below. What he remembered smelling inside the room was not gasoline but kerosene. If this is what he smelled (a second firefighter remembered only the stench of burned bodies), it undermines the supposition that a fire bomb was hurled simply to stop the police from coming through the door.

Kerosene gives off dense black smoke, as this fire did, and it is less volatile than gasoline, making it harder to light. This is why gasoline is the combustible of choice for Molotov cocktails, including the several unused fire bombs that firefighters and security forces brought out of the building. But the heavier smell of kerosene would mask the smell of gasoline, the volatility of which could have been used to set off the blaze. "No one started the fire from outside," the firefighter concluded. "It appears that [the occupiers] spread combustibles inside and then set them on fire. . . . First they spread kerosene, then they set it on fire. . . . I had the impression that the people died asphyxiated. . . . Everything there was premeditated."

Besides the chemical composition of the fire, a second factual issue that deserves more investigation is the condition of the wooden door into the office, specifically, whether or not it was intact. Unfortunately, the memories of my three sources were not consistent. Ambassador Cajal recalled that the door was a shambles from police axes and therefore could not have been a serious obstacle. In his view, the doorway was sufficiently open that the police ought to have been able to help some of the people inside the room escape—and were criminally negligent in failing to do so.

But according to the two firefighters I interviewed, the door was sufficiently intact to be difficult to push through—according to one because it was locked from the inside and according to the other because it was blocked by furniture. According to the second firefighter—the first rescuer into the room—it was hard to get through the doorway because a sofa had been shoved against the door from the inside. If the door was indeed blocked or locked, that would explain why no one else was able to follow Ambassador Cajal into the corridor. Nor could this have been accomplished by the riot police, because they were outside the door. Someone inside would have had to do it. Could floundering victims, trying to get over piled-up furniture, have unintentionally shoved it against the door and blocked their own escape? This is certainly a possibility—in a panic, anything can happen.

Or did one of the protesters, in the last decision of his life, close off the exit through which the ambassador had just escaped? As the police invaded the embassy, an occupier shouted, "We're ready to die if you don't draw back!"[28] Since the police had yet to employ lethal force, this statement is not hard to interpret as a suicide threat, as is another statement reported by Mario Aguirre Godoy, a twelfth hostage who managed to escape just before the final siege of the ambassador's office. "If you enter," one of the protest leaders told the police, "the hostages will suffer the same fate as us."[29] Since no one on the street below saw the police project an incendiary device into the room, and the flames leaped out the windows, one interpretation among horrified onlookers was that the protesters were committing suicide.

Students and Peasants

> *Covered in revolutionary wall-paintings, [San Carlos University] functioned as a virtual liberated area on the outskirts of the city, and as a meeting place for clandestine organizations. In a four-month long orgy of violence, 400 students and teachers would die.*
>
> **—George Black, *Garrison Guatemala*, 1984**[30]

Just because some of the protesters carried fire bombs, it should not be assumed that all knew such weapons would be brought, agreed how they would be used, or even understood what they were. *I, Rigoberta Menchú* turns Molotov cocktails into part of the village self-defense repertoire, but this is something I never heard about in northern Quiché.[31] The occupation plan found by the police mentions the importance of correctly handling "self-defense materials," including distributing them, orienting fellow occupiers about them, and "maintain[ing] a certain secrecy concerning their use." The phrasing suggests different levels of knowledge among the heterogeneous protesters. The intended readership of the plan—"we must keep in mind that those who need to talk are fundamentally the peasant compañeros"—underlines that it was written for educated people, who would not have included the peasants.[32] Even if the Quiché peasants knew that gasoline was being brought along, they would have been less likely to understand the implications. In the panicky atmosphere of the ambassador's office, there was no time to debate contingency plans, let alone undergo a democratic procedure, particularly with comrades who spoke little Spanish.

Not all the peasants who came to the capital with Vicente Menchú entered the embassy. Some went home a few days before. Others waited in the street outside the embassy, then marched in the funeral two days later before slipping away. Years later, when I began asking for survivors of the delegation, the first answer was that they all died in the violence. Some indeed did, but not all. What do they have to say today? One woman on the expedition denied having understood its purpose, even though it took the life of her husband. According to this embassy widow, the journey originated in a wedding party at the Catholic church in Uspantán. Two days after the ceremony, the wedding party moved on without revealing its purpose or destination—even to her. "The *señores* said they were going to the coast, but they arrived at the capital," she told Barbara Bocek and me in K'iche' Maya. Barbara and I were incredulous: Wouldn't the trip's purpose have been explained to everyone? "Maybe among the men, but not among the women," the widow insisted. "In pueblo San Carlos [the university] we found lodging. The students gave classes in pure Spanish; I didn't understand."

Another embassy widow, who did not go to the capital, claimed that her husband simply "went with the [village] committee to deal with legal papers. They said they had to go arrange the title for Chimel. We women don't understand these things, as the work of women and men is different. Work outside the house is done by men; we don't know about it. The man goes to his meeting, and when he returns we don't ask. It's true that at a meeting, Vicente said: 'Now is the time to demand our rights.' But he was the only one to speak, because only he was the leader, not [my husband]."

Obviously, the two widows could be afraid to acknowledge what they remember.[33] But their denials also suggest how some of Vicente's followers—monolingual peasants visiting a large city for the first time—could have been bewildered by the context into which they were led. This is suggested by a survivor who, while exhibiting a better grasp of the situation, also expressed puzzlement over why events took the direction they did. "Upon arriving at San Carlos, Vicente talked to us. 'Now we've arrived, and we're going to demand our rights at the embassy.' The people didn't know what an embassy is or what Spain is. They just heard him say: 'Now we're going to demand our rights at the embassy of Spain.'"

"It's true that the leaders [of the occupation] were not Indians," a student who accompanied the delegation at the university told me, "but they entered the embassy out of desperation. I suppose that the campesinos didn't understand where it would all go. Vicente Menchú wasn't the leader; he was led. They acted more out of euphoria, out of incitation. Perhaps they realized that it would be dangerous, but they felt supported by their position [i.e., the justice of their cause]. When you're desperate, in a crisis, you look for support from the first people you find, and it was the [San Carlos] students who took advantage of them."

Vicente Menchú was not the only leader among the campesinos, according to this source, but "he was the leader with whom the students dealt. Don Vicente became a spokesman for the Robin García Revolutionary Student Front, and a very little bit for the CUC. They would tell Don Vicente, 'Say, "The people united will never be defeated,"' and Don Vicente would say, 'The people united will never be defeated.' They would tell Don Vicente, 'Raise your left hand when you say it,' and he would raise his left hand." The peasants were lodged on the third level of a university building. Strategy sessions were held on the second level, in a small room under a stair, and included FERG and CUC but not the peasants from Uspantán. When a San Carlos student from Quiché asked to join the deliberations, the CUC representatives agreed, but not the FERG.

The ideological contrast between students and peasants is suggested by the recollections of another survivor from Uspantán. Just thirteen at the time, he told me that he joined the expedition as a lark, to see what it was like to travel on a bus. In the capital the trip turned serious. They went to many places to protest, as decided by Vicente and the students. There was never any talk of weapons or violence, he and another survivor told me. But he returned to Uspantán early, along with twenty neighbors. One reason was the violence of their new urban allies: When cars refused to stop for demonstrations, the students smashed the windows. Another reason was the announcement that occupying the Spanish embassy would be dangerous. "Those who want to come, come along, but those who don't—there's nothing obligatory," they were told before each action. "We're going to demand our rights, and if we die, we die," both Vicente and the students said.

Soon after the embassy massacre, the Lucas regime smashed into the San Carlos networks. The terrible fate of the regime's victims, typically tortured before they were killed, suggests an obvious motive for revolutionary suicide. Aside from fearing a slow, hideous death, militants did not want to betray their comrades. Hence the practice of guerrillas killing themselves to avoid capture, reinforcing the Guatemalan left's cult of martyrdom.

At the Spanish embassy, the few protesters who decided to ignite gasoline in a small interior space were conceivably ignorant of the consequences. Perhaps they just wanted to force the riot police out of the building. The other possibility is that they intended to immolate themselves and everyone else in the room. Ambassador Cajal still doubts this was the intent. No one would have been killed, he points out, if the Lucas regime had been willing to negotiate with him. Nonetheless, a terrible possibility remains: The massacre at the Spanish embassy could have been a revolutionary suicide that included murdering hostages and fellow protesters.

7

Vicente Menchú and the Committee for Campesino Unity

My father came back very proudly and said, "We must fight the rich because they have become rich with our land, our crops." That was when my father started to join up with other peasants and discussed the creation of the CUC with them. A lot of peasants had been discussing the Committee but nothing concrete had been done, so my father joined the CUC and helped them understand things more clearly.

—*I, Rigoberta Menchú*, p. 115

Vicente Menchú's struggle for land, culminating in martyrdom at the Spanish embassy, makes him the most heroic figure in his daughter's book. Memorialized in the pages of *I, Rigoberta Menchú*, he became the most widely known founder of the Committee for Campesino Unity, whose importance is hard to overestimate for the left's understanding of the war. For a movement led by ladinos, CUC proved that the revolution was developing a broad base of support among Indians. After visible support for the guerrillas was crushed in 1982, CUC carried on the struggle abroad by mobilizing international opinion against the Guatemalan army. This was the organization that Rigoberta joined, in whose name she spoke on international tours. In the vision of Guatemala propagated by revolutionary exiles, Rigoberta and CUC represented the peasants who had been silenced by the army's counterinsurgency campaigns.

CUC was born in southern Quiché, around the department capital of Santa Cruz.[1] This was a more developed, densely settled region than Uspantán, in greater contact with national life. Peasants were abandoning hopes for self-sufficient farming as population growth crowded them into tiny plots. They were becoming weavers and itinerant merchants instead of working for plantations. More were going to school, and they were joining new kinds of organizations that encouraged such trends. From the

1950s to the 1970s, the most important of these modernization vehicles was Catholic Action, started by a new generation of priests from Spain. The idea was to revitalize long-neglected parishes by weaning Mayas from folk Catholicism and training them to be catechists. But soon catechists became involved in organizing cooperatives and running for political office. Some of the priests who started Catholic Action had fought for General Francisco Franco during the Spanish civil war; they intended the new organization to be a counterreformation that would protect their parishioners from the lure of communism. Instead, they and their catechists collided with the patrón-client structures of rural Guatemala, turning the Quiché diocese into the local outpost of liberation theology.

Revolutionary movements are often attributed to rising expectations and antiquated structures. In this case Catholic Action was modernizing leadership in villages. K'iche' peasants were breaking out of the trap of seasonal plantation labor. But their municipios were still controlled by ladino patróns. On guard after the attempted land reform of the early 1950s, the patróns of Santa Cruz were quick to report challenges to the dictatorship, which would jail the troublemakers or expel the priest advising them. The paranoia increased after 1974, the year that the reformist Christian Democrats attracted enough K'iche' voters to win a number of town halls. The conservative reaction was nothing like the holocaust at the end of the decade. But with the Guerrilla Army of the Poor launching its first raids in the northern part of the department, rumors swirled. Meanwhile, the army's theft of the 1974 presidential race suggested that electoral politics was futile.

Santa Cruz del Quiché was a more polarized setting than Uspantán, and it was from the left wing of its Catholic Action that many of CUC's several dozen founders came. The other CUC founders were like-minded men from Chimaltenango, Huehuetenango, Baja Verapaz, and the Pacific coast. Most surprising about the new organization was its broad vision of representing "all rural workers." With the help of *concientización* (consciousness-raising), a pedagogical technique associated with liberation theology and the Catholic left, CUC wanted to bring together different categories of peasants. It wanted to unite rural proletarians and smallholders, the landless and the land-strapped, ladinos and indígenas. But its priority was organizing the migratory labor flows from the highlands to the plantations. Guatemalan peasants had relearned deference after the 1954 counterrevolution. Starting in 1978, CUC denounced the oligarchy in no uncertain terms. It wanted living wages and the distribution of estates.

In February 1980, just after the Spanish embassy fire, CUC set off an unprecedented wave of strikes on the Pacific coast. The cotton and sugar harvests were stopped in their tracks. Plantations owners felt so helpless that the Lucas García regime agreed to triple the minimum wage. Once the strike was over, the security forces kidnapped every organizer in reach. Meanwhile, CUC erupted in the highlands and joined the guerrillas. Because of the 1980 strike and the rapid spread of the insurrection, CUC is usually presumed to have been broadly based and expressed the demands of Mayan peasants. But because it operated in semisecrecy, the dimensions of the movement remain hazy. Another reason for uncertainty over its actual reach is that it lost so many members. By the end of 1982, it had been almost exterminated inside Guatemala. CUC's destruction is also a plausible reason why I could find no recollections of it in Uspantán, let alone of Vicente Menchú as one of the founders.

What, then, was Vicente's relation to this legendary organization? Did it really originate as a grassroots movement? Were its founders deeply exploited peasants with their backs to the wall, as *I, Rigoberta Menchú* would have us believe? Whether they were or not, CUC has found a place in the popular imagination. Vicente Menchú has, too, beyond the pages of his daughter's book, in the stories that are told about his traveling through the highlands and telling other peasants about his life. So what have CUC and Vicente Menchú come to mean in their symbolic afterlife?

To answer these questions, let us look closely at how CUC emerged in southern Quiché in the mid-1970s, announced itself in 1978, and joined the Guerrilla Army of the Poor in 1980. Its rapid rise and fall includes adobe brown villages in the highlands, study groups led by Jesuit priests, heated labor debates in the capital, violent strikes on coastal plantations, and the brave but poorly armed peasants who confronted the army in the early 1980s. It is a national story, of an organization that tried to represent all the country's rural poor, in a way that Rigoberta would echo when she claimed to speak for all poor Guatemalans.

Uspantán Memories of Rigoberta's Father

> *My father was in clandestinity from 1977 onwards, that is, he was in hiding. He left our house so he wouldn't involve us. He left his family and went to work with the peasants in other regions. He came back now and again but had to come via the mountains because if he passed through the town the landowners would know he was at home.*
>
> —***I, Rigoberta Menchú*, pp. 115–116**

According to Rigoberta, her father's conflicts with plantation owners and INTA prompted him to help start CUC and become a full-time organizer in other areas. He was able to return home only occasionally and in secret. Meanwhile, even before Petrocinio was kidnapped, army patrols forced Chimel to organize for self-defense. The villagers set up lookouts, secret signals, and emergency exits; built a secret camp to hide from the army; and dug traps for soldiers to fall into. After soldiers beat their dogs, killed their animals, and looted their houses, the villagers armed themselves with slingshots, machetes, stones, sticks, chile, salt, and Molotov cocktails.[2] Guerrillas never walk onstage in *I, Rigoberta Menchú,* but they hide nearby and are regarded as defenders, making Chimel sound as if it was involved with them as early as 1977.

Still, the chronology of how Chimel becomes a militant village is perplexing. Rigoberta presents the community mobilizing to get Vicente out of jail after his second arrest in 1977 (actually 1978), then describes Chimel as being so well organized that it captures an army straggler, but goes on to say that "the community acted together for the first time" after Petrocinio was kidnapped in September 1979.[3] This is not the first point where *I, Rigoberta Menchú* becomes confusing, yet such inconsistencies do not necessarily mean much. Since Elisabeth Burgos rearranged Rigoberta's stories to put them into chronological order, it would be easy to make mistakes, quite aside from the contradictions to be expected in any life story. The more serious problems crop up when we step outside Rigoberta's account to compare it with others. According to local testimony, the army did not send troops to Uspantán until after the guerrillas visited the town in April 1979. No one recalled army violence until after the EGP's assassination of Honorio García and Eliu Martínez in August 1979. As for village self-defense, there is no hint of it in local testimony until after these events.

What about the Committee for Campesino Unity? Should you ask after this organization in Uspantán, the usual response is denial of its presence. "Neither CUC nor union activity was here. I don't recall anyone calling a CUC meeting," an ex-mayor told me, as did human rights activists and other sources who were forthcoming on sensitive issues. The organization was always semiclandestine, of course: Everyone who knew about it locally could be dead, gone, or denying it. Yet human rights activists eager to claim CUC's legacy for Uspantán were at a loss for personal knowledge, nor does it show up in human rights reports or the recollections of Rigoberta's family. Although a few people affirmed that it had a local history, their source of information was the Nobel laureate's book. No one claimed firsthand experience with CUC.

Many Uspantanos recalled an earlier peasant organization with which Vicente Menchú would have had contact, the Peasant Leagues. They were started around 1965 and combined technical assistance with talk about land reform. Not much seems to have been accomplished in Uspantán. A few people say that Vicente helped start the local branch, but relatives and old associates either deny it or profess ignorance. According to one of Vicente's children, he may have gone to a meeting once. If he was looking for help with his land claim, the affiliation does not show up in his petitions to INTA, suggesting that any involvement was fleeting. Nor did he or his sons belong to the two cooperatives started in the 1970s, one as a savings and loan and the other to help farmers with agricultural inputs and marketing.

However, Vicente and his family were involved with other organizations to which Rigoberta does not refer, apparently because they would be difficult to reconcile with her version of events. Although she describes a stoutly isolationist Chimel, suspicious of outside influences, others recollect a peasant village that, like so many others, was infected with the ethic of *superación* (getting ahead), through acquiring useful knowledge from the outside world. As a village led by catechists and petitioning for land, Chimel was particularly open-minded in this regard. Rigoberta does refer to a development program of the kind that proliferated during her childhood, but it ends in failure: "Some Europeans were helping us too. They sent us a lot of money. They were people who had worked for a time teaching the peasants how to farm. But the way they plant isn't the way we do it. Indians reject the chemical fertilizers they tried to teach us about. They weren't really welcomed so they left, but they were very good friends of my father and helped us."[4]

The reference to "some Europeans" sounds like a veiled reference to a program in which the Menchús were enthusiastic participants. Dr. Carroll Behrhorst was a Lutheran medical missionary from Kansas, so well known that he was regarded as Guatemala's answer to Albert Schweitzer. After starting a hospital in Chimaltenango, he expanded his health and agricultural programs to Uspantán, including the village of Chimel. At least three young North Americans—two Peace Corps volunteers and a former volunteer, all associated with the Behrhorst Clinic—worked with the Menchú family and their neighbors in the 1970s. Vicente served on committees, and his two oldest sons took a two-year training course to become Behrhorst promoters. Besides setting up a village clinic and distributing medicine, the Menchús also experimented with vegetables and received a variety of breeding stock, including chickens and goats, as well as cows from the U.S.-based Heifer Project. "He was a real progressive farmer," one of the Peace Corps volunteers said of Vicente. "Everything we had to offer, he would try it out, and he was good. The one disagreement we had was the way he cut and burned up the mountain slopes. That's no way to farm, but that's the way he wanted to do it."

Rigoberta was not a Behrhorst promoter herself, but she used to pick up supplies for her brothers at the project's clinic. Were the Menchús involved in radical politics? None of the three volunteers I talked to could recall that they were. "I don't think it even entered their minds," one responded, based on frequent visits to Chimel between 1976 and 1978.

"They were concerned with being left alone and getting legal rights to the lands where they'd been squatting and clearing. . . . They were some of the more active people, but not revolutionary in any sense. . . . They were little tiny capitalists trying to make ends meet, make a buck, and get ahead. They were so isolated and remote out there. It never seemed like they were trying to hide anything; they were always taking me off somewhere to show me something." Rigoberta might be correct that the agricultural projects were a failure. But that is not how one of her relatives recalled them. Instead, he described the projects with deep nostalgia. "We taught ourselves about all kinds of crops and animals. He [one of the North Americans] helped us a lot. This kind of work enchanted me. How many heads [of animals] we had! Where will we get them now? There aren't any. This *señor* showed us everything so that we wouldn't fail. How to vaccinate a cow. Nearly two years of training we had. When he left, really, I cried."

Vicente's commitment to working with the U.S. Peace Corps is not the only way in which the farmer recalled by neighbors is difficult to reconcile with the underground organizer described by his daughter. Everyone I talked to denied that he was missing from Uspantán after 1977, when his daughter says that he went into clandestinity.[5] Obviously, he was not underground when he and his sons worked with the Behrhorst Clinic and Peace Corps volunteers, from 1973 to 1979. Nor was he underground when Chimel submitted its final census at the town hall, in November 1978, whereupon the Tums had him jailed. Or when INTA helicoptered in Chimel's land title in December 1979, a month before he died. Judging from local accounts, only after Petrocinio's kidnapping in September 1979 did Vicente regard himself as a hunted man. Even then, when not risking his life by protesting in the capital, he was holed up in Chimel. Old friends and neighbors also denied that Vicente was interested in *política*. What they do say is that he always *pidió su derecho*—insisted on his rights.

Significantly, Vicente was never identified with CUC as a founder or member until his daughter told her story to Elisabeth Burgos in January 1982. In the earliest account of Rigoberta's life that I could find, dated December 1981 and published by a revolutionary news service eager to promote CUC, she makes no reference to her father's association with it.[6] Until Rigoberta's trip to Paris, Vicente was never identified with the group except to have died alongside five of its members at the Spanish embassy. When *Voz del CUC* published obituaries of the embassy martyrs, it described them as "a group of Ixil and Quiché compañeros, accompanied by five compañeros of CUC"—suggesting that the Ixils and Quichés were not members. If there is a single CUC publication that claims Vicente as a member, let alone a founder, I have yet to find it.[7] More recently, Rigoberta has waffled on the question of her father's affiliation. Although sometimes continuing to describe her father as a founding member, in 1992 she conceded that he never was that, just "a very active member." When Rigoberta and CUC published a book about the organization that same year, they made no reference to Vicente as one of the founders.[8]

CUC and the Jesuits

Why does it matter if Vicente Menchú was not part of the Committee for Campesino Unity? The organization was Rigoberta's vehicle for generalizing the experience of her father and village to that of all poor Guatemalans. Her 1982 story vouched for the imagery surrounding CUC, including the idea that it represented peasant masses eager to take up arms against the state. That Vicente could become CUC's best-known founder even though he had nothing to do with it until the last days of his life suggests the importance of Rigoberta's story. It also suggests the need to ask whether CUC actually represented a revolutionary groundswell. To answer the question, let us go back to the origins of the group that Vicente's daughter joined even if he did not.

Like Vicente, many of the men who started CUC were Catholic catechists, making his daughter's association of the two plausible. Yet he was from a different corner of Mayan society than the CUC founders. As a first-generation catechist, he never had the chance to go to school and remained a farmer all his life. His central achievement was to rise from an impoverished youth to become a substantial landholder. The founders of CUC were mainly from southern Quiché, belonged to a younger and more literate generation, and had little or no land. One, a catechist from a village near Santa Cruz, has provided a frank account of the difficulties he and his comrades faced. Domingo Hernández Ixcoy led CUC's 1982 occupation of the Brazilian embassy, which came up briefly in the previous chapter. In exile he became intimate with his organization's new international celebrity, Rigoberta, but left CUC and the revolutionary movement a few years later. The K'iche's of his municipio were not the poorest of the poor, Hernández conceded in a 1982 interview with the anthropologist François Lartigue. Contrary to CUC's usual imagery of hyperexploitation, none of his neighbors went to the coast anymore because they had found better alternatives closer to home. Hernández and his companions therefore faced indifference from the people they wanted to organize. "By living so far from their exploiter, they didn't know him," he observed—in contrast to the factory workers, whom he presumed to be more politically conscious.

In the villages of Xesic, Xesic Cuarto, and Chajbal, the activists won credibility by capturing a gang of bandits, K'iche's who donned military-style uniforms to rob and rape. People began flocking to their meetings; even wealthy men were impressed. But law and order was not exactly the goal. Instead, Hernández and his companions were learning about the guerrillas up in Ixil country, and they liked what they heard. "There has to be a vanguard to protect us; we felt this clearly because the people, the mass, we compañeros who were organized were asking, . . . 'The EGP, the FAR, isn't there any communication with them? Can't we open communication with them?' The only thing told them was, 'We don't know, but perhaps farther down the road we'll meet up with them.' That's the way it was, what was said among part of the people."[9]

This account is fascinating because it shows the proto-CUC making a very different appeal than it would when it became famous, as a class-based organization fighting exploiters. After acknowledging the difficulty of recruiting a less-than-desperate population, Hernández suddenly speaks for "the people, the mass" before retreating to "we compañeros who were organized." Quietly nursing hopes for linking up with the guerrillas, a nucleus of militants must contend with the lack of a local exploiter worthy of their radical politics. Before educating neighbors about the larger enemy—plantation owners for whom they are no longer forced to work, an army that has yet to arrive, and a capitalist system that allows them to improve their lot in small, incremental ways—they must find a meaningful enemy in local terms. Bandits are the solution. By organizing to protect the property of smallholders from common criminals, they broaden their appeal. It is after scoring a victory for law and order that they step up their literacy classes and consciousness-raising, to lead their neighbors down the path to a far more dangerous objective: confronting the army.

Hernández's memoir also suggests how dramatically CUC would stand out from other organizations in the peasant milieu. As the sociologist Yvon Le Bot has pointed out, its confrontational attitude toward the national power structure was not as natural or inevitable a development as many have presumed.[10] Certainly, many Guatemalans were frustrated by the army's stranglehold on power. The left had already lost thousands of activists to repression of the guerrilla movement, especially in eastern Guatemala. Following the EGP's announcement of its presence in 1975, death squad kidnappings also began in Quiché. But most of the population does not seem to have felt very threatened by them for several more years. Like other evidence from the period, Domingo Hernández Ixcoy's story suggests that repression was not experienced by most of his neighbors as a serious issue until it came to their door.[11]

If CUC's vision did not originate in the shared experiences of an oppressed population, where did it come from? What distinguished the founders was their involvement in Bible studies, but not just any Bible studies. They were practicing the "pedagogy of the oppressed," in the celebrated phrase of the Catholic educator Paolo Freire, the use of consciousness-raising to mobilize the poor for political action. By studying the Bible, pastoral workers and parishioners were supposed to learn from each other about structures of domination, then formulate a course of action to change them. Around Santa Cruz the consciousness-raising effort was led by Jesuits and their student helpers from Guatemala City. Known as the "Jesuits of Zone 5," after their house in a poor neighborhood of the capital, they did not wear clerical garb, nor did they charge for mass as priests ordinarily did. They taught that the Church was not just in the church, and they were insistent about raising political issues.

Because Jesuits report directly to Rome, they are not under the thumb of the bishop in whose diocese they operate. Within a few years of its 1972 arrival, the Jesuit pastoral team was having conflicts with the Sacred Heart priests from Spain who ran the parishes. Opinion was particularly divided over a young Jesuit named Fernando Hoyos, also from Spain. To his many admirers and detractors, Hoyos incarnated the new currents of thought and action in the Catholic Church known as liberation theology. If liberation theology could be boiled down to one proposition, it would be that the mission of the Church is to help the poor build the Kingdom of God on earth. Although most practitioners stopped short of the lengths to which Hoyos went, his goals also reflected the newly inverted priorities of the Jesuits in Central America, from ministering to the upper classes to organizing the lower classes, and from defending the faith to fighting social injustice. What remained constant in the Jesuit mission, whether educating upper-class children or training peasant activists, was the spiritual formation of future political leaders.

Consciousness-raising did not appeal to all the Santa Cruz catechists. Instead, it divided them. But those working with Hoyos and the Jesuits did well in elections for the leadership of Catholic Action. They gained a wider audience through the diocesan radio station and benefited from the 1976 earthquake that took so many lives. The relief effort opened distrustful villages to Catholic Action. Foreign donors channeled resources through it.[12] Meanwhile, the army's capture of the state provided a powerful rationale for extralegal courses of action. There was not much point to elections if the army could be counted upon to steal them. The Jesuits, their student collaborators, and the catechists under their influence felt the same about development programs, which were running into the usual difficulties. As a result, the Jesuits directed their message "not to solve economic problems through a new technology or financial organization . . . [but] to free the mind from traditional constraints, the . . . most profound being respect for the authorities. It was a message which subverted the law."[13]

Fernando Hoyos's skill at consciousness-raising led his listeners to ask, What next? The Committee for Campesino Unity was the answer, but it came into existence as such only after a 1978 schism in the national labor movement. At issue for unionists was whether to work with rather conservative U.S. labor organizations (which worked with the CIA) or more militant bodies (which were being steered by guerrilla organizers). The dispute ramified into the labor movement's peasant affiliates, which also split. At this point the more militant peasants organized CUC.[14] Suspicious of which way the wind was blowing, the security forces had already tried to kidnap Hoyos in 1977. Three years later, as they hunted down Catholic leaders suspected of collaborating with the guerrillas, Hoyos left the Jesuits for the Guerrilla Army of the Poor. He became a member of the EGP's national directorate and joined one of its columns. In 1982 he died after being trapped by one of the army's civil patrols, composed of the Mayan villagers that he hoped to liberate.

The year before Hoyos's death, the army kidnapped two of his associates and extracted confessions of their involvement with the EGP. Emeterio Toj Medrano was an announcer for the diocesan radio station in Santa Cruz del Quiché. He had worked closely with Hoyos and become a CUC founder. Not long after abjuring his career as a subversive in an army press conference, he escaped with the EGP's help, made his way to Mexico, and described how he had been tortured. The army's other catch, Luis Pellecer, was a young Jesuit from the Guatemalan upper class. Unlike Toj Medrano, he never retracted his statements, even though he was soon given enough liberty to escape. Instead, he resigned from the Jesuits and became one of the army's key advisers. His more sweeping descriptions of Catholic-Marxist conspiracies seemed to reflect the theories of his captors, but what he said about his personal experiences was plausible, including the claim that the Jesuits were the "real founders" of CUC.[15] The order denies it,[16] and there is no doubt that CUC's indigenous founders included men of ability, but the Jesuit connection is inescapable. The radical departure which CUC represented, from the usual level of peasant consciousness in the 1970s, suggests that its Jesuit advisers provided more than a little inspiration.

An Organization Born for War

CUC was born for war. From the beginning, issues were raised which implied a profound, structural, revolutionary change. We can say, then, that the strategic objective of the organization is to prepare the masses for insurrectional opportunities, for the final stages of popular war. . . . [CUC] is a revolutionary organization of peasant masses.

—"Compañeros of CUC," September 1982[17]

The other association that emerges from the story of Padre Fernando Hoyos is between CUC and the Guerrilla Army of the Poor. In 1980 CUC announced that it was joining the insurgency. The usual explanation is that it was obliged by government repression. Of the repression, there is no doubt. But it would appear that some of the Jesuits and Santa Cruz catechists were preparing for guerrilla warfare even before they organized CUC. According to a book by Hoyos's sister, he was a member of the EGP from 1976.[18] From the premise of liberation theology, that the Church could use consciousness-raising and popular organization to build the Kingdom of God on earth, it was but a short step to the premise of the Guatemalan guerrillas, that they could jump-start a revolutionary movement even if the masses were not aware that they needed one.

That CUC was indeed "born for war" is also suggested by a 1982 interview with the EGP's commander in chief. Rolando Morán (the nom de guerre of Ricardo Ramírez) was talking with the Chilean revolutionary journalist Marta Harnecker. One reason for Morán's candor was doubtless that the Guatemalan army already knew what he was saying. Still, he may have said too much, as the interview reportedly became required reading at Guatemala's military academy.

"The masses form and enrich the guerrilla units," Morán said of the military role that the EGP assigned the civilian population. "The masses organize themselves and become the great paramilitary units . . . and people's self-defense units. These are all the military forms in which the masses participate in the war. They also participate in the economy of the war: they produce for the popular army, and they also produce for the clandestine political organisms that cannot survive without this support from the masses." The "leadership of all our mass organizations is a secret leadership," he added, as in the January 31st Popular Front and its best-known member, the Committee for Campesino Unity, which he described as "a peasant organization related to the EGP." "For example, an initial group of CUC forms in a village, a secret committee which develops a propaganda effort until it wins over the majority of the village and incorporates it into CUC's mass work. This can only be conceived in a country like Guatemala, where the degree of repression, the sharpening of the class struggle has so polarized the forces in conflict that . . . the people accept this solution as the only way to defend themselves. . . .

"In the Luis Turcios Lima Guerrilla Front on the country's South Coast, we now have some regular guerrilla forces. What are these forces based upon other than geography? In the villages of the region function mass revolutionary organisms, there are local assemblies of CUC which permit the emergence of guerrilla forces. . . . They are not all armed, but they have their self-defense groups which are indeed armed. On another level, that of the EGP itself, we have local guerrillas that are like militias, then regional guerrillas and then the Regular Army."[19] Morán did not go into how the strategy originated, but he is describing CUC as an integral part of the EGP, not a separate organization, which uses clandestine cells to enlist villages. In view of the EGP leader's confident explanation, Domingo Hernández Ixcoy's description of how the guerrillas were referred to during CUC's early days ("the only thing told them was, 'We don't know, but perhaps further down the road we'll meet up with them'") suggests that he knew more than he was telling his comrades. As Le Bot describes the implications of clandestine organization, it was "an avant-garde of restricted access which, for evident reasons, maintained itself in clandestinity and distilled vertically a fragmentary and coded information."[20]

Whether CUC was a guerrilla vehicle from the beginning or only after repression deepened is a moot issue for many of its members because they are now dead. But for those trying to learn from their experience, the question should be important. If CUC was a guerrilla front from the start, this raises troubling questions about its claim to speak for the broader population. An organization launched as a vehicle for guerrilla warfare, without explaining this purpose, is an instrument for luring peasants into a high-risk strategy without giving them enough information to understand what they are getting into. Only a sector of the masses can be mobilized, Morán explained to Harnecker. For example, if there are eight hundred people in a union, only four hundred can be mobilized. Of these, only a hundred are "the advance guard of the masses"—by the EGP's definition rather than that of the other seven hundred, who evidently are not in full agreement with the direction their organization is taking.[21] In the case of CUC, Morán mentioned "win[ning] over the majority of the village," but this was a recruiting mechanism steered from above, not an organization that came from the grassroots or set its course through community decisionmaking. There is also the implication that part of the village will be left behind, to be cast in the role of disloyal opposition once the violence begins.

As the government stepped up terror and recruits flocked to revolutionary organizations in 1980, "armed popular self-defense" became the issue debated by the Guatemalan left. Would bringing activists and communities into the armed struggle spread the revolutionary movement? Or would they be destroyed by the inevitable reprisals? In eastern Guatemala fifteen years before, guerrilla attempts to set up rural self-defense zones had been a disaster. Gustavo Porras, an EGP intellectual who worked with CUC, recalls what happened next as an unstoppable social confrontation. Provoked by government kidnappings, support for armed struggle in southern Quiché swelled so quickly that it overflowed the EGP's capacity to channel it. Until this point, the EGP had been slowly and carefully recruiting individuals to build a disciplined army for a prolonged war. Now it was suddenly incorporating masses of recruits and rushing into a strategy of popular insurrection.

By 1981 southern Quiché was in a state of rebellion. Angered by government killings, most of the population seemed to support the Guerrilla Army of the Poor. According to one source, over a thousand people from the municipio of Santa Cruz alone joined the guerrilla forces. Organized by CUC and incorporated into the EGP, they mined roads, burned government vehicles, blew up electrical infrastructure, fired on helicopters, ambushed government patrols, and attacked bases.[22] They also practiced self-defense by setting up warning systems and digging booby traps. But the insurgents did not have enough firepower to protect themselves from the army, which was soon burning their villages. Homeless and starving, survivors could only escape or, more often, surrender, which meant being conscripted into the army's new system of civil patrols. Cut off from their supporters, or what was left of them, the guerrillas pulled out of southern Quiché to regroup in the north.

In postmortems of where the EGP went wrong, it has been criticized for pushing the popular movement into armed struggle before it could protect itself.[23] Yet there were also peasants who wanted to take the initiative, who demanded weapons from guerrillas who had none to spare, as if the EGP were being pulled into a mass uprising before it was ready to lead one.[24] Guatemalan guerrillas may never have experienced such an outpouring of support as occurred in southern Quiché and neighboring areas in 1980–1981. Perceiving it to be unstoppable, the EGP ignored earlier experiences in eastern Guatemala, where the army had demonstrated its willingness to kill any number of peasants. Now the same thing happened again, on a larger scale. As for the civilians who welcomed the guerrillas and even demanded weapons, nothing in their experience had prepared them for the army's response. In the neighboring department of Baja Verapaz, the army's reaction to CUC roadblocks was so savage that some of CUC's surviving members, from the village of Xococ, changed sides and helped the army massacre one unarmed village after another.[25] When the army demonstrated its willingness to slaughter hundreds of men, women, and children in a single day, in the words of Gustavo Porras, peasants "completely changed their criteria."

What also happened, Porras acknowledges, is that the EGP underestimated the profundity of local contradictions—old feuds, often invisible to outsiders, that walled off part of the population from revolutionary organizers, even in villages that were joining the cause.[26] What was visible were crowds of peasants, welcoming organizers and demanding action against government killers. What was invisible was another population that remained silent, behind closed doors or out in the fields. They were too distrustful to become involved. Although a few could be singled out as army spies, to be killed or driven away, most could not. From these wary bystanders the army would, once it had rolled over the EGP's weaker forces, start the civil patrols and impose rigorous controls.

The reason CUC attracted so much attention, nationally and internationally, was that it claimed to speak for all Guatemalan peasants. Even if its accomplishments were substantial, the claim went far beyond what any organization has ever achieved. But CUC appeared at a time when the Guatemalan left and its international supporters wanted to identify a single group that could say just that. The impression of a large organization was created by the scale of the 1980 strikes on the South Coast. But these were not just the work of CUC (older organizations were involved), and they were never repeated. Nor was repression the only reason. Even in the proletarian context of plantations, the great understated problem was that of raising the consciousness of the seasonal laborers from the highlands whom CUC was supposed to represent.[27]

Vicente Menchú as Peasant Hero

Don't be a Menchú!

—Mother admonishing a rebellious child, 1993

If the plantation context was difficult, so was that of highland villages. Here campesinos were small landowners who tended to reject outsiders, unless these arrived via a trusted institution like the Catholic Church. In her 1982 story, Rigoberta skirts the problem by identifying her father as a pauperized seasonal laborer, who combines the consciousness of a rural semiproletarian with that of an independent peasant who is homesteading public land and defending himself against expropriation. This transforms Vicente into a universal peasant, a symbol that has undeniable appeal to campesinos and their sympathizers but, like any powerful symbol, condenses so much particularity that it can conceal a great deal.

Still, even if Vicente's life was rather different than described by his daughter, he has come to represent something much larger, a transformation of consciousness that seventeen years after his death is on display throughout the Mayan population. Something similar can be said of the organization to which Vicente never belonged, the Committee for Campesino Unity. Even if CUC started as a guerrilla front, even if it was far less broadly based than claimed, it has become a legendary instance of struggle, invoked even by Mayan ethnonationalists who have little patience with guerrilla comandantes.

This calls for a friendly word on consciousness-raising. Marxists used to assume that the working class would inevitably become conscious of its exploitation. Peasants were problematic because, as small proprietors, they were not completely dispossessed. Therefore, they would require leadership from the urban working class, that is, Marxist intellectuals. Indigenous peasants, owing to their consciousness of themselves as peoples apart, were even more problematic. To communicate with indígenas, the Guatemalan left borrowed the doctrine of *concientización* from liberation theology. Consciousness-raising was couched in a language of mutuality, in which peasants educate their middle-class pedagogues as well as vice versa, and it did contribute to the emergence of new grassroots organizations. But the approach also implies that previous consciousness is backward; it is a way for radicals to bridge the gap between the characteristic ameliorationism of the poor and their own confrontational agenda. In Guatemala the EGP turned it into a cover for transforming catechists into guerrilla organizers.

The Committee for Campesino Unity is no longer a major actor on the left, but the imagery surrounding it may appeal to more indígenas now than it did in 1980. Deserving part of the credit for this surprising development is the story Rigoberta told in Paris, less through the book (which few indígenas have been able to read) than oral transmission. One of Rigoberta's favorite themes is consciousness-raising (in Spanish the book's title is "My name is Rigoberta Menchú, and this is how my consciousness was born"), which she links to her family's militancy in CUC. Even if her father and village never belonged to the organization, the story appeals to indígenas because it expresses their experience as a people, along the lines of: (1) they took our land, (2) now we're smarter, and (3) we're not going to let them do it again.

After Rigoberta's story became known, campesinos in the popular movement started to add their own, about how Vicente himself had shown up to tell them about his experiences. One story dates to shortly after Rigoberta gave her testimony in Paris, at one of the first conferences where she was put forth as a representative figure. "The period when more people from La Estancia [a village near Santa Cruz] joined the CUC was when Don Vicente Menchú and one of his sons sought refuge with us. They told us about how they lived in the north, about the misery and hunger that were worse than in La Estancia. They told us that it was no longer possible to live in northern Quiché because of the repression. When the army of the rich arrived in the hamlets and villages, it killed everyone. They told us how the soldiers stole everything, and raped the women. They said this was war, that the war would not end until everyone became organized and began to struggle for their rights. We would win the war because we had truth and justice, and we were the majority of the population."[28]

Another story comes from one of the few CUC founders still alive and active in the popular movement, a merchant from Chichicastenango named Sebastian Morales. Two or three months before Vicente's death, according to Sebastian, he "arrived directly at my house. Because he was persecuted, he spent a week with me. What he told me was his history, that he had his land, that the army or the authorities came, and they kicked him out of his house to give it to a landlord. As they were not about to give up, they arrived in [Santa Cruz del] Quiché, then [Guatemala City], always demanding their rights."[29]

Could these stories be historical? Apart from Rigoberta's testimony, the La Estancia story is the only period evidence I have been able to find that Vicente Menchú was associated with CUC. Interpreted literally, it suffers from the fact that life on the abundant lands of Chimel was not hungry and miserable, nor did the army commit village massacres in Quiché until after Vicente's death. Still, just because the story is couched in hyperbole does not mean that Vicente never visited village catechists in the southern part of the department, especially during the last months of his life when he organized two delegations to the capital. Yet when the Vicente of these stories is compared to the one recalled in Uspantán, the contrast suggests the need for caution, as underlined by the Vicente of yet another story who visits Rabinal, Baja Verapaz.

According to the narrator, a Rabinal catechist speaking in the early 1990s, he was one of a group who was *concientizado* by Rigoberta's father. Vicente "read a phrase from the Bible that said that we mustn't just accept injustice, that it was necessary to intervene to change the situation. That's how he convinced me, with something that simple. Afterward I convinced others the same way, because people like to hear the truth." "We have to organize ourselves to be able to receive help from outside," Vicente is also supposed to have said. "It doesn't matter where it comes from, if it's from abroad, if it's from the government. What is important is that the people get out of this misery, and this will be achieved only if we work together and take advantage of the resources offered to us. Any opportunity has to be seized, to train ourselves, for projects, to build, for whatever. CUC cannot reject what comes from the government. To the contrary, it has to be used correctly, to benefit the people."[30] This reincarnation of Vicente hardly sounds like the isolationist of his daughter's book, but he does sound like a man who would be willing to work with the U.S. Peace Corps. Meanwhile, back in Quiché I have heard other peasant storytellers put Vicente or Rigoberta into uniform as EGP combatants.

The plasticity of stories about the Menchús shows that they have attained the status of myth, in the sense of a charter or template rather than falsehood. According to Claude Lévi-Strauss, myth consists of the "'remains and debris' of historical events arranged into a structure."[31] If myth consists of symbolic formulas for resolving conflicts, again following Lévi-Strauss, what are the contradictions addressed by the mythic Vicente

Menchú? Obviously, the EGP had to show that it represented Guatemalan peasants, but that would explain only why a symbol like Vicente emerged in the revolutionary movement, not why he has appealed to other constituencies. For Uspantán detractors, the image of Vicente and his family as guerrilla fighters makes it possible to blame them for the army's arrival in Uspantán. But the most popular imagery of Vicente, as a CUC organizer defending his community from ladino landlords, transcends one of the chronic dilemmas facing Mayas: competition among themselves, especially for land. As resurrected by Rigoberta, her father stands above internecine feuds because he is defending his land from ladino plantation owners, not from other Mayas. In the person of Vicente Menchú, the Committee for Campesino Unity represents a moment when peasants overcame their differences and united to defend their rights.

8

Vicente Menchú and the Guerrilla Army of the Poor

They talked about God, they talked about how Jesus was born poor like us, and he suffered for us, and he died for us. This is why we must struggle against the rich, because he was poor and suffered and died for us.

—Uspantán widow recalling village meetings with the EGP, 1994

The Vicente Menchú I learned about in Uspantán—a Peace Corps–advised farmer with title to 2,753 hectares of land—seemed quite a contrast to the persecuted militant described in *I, Rigoberta Menchú*. Yet at the end of his life, Vicente was accused of being a guerrilla collaborator, went to the capital to protest, and became a martyr for the revolutionary movement. If my portrait of the previolence Vicente is accurate, this was quite a change of direction. Explanations are available from Vicente's relatives and neighbors, but they are hardly of one mind. There are richly incongruous memories of why he ended up being persecuted by the army and dying at the Spanish embassy. Some recall that Vicente was protesting the kidnapping of his son; others say that he died for his land, with some pointing to his conflict with the Tums and others blaming his ladino neighbors the Garcías.

A few cite his daughter's book as proof that Vicente was an active member of an invisible CUC underground. More associate him with the Guerrilla Army of the Poor—some simply because he had the misfortune to live where guerrillas roamed. Others believe that he welcomed the guerrillas to his village and agreed to collaborate with them. A former vigilante insisted that, years before the guerrillas manifested themselves, Vicente turned Chimel into a secret training base for subversion. One reason for the cacophony over Vicente's last days is the ambiguity of irregular warfare, in which responsibility is unclear and the main source of knowledge is rumor. Another reason is bitterness over the loss of life. Even if

CUC was never in Uspantán, the EGP was, and its confrontation with the army left behind strong feelings, not just against the army and its collaborators, who did most of the killing, but against the guerrillas and their presumed collaborators, whom many blame for the army's arrival.

There are enough conflicting versions, and enough gaps in my information, that I cannot be definitive about Vicente's feelings toward the guerrillas. But the contradictions dramatize the quandaries facing peasants as the EGP and the army turned their mountains and valleys into a battleground. The stories also suggest probabilities. Many of my sources, especially rural folk who suffered indiscriminate repression, regard the Menchús as innocent victims. Others blame the Menchús for inviting the guerrillas to their village and provoking the army's rampage. If the latter camp consisted mainly of town dwellers who escaped the full force of the repression, it would be easy to dismiss. Yet it also includes some of the Chimel survivors. Were the people blaming Vicente to consist mainly of ladinos, with most of his fellow indígenas exonerating him, it would be easy to dismiss the accusations against him as ethnic scapegoating. Unfortunately, while some ladinos vouch for Vicente's innocence, some of his fellow indígenas join in the condemnation. Even among old associates, opinion is divided. What can be surmised from the contradictory stories? Is there any way to reconcile the many testimonials to a peace-loving Vicente with the stories about him welcoming the guerrillas? To answer this question, let us return to why his village was blamed for the EGP's August 1979 raid on Soch.

The EGP Visits Chimel

A sudden visit by guerrillas leaves behind questions. Where did they come from? What villages did they pass through? Who might be helping them? If the guerrillas kill, a rapid departure means that someone local will be blamed. With responsibility unclear, suspicion follows the deadly old rule: Who had something to gain? In the case of Honorio García, it was easy to imagine two different groups who might have denounced him to the guerrillas. One consisted of his own farmhands, who tend to come under suspicion when a patrón is killed. Hence the story that one day the guerrillas encountered some of Honorio's laborers, asked what kind of patrón he was, and were told that he paid the lowest of wages.

This is the version of events prevailing in San Pablo and Chimel. Honorio was a demanding patrón. It could have been easy to elicit a complaint from his workers. But the explanation could also be apocryphal, and Honorio's sons looked elsewhere, blaming instead the independent village of San Pablo because of the dispute over the path described in Chapter 4. The latter supposition is the one shared by a human rights activist of the

1990s who told me: "One or two only accused [Honorio], not all the people. The guerrillas came through, asking if the community was doing well, and they said no, that the señor had closed off the path, so [the guerrillas] went to kill him." Even if San Pablans did complain to the guerrillas, there is no reason to suppose that they intended to give Honorio his death sentence. Political killing was not a local practice.

Honorio's sons also blamed Chimel for the raid. When the justice of the peace came out to inspect the two bodies, Honorio's sons said that Vicente's sons had been spotted among the guerrillas. Twelve years later, in reaction to the Nobel award, Julio García stated that the raiders had been led by Vicente himself.[1] Yet other Soch witnesses do not echo this allegation, instead describing the perpetrators as *gente desconocida* (unknown people). Still, the fact that the killers charcoaled or masked their faces must have encouraged the idea that they were local.

It would be easy to understand why the Garcías suspected Chimel if they were quarreling with it over the southeastern corner of the 2,753 hectares. Some of the village's younger people believe this to be the case, and I also heard it from an embassy widow. But it is absent from the petitions to INTA, and it is denied by more senior villagers, who say that boundary problems with the Garcías began only later. Many more people suppose that Chimel was blamed for the raid because one of its energetic young men—Vicente's son Victor—had a village pharmacy sponsored by the Behrhorst Clinic. Most recollections of Victor's medical work are full of appreciation; otherwise, his patients had to go all the way to Uspantán or Chicamán for help. Unfortunately, the army often suspected health promoters of giving medicine to the insurgents, especially when they were catechists, and Victor Menchú was both.

Like his father and older brother, Victor was active in Catholic Action. Aside from teaching church doctrine, lay leaders like Victor served on committees to build roads and schools, joined cooperatives, and solicited development projects. Under the auspices of Catholic Action, soccer teams and musical groups visited nearby villages; young people met members of the opposite sex; and their parents discussed local affairs. When villagers wax nostalgic about life before the war, they give Catholic Action the supreme peasant compliment—it was *alegre* (joyful). Catechists were usually men who had experience in the outside world and could speak Spanish. Accustomed to dealing with outsiders, they were a logical target for guerrilla recruiting. Even if catechists were of two minds, the army's suspicions meant that more than a few ended up in the EGP to save their lives. Still, Chimel's catechists might have escaped persecution if it were not for a lethal rumor. It was that the guerrillas had held a meeting at Chimel, some time before their raid on Soch, and been welcomed by Vicente Menchú.

The rumor could have originated in a misfortune of geography. Chimel lies in a mountain valley where two watersheds diverge, one dropping west to the Finca San Francisco in Ixil country and the other dropping east toward the Department of Alta Verapaz. That puts it in a corridor that the Guerrilla Army of the Poor used between its forces in Ixil country and its budding activities in Verapaz. Around Uspantán everyone agrees that the EGP was moving through the area in the months before it killed Honorio García and Eliu Martínez. It is also widely agreed that the guerrillas stopped at Chimel during this period. What is not agreed is whether Chimel welcomed them—even if we turn to accounts of the visit from four people who say they witnessed it.

"The guerrillas only passed through," a woman from Chimel told Barbara Bocek and me in K'iche'. "They came here to call together the people, like at two in the afternoon, but the people didn't come together. . . . Vicente Menchú was not here. . . . 'Do us a favor, call the people together for a class,' the guerrillas said. They said they were the Army of the Poor, but what is that? One doesn't know; it isn't clear who they are. A couple of people arrived and the guerrillas asked them, 'Do us a favor and go find food'—just to be given [rather than paid for]. But there never was a *clase* [meeting] because people didn't show up. They asked for food, saying that they were the poor, too. Then they went off, and one, two, three months later the plaza in Soch is full of guerrillas."

How many were they? I asked. "Like a hundred showed up, with the language of Chajul [Ixil], but more ladino than indígena. Women, too, dressed just like soldiers but in a darker color. They didn't stay; they came at two in the afternoon. They didn't eat here because they didn't get any food, because there wasn't anything to buy, and they left by 2:30 or 3. They didn't stay." Why didn't anyone in Chimel complain to the army? "After the EGP showed up, there were Monday classes where [catechists] imparted the Word of God. Some people thought they should abandon the village; I said no. If the army arrives, maybe it will kill people. The same if the guerrillas arrive, maybe they will kill. Only God knows, so [the people did] nothing." Like a number of people Barbara and I interviewed, this woman lost a relative at the Spanish embassy. "Because guerrillas had passed through, in Soch they said that everyone here was a guerrilla," she concluded. "The people here committed *k'o ta kimak* [no error or sin], but they were all getting killed." *K'o ta kimak* became a refrain in our interviews with village survivors, particularly widows describing how their husbands died.

A second woman from Chimel, who also lost a relative at the embassy, gave us a somewhat different account of the EGP's visit. "The guerrillas passed through on May 3. They asked for food, and the people prepared it." What did the guerrillas say? "Because they spoke in Spanish, the only thing I understood was, 'Don't let your children be grabbed for the barracks.' Everyone in the village listened to them. Some understood, others no. I didn't hear everything because I went back to my house to make coffee and bring it back in a big kettle." Although the villagers brought food for the guerrillas and listened to them, according to our second source, she insisted that neither Vicente Menchú nor Chimel became involved with the guerrillas.

Our third and fourth sources, two men from Chimel, described Vicente welcoming the EGP. "I heard that Vicente was in [the] town [of Uspantán] when the guerrillas came, when they came for the first time [on April 29, 1979]," the third told me. "What I heard is that Vicente talked with them there. Later they came down from [the direction of Laguna Danta]; they came here and held a meeting over there in the chapel with Vicente. At the meeting Vicente explained to the neighbors that they are helping us, that they are here to support us. . . . I was watching from a distance, became worried and didn't stay. There were lots of them, in uniforms with weapons. . . . At [a later] meeting, Vicente said that if there is someone who doesn't want to come to the meeting or who wants to inform the army or the military commissioners, this is called a reactionary, this is called an *oreja* ["ear," or spy], and he is killed. He said that, if one goes to the army, the guerrillas will come another time to kill him. There were several meetings. They [the guerrillas] came several times."

Our fourth source is among those who left Chimel in 1980 because of alarm over the direction it was taking. He reported seeing guerrillas in Chimel many times, women as well as men wearing dark green uniforms, with the first time dating to before the death of Honorio García. "The guerrillas showed up here after occupying town, to say they were here 'to defend the life of the campesino.' The guerrillas said they were here to help us defend ourselves, because the government enslaved us. Nearly everyone in Chimel welcomed them, [but] in Laguna Danta just some households, maybe half of them. There were lots of guerrillas, thousands of them, more than I could count." Because this source also claimed that Vicente welcomed the guerrillas, I asked what he heard Vicente say. "'That's good,'" he said. "'There are lots of enemies on this earth. We want to finish off the ones filled with envy to be in peace.' How many enemies he had. He wanted a new life, but he embraced evil."

Covering Up the First Political Killings

The mayor [of Uspantán] said that he had nothing to do with the campesinos . . . so then we came here, also to [Santa Cruz del] Quiché with the head of the military base. He also said that he didn't know anything. And we sent another telegram here, to the Ministry

> *of the Supreme Court of Justice. It also said that this only had to do with the police, with the campesinos it has nothing to do. Also here with an office of the workers, the FTG. And one day we told them that we want to go see [President] Lucas and we want to talk with him there: "What crime has the indígena committed?" We want to know what crime, because are we so insane that we're going to demand things when we know that we're guilty of something? Since in that case we can't demand anything. But we know well that nothing is owed because he's a boy of seventeen years. And Lucas said no, that I have to go to other states and won't return until next week.*
>
> **—Vicente Menchú to a journalist in the capital, January 26, 1980[2]**

Much of the power of Rigoberta's account comes from the dramatic equation between her father's struggle for land and his decision to join the revolution. If identifying Vicente with CUC gave him a radical genealogy, blaming his land conflict on plantation owners gave him a cause that fitted perfectly with the guerrilla movement's definition of its struggle. Yet my research failed to confirm a close connection between Vicente's land claim and the violence that engulfed him. After several months of interviewing in Uspantán, punctuated by a review of the INTA files, I was confident that the violence around Chimel had not sprung from conflict over land.

The recollections of family members, town officials, and neighbors coincided with decades of petitions and counterpetitions by Vicente and his antagonists. Contrary to his daughter's story, Vicente's main problem had not been with ladino landlords named Brol, García, or Martínez. Instead, it had been with his own K'iche' in-laws, the Tums of Laguna Danta. When the violence came, it was triggered by the EGP's attack on two ladino families with whom Vicente did not have serious difficulties—this was what I thought I had established.

Yet there were complications. Although everyone agreed that Vicente had a lengthy feud with his wife's family, some of my sources believed that a post-1987 conflict with the García family, over the southeast corner of Chimel's 2,753 hectares, dated to before the violence. Instead of going to the Spanish embassy to protest the army's kidnappings, in their view, Vicente was defending Chimel's boundary from the Garcías and their Martínez in-laws. Hence, Vicente had died for his land. One of my most informed sources, a man deeply involved in Vicente's claim, denied that there had been a boundary conflict with ladinos at the start of the violence; was well aware that Vicente had just received the provisional land title; but also sometimes said that Vicente died for his land.

My unease was ratified by a clipping from the *Washington Post*. By pure chance a reporter named Terri Shaw had accompanied the INTA delegation delivering Chimel's land title in December 1979. After the massacre at the Spanish embassy called for more reporting on Guatemala, she used her Chimel visit to write up a background story, without being aware that the embassy victims included people from the same village she had visited. Like the accounts I collected fifteen years later, Shaw described how the villagers were too afraid to come to town to receive their titles, obliging the INTA delegation to helicopter to Chimel. "The Indians talked among themselves mainly of their friends who had been taken away by the military police and never returned," Shaw wrote. "After they accepted the new titles the Indians tried to work with the officials to sort out some of their past grievances. They showed Rubén Castellanos, second vice president of the National Institute of Agrarian Transformation, a map indicating where a large landholding family had encroached on their holdings."

This sounded like the Garcías or Martínezes, at an inconvenient date. To continue with Shaw's report, the villagers believed that government kidnappers were helping wealthy property owners seize their land. Could she have misunderstood who they were complaining about? No, because the *Post* story had much in common with the denunciations Vicente would make in the capital. First, the *Post* made no reference to the EGP's assassination of Honorio García and Eliu Martínez. Even though the army's kidnappings were reprisals for a guerrilla raid, no one mentioned that fact to the reporter. Second, the villagers attributed the army's aggression to plantation owners invading their land, as they would in the capital.[3]

After the EGP's execution of a García and a Martínez, there is no doubt that several relatives decided to avenge them by collaborating with the army. By December 1979 Chimel could blame various Soch ladinos for kidnappings. But why would Chimel accuse them of invading land, and neglect to mention the EGP's role, if not to avoid the issue of how the killing had really started? Just that is suggested by an interview with Vicente's delegation in Guatemala City five days before he died at the Spanish embassy. "The repression began over a property that we of us here from Quiché petitioned for," states a campesino who soon identifies himself as the father of Petrocinio Menchú. "A property in San Miguel Uspantán that is public land. A repression was started by the army and some finqueros who are near this public land. And because INTA began to survey this land for us, we campesinos who are there, INTA gave us possession, [but the finqueros] are inside the public land [i.e., our boundaries]. . . . They gave us the registration, everything, it took us twenty-eight years petitioning for this land. But the finqueros of Soch were always looking for a way to oppress us. After the land was released to us, they accused us of I don't know what crimes, to the army, and they want to take possession of all our crops. . . . It's because of these problems that they kidnapped our comrades in Uspantán, nine campesinos who are in charge of that land claim."

When the interviewer asks whether the town of Uspantán had been occupied by guerrillas, Vicente answers: "That's what they said, but as we live twenty kilometers from town, and as we don't come much to town, we didn't notice. The news we heard, yes, but we didn't see it." As to whether guerrillas are active locally, Vicente responds: "Well, not there. They only took Uspantán, yes I heard that, but I wasn't there when they came through, as I live far from town. Where we live, we have never seen any unknown person. People are always arriving but we know them, and we haven't seen anything either. Then those persons accuse us like that, but what are we going to know? Well, if they had passed through or there had been talk with them, then it's important and one has to say, but no." With the interviewer pressing him—why would the army treat peasants so badly if there were no guerrillas around?—Vicente responds: "Perhaps the finqueros have paid something to [the soldiers] because they want to scare us or want to exploit us on this property where we are, so that they can take advantage of it, right? So putting fear into people, they want us to abandon it. Already many have left Chimel out of fear, some thirty campesinos from Sacapulas, Parraxtut, they left."[4]

This was far from a straightforward presentation. First, as everyone now agrees, the EGP had definitely visited Chimel. Second, the kidnap victims had not been in charge of its land claim. Even if Petrocinio played a secretarial role, most of the victims were from another village. Third, the Parraxtut settlers had left Chimel years before owing to disagreements with Vicente himself, over how he ran the community and refused to compromise with the Tums. Clearly, Vicente was not acknowledging the EGP's role in starting the violence. Perhaps he regarded the guerrillas as friends, but that is not the only possibility. His urban advisers could have warned him against mentioning the EGP, on the grounds that doing so would raise thorny questions and get him in deeper trouble. Or he could have been denying what he knew out of fear, of the guerrillas as well as the army.

Vicente and his delegation were not alone in omitting the murder of two ladinos. None of the documents distributed by the left in conjunction with the protests in the capital mentioned the first political killings in Uspantán.[5] When solidarity reports did mention the execution of Honorio García and Eliu Martínez, it was with false rationalizations, that the victims were military commissioners or had threatened to shoot peasants.[6] Not even the Catholic Church mentioned them in its communiqués.[7] Because of the influence that guerrilla cadres and sympathizers attained in human rights reporting, Honorio and Eliu never received attention as victims of political violence. They were kept off the human rights map by the guerrilla movement's success in stigmatizing them.

Why Welcome the Guerrillas?

Many in Uspantán disbelieve that Vicente Menchú would do what some of his associates claim that he did: welcome the EGP to his village. The character witnesses include two ladinos active in the conservative wing of Uspantán politics, two members of the Martínez family, and three other ladinos I interviewed. Unlike the Vicente of his daughter's 1982 story, the man they describe maintained a demure deportment on wider, ladino-dominated stages of power. Given the charged racial politics of *I, Rigoberta Menchú*, their inability to recall confrontational behavior toward ladinos is noteworthy. If anything, the majority of the ladinos I interviewed were perplexed over how Vicente met his end.

As a member of a subordinate group, Vicente would not have expressed the full range of his personality in interactions with ladinos, whose good opinion was so important in his legal struggles against other K'iche's. But for what it is worth, Vicente's ladino defenders find it hard to believe that he would collaborate with the EGP unless obliged by the army's overreactions. One argued that it was completely out of character for Vicente to ask someone to kill his enemies. In visits to the town hall, according to this ex-functionary, Vicente always exhibited a tranquil personality. He spoke slowly and politely. "'Look, sirs, we are from Chimel, and we would like this, this, and this,'" he would explain patiently and tactfully. "He was not a revolutionary," this source insisted. "He had a mentality of peace, of searching for peaceful solutions. I continue to believe that his intentions were peaceful."

If it was out of character for Vicente to cast his lot with the guerrillas, at least unless forced to, why would he welcome the EGP to his village *before* the army began kidnapping men from Chimel and San Pablo? One possibility is that Vicente was less enthusiastic about the EGP's arrival in his village than some accounts indicate. The generally favorable image that the revolutionary movement achieved internationally has obscured the fact that villagers could feel just as intimidated by the arrival of guerrillas as soldiers. As community leader, Vicente's duties included negotiating with whatever authority or force presented itself, and Mayan elders are skilled at dissembling their feelings. "When [the guerrillas] show up here," an elder in a nearby village explained, "one cannot reject them, because it is necessary to humble oneself. To defend our own life we have to humble ourselves. If not, they can kill us. It's the same if the army passes through."

Yet if Vicente was a reluctant host, why not report the EGP's visit to the army? It is not unusual for village leaders, who now maintain that they had mixed feelings about the guerrillas, to say that they opted for silence to avoid the inevitable complications—patrols by the army, demands for more information, and identification as an informer by the EGP. That, too, was a death warrant. Just because Vicente never acknowledged that guerrillas visited his village does not mean that he was pleased by their arrival. One day a man living near Chimel was summoned to a meeting there, with fifty strangers in military gear. "You're treated like burros, like animals, but we're going to get rid of all the patróns, all the finqueros, all the gringos who exploit you," the strangers said. Although our source did not know Vicente by sight, he did remember an older man's saying, "Si ustedes trabajan conformamente con nosotros, nos estamos de acuerdo" (roughly, "If you live up to your word, we are in agreement"). Interpreted literally, this is a conditional welcome, and perhaps only a reluctant one.

But that is not what Barbara and I heard from two of the four villagers who said they witnessed the guerrillas visiting Chimel. According to the two men quoted earlier, Vicente told his neighbors that the guerrillas would support them. This other possibility is corroborated by stories about serious differences between the Menchús and some of their in-laws over the EGP's visits. From two men related to the Menchús by marriage, I learned that one of Vicente's in-laws departed after someone stoned his house and tried to break down his door in the middle of the night. Another in-law reportedly left Chimel after he refused to support the guerrillas and Vicente accused him of being an army informer. These conflicts occurred after the death of Honorio García, I was told, and they resulted in the departure of three families from Chimel before it was destroyed. At the very least, there was enough discord over the EGP's visits to prompt a breakaway, by families who had sided with Vicente in his long struggle with the Tums.

Until the stories about Vicente supporting the EGP began to accumulate, I found it hard to believe that he would join an armed rebellion just as he was obtaining title to 2,753 hectares. It did not seem to flow logically from the prospects for his family and village, as owners of a tract of which most campesinos only dream. But Vicente's good fortune was hardly incompatible with joining an insurgency. Revolutionary movements usually claim to represent the most oppressed members of the population. This is the kind of imagery that has an international impact, as exemplified by *I, Rigoberta Menchú*. But it is usually not destitute peasants who join insurgencies. As Eric Wolf has pointed out, the most oppressed do not have the resources and maneuvering room to confront the power structure so directly.[8]

Instead, revolutionary peasants tend to come from better-off strata, whose rising expectations collide with inflexible power structures. In the Ixcán lowlands northwest of Uspantán, the EGP recruited members of rather successful, Catholic-financed cooperatives. Among the Ixils of Cotzal, the first men to welcome the guerrillas were relatively well-off political activists. In the Ixil town of Chajul, the guerrillas first appealed to small proprietors under siege from cattle rustlers. For an example of how peasants defending their property can become revolutionary martyrs, let us look briefly at the events that sent Ixils from Chajul to the Spanish embassy.

The Story of Gaspar Vi

It has been very difficult to know the real base of the guerrillas. . . . It is not known how far they reach, where they don't reach, who they relate to.

—Rigoberta Menchú, 1992[9]

One risk of dissecting the left's imagery about army violence is the implication that it is unfounded. This is far from the case, as will become clear in the next two chapters. Moreover, even if Rigoberta's portrait of her father differs markedly from local memories of him, at the Spanish embassy there was another catechist who, in certain ways, embodies the persecuted Vicente of *I, Rigoberta Menchú* more than the historical one. Gaspar Vi was one of three Ixils from the town of Chajul who perished along with Rigoberta's father. A vice president of Catholic Action, he was appreciated for his skill in mediating local conflicts. A few months before he died, he was kidnapped by the army, beaten badly, and released thanks only to pressure from the Catholic Church.

When I asked after Gaspar in Chajul, a man who knew him told the following story. "There were robbers here, together with military commissioners who were their accomplices. They had their group; they would steal things. And if they were accused, they would make counteraccusations and back each other up as witnesses. Once there were five of them, drunk, who demanded a drink from Gaspar Vi. He refused. Drunk, they told him, 'You're going to pay for this.' They took one of his cows; just the hide was left. Gaspar Vi went to the town hall. 'Who robbed it?' they asked. 'I don't know,' he answered. 'Well, maybe, these señores.' 'Do you have proof?' they asked. 'No.' 'Well, we can't do anything,' they said.

"So Gaspar Vi and twenty other men formed their own group. He and Gaspar Mendoza were the leaders, because they spoke Spanish, plus others who had lost cows. 'You've lost three; you've lost one'; that's how it went. They went out to the army base at Juil to present their problem. The army asked them to put their names and identification numbers on a list, and who's there but Otomero Galindo, the military commissioner. When the army confronted him with the accusation, he said that he was a hardworking man, that he worked for the army, and that these twenty men—from the Catholic Church, from the Christian Democratic Party, leaders of the pueblo—were guerrilla collaborators. Okay, the army said and grabbed Gaspar Vi and his son Baltazar. It dragged them off to Cotzal. Six days later they came back, with their wrists and necks swollen, perhaps from the ropes."

"'We're screwed,' Gaspar said. 'We're on the list. We're all on the list. No more political parties, organizations, cooperatives.' He withdrew to his land in Tzitzé and no longer came to town. In Tzitzé the guerrillas began to visit him, not uniformed like guerrillas, but like cattle owners with ropes across their chests looking for their cows. They asked to buy chickens, cows—'How much is this cow worth?' 'It's worth 500,' he said. 'Is that your final price?' they asked. 'It's my final price.' 'Well, maybe we'll come back in a week to see if we have enough money.' So they kept coming back. Finally they asked him, 'Do you have a house in town?' 'Yes,' he said. 'Why don't you ever go there?' He told them what happened. And this is how they gained his confidence." So was Gaspar an EGP collaborator before he went to the capital to protest? "Maybe so," my source replied. "Our people don't know what an embassy is. They don't know what a demonstration is. They don't lend themselves to that kind of thing."

On earlier occasions, Chajules had told me that the violence began locally with cattle thieves, whom the guerrillas helped kill or drive out of town. When a Chajul mob killed two men in October 1979, they were identified both as cattle thieves and army informers.[10] As in the previous chapter, when the CUC founders won over neighbors by arresting criminals, here we have another case in which the revolutionary movement recruited peasants not by organizing them against a class enemy but by defending their rights as property owners.

"No, the guerrillas didn't talk immediately about armed struggle," another man from Chajul told me. "Instead, what they said is, 'We have to organize ourselves because we're an isolated town, and backward, and the government doesn't help us.' They organized peasant leagues [against local thieves] and the mobile military police showed up to control them. That's how the deaths began. The people and the guerrillas went after the thieves, who would rob cows, maize, who would break into houses to take clothes. [The people and the guerrillas] killed many bandits. So the mobile military police grabbed certain people to be informers. These were the same thieves who would spend all day drinking instead of working and who now accused people of being subversives. They would go from house to house demanding money and, if they didn't get it, would say, 'There's a subversive.'"

Accounts like this illustrate how hard it is to define when guerrilla organizing began. No one except survivors among the first cadre in an area may know, because it was the EGP's policy to infiltrate preexisting structures and only gradually disclose its agenda, even to the people it was organizing. What is also clear is that the Chajules were subject to outrageous mistreatment by the army. In the already quoted interview just five days before the Spanish embassy fire, Chajul protesters told of soldiers entering houses to take away young women for gang rape. Men were arrested and never returned; others were robbed at gunpoint; others were ordered to come to the plaza to see "your dead fathers"—the seven captives from Uspantán who the army claimed were guerrillas. The denunciations were in such broken Spanish that they defy accurate translation, but an older campesino with more fluency—probably Vicente Menchú—stated the following: "I was a soldier in the time of [the dictator] Ubico; these ideas didn't exist like what is happening now. . . . We always went out to inspect something for the head of our unit, but they were always watching us so that we didn't do anything against others. But now it appears that those in the army have no discipline, because they no longer respect our rights as campesino indígenas."[11]

The Tragedy of Vicente Menchú

The problem is always that of land, of authority, of wanting to take advantage. That was the big problem, the division among themselves, giving birth to the violence. Always for the land.

—Human rights activist in Uspantán, 1994

Scholars have long debated why peasants join insurgencies. Especially for those who wish to defend the legitimacy of guerrilla movements, as the vox populi of oppressed peasantries, ideology looms large as an explanation. Deepening oppression raises the consciousness of peasants, who therefore decide to fight, and *I, Rigoberta Menchú* is among the evidence adduced for this position. What has not received much attention is that once insurgents and counterinsurgents go into action, peasants have few choices.[12] If peasants do make ideological connections with insurgents, these often do not last very long, not least because so many are killed or forced to surrender. Among survivors, many decide that their revolutionary period was a mistake.

Rigoberta's father may have found reason to welcome the guerrillas. Peasants are very aware of their lack of power, so they understand the importance of maintaining good relations with whatever faction has the upper hand. The sudden arrival of a guerrilla column, in far greater numbers than government troops had ever manifested themselves, could have impressed Vicente, as could their vision of a new social order. But even if Vicente had a more radical constitution than I am giving him credit for, what he had in mind must have been rather different from what the guerrillas were planning. Peasants in this part of Guatemala had little experience with how the army treated villagers it suspected of subversion. Nor did the EGP feel obliged to tell peasants about the potentially disastrous implications of joining it. Guerrilla leaders knew what had happened to their peasant supporters in eastern Guatemala, but they were too dedicated to their cause, and too fanaticized by the sacrifice of so many of their comrades, to be very sensitive about what their strategy would cost the next population they tried to organize.

What cannot be overemphasized is the speed with which the war overtook Vicente. Only nine months elapsed from the EGP's first appearance locally to his death at the Spanish embassy. Whatever decisions he made, there was little time to make them and little or no chance to take them back. Only after Chimel had compromised itself by receiving the guerrillas did the consequences suddenly manifest themselves, in the EGP's two executions followed a week later by the army's first kidnappings. Suddenly, Vicente was up against the wall. Now he was committed, whatever his intentions had been, whether he liked it or not, and Chimel was overtaken by anxiety.

"If there is someone who doesn't want to come to the meeting or who wants to inform the army or the military commissioners," to repeat how Vicente has been quoted above, "this is called a reactionary, this is called an 'ear,' and he is killed. . . . If one goes to the army, the guerrillas will come another time to kill him." As in-laws refused to follow his lead, Vicente learned one of the lessons of joining a clandestine organization: Since breaking away endangers the group's security, changing your mind is punishable by death. Should you try to recruit a trusted friend who turns you down, he can suddenly become your worst enemy.

If Vicente indeed welcomed the guerrillas, what could he have hoped to accomplish? If we take *I, Rigoberta Menchú* at face value, the answer is simple, because Chimel is under siege from plantation owners and guerrillas will protect it. But if Vicente's unending conflict was instead with Laguna Danta, could he have wanted the EGP to protect him from his own K'iche' in-laws? When the guerrillas appeared in 1979, INTA was about to title the 2,753 hectares, but it refused to include the 151 hectares around Vicente's house and settlement. Ownership of the latter tract was still unresolved, to the ire of both parties. Only months before, in November 1978, the Tums had cast their shadow over INTA's final census by having Vicente thrown into jail. Although he was free within a few weeks, the court case was still hanging over his head, and his possession of the ground where he had lived for thirty years was still not secure.

That Vicente hoped guerrilla muscle would help him against the Tums is only a hypothesis, and not a pleasant one. But it would be compatible with a long history he shared with the Tums, of appealing to external institutions against in-laws. As for the EGP, it did not wish to side with one peasant faction against another. Instead, it wanted to bring them together against their class enemy, who would usually be ladinos. If Vicente wanted to use the EGP against his K'iche' rivals, this never came to pass. Yet when guerrillas organize smallholders whose most pressing enmities are against each other, what happens next can be motivated by the internecine quarrels, not the larger cause that peasants are supposed to embrace.

When I visited Laguna Danta in 1991, the various Tums who received me were not pleased by my questions about their feud with Chimel. Although still bitter over it, they denied any connection with the political killings that ravaged their own village as well as Chimel in the early 1980s. Again and again, an old man who had spent much of his life sparring with Vicente fast-forwarded to the latter's death at the Spanish embassy. He did so obsessively, as if it had been as great a shock to him as it was to Chimel. The Tums did not want to be blamed for the persecution of the Menchús, and I never heard anyone associated with Chimel do so. However bitter their differences, some unacknowledged denominator of solidarity may have prevented the kind of accusations, of working for the army or the guerrillas, that piled up so many victims elsewhere.

The first person to mention a skeleton in the closet was a ladino from Soch. Though more than willing to blame fellow ladinos for their part in the violence, he did not stop there. The Menchús "had a supply of medicine in Chimel, put there by the [Catholic] priest, and would also come down here [to Soch] to sell medicine at the market. When guerrillas showed up [in Chimel] and demanded medicine, one of the Tums told the army, which decided that the Menchús were guerrillas."

Later Barbara Bocek and I were interviewing one of Vicente's old friends, an elder with kinship ties to both sides in the Tum-Menchú feud, who mentioned something about *zahorines* (Mayan sorcerers) working against Vicente. Then he referred to Nicolás Tum Castro—a cousin of Vicente's wife, Juana Tum Cotojá. From his home in Laguna Danta, Nicolás led the struggle against Vicente, especially after the death of his father, Antonio Tum. As INTA titled the 2,753 hectares to Chimel in the late 1970s, Nicolás continued to protest the occupation of the other 151. Thirteen months after Vicente's death, on February 28, 1981, at 4:30 in the afternoon, Nicolás was murdered as he emerged from his sweat bath, along with a nephew named Antonio Hernández Lux.

Laguna Dantans told me they did not know the precise reason for the two murders, but they blamed the guerrillas. Now a K'iche' elder in another village was making a connection we had not heard before. "Nicolás Tum was telling the army every time the guerrillas passed through. He said that he had influence with the army, by telling it about their movements, and that the guerrillas could not touch him, that they were not capable of it. Yes, he was a Catholic, married by the church [and therefore at least nominally a member of Catholic Action, which opposes witchcraft], but he also liked his oracle, his book. Yes, that made him a *zahorín*. Surely he was doing bad things with his oracle against Vicente. That's why Vicente burned to death at the embassy."

That a Tum elder was an informer and a sorcerer is just another version of events. It is not necessary to explain what happened, and it is perhaps without any basis. But it is true that where peasants refrained from denouncing each other to the army and the guerrillas, many fewer died than where they did. Welcoming the guerrillas was fatal. If Vicente indeed embraced the guerrillas, it was probably because he hoped they would help him against the Tums. In this tragic sense, it is possible that Vicente died for his land, along with his old enemy Nicolás Tum Castro. They would have died not because ladino planters coveted their land but because they could not resolve their differences. If Vicente had a weakness, this was it. Whatever demons he harbored, they were directed against other indígenas who challenged him.

How about Vicente's relation to the EGP? What can be established is that guerrillas held meetings in Chimel, but not much else. The question of how Vicente felt about the rebels has several possible answers. One is that he thought they could help him against his local adversaries. Since assassination had yet to become a factor in local politics, there is no need to assume that this was what he had in mind. A second possibility is that Vicente gave the appearance of welcoming the guerrillas because he was playing for time, pondering them as a new factor in local affairs or even hoping that they would go away, only to be trapped by the EGP's precipitous decision to execute two of his neighbors. Even if Vicente had not perceived a clear benefit to working with the guerrillas, the unjust kidnapping of his son, then the discovery that the only support he could find was from students in Guatemala City, could have convinced him that he had no choice but to follow their advice, as demonstrated by the way he presented the situation in the capital.

Either of these possibilities is compatible with a third—that like many peasants in nearby Ixil country, he was attracted to the promises of the Guerrilla Army of the Poor without realizing that its agenda could easily require the sacrifice of his community. When the guerrillas visited villages like Chimel, they talked of a new society where wealth would be redistributed, indígenas would be equal with ladinos, and the government would be run by the people. What they did not dwell upon was the enormous risk of armed struggle, of turning peasant families and villages into a logistical base for military activities. That came later, after the army's responses made it clear that peasants had no choice but to defend themselves.

We should not suppose that because there was a meeting in Vicente's village, there was a meeting of minds. It cannot be assumed that guerrillas and villagers were candid about their respective objectives, let alone arrived at a shared understanding of what future cooperation would mean. Even if their first meetings went well, the creation of a middle ground between two such different groups takes time.[13] Of that there was little before, suddenly, defense against the army's reprisals took precedence over all else. Henceforth Vicente was trapped in a struggle for survival that had little to do with his previous aspirations.

9

The Death of Juana Tum and the Destruction of Chimel

The best and most active, nearly all of them died, because they didn't know how to defend themselves. They died innocents.

—Chimel survivor, 1995

For the revolutionary movement, the people who died at the Spanish embassy were martyrs whose example was rallying Guatemalans against the dictatorship. The triumphalism did not extend to the most bereaved. According to Rigoberta's 1982 account, the loss of her father was so unexpected that it left her profoundly demoralized.[1] She was not completely confident of the left's explanation for the fire, which would have made it harder to submerge her feelings in righteous indignation. In Chimel, villagers were not steeled to new heights of militancy by the news. Instead, they recall being "shocked" and "demoralized." One woman has the nightmarish memory of hearing the victims scream "Open the door!" over the radio.

Outsiders in search of clarity can easily overestimate the coherence, and underestimate the ambiguity, experienced by people trapped in a civil war. In Uspantán the common denominator in memories of the violence is confusion. People of all categories were surprised by the sudden eruption of violence. They were not prepared for political killing by a long history of agrarian violence as described in *I, Rigoberta Menchú*. Whatever use of force Uspantán had seen, it remained below the level of homicide. Suddenly, the routines of earning a living, caring for children, and going to town were interrupted by senseless murders, impossible to explain within the old order of civility. A predictable world dissolved in chaos. The confusion was less over responsibility for particular killings (although that was sometimes the case) than why they were occurring in the first place.

"It was not known what a guerrilla was. We didn't even know what kind of institution it was," a human rights activist told me. "We just heard the word but didn't know what it was. When they arrived on April 29, 1979, we thought they were the army. They spoke only in Spanish. . . . They invited the people and, as you know, when the army makes an invitation, the people attend because they are very *educado* [polite]. Then [the guerrillas] established themselves in the mountains and the calvary began for our campesinos. The campesinos were in their houses. When the guerrillas showed up, they said, 'We're good people and we're going to destroy the army.' Our people are naive, so some said, 'Very well,' not knowing what this entailed. Then the army came, and when it realized that some family had given food to the guerrillas, these people were taken away. . . . There was a confusion. The army was in uniform, and the guerrilla was in uniform. There was no life with the army, and there was no life with the guerrilla."

Just as Petrocinio Menchú was the first person from Chimel kidnapped, his mother was the second. Rigoberta places Juana Tum Cotojá in the capital just before the fire at the Spanish embassy; then has her both return home to Chimel and travel across the highlands, organizing women with the story of watching her son burn to death at Chajul.[2] According to everyone I asked, Juana was in Chimel caring for her two youngest children after the death of her husband. Meanwhile, the Guerrilla Army of the Poor stepped up its activities. On April 18, 1980, it occupied the nearby village of Caracol, to call on the inhabitants to join the war against the rich. An EGP communiqué makes no reference to violence, but the guerrillas executed two campesinos serving as military commissioners, for reasons that villagers found difficult to apprehend.[3]

"My uncle Miguel López asked [the army] to [let him] resign, because he could see that things were getting ugly and he wanted to get out, so he passed [the job] to my in-law Isidro," a Caracol man told me. "The next day the guerrillas captured Miguel at his house and brought him to the chapel tied up. That same afternoon, Isidro had hurt himself with his ax and came back from work carrying one of his children. He hadn't done anything; he just had the job for one day. There was no talk to the people [by the guerrillas]. They just captured [Miguel and Isidro], ignored their pleas for mercy, and shot them in front of the church." How did the villagers feel about this? "The people were afraid. In neither side did we have trust." According to another man from Caracol, "For us the two military commissioners hadn't done anything wrong. Yes, it surprised us a lot. . . . [and] made us afraid of the guerrillas. But where is one to go? Either of the two groups can kill you. But who commits more massacres is the army, not the guerrillas."

The two bodies had yet to be taken away when, the following day, Juana Tum passed through Caracol on her way to town. *I, Rigoberta Menchú* does not describe how Juana was kidnapped on April 19, 1980. A few Uspantanos repeat the army's improbable claim that Rigoberta's mother was captured with a gun under her clothing. More say that she was kidnapped in front of the church as she left mass. But relatives say she was taken from a house, the place where she and her husband were accustomed to ask for *posada* (lodging) when visiting town. According to a family account, "She had come out of mass and was eating supper when people came to the door and said they wanted to talk with her. 'Who is it?' she asked. [Her host] couldn't say, because it was completely dark outside. So she came to the door, they took her, and dragged her past the church. They found her clothes in the street; she'd just been dragged away." According to another family member, Juana went to town "for necessity, because the children were suffering for lack of sugar. It's very sad: [one of her adult sons] wanted to go, but she said, 'No, I no longer have small children, but you have a baby.' She went to buy things like sugar. When she came down to town at eleven at night, they took her from where she was staying."

Rigoberta's description of the death of her mother was, like that of her brother, nightmarishly precise. "I want to say in advance that I have in my hands details of every step of the rape and torture suffered by my mother." The account concludes with the astonishing image of her mother being exposed on a hillside and "eaten by animals; by dogs, by all the [vultures] there are round there, and other animals helped too. [The soldiers] stayed for four months, until they saw that not a bit of my mother was left, not even her bones, and then they went away."[4] Given the lack of information about the fate of most kidnap victims, Rigoberta claims such a remarkable level of knowledge that the literary scholar John Beverley refers to it as magical realism.[5] The obsession with what happened to her mother's body can be explained in terms of the horrible uncertainty felt by relatives of the "disappeared." Visualizing her mother's death so graphically might be the only means of closure.

However improbable some of the details, there are two reasons to believe that Rigoberta's account is basically true. First, in the early 1990s relatives who were remarkably ignorant of *I, Rigoberta Menchú* told me essentially the same story. "When they got there, the soldiers raped her," a family member said. "First they asked her, 'Are you really Vicente's wife?' 'Yes,' she said. 'How many of your children are still alive?' She told them. After raping her, they began to torture her. She suffered for eight days before dying. Right there they threw her into the pit, at Xejul." Like Rigoberta, this family narrator said he learned about Juana's fate from local men who were in the army. Unlike Rigoberta, relatives presume that Juana died at the army camp at Xejul some days after she was captured, although they are hardly certain.

The second reason Rigoberta's story is credible is that the army murdered thousands of helpless prisoners. The pit *(hoyo* or *sótano)*, typically a hole in the ground covered with logs or planks, was a regular feature of army camps. Into it prisoners were cast to die of hunger and wounds, atop the remains of others who had already died. "What shouts and laments he heard from the pit," a woman said of her father's experience at the army's Uspantán garrison in 1984. Victor Montejo, a Jakalteko Maya schoolteacher who is now an anthropologist, has described how he was nearly cast into the pit at the army garrison in Huehuetenango, in 1982 under the administration of General Efraín Ríos Montt. He was dragged "to the rim of a foul cesspool filled with mud, water and garbage. As they held me at the rim I heard a muffled cry rise from the depths and a head broke the surface, struggling to free itself from that horrible captivity. I could not make out the features of that unhappy wretch, who screamed with clenched teeth from the edge of that pit, exposed to the cold night wind and freezing rain. 'T-t-take me out or shoot me, but don't leave me in here,' he wailed pitifully. One of the soldiers leaned over the rim the man was clinging to and hit him in the face with his rifle butt, sinking him once again into the dark murky waters of the pit. 'Shut up, turd.'"[6]

Rigoberta's account of her mother's death also summons up the ghastly body dumps that became an institution in Guatemala and El Salvador. Except by mistake, victims were not left alive in these carrion piles. Two became well known in Uspantán. One was at the west end of the airstrip just south of town. Here a truck could be driven close to the rim of a gorge. A man living nearby would often see the headlights of a vehicle late at night, then hear men throwing people over the edge—a hundred or more, he estimated. After the body tumbled to the bottom, it would be washed away during the rainy season. The other dump, called Peñaflor or Paso de la Muerte, was also at the lip of a gorge, this one along the road to Chicamán, at a bend that the Catholic Church has marked with a cross.

"The people there are uncountable. They arrived by truckloads. Some were set on fire alive," a widow told me. "We will never know how many people because there's a river, and when there was a lot of rain they were swept away by the current. There's a woman who says that some are buried. Not just men: There are women; there are children; there are even women hugging babies. From being set on fire, some are carbonized. It will never be known how many people. Some victims were identified by family members and buried there. On the Day of the Dead, people who know relatives died there come to leave wreaths of flowers."

The Burning of the Villages

Yes, there's a lot to remember in Chipaj.

—Old man, 1995

The kidnapping of Petrocinio had not severed Chimel's relations with town. But after the death of six members at the Spanish embassy, the villagers stood branded as guerrillas in the eyes of fearful neighbors as well as the army. The isolation of the village was completed by the abduction of Rigoberta's mother. "When Juana died," a family member told me, "we couldn't leave at all. No one came out any more; no one left to buy what they needed. The children became listless. Soldiers arrived to destroy the maize and kill animals. The people fled whenever they saw soldiers."

Before the fire at the Spanish embassy, the army visited Chimel once, but the houses were empty and the soldiers only talked with a ladino schoolteacher before departing. After Juana was kidnapped, the village seems to have been left alone for the next eight months. When it was finally attacked, the assailants came up from Soch, on Christmas Eve 1980. There were about fifty of them, armed with shotguns, machetes, and axes, and they seem to have included the sons of Honorio García, other ladino vigilantes, some of their indigenous laborers, and perhaps soldiers. "Gosh, there's lots of flames out there," one villager said as he rubbed the sleep out of his eyes. The men fled; women shrieked; two teenage girls were raped. "There was no defense because we were taken by surprise," another man told me. "There were no dead, although people were cut up and injured as they fled. They set all the houses on fire, took the pigs, plus cows, horses, chickens, and money. They robbed the houses of radios, clothes, and maize and stayed maybe two nights before leaving."

The self-defense tactics described by Rigoberta, such as putting traps along paths and in houses, were indeed employed by EGP-advised villagers.[7] In the case of Chimel, several survivors denied having been "organized," but another said they followed guerrilla instructions to dig stake pits and post lookouts. When a neighbor arrived to harvest maize just before the Christmas Eve attack, he was confronted by four young men from the vicinity. They were armed with a hunting rifle and a pistol, identified themselves as the EGP, and said they were fighting for a time when there would be no more poor people. They also warned the visitor against giving information to the army, because he would be watched. The next time he came to harvest, just after Christmas 1980, many houses had been burned. Chimel therefore seems to have been "organized," but it does not seem to have been organized very well.

The guerrillas could suggest ways to save lives, but not the way of life necessary to sustain those lives. From a survivor of the nearby village of San Pedro La Esperanza: "Like [the guerrillas] showed us, we kept our maize, our salt, our soap out in the brush, but the army found everything and took it all. We had to eat greens without salt, and *guisquil* [a vegetable], but when the army saw that the people were eating *guisquil,* it cut everything down, even the peaches. Lookout duty, too, that's the only reason some of us are still alive." The main defense from army raids was dispersal. "Everyone went somewhere different," a Chimel survivor told me. "It was better for everyone to spread out, because when there are a lot of people together there are children yelling, there's fire, there's smoke, and people leave trails. But if there are just a few people, they don't leave signs; they're more hidden."

This is a more passive approach to community defense than the one described by Rigoberta. It would appear that the EGP did not have a strong presence in the burned villages of Uspantán. After your houses were destroyed, I asked one Chimel survivor, did the guerrillas show up to give you advice? "Que esperanza!" she replied (roughly, are you kidding?) "Nothing. They came through, but they liked to grab animals, any chicken, even before the village went to the *montaña* [forest]. They liked to grab things, they didn't pay because they said they were also poor." Judging from available reports, most of the fighting around Chimel dated to a brief period between September 1981 and February 1982.[8] If the EGP tried to defend Chimel, it was not very effective. One of the most common misapprehensions of guerrilla warfare is that it protects communities from repression. It is an idea that I have heard draw bitter laughs in Uspantán. "No, the guerrillas never defended Chimel," a survivor told me. "Combats didn't last long, just ten to fifteen minutes, because [the guerrillas] were few."

True to Rigoberta's account, at least a few villagers joined the insurgency as combatants. Because recruits needed to be tough and malleable, they could be even younger than some of the army's notoriously underage soldiers. Many were orphans, including Rigoberta's two younger sisters. According to her story in Paris, one sister chose to join the guerrillas before her parents were killed.[9] But according to Chimel survivors, the two were "very small" and stayed at home with their mother until she, too, was taken from them. "They went with the guerrillas only because they were orphans, for protection; there was no life in Chimel," an old neighbor said.[10] In Nebaj I met three amnestied guerrillas who remembered Ana and Rosa Menchú as political cadres during the mid-1980s. "Josefina" and "Angelina" were part of a twelve-person Education and Promotion of Popular Organization (EFOP) unit, which visited EGP columns to give political talks. Although they had noms de guerre like everyone in the organization, they told about their family and their sister's international work. A member of the Communities of Population in Resistance (CPRs), which held out against the army in the northern reaches of Ixil country, told me he became a compadre of Ana Menchú, that is, godfather to her son, who was two or three years old around 1987.

Obviously, survivors are not likely to provide a glowing account of their experience with a defeated revolution. They emphasize suffering and disillusion with guerrillas who failed to protect them. How they might have responded favorably to the EGP, at least for a while, comes up only occasionally. Doubtless some of my Uspantán sources were more involved with the guerrillas than they feel free to acknowledge. Still, compared with my interviewing in Ixil country, I was struck by how hard it was to hear about local revolutionary leadership in Uspantán. From Ixils I learned of dozens of people who became commanders, combatants, or cadres. By 1989 some were living under amnesty in government-controlled towns and evinced a certain pride in talking about their experiences with the EGP. In Uspantán the names never came up. As far as I can tell, the guerrillas did not have a clandestine network in Uspantán before the first columns appeared. Few refugees held out after 1983 and became part of the CPRs, the refugees beyond government control who supported the guerrillas into the 1990s.

Even if Uspantanos had fewer ties to the guerrillas than Ixils, the suffering was comparable. Chimel was just one of a belt of mainly K'iche' villages along the mountain ridge north of town that came under attack in late 1980 and early 1981. Another was Xolá, the prosperous village near town where Rigoberta's mother was born. Unlike Chimel, it was never physically destroyed, but its savvy K'iche' farmers and traders lived in terror of kidnappers for several years. "The guerrillas came by here. Lots of them showed up and wanted to talk with the people," a Xolá human rights activist told me. "But the people didn't want to; they were afraid and went into their houses. Then the judiciales [army-sponsored vigilantes] came and organized their group. Money is what they wanted, so they began to kidnap people. . . . People just had to stand by with their arms crossed while the judiciales took whatever they wanted, because if they didn't the judiciales would kill them or throw a bomb." One source ticked off the names of nineteen men whom judiciales kidnapped from Xolá, never to be seen again. "It was just calumnies," he claimed. "We don't know what kind of people guerrillas are. Just for *envidia* [envy]. A man has his land, his business, his women, his boundaries, his animals—that's why [they died]." Most of the men who committed these crimes were indígenas.

Xolá had been particularly active in starting Uspantán's two cooperatives, one for selling agricultural inputs and the other for making loans. The co-ops were led by Catholic catechists. That made them a target both for the army and for neighbors envious of their success. Another village active in the cooperatives was Macalajau. One day an army captain arrived, called a public meeting, and claimed the guerrillas were lurking nearby. "'Here in Macalajau there are people who collaborate with the guerrillas,'" he is quoted by a survivor. "'They've gone far enough for it to be known who they are. Not many, just five or six are collaborating with the guerrillas. To whoever clarifies who they are, we're going to pay two or three hundred quetzals [US$200–$300].' No one came forward. Just one man replied: 'We're campesinos, working for our daily bread. How are we going to know about this?'" Not long after, on a November night in 1980, two village informers led soldiers to various houses. Someone had decided to help the army after all. Seven men, including two cooperative leaders and three brothers of a man who died at the Spanish embassy, were killed or kidnapped. Subsequently, the captain sent a local functionary to announce that loyal Guatemalans must come live in town. Some did. Others did not, with the result that they were attacked by masked soldiers and vigilantes who burned their houses.

Two other villages, San Pablo El Baldío and San Pedro La Esperanza, were destroyed by the army in early 1981. From San Pablo I interviewed three survivors who acknowledged that villagers had contact with the EGP but denied that it ever held a community meeting. "The guerrillas didn't come before the death of Honorio," one claimed. "Afterward they took a turn through here and spoke with some people, asking for collaboration, asking for food. . . . Some people said yes, but they didn't realize what was going to happen. Once they realized, some repented, but by then it was too late." Even though eight men from San Pablo were kidnapped after Honorio's death, another year and a half passed before the army burned the houses in 1981. The fincas in the valley below were burned later that year, apparently by the guerrillas. Starving in the dank surrounding forests, most San Pablans surrendered to the army in 1982–1983, one or two families at a time.

San Pedro La Esperanza, west of San Pablo and Chimel along the same forested ridge, seems to have been a less conflictive place before the war. This enabled it to receive a provisional title from INTA in 1975, to more than thirteen hundred hectares. There were sixty-seven families, including ladinos as well as K'iche's, who built a school and set up a Wednesday market. "'We don't want the army to kill people; you have to unite to defend yourselves,'" a widow recalled the guerrillas saying. "They said that in Guatemala there are rich and poor; the president is in his palace with his money; we have to be united in order to struggle—this is what God wants. We know that the army kills us, and this is why we have to be united. 'Better that we go so they don't burn the village,' the guerrillas sometimes said." Unfortunately, continued the widow, "The time between visits of the two sides was short, sometimes the same day. . . . Because the guerrillas would run away, there were no guerrillas there to kill, so they killed the people. . . . All the houses the army burned; all the clothes they burned. We were left without clothes for two or three years. We were left without our identity documents. We were left without a place to sleep. We slept off in the brush for two or three years, with the animals around us. How we suffered!"

The Death of Victor Menchú

Chimel is never destroyed in the pages of *I, Rigoberta Menchú*. When Rigoberta told her story to Elisabeth Burgos, she did not know what had befallen her neighbors. If she had, how would it have affected her attitude toward the guerrillas, her story, and the subsequent evolution of her career? Soon after the 1982 testimony was published and became an unalterable declaration of commitment, many of the indígenas who had joined the revolutionary movement during the same period as Rigoberta left it. They had reacted to army atrocities as she did, by resolving to fight back, but in the belief that the guerrillas could win. Once that was impossible, they began to think differently about how the killing started. Blame that they had focused exclusively on the army, for the obvious reason that it murdered their relatives, they now extended to the guerrillas, for luring indígenas into a hopeless cause.

Certainly this was the case in Chimel, to whatever extent its people chose to join the guerrillas in the first place. Afraid to come to town, Rigoberta's neighbors subsisted amid the wreckage of their houses, under shreds of tin roofing without walls, and slept in the nearby brush and forest every night. When enemies approached, they hid in dugouts that were big enough for a family, as high as a person and two meters deep. After Vicente's death there was still a village committee and some sharing of food—if there was any to share. In forest clearings they kept growing maize, but soldiers and civil patrollers arrived to destroy it, making it harder and harder to find anything to eat. "We went six months without tortillas, just eating raw *pacaya*," a widow told me of a bitter-tasting root. "This is why my three children died."

Another widow described how a son had his throat cut by a civil patrol leader; how the four-year-old boy with him was "chopped up like a tomato"; how another son was killed by soldiers and civil patrollers; and how three others died of hunger in the forest—all this after losing her husband at the Spanish embassy. "When the patrol showed up, there were lots of them, God help us. So many times it's beyond counting. Three, four, or five days later they would come again," forcing the refugees into one evacuation after another, until they could no longer run. "In Chimel there was no longer life. Every time we put the house back together, they returned to burn it again. This is why we went to Guacamayas, but the soldiers came there, too."

Las Guacamayas is northwest of Chimel, across a ridge in a warm valley bordering Ixil country. Refugees from Chimel were among a thousand or more who fled there in 1981, to subsist on bananas and roots. EGP cadres arrived to teach them how to survive. "They told us that we shouldn't go back to town, better to hold out, that hiding we could struggle on. They told us what we ought to do, but we didn't know [if they were right]," a widow told me. Because Guacamayas was just a few hours from the army-held Finca San Francisco, it turned into another trap. By 1982 soldiers and civil patrollers were showing up every few weeks to flush out refugees, capture them, and shoot anyone who tried to escape.

"The army just kept coming, with airplanes, too," a Guacamayas refugee told me. "Where smoke rose the soldiers called in an airplane; then they came, too. Also helicopters with machine guns. Some managed to flee; others were left dead. So by 1982 we had to hide somewhere else, but always in Guacamayas. Bit by bit more people were showing up. Among us are those who have a few ideas, who have studies, so among the youth we organized a lookout system to defend ourselves. Edible wild plants ran out. . . . All the maize had been burned. Many died of hunger; entire families died. I knew a family of eighteen of whom none survived. If we found bones, we buried them a little."

Survivors fled downriver, then into the gorges of northern Chajul, where they organized the Communities of Population in Resistance. When I visited in early 1994, only eight people from Chimel were living there—a low number considering that the CPRs are just two days' walk from Chimel, and one more indication of how the guerrillas failed to provide a credible alternative. Many more of the Chimel refugees stayed closer to home, hiding along the ridge above the village, until the army starved them out or they heard of the amnesty offered by the new regime in the capital, that of General Efraín Ríos Montt.

By the time *I, Rigoberta Menchú* appeared in 1983, most of Chimel's survivors had surrendered or been captured. They included Rigoberta's two older brothers, the last two men in the family. One of them was Victor. Born in 1953, he had a wife and three small children. Like his older brother Nicolás, he was a peasant farmer and catechist in his father's mold, who worked on Peace Corps farm projects and served as a health promoter. His wife, María Tomás Lux, died mysteriously before Chimel was destroyed, late in the evil year of 1980. Having run out of maize, she went down the valley to El Rosario to obtain it from friends. When her body was found weeks later, she was wearing ladino clothes. No one in Chimel seems to know what happened: Perhaps she tried to change her appearance to escape from a trap.

Once the village became uninhabitable, Victor took refuge in the forest to the north at a lower and warmer place called Cuatro Chorros. Twenty-eight months after Chimel burned, in April 1983, he presented himself and his children to the army at its new garrison in the middle of town. Among those who now blame the Menchús for the violence, some say that Victor died because he was still committed to the guerrillas. "He showed up really malnourished, so they took care of him at the garrison, cured him, gave him an injection, and he asked for permission to go to the toilet. He found a metal tube and hit the soldier who was watching him on the head. The soldier fell. Victor grabbed his weapon, put on the uniform of the soldier, and went out with the Galil [machine gun], shooting at the sublieutenant. He wanted to go back to the montaña. There was a sentry who shot and killed him." Why would Victor try to escape just after surrendering? I asked. "He was of that mentality. . . . The officer was going to let him live; he was going to get information from him. [Victor] walked in the street with the officer; [the officer] was taking care of him. But [Victor] was frustrated when he left the montaña and decided to go back."

A more convincing explanation of Victor's death came from his brother Nicolás. Victor always liked to listen to the news on his radio. Somehow he was able to obtain batteries and hear about the amnesty that Ríos Montt was offering over the radio. Nicolás urged him to wait, but Victor refused. "If we stay here, we're all going to die," he said. Full of trepidation, Nicolás followed a month later. "When we showed up all together—myself, my wife, the children, and two little ones—the commander was surprised," Nicolás told me. "'You're from Chimel?' he asked twice. He came over and checked my hands to see if they were calloused from work. 'No one captured you on the way?' he asked me. 'Why did you come?' 'I came for the sake of my children,' I told him. . . . 'Do you know where your brother is?' he asked me. 'No, my officer,' I answered him. They took the children aside, one by one, to ask them questions. 'Does your papa use this kind of weapon? Or this kind?' [The soldiers] showed [the children] their weapons. One by one, the kids said that their papa used only an ax and a pick. 'How many days was he away from the family?' [the soldiers] asked them, one by one.

"'Where is your brother?' the officer asked me again. 'Excuse me, officer sir,' I answered, 'right now I don't know if he is alive here on earth or in heaven. 'When are you going back to your land?' the officer asked. 'Excuse me, officer sir,' I answered, 'but now I am under your control. I'm like your prisoner, and you decide where I go.' Then the officer took me up the street toward the market, telling me that he was from Uspantán and that his own father had been a good friend of my father. 'Your father, your mother, your brothers have met their ends,' he told me, 'but not you.' Then he asked me to turn around, where the cement block had been shattered with bullets. 'Your brother died here,' the officer said. 'This is what brought him peace, but not his end,' I said. 'I'm not afraid to die.' The officer put his arm around me and promised that I was not going to die."

At this point in his story, Nicolás broke down, and so did I. "Excuse me. It left me in rage. Everything here left me in a rage, but we came back. This rage I will never forget.'" Once Victor was jailed at the garrison, Nicolás learned, "bad soldiers from Xolá" began to taunt him. "We're going to eat fresh meat tonight," they threatened. That evening at nine, the K'iche' soldiers told Victor, they would take him out of his cell to kill him. As Victor awaited his death, he cried and prayed. At 8:30 he asked the guard to let him use the toilet, where he found a bit of metal pipe, which he concealed inside his clothes and smuggled back to his cell. When soldiers arrived at nine to take him to another interrogation, he hit the one in front with the pipe, ran out of the garrison, and was shot down as he ran toward the market, unarmed.

Knowing as Victor did what the army could do to prisoners, it is hard to overestimate the courage that was necessary to surrender. He must have done it, as Nicolás said of his own decision, for the sake of his children, whom the army would be less likely to kill. It is also hard to overestimate the fear that Victor must have felt at the garrison, in the power of his enemies. As a ladino commiserated, "He saw the Garcías there, the Canos, many of the vigilantes around here. He became terrified, and they killed him." Who's to blame? I asked Nicolás. "I blame the people of the very town for having a tongue so long it cannot be measured," he answered. "The officers and soldiers don't come to kill; the people finger [the victims]. When the people came to town, there was Vitalino Cano sitting there by the garrison. 'This one is a guerrilla,' he said. 'That one is a guerrilla,' he said. They killed many people.'"

Nicolás and his family escaped this fate, but just barely. They were lodged in the town auditorium, with a multitude of refugees who had surrendered or been captured. Living in such close quarters, many fell sick. Even though a sister took charge of Victor's three daughters, two of them soon died: Juana was five years old, Cristina just three. Because Nicolás remained healthy, an officer decided that he was a well-fed guerrilla and sent him in a helicopter to the dreaded military base at Santa Cruz del Quiché. When soldiers started to blindfold him with a bloody rag, a colonel reprimanded them, saying: "You are not going to mistreat this man. He hasn't done anything terrible; he's just here to give information." "Not a kick or a blow in two months," Nicolás told me, with some wonderment. "At the recommendation of the colonel, they gave me the same food as the officers."

An uncle—one of Vicente's brothers—also escaped Victor's fate. According to a son who surrendered with him, "They locked us up in a room and said that we were guerrilla leaders. They began to ask if we carried weapons or not, extracting information. We were treated badly, threatened but not beaten, because my father was well known in town and people came to visit. We were released after eight days in the garrison."

Menchús living in town were pressed into the army's civil patrol and obliged to join expeditions to Chimel to rob the maize harvest. Three of Rigoberta's cousins and nephews joined the army, two because they were obliged to and the other voluntarily. "There's no humanity there," one said of the experience. "They took me away by force. For being a Menchú, they told me: 'You're leader of the guerrillas.'" After the usual two and a half years of duty in 1982–1985, he came back to Uspantán, only to feel less safe as a civilian. "The violence was still bad. There were lots of resentments and accusations here," he said. Shortly he rejoined his unit, preferring to trust in soldiers and officers rather than old neighbors. Ten years later, after returning to civilian life, he was one of Uspantán's best-known human rights activists.

The Gulf Between Guerrilla Strategy and Popular Consciousness

When the army came, and the guerrillas, it was like when a coyote gets in with goats. They ran this way; they ran that way. There was no way to escape. How many people died that way.

—Villager near Chimel, 1995

From the quantity of killing committed by the Guatemalan army, many observers have assumed that the insurgency was a popular uprising—why else so much bloodshed? But in Uspantán, corroborating evidence is hard to find. Some idea of the EGP's lack of presence is suggested by the fact that during the entire war, it attacked the security forces just once in town, on April 25, 1980, when two plainclothes agents were shot near the plaza. The local support the guerrillas won seems to have been mainly in besieged villages that were soon destroyed. Survivors became refugees on the run, most of whom were killed, captured, or forced into submission, leaving only a handful to flee north to the Communities of Population in Resistance.

If survivors are still afraid of the army, can we rely on their accounts and conclude that the revolutionary movement never was strong in Uspantán? My conclusion can only be tentative. But any skepticism about my argument should extend to the EGP's claim that it was embraced by the indigenous masses. Surely the crucial silences that can obtain between peasants and an anthropologist armed with a notebook can also occur between peasants and outsiders armed with guns. Arriving at a similar conclusion was a man who helped start the war in the western highlands with a gun and who helped end it with a pen, the guerrilla commander and author Mario Payeras.

After leaving the EGP in 1984, Payeras criticized the choice of northern Quiché as the first theater. He and his comrades had been attracted by the region's geographic advantages, but they underestimated "the very social backwardness of a marginal area of the capitalist system. The immediate consequence of this backwardness translated into slow rhythms of accumulation of forces and huge difficulties, particularly in the formation and reproduction of cadres. . . . The fundamental energy of the guerrilla force, during the years of implantation, was consumed in organizing, explaining, politicizing, trying to compensate with sermons and examples the lack of factors that are the historical product of social practice, above all, the class struggle." Bluntly, most of the population had no idea that they needed a revolution, and it was hard to convince them that they did. As Payeras puts it, "Except in some zones of the montaña and for some periods [such as after the army destroyed their villages], the different preconceived stages of the war . . . emerged out of phase with the struggle and real movement of the masses."[11]

Payeras attributes the gulf between revolutionary strategy and popular consciousness to *foquismo,* the Cuban doctrine that with little or no previous political work, small *focos,* or bands of professional guerrillas, could trigger peasant revolutions. The failure of foco theory was widely recognized after the 1967 demise of Che Guevara in Bolivia. Interning himself in the bush with a small band of professional revolutionaries, Che was unable to win over suspicious peasants, who instead reported him to the authorities. Fifteen years later, the EGP claimed to have transcended the errors of foquismo by engaging in long and careful cultivation of a popular base in northern Quiché. But they did not do so in Uspantán, and probably not even in the Ixcán and Ixil country to the extent that the guerrillas believed.

Payeras and myself are not alone in sensing a tenuous connection between the EGP and peasants in the group's supposed heartland; other Cuchumatanes fieldworkers have derived the same impression.[12] In *La Guerra en Tierras Mayas,* first published in French in 1992 and too often ignored, the sociologist Yvon Le Bot pointed out the inability of the Guerrilla Army of the Poor to deal with the complexity of indigenous communities, that is, their actual felt needs. Armed struggle was not a solution to the intensely local conflicts dividing Chimel and its neighbors. Instead, it was a strategy for seizing power at the national level that required the sacrifice of the communities it was purporting to defend.[13]

The stories I heard in Uspantán suggest that peasants were not very organized when the repression hit. Certainly they were far less militant and prepared than the revolutionary exemplars of *I, Rigoberta Menchú*. What I heard in Uspantán was almost more awful than what so many have read in those pages, where at least campesinos die for a cause that is their own.

What I heard about in Uspantán was a preemptive slaughter of peasants who had little or nothing to do with the guerrillas, who at most had listened to a few speeches, and who had little conception of the larger cause for which they were dying. Surely they died for something, but what that might be is still being worked out by the families they left behind.

10

The Death Squads in Uspantán

He was a victim of the violence like so many others. He was overwhelmed by what happened; he was swept away. This is why he sought vengeance.

—An enemy of Chimel described by an old friend, 1994

However much the violence perplexed the people of Uspantán, they are not confused about the identity of the killers, especially if they were local. Dozens of people told Barbara Bocek and me about the army's *orejas* ("ears," or informers), *confidenciales* ("confidentials"), *judiciales* (judicial police, who functioned as marshals and detectives), and *comisionados* (military commissioners, in charge of conscription for the army). Except for some of the judiciales, these were local men the army appointed to track down subversives in a defenseless population. Although the most notorious were ladinos, more than a few were indigenous. Because they functioned as state-protected killers, I refer to them as vigilantes—ostensible upholders of law and order who engage in extrajudicial killing. For human rights groups, the crucial fact about vigilantes is that a state authority (like a military officer) deputizes them to violate the state's own laws.[1] Because their license to murder came from the army, that institution is responsible for what happened. But for some of my Uspantán sources, the local collaborators bear more of the blame, either for the actual killing or accusing neighbors of subversion.

The willingness to identify responsible parties, even before the human rights movement was institutionalized locally in the mid-1990s, is a redeeming note to the terrible experiences this chapter relates. Even after death squads made it unsafe to go out at night, even after the Catholic Church was shut down and every man within reach was forced to join counterinsurgency militias on pain of death, some Uspantanos had the courage to complain to the only available authority—the same army that was sponsoring most of the violence. Backing them up was the weight of public opinion, which showed little enthusiasm for either side and brought political killing to an end long before monitoring committees could be set up.

We might assume that the men who became vigilantes had reputations for violence before the war. This is not the case, at least in Uspantán. Almost to a man, the killers of the early 1980s were known as *gente pacifica, gente trabajador* (peaceful and hardworking people). Another common theme, though not held to excuse the lengths to which they went, is that they were reacting to EGP assassinations of their relatives or friends. I heard of far fewer guerrilla killings in Uspantán than in Ixil country, but there were enough to justify a retaliatory holocaust. The three sons of Honorio García are an example of how victims turned into victimizers. No one I talked to would agree that the Garcías carried firearms before the war. Told to leave the valley or die like their father, the sons fled to Chicamán with their mother, who sold a young bull to buy the family's first firearm—a shotgun. One son went on to join the army's G-2 (intelligence and death squad) section, which sent him elsewhere, while his two brothers worked with the army locally. Of the latter, Antonio García Martínez was killed in December 1981 by friendly fire. He had joined an expedition to find a local youth, a military cadet coming home for the holidays whom the EGP took off a bus and executed. In the darkness and confusion, one search party fired on the other, and Antonio died, too.

Another example of the high price paid for the EGP's relatively few murders were the "Aarones." This was another trio of brothers, known by one of their first names (Aaron), who were reacting to the death of their father. The Aarones were poorer than the Garcías: They did not employ indigenous laborers to cultivate their land in Chipaj, which is along the road to Soch. "Before the violence they were hardworking people," the father of a victim told me. "As youth they attended an evangelical church. Their father was active and their grandfather a church leader. This is why I say they were dragged down by Satan. . . . People say that the guerrillas killed their father, Gonzalo [or Belisario] López Gamarro. He was accused of making deals with the guerrillas, then he went over to the army's side, that's why the guerrillas killed him."

A relative of the Aarones provided a more detailed story. "The guerrillas got ahold of their father, Belisario López. He got involved with them and organized his own group. Then this Aaron was in army service in Huehuetenango, realized that his father was involved, and told him that if he didn't abandon the group, he was going to kill him. So Belisario began to identify the people in his group, some twenty of them [who unlike the ladino Belisario, were K'iche's]. Then the real guerrillas showed up. As he had rebelled against them, they did their justice and killed him, too. The others had already died because of his big mouth. Now the sons were angry with the people and began to kill them."

The Persecution of the Catholic Church

The peril posed by the guerrillas cast a pall of suspicion over the indigenous population. It gave the vigilantes a reason to personalize the conspiracy theories on offer in Guatemalan society, translating fear of Indian uprisings into fear of communist subversion. The invisible guerrilla menace also created a cloud of suspicion over the Catholic Church. The Uspantán clergy were no radical vanguard, as suggested by Rigoberta's complaints that they fostered political passivity.[2] But they clearly sympathized with indígenas and, owing to the dearth of militant peasant organizations in Uspantán, were also one of the few aboveground institutions that was available to be blamed. Nor was the Catholic-EGP association a figment of the imagination. Since catechists like Vicente Menchú were village leaders, they were sought out by the guerrillas. Catholic clergy in other parts were working with revolutionary fronts like CUC; although not necessarily numerous, they and their activities tarred the entire Catholic Church. Finally, even parish priests trying to keep to the middle of the road felt compelled to speak out against the army's kidnappings. Their denunciations included the army's first abductions in Uspantán, of the men from San Pablo and Chimel.

When the fire at the Spanish embassy sealed the Lucas García regime's evil reputation, it blamed the Catholic Church as well as the guerrillas. A month later, in early March 1980, a parish priest witnessed one of the first massacres in northern Quiché, when soldiers machine-gunned an angry crowd in Nebaj. Wishing to prevent further such reports, the army decided to drive the Catholic clergy from the department. Even if Uspantán had been completely quiet, the parish probably would have been shut down like the others. As it turned out, the army attacked after the EGP shot two agents near the church on April 25, 1980. Shortly thereafter two grenades sailed over the wall of the parish compound. When the priests and nuns failed to get out of town, the compound was machine-gunned.

In June 1980 the army murdered the parish priest of Chajul and his sacristan as they came up a trail. In Joyabaj, in southern Quiché, assassins killed the parish priest at his desk. Other hit men trailed the bishop. To call the attention of the world (including Pope John Paul II, who was inclined to blame liberation theology for the persecution), the Quiché clergy decided to close the diocese. The decision was not made without heated debate; some priests argued that leaving the department was tantamount to abandoning their flocks. To stand by their parishioners, several joined the Guerrilla Army of the Poor. Others started a revolutionary support group, called the Guatemalan Church in Exile, which operated from Mexico and Nicaragua. Still others made plans to return to Quiché "in the catacombs," by accompanying refugees hiding from the army.[3]

Perhaps the most courageous of the diocesan clergy were a handful who decided to reopen parishes, even though the pace of killing was accelerating. One was a Spaniard of the Sacred Heart order, Juan Alonso Fernández, who returned in the hope that his apolitical record would protect him. On arrival in Uspantán, he had to ask the army commander for the keys to the rectory. When the officers mocked him, he replied indignantly that he had fought communists in the Spanish civil war, but they only mocked him more. Two days later, on February 15, 1981, he was stopped in the great ravine between Uspantán and Cunén by several masked men. They dragged him off his motorcycle and into the woods, tortured him for a while, then put three bullets in his head.[4]

For the army of Lucas García and the local men operating under its command, Juan Alonso represented a vast conspiracy that justified their response. Consider what a vigilante told me thirteen years later, as if to justify the hunting down of catechists: "All the people who were involved with the priests, every last one was involved with the guerrillas. The Colegio Belga brought up girls from the capital [Catholic secondary students doing social work in villages], who bathed nude in the river and deranged the people. Victor Menchú was a medic for the guerrillas, trained in another country. He visited the plaza at Soch for espionage. After the guerrillas burned out [the evangelical missionary at Las Pacayas], they went past the [Catholic] nuns at La Peña and didn't touch anyone. When the guerrillas occupied the town of Uspantán, the nuns were there, pleased to be listening.

"Every day there were twenty to thirty [catechists] on this road, going to a training course in Chicamán, about the poor against the rich, about *indios* against ladinos, about ladinos who steal land, about the Mayas. This is why so many left for evangelical churches, because the priests got involved in so many things. They've lost a lot of ground. Their followers would stage raids here, then take a course in Chicamán, but only for the peasants. The arms were smuggled in by the priests in their cars: who else doesn't get searched here? No one can search the *señor* priest. Lists of catechists were found in the knapsacks of guerrillas—this is how I know the Menchús were guerrillas—but the army has [the lists] now, not me. Everybody knows this."

The Massacres at the Finca San Francisco and Calanté

When my sister went down to work in the Brol's finca, she found that most of the Brol's labourers were guerrillas.

—***I, Rigoberta Menchú*, p. 243**

Some hours' walk from Chimel is the Finca San Francisco, one of the most obvious political opportunities for the guerrillas in northern

Quiché. The Ixils of Cotzal felt that this large, profitable coffee estate was on municipal land, but their claim had been overridden by the Brol family's purchase of national land titles. Thanks to the long-standing grievance, at least a few Cotzaleños were working with guerrillas at the early date of 1969. Then there was the finca's permanent labor force. As a mix of Ixils, K'iche's, and ladinos, among whom Spanish was the lingua franca, the resident workers were relatively accessible to organizers. But hundreds of the most independent-minded were expelled when the finca broke a union organizing drive in the early 1970s; the EGP may have arrived too late.

This left the seasonal workers, the most precarious and exploited of the finca workforce, whom the Committee for Campesino Unity (CUC) tried to organize. "The people of the finca [the permanents], we just wanted to work," a man told me of labor turmoil around 1980. "But among the seasonals, who arrived for the harvest, fliers would appear at night. They wanted their raise. They were from CUC. On going to work, they would block the bridge so that the others could not pass, demanding a higher price." Even if CUC activists managed to organize work stoppages, such mobilizations could only be short-lived, as temporary workers soon went home or moved to another finca.

If the EGP had little support on the finca, this would help explain why it resorted to military rather than political pressure and put the finca under relentless assault. In 1978 guerrillas kidnapped one of the finca's owners, Edmundo Brol, and extracted a high ransom for his release. The following year, on January 21, 1979, the EGP occupied the town of Nebaj and killed Edmundo's brother Enrique when he resisted capture. The following day, the same column occupied the finca and killed three government security agents.

Whatever network the EGP had on the finca probably succumbed to the army's raid on May 24, 1981, one of the two largest massacres recalled by the people of Uspantán. There was a Sunday market in the finca that day, to which peasants from the surrounding area continued to come, if only because necessity prevailed over fear. The action is said to have been carried out by a joint force of vigilantes from Uspantán and soldiers from the Cotzal garrison who wore masks and gloves instead of uniforms.

The following account, though secondhand, captures typical procedures of the Guatemalan army: trapping a crowd on market day, then introducing an *encapuchado,* an informer wearing a hood like a judge in the Spanish Inquisition, who picked out suspects to be taken away for torture and execution. "They came into the market, shouting three times, 'We are the Guerrilla Army of the Poor! We are guerrillas!' No one responded. Then they told the people to put themselves in rows, with men, women, and children apart [often the first step in a massacre]. While the people were forming up, a shot went off and everybody fled. Everybody scattered. The armed men began to fire, and many people died. Others fell into the river; others fell wounded in the montaña. It turned out that the finca was surrounded by the army. . . .

"'Get up,' the army said to the people who had hidden. 'But if you flee, we're going to shoot.' They gathered the survivors in the finca a second time, in a structure with an office, where there were two encapuchados. They called the administrator, but he didn't show up, so at last they brought him. Three times the army asked the people whether he should be killed. They struck him in front of the people, but the people didn't say anything. Afterward the administrator took out a cigarette and lit it, but he was trembling.

"Then the people were brought before the encapuchado, one by one. He remained silent, just moving his head to indicate whom he chose and whom he did not. Many were taken to the truck that was waiting, perhaps more than forty or fifty. Afterward, those who remained were given a lecture. 'We are the Guatemalan army. If you have a member of your family in the truck, forget about him, because he's bad seed. Those of you who remain are the good seed; nothing is going to happen to you. Everyone who has gotten involved with the guerrillas, they're gone, forget about them.' When they picked up the bodies [from the earlier shooting spree], there were thirty-nine. There were also many who died in the bush and were eaten by dogs."[5]

The following year, on March 31, 1982, the guerrillas killed two administrators and a truck driver, burned the patronal house, and destroyed much of the year's harvest. Later that day, soldiers arrived with a list, extracted ten men from their houses, and took them away blindfolded, never to be seen again. All told, according to a member of the Brol family, the finca lost seventy-five supervisors and workers in the violence.

With the Catholic Church shut down, the majority of murders were probably never reported to the outside world, so they are still difficult to date and quantify. But one massacre occurred at the town's back door, a few kilometers up the ridge at a place called Calanté, and it is the largest documented killing near Uspantán. On February 14, 1982, families who had taken refuge in the town—that is, submitted to the army—went out to harvest their fields. Just beyond Calanté, they were intercepted by a group of men dressed in green and carrying large knives. Many of the victims were found lying in rows, with their hands tied and throats cut—fifty-four in all.[6] The army was quick to fly in journalists and blame the guerrillas, who supposedly had mistaken the campesinos for a supply column to an army detachment. But most Uspantanos blame the army.

Ríos Montt, the Civil Patrols, and the Downfall of the Vigilantes

Some evangelicals say, "Because I'm a Christian, I am not going to get involved in this." But how can Christians not struggle against wrongdoing? That's just nursing evil.

—An evangelical on why he confronted vigilantes, 1994

A month after the Calanté massacre, on March 23, 1982, junior army officers overthrew the regime of General Romeo Lucas García. As far as they could see, the ruling clique was more intent on enriching itself than winning the war. In the capital, the security forces were degenerating into extortion rackets preying on the upper classes they were supposed to protect. The year before, they had destroyed the guerrilla underground in Guatemala City, but in the western highlands the war was not going well. Chaotic reprisals had angered a population that previously showed little interest in national affairs. Peasants were welcoming the guerrillas as a way to defend themselves. More army patrols were falling into ambushes. To lead the new junta, the junior officers appealed to their former superintendent at the military academy. General Efraín Ríos Montt had been elected president in 1974, as a Christian Democrat, only to be humiliated when the high command imposed another general as the next executive. Since then, he had retired from the army and become a born-again Christian. Now he suddenly reappeared and took command. Nursing old grievances, he ejected the two other members of the junta from the national palace, appointed himself president, and in rambling sermons over the airwaves, announced that he had been appointed by God to save Guatemala from immorality and communism.

Ríos Montt's most obvious accomplishment was to rein in the death squads around the capital. Unfortunately, his declarations of law and order did not have much impact on how the army was waging the war in the highlands. Some of the largest massacres—in Ixil country (three hundred or more victims in six villages of Chajul), in the Ixcán (seventy-one in Canijá), in Huehuetenango (302 at the Finca San Francisco of Nentón), and in Rabinal, Baja Verapaz (268 at Plan de Sánchez)—occurred during the first four months of his government. At the time, Ríos Montt's defenders said that he needed several months to bring the army under control. Since then, exhumations have documented later massacres like the one at Dos Erres, Petén, in December 1982 (at least 250 dead). In the municipio of Uspantán, the largest known killing occurred under Ríos Montt, at a place called Agua Fría on September 14, 1982. In what is now the municipio of Chicamán, some hundred Achí Maya refugees from Baja Verapaz were slaughtered by soldiers and their civilian auxiliaries.

Massacres indeed tapered off under Ríos Montt, but probably not because he had brought the army under control. Although he did transfer a few abusive commanders and announce an amnesty that gradually took hold, he had such a weak grip on the officer corps that it ejected him from the presidency after seventeen months. A more important change was in the attitude of peasants toward the guerrillas. As the army escalated killing to the crescendos of 1982, it showed campesinos that the guerrillas could not protect them. Many who had looked to the rebels for protection now turned against them, hastening their withdrawal from many areas. Only here and there did the guerrillas hang onto pockets of supporters, most of them hiding in forests and starving. Within a year, many of these, too, had surrendered. Once the population was intimidated, the army reined in its killers.

The most effective technique for turning hostile peasants into reluctant collaborators was the civil patrol, an institution started under Lucas García but expanded under Ríos Montt. Many observers have noted that the patrols were inspired by counterinsurgency militias in other countries. Few have noted their unsung predecessors in the Local Irregular Forces (FILs) of the EGP, the peasant auxiliaries it organized to carry supplies, evacuate casualties, spy on the army, and harass it. The FILs date to before the civil patrols, and the EGP was so proud of them that it published photos of their members lined up remarkably like the army's civil patrollers would be for the next decade.[7] In Ixil country it was not rare for civil patrol leaders to be former FIL leaders whom the army had given an offer they could not refuse.

Once the army arrived in overwhelming force, the only way peasants could prove that they were not subversives and escape the corresponding death sentence was to join the patrols. By 1983 the army said there were 900,000 men in them. That would mean virtually all males in militarized areas of the highlands from the age of fifteen to sixty, including ladinos as well as indígenas. Most were not very enthusiastic about their duties, but the army forced them to join expeditions to suspect villages like Chimel. Their main job was slashing maize crops and burning houses, but patrollers also murdered some of the refugees they caught, often under the orders of a berserk vigilante. In the stories I heard, Uspantanos tended to blame one or two individuals who already had a history of killing. They also distinguished between orejas, collaborators, and judiciales, as committed killers, and civil patrollers, as conscripts who were obliged to join. Obviously, the distinction might not mean much to victims.

Around Uspantán, as in so many other towns, there are stories of the army calling all the men to a mass meeting at which they are told, "Everyone is going to serve in the patrol, and anyone who doesn't patrol is a guerrilla." Then the threats against resisters: "We'll throw you into the pit!" However, some Uspantanos inject a note of communal solidarity into the coercion. "We organized the civil patrol under Efraín Ríos Montt so that the soldiers would not come to kidnap," one of Rigoberta's relatives told me. "We were just like sheep, frightened and waiting [to be grabbed by soldiers and vigilantes], and this is why we organized, so that they would not take away more people." After all the surviving men in Xolá were serving in the patrol, he said, "only two or three patrollers were taken away."

Significantly, ex-patrollers are more likely to invoke solidarity against the army than against the guerrillas, whom most say they experienced only as a phantom. When I asked an early kidnap victim why the patrol was organized, his answer was: "Because there were military commissioners in each village. Because they used to drink, to take advantage of people, to accuse them of being guerrillas and take them tied up to the garrison. So we formed the patrol to watch out for everyone, so that they could no longer be accused of being guerrillas or have their money taken." A ladino acknowledged the patrol's communal intent but expressed less satisfaction with the results. "It was born before Ríos Montt, in the community of Xolá, so that there would not be more kidnappings and murders, to keep watch, to be united with the army and the army's peace, but it was worse. Because it went out into the communities to take advantage, to rob and commit massacres, big and small."

To this day, Ríos Montt does not enjoy the aura in Uspantán that he has next door in Ixil country, where his law-and-order party won thousands of votes in the 1990s. A few Uspantanos do claim that kidnappings stopped under his administration in 1982–1983. "Lucas would have finished us off completely if it were not for the coup d'état [that brought Ríos to power]," one elder told me. But Riosmonttismo is weaker than in Ixil country, and objections are raised more often. "No, Ríos Montt didn't change things," a man who had to flee Uspantán under his regime told me. "Under Lucas García, they kidnapped people and left their cadavers in the road. Under Ríos Montt, they kidnapped people and buried them." "The hole is already dug. Say good-bye to your house because you won't come back," civil patrollers told him. "Ríos Montt improved the situation a bit," a human rights activist conceded. "They declared the amnesty, many patrollers went up to capture people, [but] many fled and were shot. So it was just taking advantage. The violence continued. It's not true that it simply calmed down under Ríos Montt."

If few in Uspantán associate the born-again dictator with a dramatic reduction in army violence, the reason may be that local commanders failed to break with the policies of the preceding regime, even by the standards of Guatemalans accustomed to military rule. One figure that recurs in Uspantán stories is a Captain Sosa who gave several military administrations a bad name. He often became *bravo*—angry. He is said to have made off with reconstruction materials after the town was struck by an earthquake. And he is accused of using the same methods as before, albeit on fewer victims. I heard stories about unknown prisoners being kept in the pit at the town garrison as late as 1984–1985.

Soon after the army organized the civil patrols, it turned against its most murderous collaborators, as if to stave off a popular reaction. One scapegoat offered up was the terrible Aarones trio. Eventually I stopped asking about the three brothers because the stories about them were so sickening. "They would tie up a husband, rape his wife, and then shoot the man—this was their practice. It's said that when they had someone in a room in their house they were going to kill, they would ring the bell of the Catholic church to summon the people. If someone didn't arrive, they would order him brought, and he would suffer the same fate." On one occasion they soaked two brothers with gasoline and set them afire in a schoolyard full of children, "to be an example so that the children don't get involved with the guerrillas." Before another group of horrified bystanders, they executed a teenager denounced as a guerrilla, even though they knew he was severely retarded because he was their own cousin.

A few days after the Aarones killed their cousin, the army disarmed them. Stories vary about what happened next, but each version is told with considerable satisfaction. According to the father of a victim, their capture was ordered by Captain Sosa. "It's said that they were taken through all the villages tied up, so that they themselves could tell what they had done. What happened is that every time they were presented in the plazas, the people would ask that they be killed, and the army would whip them with a rubber tube. They were taken through all these plazas—Chipaj, El Pinal, San José El Soch. Then they were brought back, and it's known that they were kept in a small cell where they had to stand in water. This Sosa sent them to a court-martial. It's said that there was a lieutenant at the base in Cobán, and it's said that he had an amorous relation with a sister of the Aarones. It's said that the lieutenant exerted himself to prevent them from being shot, because the army here would have killed them." When survivors asked Captain Sosa what to do if they returned, his response was: "If you see them, kill them!"

The army also turned against a ladino whom some blame for the Calanté massacre. Oralio Cano was notorious for extorting money, chickens, and land. If his victims did not cooperate, he would denounce them as subversives. Then the army decided enough was enough and gave him twenty-four hours to leave town. Again, stories vary about Oralio's subsequent fate, but they are all told with thinly disguised relish. According to one version, he made the mistake of returning to Uspantán for Holy Week, the annual observance of Christ's crucifixion and resurrection that Guatemalans celebrate so lavishly. Unfortunately for the handsomely accoutered Oralio, he reminded his neighbors so much of Judas that they tried to lynch him. According to another version, he died of blows administered by furious émigrés from Uspantán in the Ixcán, and according to still another he was beaten to death in Alta Verapaz after trying to repeat what he had done back home. The most inclusive version of Oralio's subsequent fate, derived from a relative, has him serving two years in prison. Once free, he goes to the United States but cannot find work. On his return, neighbors invite him to drink with them at the house of one of his relatives and beat him up. Next he goes to the Ixcán to live, where Uspantanos beat him up again. He finally meets his end after an unsuccessful prostate operation. Whatever the version, Oralio's victims manage to pay him back.

Stories about the downfall of vigilantes suggest that even though they committed appalling crimes, these did not destroy the capacity for protest. This is also evident in stories about opposition to the civil patrols. After 1985, under a new national constitution, the army could no longer compel men to serve. When I visited Uspantán for the first time four years later, however, the patrol continued to be compulsory in some villages. "People still fear informers who say that if a man doesn't patrol, he's going to be on the list, so many continue to patrol," a human rights activist said. "He who mentions human rights is from the subversion," officers told patrollers into the 1990s.

Some of the more dedicated patrollers contributed to the institution's eclipse by taking advantage of their night watches to commit burglaries. The most notorious was a radio repairman turned vigilante and civil patrol chief, with enough influence to confront army officers. "Eugenio Juarez dedicated himself to stealing clothes from the stores of merchants," one source related. "Then he would stage a gun battle and say that it was the guerrillas." When K'iche' storeowners complained to the local army commander, Eugenio appealed to the colonels in Santa Cruz del Quiché. Suggestive of Eugenio's pull with the army were stories about officers trying to get him off the hook, even as the town's K'iche' businessmen persuaded the national police to arrest him. When he was finally brought to trial, a colonel conscripting character witnesses from the civil patrol told them, "All the things that you saw in 1980, 1981, 1982, 1983 you're going to deny. If not, you will go in place of Eugenio." Finally an exhumation of some of his victims led to an eight-year prison sentence.

Even in the villages, active patrolling stopped in 1992, after the Uspantán patrol commander died in a confrontation with the guerrillas. In another morality story, Uspantanos do not attribute his end to the mere fortunes of war. Instead of robbing stores, extorting money, or betraying victims who failed to pay up, he and his men are said to have captured and murdered a fifteen-year-old girl serving as an EGP courier. From her they are said to have taken Q65,000 (about US$13,000), an act comparable to stealing a mafia payroll. The commander's next mistake was to set aside Q20,000 for himself, while dividing the rest among eighteen comrades and trying to keep other patrollers in the dark. His standard of living rose. But the division of spoils generated such resentment that it reached the ears of the EGP. One day in December 1992, the guerrillas made themselves known on a ridge west of town and challenged him to come out for a fight. That he did, only to separate from his men and be found slumped over a log.

Why Such Brutality?

Here in the village of El Desengaño there were 85 houses with a total of five to six hundred people. . . . According to the information I was able to collect, the number of dead and disappeared reached 185. There were also families burned inside their houses. [A long list of names follows.] Only 116 are here [I count 123]. As you can see, these are the persons who were victims of the violence. There are also displaced people and some refugees in Mexico, around thirty to forty. There are still more persons but I couldn't remember them all. These murders were by the government and the patrollers.

—Handwritten note from a widow, 1994

In Uspantán the destruction of villages and displacement of refugees was not as massive as in Ixil country to the west. But it was substantial. Villages that were destroyed completely include Chimel, El Desengaño, San Pedro La Esperanza, and San Pablo El Baldío. "Everyone from before disappeared," a new settler at San Pablo told me when I came looking for survivors. "Some died, others left. Only the grinding stones and blocks remained, but broken." These were predominantly indigenous homesteading communities, but only San Pablo had a serious conflict with ladino landowners, suggesting that this was not the main reason for their destruction. Instead, they shared an unfortunate location, in the mountains and along an EGP corridor, which gave the army reason to believe rumors that they were "organized."

Villages that were only partly destroyed include Calanté, Macalajau, Laguna Danta, and Caracol, probably because some of their inhabitants were cooperating with the army at an earlier date. Villages that were not burned include Los Canaques (about half ladino), Joya Larga (which was also heavily ladino), the Finca Los Regadios (owned by the Brol family), and Xolá (which was mainly indigenous but also very close to town). The small fincas of Soch were left in ruins. The Garcías and Martínezes were unable to afford the high-interest loans needed to rebuild, and the majority of their laborers sought livelihoods elsewhere.

The first man I met from Chimel said that nearly everyone there had died—a hundred killed by the army and its collaborators and another 250 from hunger. Only about twenty had survived, he said. Fortunately, I soon met more than that. INTA's November 1978 census provides the names of the seventy-nine men and women who headed each household in Vicente's claim, along with the number of children still living with them (142), for a total population of 221.[8] When two survivors went through the seventy-nine named individuals with me, they said that one died of illness, twenty-one died in the violence, and thirty-eight were still alive. Of the fate of the other nineteen, they did not know. A third survivor corroborated the information provided by the first two sources and added more. Of the nineteen persons still unaccounted for, he said four died in the violence. Of the remaining fifteen, two reportedly had died of illness, a third for a reason he did not know, and the other twelve he believed to be still alive. This information suggests that fifty of the seventy-nine persons named in the 1978 census were still living, twenty-five died in the violence, and four others died of unknown or other causes.[9]

The avalanche of violence in the previous two chapters has probably been difficult for readers to comprehend. If Uspantán was relatively peaceful, how could the execution of two ladinos unleash so much brutality? Since much of the killing was authorized by the army, let us now think of the problem in terms of army officers, usually in Uspantán only for short tours of duty, and consider why they would react to guerrilla raids with such sadism. Scholars and activists have been wrestling with this problem for years, as they do whenever a seemingly peaceful milieu dissolves in carnage. One argument, put forth by the revolutionary movement, is that a regime of plantation owners and army officers was unwilling to tolerate any assertion of economic independence by peasants. Therefore the simple fact that indígenas were organizing cooperatives was enough to trigger reprisals, with the aim of throwing them off their land and freeing up their labor for the plantations.

This is an explanation based on political economy, but it is not a very good one, either for Uspantán or the region. Plantation owners had little interest in most of the land remaining in Mayan hands; it was too marginal. By way of confirmation, only occasionally did finca owners use the mayhem of the early 1980s to expropriate peasant land (Chimel itself being an example, as we shall see in Chapter 18). The war certainly fomented agrarian conflict, but most disputes were between peasants displaced by the violence. As for the wider argument, that military officers and plantation owners were unwilling to tolerate a peasantry pulling itself up by the bootstraps, some of the most prosperous Mayan areas, like Totonicapán Department, largely escaped the violence. What hard-hit areas had in common was a factor that the political economy argument downplays—clandestine organizing by guerrillas.

But if army violence was usually a reaction to guerrilla moves, why was it so extreme, to the point of counterproductively pressuring some peasants into joining the guerrillas? Ladino racism toward indígenas is another common explanation, but not one that goes very far, because army officers could treat ladino peasants the same way, as they demonstrated in eastern Guatemala in the 1960s. Any doubts should be dispelled by the exhumation at Dos Erres, the Petén village where the army killed at least 250 ladinos in 1982. The widespread idea that the Guatemalan violence was an "ethnic holocaust" dodges the crucial factor in army violence, that it was a reaction to an insurgency, as well as the fact that indigenous civil patrollers played an important role in army strategy.

Another explanation for the army's brutality is the institutional culture of its officer corps—a distilled version of the authoritarian streak in Latin American culture. One way of understanding the subculture is in terms of the ideology of male honor, which turns forbearance and compromise into a lack of manhood. Another is in terms of historically weak political institutions, which fail to inspire confidence that opponents will play by the rules. Weak political institutions prevent the idea of loyal opposition from taking hold; opponents are perceived as enemies against which any means is justified. Certainly political culture is part of the explanation for what happened in Guatemala, but it could be hard to find any cultural tradition where this kind of behavior has not occurred.

Two other explanations for the brutality are more precise. The first, often ignored by analysts who sympathize with guerrillas, is the paranoia generated by irregular warfare, in which insurgents seem to melt back into the civilian population. Whether they are really farmers during the day and guerrillas at night is beside the point. The mere perception that civilians support guerrillas is enough for them to be identified as the otherwise invisible enemy. By claiming to represent a civilian population that is typically mute, terrified, and divided, insurgents muddy the distinction between themselves and noncombatants. This hardly justifies government reprisals against noncombatants, but it suggests why they are a sociological probability.[10] It is also why guerrilla warfare is so risky for the movement practicing it. Sooner or later, civilians are likely to perceive that their supposed defenders are using them as cannon fodder.

Only strong institutional controls can discourage panicky soldiers from conflating an invisible enemy with the visible population. The Guatemalan army had a centralized command structure, but controls on killing noncombatants were not much in evidence in the early 1980s. To the contrary, the army learned that terror works—a second reason why brutality toward noncombatants is so characteristic of irregular "popular" warfare. If the guerrillas were fish swimming in a sea of peasants, army officers fondly quoted Mao Zedong, they would dry up the sea.[11] So massacres became policy, not just a reaction to guerrilla ambushes. The army's application of collective guilt to nearby civilians had several advantages. Besides eliminating actual collaborators, it ran off other peasants who might be tempted to follow their example and intimidated still others into becoming army informers. Since the army held the reins of power in the capital, it did not have to worry much about accountability. As for survivors driven into the guerrilla movement, their number was usually much smaller than the number warned away.

By the time the guerrillas arrived in Uspantán, the army was an experienced killing machine, all too ready to retaliate against possible civilian collaborators because it knew that was the way to defeat the guerrillas themselves. No doubt the officers directing the killing harbored racist attitudes toward Indians. No doubt they believed they were defending the fatherland against an international communist conspiracy. No doubt such ideas made it easier to kill larger numbers of people. But other thoughts could have occupied their heads, because brutality toward civilians is the predictable result of irregular war.[12]

PART THREE

Vicente's Daughter and the Reinvention of Chimel

11

Where Was Rigoberta?

When I was older, my father regretted my not going to school, as I was a girl able to learn many things. But he always said: "Unfortunately, if I put you in school, they'll make you forget your class, they'll turn you into a ladino. I don't want that for you and that's why I don't send you." He might have had the chance to put me in school when I was about fourteen or fifteen but he couldn't do it because he knew what the consequences would be: the ideas that they would give me.

—*I, Rigoberta Menchú*, p. 190

Now that Rigoberta's community has been swallowed up, the reader may well ask, What happened to the central figure in our story? Why has a person who played such an active role in Chimel gone virtually unmentioned? The reason, according to those who knew her, is that Rigoberta did not live there after the mid-1970s. The narrator of *I, Rigoberta Menchú* is widely remembered, but not as a catechist or organizer. In a peasant society ruled by elders, where girls reaching puberty are kept under close watch, it would be very unusual for a person of her age and gender to play the leadership role she describes. She did stand out from other Mayan girls in one respect. Although Rigoberta has often said that she grew up monolingual and illiterate, this is not how she is remembered in Uspantán. What distinguished her was that Catholic nuns took her away to boarding school. Not only is this no secret in Uspantán, but anyone who remembers Rigoberta at all remembers that she left Uspantán for her education, which is held in such high esteem that some think she went as far as San Carlos University.

Actually, *I, Rigoberta Menchú* makes a few references to living in a convent and being taught by nuns. But such hints are overshadowed by the repeated claim that she never went to school and learned to speak Spanish only recently, as if this was a point of pride. In the same vein, Rigoberta tells how her village sent away two government teachers, to prevent them from alienating the children with a ladino education, and how her father refused to send her to school.[1] What I heard in Uspantán was rather different. Like many village leaders, Vicente Menchú appreciated the value of education and tried to obtain it for his children. At the end of the 1970s, a government teacher worked in Chimel until the violence forced her to leave.

Earlier, during Rigoberta's childhood in the 1960s, educational opportunities in Chimel were very limited, to the point that some deny there were any at all. Others say that literacy work was sponsored by the Catholic Church. One of Rigoberta's cousins told me that he was her *animador* (tutor) for four years, until nuns took her away to continue her education. The limitations of memory make it hard to specify dates, but local testimony leaves no doubt about the general picture. According to two siblings, Rigoberta left Chimel at the age of six or seven. One recalled that, destined for the Catholic boarding school at Chichicastenango in southern Quiché, "she cried a lot when she left. A disease infected her eyes; she was scratching a lot, but little by little she got better. She spent a year and a half in Chichicastenango."

Rigoberta then returned to Chimel for some years before resuming her schooling, this time in the town of Uspantán at the age of twelve to fourteen (1971–1973). Everyone agrees that the endeavor was supported by the parish nuns from the Belgian Order of the Sacred Family, which specialized in educating young women. Sometimes she lived at the convent, other times with nearby relatives. She also worked for at least two ladino women. One was a friend of Rigoberta's mother, who placed her in the job. It involved serving meals at the Guatemalan equivalent of a lunch counter. The other employer I was not able to interview, because she and her husband were blown up in the late 1980s when a drunk set off a grenade in their bar.

Among Rigoberta's activities was a Catholic youth group that met every week. "I knew her in 1972–73–74," a K'iche' schoolteacher recalled. "She was nice. She played basketball; she threw her baskets and came every Saturday, coming down [from the village] to attend religion classes at the parish. She didn't know about politics. Few did." According to another member of the youth group, she was "very intelligent, active, and obliging. She made friends with people very quickly and was always ready to help. If there was sweeping to be done, she would do it. If someone had to start a game, she would do it. . . . Spanish she spoke easily and well. . . . She was neither very poor nor well-off, just in between."

The nuns also sponsored Rigoberta at the government primary school a few blocks from the parish compound. When I asked the director to confirm the dates, he recalled spotting her name in a register and we undertook a search. Unfortunately, the records were in disorder and we never found her name. But he and a schoolmate remembered her teacher as the late Pompilio Godínez. Rigoberta herself is remembered as the fastest student in his class. After first and second grades in Uspantán, the next stage of Rigoberta's educational journey was at the Colegio Belga in downtown Guatemala City. Administered by the same order of nuns that served Uspantán, the *colegio* is a well-known secondary school for girls from wealthy families. It was also noted for its social work in Uspantán, making it one of the sympathetic institutions where Vicente Menchú and his delegation held protests on the way to the Spanish embassy.

When I stopped at the colegio in 1991, an administrator said that Rigoberta only had worked there for a few months, not studied. Four years later, after some hesitation, another administrator acknowledged that Rigoberta completed two years of primary school there. According to several classmates, she worked for room and board while thriving in an accelerated program for older girls. Kept busy from dawn to late at night, she and her companions began the day by attending mass, then turned to their studies, before cleaning and mopping the rooms of "the students with money." That might help explain her withering portrayal of working as a maid for wealthy ladinos.

The schoolmates agree that Rigoberta spent at least two years at the Colegio Belga in the late 1970s, enabling her to advance from the third through the sixth grades. It is also possible that she spent a third year at the school simply working. Next the nuns sent her to another of their institutions, in the prosperous ladino town of Chiantla, Huehuetenango. The Colegio Básico Nuestro Señor de Candelaria is a walled compound occupying an entire block. As an exclusively female *internado,* or boarding school, it brought together Mayan girls from a wide area of the highlands, along with a few ladinas. Given the repression and misrule of the late 1970s, the school could have been a political hotbed. Certainly the security forces thought it was. Yet the alumni I interviewed, six in all, insisted that it was not. The only remotely political activity they described was accompanying nuns on charitable expeditions, to hand out food and clothing to the poor.

Otherwise, the nuns isolated their students from the outside world with a strict regime. Confining indigenous youth in boarding schools is an old Catholic practice that is often blamed for deculturating them. In the case of female students, one reason is to prevent them from becoming pregnant. Not only did the nuns hope to guide some of their charges into a celibate career with the Sacred Family, but there was no greater embarrassment than sending one home with an infant, to parents who distrusted the idea of educating their daughter in the first place. Boyfriends were therefore anathema. The girls were given an hour of liberty every week, to go to market. According to one alumnus, even their correspondence was read. "We were under lock and key," said another.

Several schoolmates did tell me that Rigoberta was interested in politics at both boarding schools. But with little access to the outside world, there was little to protest except the nuns themselves. "She always had the idea of struggling for the less fortunate," a Chiantla schoolmate told me. "And also against injustices. We revolted a bit against the *madres* by questioning things like the food, the schedule, the punishments. The internado was hard. The nuns kept the best [food] for themselves. If they were so dedicated to us, why was there so much difference? If a professor didn't do a good job of teaching, if she gave us too much work, we protested. This is why we became more critical about the status quo; this is what brought us together. The idea of struggling against injustices brought us together. Perhaps we were something like leaders."

According to this friend, Rigoberta never talked about the Committee for Campesino Unity. Instead, she wanted to become a *madre* herself. "Not to be a teacher, not to have a career," a cousin said of her ambitions when she still lived in Uspantán, "but to lead a Christian life, to be a good person. She wanted to be a nun. She would study until eleven at night or two in the morning." Unlike some students, she attended daily mass faithfully. Yet if she saw her teachers as role models, she also became disillusioned with them. "At the beginning Rigoberta wanted to be a nun," another schoolmate said, "but upon seeing the inequalities . . . she took off her blinders and had strong commentaries."

Could schoolyard sedition have been the first sign of Rigoberta's revolutionary consciousness? Certainly the references to Catholic clergy in her 1982 story attest to mingled feelings of gratitude and hostility. But what about her three months of vacation every year, from October to January? Away from the internado regime, she could have found the freedom to become a political activist. She could have been the missing link between her peasant father and the student revolutionaries at San Carlos University. She even could have gone to work for the insufferable, upper-class housewife pilloried in *I, Rigoberta Menchú*.

A schoolmate believed that Rigoberta spent her Colegio Belga vacations by continuing to work there, to earn her keep. For her single vacation from Chiantla, starting in October 1979, another friend recalled Rigoberta urging her companions to return with her to the capital—not to engage in political protests, but to work at the Belga once more, earn money for the coming year, and enjoy Christmas in the city. If so, Rigoberta and her friends spent their last school vacation at the Colegio Belga in downtown Guatemala City, a few blocks from where her family had just risked their lives to protest the kidnapping of Petrocinio. Then Rigoberta and her friends returned to Chiantla between January 13 and 15, 1980, just as her father and brothers came to the capital for a second time to protest.[2]

The Last Visit Home

> *I had to face some terrible moments. First, when the news came that the bodies were unrecognizable and I thought that my mother and brothers were there. What I couldn't bear was the idea of them all dying together. . . . I couldn't bear it. I couldn't bear to be the only one left. I actually wanted to die.*
>
> —*I, Rigoberta Menchú*, **pp. 185–186**

Rigoberta's education had taken her away from her family in its moment of destruction. Relatives date her final visit home differently, perhaps because they saw her for the last time on separate occasions. A certain emotional distance (hardly surprising in a nineteen-year-old) is suggested by a sibling's belief that the last time she visited was in 1978. But he recalled the occasion with affection; "Her way of talking was no longer that of ours. She could speak Spanish well. . . . She admonished us to speak correctly. She always shared what she was studying there. . . . We were always taking it in, in case there was some court or lawsuit to attend. She always explained things to us. When she left, we were always sad."

Another sibling recalled that Rigoberta's last visit was five months before her father's death. That would date it to September 1979 (or to the next month, at the start of the October–December school recess). "My father only went around hidden at that time because his enemies wanted to kill him," the sibling told me. "Finally you've come to me," Vicente tells his daughter as he sits in a chair to receive her, in town rather than Chimel. "I'm going to die because my enemies are persecuting me." Both his children cry. "They're going to shoot me," Vicente continues. "But you're going to finish your studies." If these were the last words Rigoberta heard from her father, they would explain why she did not join the protests in the capital. They would also vouch for her portrait of Vicente as a figure of defiance who knew his days were numbered.

In her 1997 life story, Rigoberta dates her last visit to Chimel to early October 1979. Her father is not home, but her mother is—devastated by Petrocinio's fate and relieved to see her alive.[3] If this was the final time Rigoberta set eyes on Chimel, it apparently was not her last visit to the municipio. According to yet another relative, the last time Rigoberta visited Uspantán was after the death of her father and the disappearance of her mother (therefore after April 19, 1980) but only for a short while, perhaps a week. "When she realized that she, too, was being pursued, she left again."[4]

The most inconvenient datum I came across was in an obituary for Vicente Menchú. "His daughter is currently persecuted," stated a revolutionary publication with the date April 1, 1980, "for which reason she has to move in clandestinity." If this is a reference to Rigoberta (the only one of Vicente's six daughters living away from Uspantán at the time), it is the first published reference to her that I have been able to find. Since the mere fact that an indigenous youth was getting an education could attract government killers, it may refer simply to Rigoberta's vulnerable position at boarding school.[5] Interpreted literally, it would mean that she was underground even before the death of her mother, contrary to the recollection of schoolmates.

Escape from Chiantla

According to one of the teachers at Chiantla, the school has a record of Rigoberta's finishing *primero básico* (seventh grade) in October 1979, but no record of her for 1980. Yet five schoolmates remembered Rigoberta starting her second year at Chiantla, only to leave midway through the 1980 term, so it would appear that her name was expunged. It is not hard to understand why. Like the rest of Guatemala, the Chiantla school was under siege in the early 1980s. Because the nuns worked in counterinsurgency zones and were part of a clergy that was reporting human rights violations, they were in the army's gun sights. The school's Belgian director received anonymous threats. Without explanation, soldiers would surround the compound for a day or two. Then they would go away, to return on a later occasion. The nuns told their students to stop addressing each other as *compañera* (which could be interpreted as guerrilla talk) and drop to the floor at the sound of a whistle.

It was under such conditions that Rigoberta left the internado one night, unannounced and bound for exile. After learning of her parents' deaths, she spent much of her time alone in the chapel, on her knees crying and praying. "I'm not going to just let this happen," she told a friend. "I have to see what I'm going to do."[6] "We took religion very seriously. We really believed that Christ was there in the Eucharist," another friend explained, "so that when her family members died, she took it to the chapel. There were moments of rebellion when she shouted: 'Why is it that my family has to disappear!'"

Some of her schoolmates believe that soldiers surrounded the internado looking expressly for the future Nobel laureate. According to one, the soldiers had been watching them closely on their daily procession from the residential compound to classrooms next to the church. Then one night the nuns prohibited talking at dinner, ordered the students to bed, and imposed a blackout. That was the night Rigoberta vanished. She was said to be over in the chapel, praying for her family. But she never returned, and the next day the girls noticed that the soldiers were even more vigilant, as if they were looking for someone in particular. In the words of a schoolmate, "She disappeared. Some days later I don't know how many [army] commandos surrounded us, looking for someone by the name of Menchú"—and searched the entire compound for her.

The most obvious problem with this version of events is that the army searched the boarding school at Chiantla only once—under Ríos Montt's state of siege in 1982 or 1983. The raid was a traumatic experience, with soldiers lining up students and nuns as if making preparations for the worst.[7] According to two other schoolmates, Rigoberta left the compound on a night when soldiers were not surrounding it. She went to bed as usual, but in the morning the bed was made and her things were gone. She may have been able to say good-bye to a single friend, who later died in the violence. The nuns never explained her disappearance, and the students dared not ask. From the kitchen staff, they learned that Rigoberta had been smuggled out in ladino dress and taken to the capital, where a passport was obtained for her to leave the country.

Looking for Bernardina

> *One day about eight years ago, I was told she was in the town square at Mixco, but we couldn't go. A year ago, a little girl said she was alive, but she didn't know where. I'm on the bus and I see a girl who looks like her. I turn around to see if it's her.*
>
> **—Mother of one of Rigoberta's friends, 1994**

Finding Rigoberta's old schoolmates required detective work. Several proved to be living around the corner, so to speak, while others turned up in the personal network of a North American colleague in another town, and still others in a city. Not all were pleased to have a gringo knock on their door with questions about their old schoolmate. One was still hiding her readings on social studies from fourteen years before. But I am grateful to each of them for helping me. Eventually I interviewed six women who studied with Rigoberta in Uspantán, Guatemala City, and/or Chiantla, plus three others who had heard stories about her.

One schoolmate from Rigoberta's hometown I was never able to find. An uncle had not seen her for ages, but he understood that she was living in Guatemala City. Surely her sister would have the address, in another town at a vague address. Following a canvas of the neighborhood, I found the sister's house. No one was there. Nor did I find her on subsequent visits. Then one day, at the offices of the Communities of Population in Resistance in the capital, I struck up a conversation with two women who looked like they might be from Uspantán. They turned out to be the mother and sister of Rigoberta's friend.

Bernardina Us Hernández was from the village of Macalajau. Her father, Reyes Us Hernández, was a Behrhorst promoter, like two of Rigoberta's brothers, and was at least as well known as Vicente Menchú. Everyone I talked to remembered him warmly. When an earthquake wrecked the village school, Reyes led the committee to rebuild it. He also headed the committee that refurbished the chapel. He was on the village road committee, ran a cooperative store, and with the help of the Behrhorst program, set up a village clinic. "Reyes Us Hernández was quick, eloquent, and knew how to speak his mind," an ex–Peace Corps volunteer recalled. "He was enormously respected by his people." "This person really struggled. [He told us] that this is our right, that we work according to the law," a human rights activist told me. "But other people resented him, they rejected him, and they accused him of being a guerrilla commander."

Reyes was one of seven men who fell victim to the army's first attack on Macalajau, on a November night in 1980. Guided by neighbors with their faces covered, soldiers broke through Reyes's door. He managed to slip out of the house through a loose plank, only to be shot in the back and dispatched with two bullets to the head. Four months later, his seventeen-year-old son Daniel was murdered in front of the family. During the same period, six other men in Reyes's family network were taken away by soldiers, never to be seen again.

Like Rigoberta, Bernardina had finished her primary education at the Colegio Belga and moved on to Chiantla. She shared Rigoberta's interest in politics and also felt obliged to leave school after her father's death, to help her mother and younger siblings. With them, she took refuge in the anonymity of Guatemala City. According to the sister I finally met in 1994, Bernardina worked as a maid to support her family and continued her studies on Sundays. She was also a supporter of the Committee for Campesino Unity but not a member, her sister told me. Three years after the murder of her father, in September 1983, Bernardina was on an errand for another displaced person when she was dragged into a car by men in civilian dress. I wonder if she had been sent on an undercover mission, of which she may or may not have been aware, which then was betrayed to the security forces. As she struggled with the kidnappers, her watch dropped into the street. Later it found its way back to her family, but Bernardina never did. That is why she was hard to track down. Her fate suggests why it was important for Rigoberta to flee to Mexico.

12

Rigoberta Joins the Revolutionary Movement

I told myself that I wasn't the only orphan in Guatemala. There are many others, and it's not my grief alone, it's the grief of a whole people, and all of us orphans who've been left must bear it.

—*I, Rigoberta Menchú*, p. 236

When the future laureate told her story in 1982, she spoke of years of experience as a political organizer. They begin around 1977 when her father goes underground to start the Committee for Campesino Unity and she helps organize Chimel against the army's first probes. In 1979 she joins her father as a CUC leader.[1] Eventually the security forces pick up her trail and she flees Guatemala, after the 1981 May Day protests in the capital. Yet if Rigoberta was in boarding school from January 1976 or 1977 to mid-1980, she could not have been an activist of this kind. Although several schoolmates described Rigoberta's interest in politics, none could recall conversations about CUC or village militancy. They also vouched for her near confinement during this period, with domestic service for the Colegio Belga occupying most of her October-to-January school recesses.

Whom to believe, particularly on these last points? Rigoberta's education is undeniable, but some readers will find it far-fetched that she had no connection to the left. Students from rural backgrounds were bridges between peasants and urban intellectuals, with much of the traffic running through the Catholic Church.[2] Could the schoolmates I interviewed know more than they wanted to tell me? Or be ignorant of Rigoberta's involvements? Or have a grudge against her? Their attitudes toward her certainly differed. Those familiar with *I, Rigoberta Menchú* were hurt or puzzled by her denial of their years together, whereas others had no idea of the omission until I told them. Two were resentful of Rigoberta's stature, another was awed, and the others were somewhere between. Yet they remembered much in common, above all the strictness of the internado regime, from which I conclude that, yes, Rigoberta was relatively isolated politically.

Rigoberta's unacknowledged school career provided the architecture for her 1982 account of the revolutionary movement's smuggling her to Mexico. Detected by soldiers in "a little town in Huehuetenango," she hides in a church. From there she flees to the capital, where she takes refuge with unsympathetic nuns who exploit her as a domestic servant, forbid her from talking to their students, and make her eat scraps off their plates. They also make her wait on a young Nicaraguan refugee who turns out to work for the secret police. Only after fifteen days of mistreatment and paranoia do her compañeros—in the revolutionary movement rather than the Catholic Church—get her on an airplane to Mexico.[3]

Recently, without retracting anything, Rigoberta has changed her story in ways that coincide with the recollections of schoolmates. "Thanks to my contact with the clergy," she told the Guatemalan newsweekly *Crónica,* "I left the country in mid-1980. Then I had the opportunity to participate in the conference of the bishops of America, in Oaxaca, Mexico, which was attended by outstanding figures like Samuel Ruiz [the bishop of Chiapas] and Bishop Méndez Arceo [of Cuernavaca]. I still spoke Spanish only poorly, and perhaps the people understood my message because of the anguish and desperation that afflicted me. That time I spoke only of the pain I was experiencing over the death of my parents. It was a testimony that touched many bishops, to the point that each one wanted to take me to his country, but I stayed with Samuel Ruiz in Chiapas and, for the first time, I temporarily forgot the trauma I was bearing. Later, my compañeros in CUC came to look for me and I returned to Guatemala at the beginning of 1981. At the end of that year, I went abroad again, to speak at a conference of Christians in Nicaragua, and I could no longer go back."[4]

Rigoberta is still dating her militancy in CUC to the late 1970s, and she is still omitting her schooling. But she attributes her escape from Guatemala to the Catholic Church, not to revolutionary comrades, and she dates it to 1980 rather than 1981. Instead of staying in Guatemala until mid-1981, whereupon she is forced into exile for the first time, her new chronology has her leaving Guatemala in mid-1980, returning at the start of 1981, then staying most of the year, before embarking on international work. If we then put into the picture Rigoberta's schooling, which occupies most of her time until mid-1980, it seems very unlikely that she joined the revolutionary movement before going abroad.

So how and when did she join? In Mexico Rigoberta was among the first of tens of thousands of Guatemalans to seek asylum in the state of Chiapas. Part of Guatemala until 1824, the Chiapas highlands are populated by Mayas and would have felt more like home than any other place of exile. Unlike the starving refugees who would flee across the border and spend more than a decade in camps, Rigoberta flew to the Mexican capital accompanied by a Catholic nun. Within days, she impressed a meeting of Catholic bishops and was taken into the household of a champion of liberation theology, Monsignor Samuel Ruiz.

Ruiz resided in the colonial town of San Cristobal de las Casas. His sister Doña Lucha treated Rigoberta like a daughter, according to the latter's 1997 life story. The future laureate became an active member of the bishop's household, to the point of organizing a birthday party for him and composing a poem in his honor. She tried to find a financial sponsor to continue her education, a diocesan worker recalls, and she gave talks at Nueva Primavera, a school run by a Mexican order called the Sisters of the Divine Pastor. The nuns taught monthlong courses in literacy and nursing to peasant girls. Since Rigoberta was from a similar background, her function was to reinforce the program's consciousness-raising paradigm: that students were oppressed but could educate themselves and join with others to change society. Like the bishop's conference she had addressed, this was a venue in which Rigoberta could tell her story.

It was also a hotbed of revolutionary intrigue. As Guatemalan peasants began to pour across the border, Ruiz and his diocese were the first to come to their aid. Proximity to the border also made Chiapas a logistical base for the Guatemalan guerrillas. For better or worse, depending on your point of view, the insurgents were able to turn the diocesan refugee program into a supply line. Ruiz can be accused of complicity, but as bishops usually are, he was in a difficult position. As the bishop of Chiapas, he presided over one of the most backward and violent dioceses in Mexico. As an advocate for the poor, he had recruited urban leftists to implement his projects for indigenous communities and defend them from conservatives (one such group would turn into the Zapatista National Liberation Army in the 1990s). With the Guatemalan army on the rampage across the border, the solidarity activists on his staff had powerful moral arguments in their favor. If ever there was a just war in keeping with Catholic tradition, Guatemala in the early 1980s seemed to qualify.

For a refugee like Rigoberta, it would have been hard not to get involved. Since the guerrilla networks in Mexico were illegal and clandestine, joining them was not an occasion for public announcements. Nor would too many questions have been asked when Rigoberta started displacing herself on political errands. In a solidarity milieu like San Cristobal de las Casas in the early 1980s, studious disattention is the prescribed attitude toward clandestine affiliations, because everyone involved needs to maintain plausible deniability. As admirers of the Sandinista revolution in Nicaragua, Ruiz and his supporters would hardly have disapproved.[5]

When Rigoberta told her story in Paris in 1982, she traced her political career back to a mythological era of village militancy. When she retold her life fifteen years later, for *Crossing Borders,* she cut out references to her involvement with the guerrillas. But a careful look at her earlier life story will suggest how she may have joined the revolutionary network in Chiapas. In Paris Rigoberta extolled the superior revolutionary consciousness of one of her sisters, who joins the guerrillas unbeknownst to her parents at the age of eight, who lectures Rigoberta on the need for stoicism, and who, after the death of their mother, goes back to Chimel to take her even smaller sister to safety in Mexico. In a suggestive passage near the end of *I, Rigoberta Menchú,* the narrator has reached Mexico and is feeling disoriented when she is visited by comrades who have just arrived from Guatemala. To her surprise and joy, they include her younger sisters Ana and Rosa. Following a family reunion, each of the three chooses an organization and goes back to Guatemala—her sisters to the guerrillas in the mountains and Rigoberta (until this point with CUC, according to her story) to a new organization called the Vicente Menchú Revolutionary Christians.[6]

According to Chimel sources, as mentioned before, Ana and Rosa were with their mother until she was taken from them. Then, like so many other orphans, they seem to have been adopted by the Guerrilla Army of the Poor. Being reunited with them in Mexico must have been a powerful experience for Rigoberta, and it could have been a decisive one, too. A person who met the two sisters in Mexico recalls that they were indeed very young (about twelve and fourteen years old) and very militant, more so than Rigoberta. With her other siblings trapped in Uspantán, the only family that Rigoberta could be sure she had left were Ana and Rosa. This is why I suspect that it was through two of the orphans who made up so much of the EGP that it recruited another. If so, then her first experience as a revolutionary organizer in Guatemala dated to early the next year, in 1981.

Rigoberta and the January 31st Popular Front

We set up barricades, threw "propaganda bombs" and held lightning meetings. We had to complete each of these actions in a couple of minutes, or it would mean a massacre. And so we were organized in such a way that the barricades would be opened, the propaganda given out, and the meeting held all at the same time. . . . We telephoned all the factories and told them that we'd placed high explosives there and that they were responsible for the lives of all those people. . . . A compañero placed a box with an aerial which looked like high explosives near a building where people could see it. The police arrived and made a tremendous fuss.

—*I, Rigoberta Menchú,* pp. 232–233

By the end of 1980, when I believe Rigoberta joined the revolutionary movement, it was approaching its apogee. The Guerrilla Army of the Poor was expecting a mass insurrection, like the one that brought down the Somoza regime in Nicaragua. The Committee for Campesino Unity was working openly with the EGP. It described itself as a "revolutionary mass organization of rural workers," whose task was to "raise consciousness and politicize so that the campesinos participate massively in the popular war." Its tactics included "sabotages, propaganda bombs, highway blockades, barricades, attacks on informers, the burning of buses, etc.—all within a strategy of massive incorporation of the people into popular war."[7]

During these first years, Rigoberta's political career must be traced through the shifting coalitions, fronts, and disguises of an insurgency fighting for its life. The guerrilla armies were trying to pull together a broader popular movement that would simultaneously obey their instructions, widen their appeal, and withstand ferocious repression. In 1979, unionists, peasants, students, church activists, and social democratic politicians had organized the Democratic Front Against Repression. Since it included a broad range of the aboveground left, the FDCR was split by desperate debates over how to react to government terror. Should grassroots groups stay within the law, or should they become guerrilla fronts? Although some predicted that joining the guerrillas would spell rapid destruction, CUC was among the groups that distrusted the coalition's "lack of security and self-defense," withdrew from it in 1980, and chose the guerrilla road.[8]

Disagreements with the FDCR obliged the guerrilla armies to organize their own popular front. About the time Rigoberta returned to Guatemala, on the first anniversary (January 31, 1981) of the fire at the Spanish embassy, three organizations announced themselves and joined CUC in a new coalition. Each of the new groups bore the name of an embassy martyr. They included the Felipe Antonio García Revolutionary Workers Nuclei, which claimed fifteen hundred members; the Trinidad Gómez Hernández Barrio-Dwellers Committee, which claimed 150 members; and the Vicente Menchú Revolutionary Christians, which claimed four thousand members. Together with two preexisting organizations, the CUC (which claimed six thousand members) and the Robin García Revolutionary Student Front (which claimed five hundred), they formed the January 31st Popular Front (FP-31).[9]

The idea was to use the imagery of the embassy martyrs to mobilize the masses for an insurrection. According to FP-31 announcements, the guerrillas were the unquestionable vanguard of the Guatemalan people and popular revolutionary war was the people's only road forward. FP-31's members did not belong to the guerrilla organizations, according to the front's declarations, but their political objectives were identical. Since not everyone could join the guerrilla war, nor were there enough firearms for everyone, the masses would have to take advantage of their strength in numbers. The resulting paramilitary forms of struggle would help establish a popular revolutionary government. According to the Vicente Menchú Revolutionary Christians, its members would "exercise openly the just violence of the oppressed against those impeding the construction of the Kingdom of God."[10]

If Rigoberta's potential was quickly recognized, this could have been one of the reasons for naming an entire organization after her father. She is sometimes described as a founder of the Revolutionary Christians.[11] But *I, Rigoberta Menchú* does not refer to her as such. Moreover, if she did not join the revolutionary movement until the end of 1980, she would have been a neophyte when the front was set up. As for why the Revolutionary Christians were named after her father, the reason could be that he had welcomed the EGP to his village, or that he was the kind of catechist whom the guerrillas wished to recruit, or that he had led the peasants who died at the embassy.

If Rigoberta was a revolutionary novice, one of hundreds who joined the movement in 1980, what would she have done for it? Away at boarding school, she could not have been one of the CUC militants who joined the plantation workforce and triggered the strikes of February 1980, as claimed in *I, Rigoberta Menchú*.[12] But if her career began a year later, she could have been part of the unsuccessful effort to organize more strikes. For a person who had not known plantation life during her first twenty-two years, the shock of a first experience would explain her eloquent descriptions of the suffering there. In 1981 Rigoberta could also have become involved in the highland village organizing that her story improbably situates in Chimel several years earlier. Her descriptions of village self-defense are detailed—but also so triumphalistic that they read like a textbook description of what was supposed to happen, rather than what actually did.

As the daughter of a revolutionary hero, after whom a new front had just been named, Rigoberta's most likely theater was the capital. In 1982 she used the present tense to describe herself as a delegate shuttling between Guatemala City and outlying locales in the revolutionary network. To whatever extent the Revolutionary Christians and the Committee for Campesino Unity were separate structures in the FP-31 network, she described herself working for the Revolutionary Christians rather than CUC.[13] "I thought a lot about whether to go back to the CUC, but I decided that the CUC had enough leaders, enough peasant members, and also many women taking on responsibilities in the organization. So, because of my Christian background, I opted for the 'Vicente Menchú' Revolutionary Christians. I didn't choose it because it bore my father's name, but because, as a Christian, it was my duty to work with the people. My task was to educate the Christian compañeros whose faith brings them into the organization. It's a bit like what I was talking about before, about being a catechist, except that I'm the one who walks on the Earth, not one who thinks that the Kingdom of God only comes after death."

Because of her Catholic education, including a dose of liberation theology from the Chiapas diocese, recruiting catechists into the revolutionary movement was the work for which Rigoberta was best prepared. Arguments for how the Bible justifies armed struggle are a prominent feature of *I, Rigoberta Menchú* and part of its appeal to the Christian left. Like the contrast between the "church of the poor" and the "church of the rich," this was part of the repertoire that cadres used against Catholic clergy discouraging parishioners from joining the guerrillas.[14] Such references put Rigoberta and her story in the middle of the central debate in the Catholic Church of the late 1970s and early 1980s: whether to support the guerrilla movements that had taken such expert advantage of its grassroots leaders and programs.

What Rigoberta understated in 1982 was just how bad the previous year had been for the revolutionary network in the capital. With the security forces dragging away suspects to horrible deaths, life consisted mainly of elaborate security precautions. The confusion and retreat emerge in her 1997 retelling of her life. With comrades disappearing left and right—some kidnapped, others going into hiding—those who remain are terrified of being captured and tortured themselves. Then Rigoberta and her sisters Ana and Rosa commit a terrible blunder. While renting a truck to move to a new safe house, they forget to tie a box, which then spills political pamphlets. The truck driver turns pale, and the possibility that he will betray them ruins the new location. Their CUC comrades tell them they are "very burned" and refuse to give them another place to live. Unable to deal with the capital on their own, Ana and Rosa return to Quiché to join the guerrillas while Rigoberta—feeling guilty for parting from her sisters—travels overland to Nicaragua to become a UN-registered refugee. Judging from the only reference to duration, she was in Guatemala "a few months" before being forced to leave.[15] Judging from another source, Rigoberta may have spent much of 1981 in Chiapas with the Catholic diocese.

A final observation may seem perverse, in view of the attention that Rigoberta gives CUC in her 1982 story and that I echo. It is that she may never have belonged to the Committee for Campesino Unity until after she told her story to Elisabeth Burgos. In December 1981 the revolutionary *Noticias de Guatemala* published Rigoberta's first testimony that I have been able to find. In it she lays out the story of her father and herself as a representative of the Revolutionary Christians, without making any reference to CUC. If Vicente is impossible to connect to CUC, if Rigoberta was in boarding school until 1980, and if her sisters joined the revolutionary movement through the Guerrilla Army of the Poor, there is no verifiable connection between Rigoberta and CUC until she makes it herself, in Paris in January 1982.[16] What makes CUC an essential referent is not that it was the cradle of Rigoberta's career. Instead, it is how she tried to connect the stubbornly idiosyncratic experience of her community to the national narrative being propounded by the revolutionary forces.

The Destruction of the Popular Movement

> *The strategy of generalizing the war transformed social and political conflicts into armed confrontations. . . . The logic of the popular war led to the asphyxiation of the social movement.*
>
> **—Yvon Le Bot, *La Guerra en Tierras Mayas*, p. 262**

As Rigoberta returned from Mexico to join the political wing of the insurgency in Guatemala, in 1981, it peaked in the western highlands. The reason was a rush of recruits from church, peasant, and labor organizations being crushed by the government. The survivors enlarged guerrilla ranks, but they did so only briefly, because the grassroots networks needed to sustain them had been destroyed. To explain the disaster, solidarity accounts customarily dwell on the army's ferocity. What they pass over lightly is a guerrilla strategy that hinged on turning unarmed civilians into military assets, against an enemy known for ruthlessness.

"With the development of mass work," EGP commander in chief Rolando Morán explained to Marta Harnecker, "we have a greater source of combatants. The mass organizations can carry out the tasks of war that don't correspond to the guerrilla forces. This complements their other functions and prepares them to be regular combatants. The same thing is occurring among the Indians, who at this time have definitively joined the revolution. There are tens of thousands of Indians in our zones working with the EGP and fully conscious of it. The CUC forms a secret committee in a community, developing educational work until they win over the majority of the population and have them join our work." The mass organizations were not all armed, Morán continued, but they did have self-defense groups that "are the seed and the bridge between the masses and the guerrillas."[17]

By the time Morán laid out this scenario for Harnecker, from outside the country in 1982, what it referred to in Guatemala was a landscape of empty corridors, burned villages, and shallow graves. In the capital, the radicalization of the labor movement peaked in a mass protest on May 1, 1980. As it disbanded, the security forces kidnapped dozens of demonstrators off the street. Within the National Committee for Labor Unity, feuding between guerrilla factions over bringing urban workers into the armed struggle was responsible for the two most devastating kidnappings in the history of the labor movement. On two successive occasions, the security forces trapped and "disappeared" a total of forty-four labor leaders, whose meetings were betrayed by an informer in one of the guerrilla groups.[18] At this point, the urban labor movement virtually disappeared. Not wishing to die and leave their families without providers, most rank and file abandoned union activity. Many of the surviving leaders went into exile. Only the most sacrificially inclined joined the armed struggle. On the South Coast, the repression that followed the CUC-led strikes of 1980 virtually eliminated labor unions from the plantations, an absence that continues to the present.[19] The idea that labor unions could become a platform for insurrection had pushed them into a confrontation with the state that destroyed them.

In the highlands, the implications of guerrilla strategy for grassroots activists were just as devastating. Even if organizations were not infiltrated by the EGP, the mere fact of doing community work in an area where guerrillas were active was lethal. "It was panic, everything started coming apart in October 1981," a Catholic priest told the journalist Phillip Berryman. The priest had gone "into the mountains and was present during a major army attack on the people. For several days during the army attack he was hiding in the fields. Observing the EGP close at hand he became increasingly disenchanted. When the people of the area had risked their lives to capture weapons from the army, the EGP going back on their word took the weapons, leaving the people more exposed. Due to the betrayal of someone in the movement, the army made a surprise attack and almost captured a major EGP commander. The guerrillas managed to escape, but they abandoned the priest, whom they had entrusted with responsibilities, and the people of the village. After three weeks the EGP escorted the priest out of the region. He later realized that internal struggles were weakening the EGP."[20] As the army decimated their support base, the guerrillas were forced "to bury arms and ammunition for want of fighters to bear them."[21]

Pulling popular organizations into the war was a disaster. By infiltrating the peasant movement, then mobilizing it, the guerrillas brought down ferocious repression. Their guerrilla columns grew temporarily, from village survivors who had nowhere else to turn, but the "popular base" from which they had expected a steady flow of maize and youth was shattered. By 1982 so little was left of CUC that it survived as an organization only in exile. Of the thirty people who founded it in 1978, no more than six survived. The organization's publications were discontinued.[22] Back in Guatemala, the question, "Where is CUC?" became a reproach.[23] Surviving leaders were out of touch with their supporters who were repudiating them and submitting to conscription into the army's civil patrols. Only abroad could CUC leaders remain active, appealing for international solidarity for a popular movement that no longer existed.

13

The Construction of *I, Rigoberta Menchú*

Paris is their soundbox. Whatever happens in Paris has repercussions through the world.

—Elisabeth Burgos-Debray, *I, Rigoberta Menchú*, p. xvii

In January 1982 Rigoberta went on her first tour of Europe, as a representative of the January 31st Popular Front. Her first stop was Paris, where she told the story that became *I, Rigoberta Menchú*. She was both better and worse prepared for the task than can be inferred from the book itself. She was less prepared because, however quick to absorb the revolutionary lexicon, she had little political experience. Yet she was more prepared because Catholic nuns had given her a distance from peasant life that is hard to achieve without schooling. Still close enough to her origin to talk about it eloquently, she was in a doorway between the preliteracy of peasant society and the wider world opened up by schooling. Poised in that doorway, she could look back on her past and recreate it for the outsiders who would shape her future.

Even if Rigoberta's school career did not give her the liberty to become a CUC activist before she fled the country in 1980, it puts her on the cutting edge of revolutionary organizing during this period, and not just in Guatemala. A Catholic education locates her among the students who were a prime constituency for Latin American guerrilla organizations. Yet if schooling was so central to Rigoberta's youth, if her family valued education, and if it helped her speak out on behalf of her people, why not claim it? The larger question is, why transform so much of her experience? One clue is the breathless, action-packed quality of her story. The narrator of *I, Rigoberta Menchú* spends up to eight months a year working on plantations, as well as a dismal period as a maid in Guatemala City, yet still has time for happy interludes of childhood in a highland village. She accompanies her father on his pilgrimages to INTA, then becomes a catechist, helps her village defend itself against the army, and becomes a traveling organizer for the Committee for Campesino Unity. She tells us that was the last time she saw her family—until she joins a sudden family reunion to witness Petrocinio's death. The story includes so many experiences that Rigoberta always seems to be running from one engagement to the next, as if she were narrating a life too busy for one person actually to have lived. Or as if she were trying to be more representative of her people than any one person could be.

But is *I, Rigoberta Menchú* really her voice? Since her taped stories were edited by the anthropologist Elisabeth Burgos-Debray, could they have been seriously distorted? Rigoberta appeared to confirm just that when, in December 1997, she told a journalist that the book was Elisabeth's, not her own. "It does not belong to me morally, politically or economically. I have respected it greatly because it played an immense role for Guatemala. . . . But I never had the right to say if the text pleased me or not, if it was faithful to the facts of my life. Now my life is mine, therefore I believe that now it is opportune to say that it is not my book. . . . Anyone who has doubts about the work should go to [Elisabeth] because, even legally, I do not have author's rights, royalties or any of that."[1] These are serious allegations. So who is Elisabeth Burgos-Debray, what was her role in creating *I, Rigoberta Menchú*, and whose story is it?

A Week with Elisabeth Burgos-Debray

When Rigoberta came to Europe for the first time in January 1982, she was not a public figure. In her hometown she was a schoolgirl and in San Cristobal an outgoing young refugee. Now her job was to represent the revolutionary movement to solidarity groups. She was accompanied by a labor unionist named Mazariegos, who by her own account would do most of the talking.[2] At the start of the tour, in Paris, someone had the idea of sending her to Elisabeth Burgos. The woman who would turn Rigoberta's stories into a book was an old friend of the Guatemalan guerrillas. From the upper class of Venezuela, Elisabeth was best known as the wife of France's most adventurous man of letters, the philosopher Régis Debray.[3] Like his equally notorious mentor Louis Althusser, the young and dashing Régis had ridden the crest of 1960s Marxism to become a world intellectual figure. His best-known work, *Revolution in the Revolution?* championed the Cuban theory of armed struggle for liberating Latin America from U.S. imperialism.

Because of her husband, skeptics have assumed that Elisabeth was a dilettante on the caviar left. But she was a political exile herself, with a long history of activism dating back to her youth under the Pérez Jiménez dictatorship in Venezuela. During the protests that led to its overthrow in

1958, Elisabeth joined the Communist Party. Five years later, as the Venezuelan communists waged an ideologically fashionable but self-destructive guerrilla war against an elected government, Elisabeth met Régis on one of his journalistic tours. When the police detected their relations with the guerrillas, they skipped out of the country; traveled around Colombia and Ecuador; were arrested in Peru, expelled to Chile, and ended up in Bolivia, where Elisabeth stayed to work for the government until it was overthrown in a coup. After being arrested again—this time in Venezuela, while trying to visit her family—she rejoined Régis in France.

In 1966 the couple went to Havana for the Tricontinental Conference, an international assembly of Latin Americans, Africans, and Asians, which issued a declaration of revolutionary war throughout the Third World. Asked to stay on by the Cubans, Elisabeth and Régis went into military training. The idea was to join Che Guevara at the unknown location where, with a small band of revolutionaries, he would unleash "two, three or many Vietnams." The place turned out to be Bolivia, where Che was about to become the unlikely Christ figure of the Latin American left. As he and his column were trapped by the Bolivian army and its U.S. advisers, Régis fell into the army's hands. Soon Che was dead and Régis was sentenced to thirty years in prison. To obtain visiting privileges, Elisabeth married him behind bars and, for the next three years, led the international campaign that won his release.

With her instinct for history, Elisabeth followed the revolution to Chile, for a lesson in the limitations of democratic change. A Marxist named Salvador Allende had been elected president and, leading a coalition of the Chilean left, vowed to build socialism democratically. Elisabeth was among the thousands of foreign militants who arrived to help. One of the presuppositions for Allende's experiment was the constitutional tradition of the Chilean military. Presumably, the officer corps would not overthrow him. As it turned out, Allende died in the rubble of the presidential palace. Fortunately for Elisabeth, her plentiful experience with military coups persuaded her to leave just before the CIA-supported counterrevolution that took the lives of so many young leftists like herself.

Over fifteen years, Elisabeth's life had embodied the aspirations, strategies, and defeats of the Latin American left. Like many others of her generation, she was disillusioned with the prospects for armed struggle. There had been so many deaths and failures. But the fate of Allende suggests why it was hard to conceive an alternative. As soon as the left began to compete successfully in the democratic arena, it would be repressed by the local military and its U.S. backers. Was armed struggle still the only way forward? This is why Elisabeth and Régis were far from renegades, especially in social democratic Europe. By the early 1980s, Régis was a foreign policy adviser to his friend President François Mitterrand. Although still on good terms with guerrilla leaders, he had disavowed Che's theories as unworkable. Instead of promoting new wars of liberation, he was trying to steer the guerrillas of El Salvador into a negotiated settlement and social democracy.[4]

Like other Marxists, Régis regarded social class as a more fundamental category than ethnicity. Obviously, indigenous groups had to be integrated into revolutionary movements, but they could not be expected to take a vanguard role, at least not without considerable leadership from other parts of society. With little in the way of indigenous political organizations, Marxists had not done much to take them into account. Compared to her spouse, Elisabeth took more interest in indigenous people and argued for their importance, as underlined by Che's inability to communicate with the peasants among whom he tried to implant his last guerrilla column. By January 1982 the Mayas of Guatemala were at center stage in the Central American revolution, and Elisabeth was in a strategic position to help them.

Elisabeth was living in Paris, raising a daughter and writing a doctoral dissertation, when she was asked to interview a young Mayan refugee. At the French government's Casa de América Latina, she had already organized a solidarity event for Guatemala. Her ties to the country dated back to the 1960s in Cuba, where she had become friends with Guatemalans in training to liberate their homeland. Among them were some who would give their lives, including the former army lieutenant Luis Turcios Lima and the poet Otto René Castillo. Other friends from Cuba have survived to this day, including Ricardo Ramírez (Rolando Morán), the future founder of the Guerrilla Army of the Poor, and his partner of many years, the anthropologist Aura Marina Arriola, with whom Elisabeth worked to set up EGP solidarity structures.[5]

Rigoberta spent a week with Elisabeth in her Paris apartment. "The first thing that struck me about her was her open, almost childlike smile," Elisabeth wrote. "Her face was round and moon-shaped. Her expression was as guileless as that of a child and a smile hovered permanently on her lips. She looked astonishingly young. I later discovered that her youthful air soon faded when she had to talk about the dramatic events that had overtaken her family." Following an old paradigm, the anthropologist gave her "a schematic outline, a chronology: childhood, adolescence, family, involvement in the struggle" before turning on the tape recorder.[6] But Rigoberta's stories flowed so freely that she took over the process, with Elisabeth asking few questions. Ultimately, the recordings went on for eighteen and a half hours. After Rigoberta's departure, Elisabeth transcribed the tapes into a manuscript of almost five hundred pages; rearranged material to keep it chronological; divided it into chapters; dropped her own questions; and turned the material into a monologue, as if it were one continuous narrative.

Disjointed elements in Rigoberta's testimony have led to finger-pointing at the editor. Some suspect that Elisabeth was responsible for introducing errors into the story, that is, interfering with it too much. Others criticize her for not interfering with it enough, that is, failing to iron out the inconsistencies that become evident to a careful reader. From a scholar's point of view, basing a book on a relationship of one week and twelve cassette tapes was a bit rash. Nor was there enough fact-checking (the first page identifies Uspantán as the capital of Quiché Department). But verifying Rigoberta's story with other survivors would not have been possible—in 1982 many were still in hiding and others could have been killed for the mere act of talking with an outsider. Given the need to arouse international opinion, it is hard to fault Elisabeth for publishing as soon as she could.

Who Authored *I, Rigoberta Menchú*?

> *It's not her life story, not her autobiography, doesn't fit her type of person. You can tell after a while that she's clearly a highly educated person, with more than a third-grade education, clearly very comfortable in Spanish, more so than if she had learned it the way she said she did. But the book is representative of somebody's life if not hers. Many people have a life like that.*
>
> **—Former aid worker in Quiché Department, 1992**

Recently the authorship of oral testimonies like *I, Rigoberta Menchú* has become controversial. Now that native people are insisting on equality, they are less willing to have their words mediated by outsiders. This includes anthropologists accustomed to speaking and publishing on their behalf. In my own case, I have benefited from twenty-four years of schooling, including generous support for my research, and can communicate with some of the most influential media in the world. The typical person I interview has a few years of education, if that; is hard-pressed to decipher a newspaper; and can barely write a simple note. This is quite a disparity in power. As more indigenous people become capable of reading what has been published about them, they are challenging what they feel is incorrect or inappropriate. Meanwhile, academic journals are full of debate over anthropological representation, that is, how we communicate the thoughts and lives of our subjects.

So who is the author of a taped and transcribed life story such as *I, Rigoberta Menchú*? The person who tells it or the intermediary who shapes it for publication? The storyteller might seem the obvious answer, as this is the oral equivalent of an autobiography, a genre known in Latin America as testimonio. But the storyteller is insufficiently literate to produce a book on her own. The many functions of the intermediary—posing the questions to be answered, transcribing the answers from a tape, reordering them to communicate with a foreign audience, editing out repetition, correcting grammar, and signing a contract for publication—complicate the question of authorship. At worst, an intermediary can take so many liberties that she becomes the author. Even a faithful intermediary has to make so many decisions that she takes on certain attributes of an author.

In the case of *I, Rigoberta Menchú,* the person who contracted with Editions Gallimard of Paris to administer world rights was Elisabeth Burgos. Her name is not on the cover of the current edition in English, appearing only on the title page as editor, but she figures prominently on earlier covers. Who authored the book is an issue that scholars have debated and readers have pondered. So has the Nobel laureate, who sometimes claims to have had editorial control of the text as well as the testimony, then sometimes disclaims it.

"The book was an idea of Arturo Taracena, a warm-hearted friend, a Latin American historian," she explained around the time she received the peace prize. "He encouraged me to write it. It was a painful task for me, having had such horrible experiences and having to relive them in the telling. I was also afraid that our stories might end up as a pamphlet, that they might be published [briefly] and then lost. That's why we decided to work with Elisabeth Burgos Debray, a wonderful woman with a well-known name. Actually, the book is the result of collective labor. The first step was to make recordings for 12 days, very difficult 12 days. At that time, my Spanish was awful. I could hardly speak it, much less read it. With the help of many friends from the Guatemalan Solidarity group, transcriptions were made and then they read the text back to me. That way, I could listen to what was written. Of course, we left out several accounts, accounts that I thought we should save for the future and not publish now. And I also was inhibited because there are things that, our parents tell us, should be left unsaid."[7]

This is quite a different version of events than Elisabeth's—and also from two other explanations Rigoberta has provided. For her 1997 life story, *Crossing Borders,* the laureate reiterated how she helped edit the final text of *I, Rigoberta Menchú*. Then, just before the new book appeared, she lost her temper during an interview and accused Elisabeth of excluding her from the 1982 editing.[8] In yet a third version, apparently to explain the factual problems with the 1982 life story, Rigoberta has blamed Elisabeth for substituting other persons' life stories for her own. Never published, this last explanation was the one available from Rigoberta's staff in 1993. According to it, Elisabeth interviewed not just Rigoberta but four or five other Mayan exiles as well. Supposedly Elisabeth then stitched together their stories under Rigoberta's name, to achieve a more dramatic testimony. Although Rigoberta and the others had gone along with the decision, now they were said to be angry about it.

This last version of events, the multiple-narrator hypothesis, would explain the wide array of personal experiences claimed in *I, Rigoberta Menchú*. A group of people telling their stories could account for experiences that Rigoberta lacked. Elisabeth would then have distilled the testimony of five or six persons into the story of one omnibus survivor and militant. Yet the book is not just a compendium of too many episodes for one person to have experienced. It also works revolutionary paradigms into one episode after another, subtracting factual elements that contradict them. To satisfy expectations that land conflicts are between virtuous Mayan peasants and evil ladino planters, someone exaggerated Vicente Menchú's problems with the ladino finca owners of Soch, while subtracting those with his K'iche' in-laws in Laguna Danta.

Who was this someone? Probably not the other alleged Mayan contributors, leaving us with one of the two people with whom we started. It could have been Elisabeth who decided to drop any reference to the quarrel with the Tums, the U.S. Peace Corps, and boarding school. It could have been Elisabeth who turned Vicente Menchú into a founder of the Committee for Campesino Unity. But if it was Elisabeth who authored the unforgettable account of how Petrocinio died at Chajul, or the grim portrait of Vicente going underground to fight for his rights, then Rigoberta would lose authorship of her story as well as the final text. Instead, she would become a mere instrument for a foreign storymaster, problematizing *I, Rigoberta Menchú* on a deeper level. Not only would it fail to reflect her life and village as remembered by so many others, but it would not even be Rigoberta who told the story.

Given the Nobel laureate's obvious gifts as an orator and protagonist, the multiple-narrator explanation is condescending. It is also implausible. Aside from still extant tape recordings, which prove that it was Rigoberta who told the story, she was telling it in her distinctive way before she met Elisabeth. Finding a life narrative that predates the visit to Paris was not easy, but eventually one turned up. For a revolutionary news bulletin dated December 2, 1981, Rigoberta describes how her father put up years of heroic resistance to "the constant outrages of the landlords"; how her brother Petrocinio was kidnapped on December 9, 1979, tortured for various days, then taken to Chajul with twenty other men to be burned alive; and how her mother was kidnapped, tortured for twelve days, then left "on a hill near the community" to be guarded until her remains were devoured by animals. She also anticipates the key claim of her Paris story: "My sorrow and my struggle are also the sorrow and struggle of an entire oppressed people who struggle for their liberation."[9] Contrary to the laureate's occasional statements to the contrary, there is every reason to believe that *I, Rigoberta Menchú* is her own account of her life.

What Elisabeth Burgos Says Today

As I found more problems with *I, Rigoberta Menchú,* it became obvious that I should talk to the book's editor. What was not so obvious was that Elisabeth would want to talk with me. In the early 1980s, she was still a supporter of the revolutionary movement, along with myself and many others appalled by the brutality of the Guatemalan army. Since then my thinking had changed because of my conversations with peasants, including many who once supported the guerrillas. Elisabeth did not have the same experience, of hearing so much testimony contradicting Rigoberta's. If it was difficult for some of my colleagues to countenance questions about the veracity of *I, Rigoberta Menchú,* what else to expect from the figure who had turned Rigoberta's story into a best-seller?

As it turned out, an old friend of Elisabeth, an anthropologist who had known her in Bolivia, assured me that she would be equal to the occasion. When I arrived at her apartment in Madrid, in 1995, she listened to my ill tidings with apparent equanimity. If I had been in her position, listening to dreadful new information that cast doubt on one of the more significant projects in my life, I doubt that I would have reacted as calmly. Nor would I necessarily be prepared to lay out my side of the story, to someone in a position to harm my reputation.

On how the book came to be, Elisabeth told essentially the same story that appears in the 1982 introduction, with the addition of fascinating details. A Canadian medical doctor living under the name Marie Tremblay asked her to interview an interesting person for a magazine article. Rigoberta showed up at her door accompanied by Tremblay, in the cold of winter, wearing the same light clothes she would back home. She was en route to a conference in Holland, had nothing planned for Paris, and proved to be completely available for what, as the story poured forth day after day, became an unexpected week of taping. At the end of the week, Rigoberta was picked up by Arturo Taracena, the Guatemalan historian finishing his doctorate in Paris.

"They had her cooking [for them] in Mexico. Even the Guatemalans didn't take an interest in her because she was indígena," Elisabeth told me. "She was anxious and didn't have the least idea of where she was. What I detected is that she wanted to express herself, to overcome her experiences and get to a broader place than where they had her. For the first time, she wasn't in a house with Guatemalans, and I was listening to her. I think it was a pleasure for her to talk with someone who took an interest in her."

Elisabeth was able to listen at such length, for the most part quietly, only because of her work with the anthropologist George Devereux and his ethnopsychiatric approach. She had studied clinical psychology at the

University of Paris VII, as well as ethnology at the School of Social Sciences in Paris, and now she was writing a dissertation on the ethnopsychiatry of French and Latin American women. "Without that training, I would not have been able to do the interviews the way I did," she told me. "You have to immerse yourself in the interviewee. You ask questions only when a block comes up, when the interviewee repeats herself a lot, for example." The questions she asked were mainly about the culture, because Rigoberta was most interested in talking about oppression.

In her 1982 introduction, Elisabeth attributed the book's genesis to a Canadian solidarity activist in Paris—the medical doctor Marie Tremblay. Thirteen years later, Elisabeth said that Tremblay had suggested only a magazine interview, soon published in the influential weekly *Le Nouvel Observateur,* from which it quickly reverberated back to Latin America.[10] It was only after Rigoberta's departure, Elisabeth told me, that she realized she had enough material for a book. Since no one else had broached the idea during the week that Rigoberta was in Paris, it had never been discussed with her. She could have had no idea that the story she was telling would acquire the weighty permanence of a book.

Without a job at the time, Elisabeth was able to devote her full energies to the project. She only would have to put off finishing her doctoral dissertation. So every day she took her child to school, came home, and worked on the transcription, assisted by a Chilean friend. Although Rigoberta's Spanish was eloquent, like some of the peasant Spanish I hear in northern Quiché, the grammar was not what readers expect on a printed page. "Her Spanish was very basic. She translated from her own language [in her head]; this is what cost me a lot," Elisabeth said. "Yes, I corrected verb tenses and noun genders, as otherwise it would not have made sense, but always trying to retain her own powerful form of expression. Rigoberta's narrative was anything but chronological. It had to be put in order. And the passages about culture that I elicited had to be inserted into the narrative of her life.

"I had to reorder a lot to give the text a thread, to give it the sense of a life, to make it a story, so that it could reach the general public, which I did via a card file, then cutting and pasting. It was hard to give it a sense of continuity in Rigoberta's own words. This is a far greater challenge than simply quoting someone as part of your own narrative. If I had wanted to do it as a professional publication, with my questions included, I could have done so, but this was not my objective."

After the manuscript was finished, Elisabeth gave a copy to Arturo Taracena, so that he could send it to Rigoberta's organization for a security check. When the manuscript returned, it came with a letter asking for the deletion of three passages, two of which now seem of little significance. The three concerned the participation of children in village self-defense, the relation between the January 31st Popular Front and guerrilla forces, and the Spanish ambassador's attribution of the embassy fire to the protesters. The reason for the last deletion, according to the letter, was that the ambassador's statements had been distorted by the government. Dated August 8, 1982, the letter was signed by a pseudonymous "Vicente." Because of personal references, Elisabeth knew (and has since confirmed) that this was the EGP's leader, Ricardo Ramírez, a friend since their days in Cuba.

What Elisabeth refused to remove were the epigraphs she had inserted under chapter breaks. This was an additional request by Arturo, who happened to be the nephew of Ricardo Ramírez's partner, Aura Marina Arriola. Arturo objected to the passages from the Bible that Elisabeth had chosen, but he was particularly opposed to six epigraphs from Guatemala's Nobel laureate for literature, the novelist Miguel Angel Asturias. His reasoning was that because Miguel Angel's son Rodrigo was the founder of a rival guerrilla army called the Organization of the People in Arms, the quotations would confuse knowledgeable readers into thinking that Rigoberta belonged to ORPA rather than her actual organization. Although the Canadian doctor who brought Rigoberta to Elisabeth's attention worked with ORPA, Arturo reported to the EGP.[11]

The person who brought Ramírez's letter and the corrected manuscript from Mexico to Paris was Rigoberta, whom the letter also authorized to participate in a documentary that appeared on French television the following year.[12] Unsure how the manuscript would turn out and reluctant to lose control over her efforts, Elisabeth did not contact publishing houses until after the manuscript was finished, around September 1982. Editorial Gallimard was the first to respond with a contract, which she signed. The book appeared the following year in Spanish, in 1984 in French and English (the two editions that have sold the most copies, with some 150,000 in English), then in German, Italian, Dutch, Japanese, Danish, Swedish, Norwegian, and Russian, plus a pirate edition in Arabic.

Rigoberta Breaks with Elisabeth

Never again did the two women experience the intimacy of that week in January 1982. Subsequent encounters were few. When Rigoberta passed through Paris in 1984, according to Elisabeth, she did not want to talk about the subject of Indians, to the point of turning down a copy of the *Popol Vuh* (roughly, the *Aeneid* of K'iche' literature) that Marie Tremblay offered her. On another brief visit to Paris, in 1985–1986, Rigoberta's attitude had changed again. "It seems that we Indians have to pay very dearly in order to learn," she said while walking to a meeting with Danielle Mitterrand, the first lady of France. Why? asked Elisabeth. "Because we've had to pay many dead."

"She was speaking very allegorically," Elisabeth remarked. "I could see that she was under pressure. After that first moment of openness, it could be seen that she was not free to speak. Since I had received news of executions within the EGP, I supposed that her lack of openness had to do with the internal divisions." Doubtless Rigoberta also felt uneasy about the dilemma into which the editor of her testimony had unwittingly led her. The story she told in 1982, the one that launched her career, had been told with the fervor of a convert. Now she was famous, but the fervor had passed, and words transformed into a book had defined her, apparently forever, as someone who she was not.[13]

In 1989 Elisabeth became director of the French Institute in Seville, Spain, removing her from the Paris crossroads where she was accustomed to interact with notables. This was also the year that she wrote a letter to Fidel Castro asking him to spare the life of General Arnaldo Ochoa, the hero of the Cuban expedition to Angola, who was suddenly arrested for drug trafficking and other crimes against the state, sentenced to death, and executed, all in the space of a month. Along with her ex-husband, Régis, who also tried to save Ochoa, Elisabeth had been friends with both the condemned man and Fidel. They did not believe that Ochoa had done anything without the knowledge of his chief, who apparently was liquidating a potential rival.

To the appeal for Ochoa's life Elisabeth attributes her subsequent exclusion from Rigoberta's campaign for the peace prize. For some readers, this will presume an overly centralized view of the relations between the Castro regime, the Guerrilla Army of the Poor (the Cuban favorite in the URNG), and solidarity committees in Europe—or at least surprising loyalty to Fidel in Rigoberta's support network. Invoking three decades of experience with the Latin American revolutionary movement, Elisabeth insists that this is why she became an outcast.[14]

There is doubtless a second reason why Elisabeth was excluded from the Nobel campaign, one that complements the first. It is evident in how Rigoberta answered a question in 1991, about her relationship with Elisabeth and how this affected the final text. After resisting the suggestion that the testimony is anything other than her own, Rigoberta acknowledges that "what is effectively a gap in the book is the question of the right of the author, right? Because the authorship of the book really should be more precise, shared, right?. . . . It's also the result of not knowing how to do a book. An author was needed, and she's an author."[15] Rigoberta's wish to claim authorship is also suggested by the curriculum vitae for the Nobel prize, which lists her as winner of the 1983 Casa de las Américas award in Cuba, when it actually went to Elisabeth as editor.

In any case, Elisabeth was never invited to any of the occasions associated with the Nobel. The absence was widely noted. Her only contribution was a new preface for the Spanish edition, as well as supportive commentaries in the press. The last meeting between the two women occurred a few months after the Nobel award, in February 1993. Rigoberta asked Elisabeth to sign over the author's rights, so that she could make her own contracts. "Before things were different," she explained. But according to Editions Gallimard, Rigoberta could not be given the rights because of the numerous contracts it had made around the world. Elisabeth also feared that her name might be deleted from new editions, just as she had been shut out of the Nobel campaign. Subsequently, Rigoberta complained to the book's publisher in Mexico, Siglo Veintiuno, that Elisabeth had stopped passing along her fifty percent share of the royalties. According to Elisabeth, she had always sent Rigoberta the full royalties (minus taxes) through an arrangement with Danielle Mitterrand and the Mitterrand Foundation.[16] Incensed by Rigoberta's accusations, she now stopped the remittances.

While I was in Madrid, Elisabeth dug a box of tape cassettes out of a closet. They were the recordings of Rigoberta's voice, from thirteen years before. Were it not for bad planning on my part, I could have listened to the entire sequence. Still, I was able to listen to the first two hours, and they left a powerful impression. From her first words, Rigoberta sounds in control. She speaks slowly, carefully, and clearly with a characteristic Mayan lilt, pausing while searching for words and never punctuating her elocution with "uh's" and "er's". She is very definitive: This happened when she was five, that happened when she was eight or twelve. She also sets up a style of telling her story that communicates effortlessly to outsiders, framed in broad categories such as "our culture" and "our people."

In the first two hours of tape, I heard little prompting from Elisabeth. Her opening question is simply: "Your life, how is the life of the indígenas?" Her only questions are to clarify details. Never does Elisabeth raise new subjects, change the direction of the interview, or prod a reluctant subject into continuing. As for Rigoberta, she begins with the famous opening lines of the published text: how this is not just her life but the life of all poor Guatemalans; how she grew up without school, on the fincas of the coast, where she worked up to eight months a year. From the start of the session, Rigoberta is creating a persona for herself as a Guatemalan everywoman, with little prompting from her interviewer. Upon hearing my findings, such as the likelihood that Rigoberta never worked on fincas as a child, Elisabeth recalled how convincingly her interlocutor detailed life there, such as how you have to pick the berries off a coffee tree ("like caring for a wounded person").[17] No, Elisabeth told me, she never doubted Rigoberta's story. After listening to the first two hours, I could understand why. Rigoberta was utterly convincing. Under the spell of that calm voice, I, too, would have believed everything she said.[18]

14

Rigoberta's Secret

I'm still keeping secret what I think no-one should know. Not even anthropologists or intellectuals, no matter how many books they have, can find out all our secrets.

—*I, Rigoberta Menchú*, p. 247

In her 1982 story, Rigoberta reiterates that she is not telling her listener everything. The secrets she refers to are ancestral ones, of the kind passed from elders to the young.[1] Literary scholars have made much of these passages, to suggest the irreducibility of *I, Rigoberta Menchú* to Western forms of knowledge.[2] Once the book is compared to other versions of events, another secret becomes all too obvious: its tangential relationship to her life, family, and village. This brings us back to key questions: Why would Rigoberta deny the schooling that was so central to her experience? And why would she transform not just her own experience, but Chimel's?

When I told colleagues about the discrepancies between Rigoberta's account and others, they reminded me that memory is always selective. Just because a story about the past is partial does not mean that it is false. Yet the selectivity of memory does not explain Rigoberta's omission of boarding school. She could not have forgotten how she spent years of her life. Nor does it explain eyewitness accounts of events that Rigoberta could not have witnessed, like the death of her brother at Chajul, or the invention of events that never happened, like Chimel organizing for self-defense during a period when her father was working with the U.S. Peace Corps.

Some scholars are quick to excuse Rigoberta from accountability on the grounds that she is from a non-Western culture, therefore must operate on a different truth standard. Obviously, no one should expect her to attain sociological detachment. But it is a mistake to assume that epistemic validity matters only in the Western tradition, as the anthropologist Michel-Rolph Trouillot has pointed out.[3] Mayan peasants often distinguish between what they know with confidence and what they have only heard is true. *No me consta,* or "I'm not sure," punctuated their conversations with me, as did the cautious *lo que dicen,* or "what people say."

Rigoberta's testimony is also defended on the basis of "collective memory"—the idea that since she is speaking for her people, it is not very important whether the experiences she describes actually happened to her, or whether they happened exactly the way she says, because they represent the collective experience of the Mayas. This argument is not without a certain validity: Even if the young Rigoberta did not watch her siblings die on a plantation, other Mayan children have. Therefore, her story may be true in a poetic sense. But the idea of collective memory dodges an important question: What parts of her testimony might not be so collective, reflecting a perspective at odds with many of her people?

Still another argument in Rigoberta's defense is that like anyone in that position, she was traumatized and obsessed by the sudden loss of her family. The breathtaking stories about how her brother was burned and her mother tortured, the degradation of bodies and the scattering of remains, have a dreamlike, feverish quality.[4] These are nightmares on multiple levels: in what the victims themselves must have experienced, in how Rigoberta imagined their deaths, and in how she retold them for her listener in Paris, breaking down and sobbing.

Under night-and-fog regimes, the cruelty that cuts deepest is the unknowability of what happens to loved ones who suddenly disappear. Aside from the shock of the loss, there are no remains to be mourned, not even a place where death can be memorialized, let alone an explanation of their fate.[5] Hence the determination of survivor associations, like the Mothers of the Plaza de Mayo in Argentina, to pry out of the authorities any gruesome fact about the fate of their relatives. Now that her mother and brother had gone to unknown graves, Rigoberta was using the slender data at her command to reclaim them in the only way she could, by visualizing their deaths in horrible detail.

Since *I, Rigoberta Menchú* is a story about a girl coming of age, there is a constructive dimension to these stories. The literary scholar John Beverley has suggested that the book can be read "as an Oedipal bildungsroman built around the working-through of an Electra complex: an initial rejection of the Mother and motherhood in favor of an Athena-like identification with the Father, Vicente, the campesino organizer; but then also an authority struggle with the Father, who does not want his daughter to leave home and become educated; then the death of the Father at the hands of the repressive apparatus of the state, which leads to a possibility of identification with the Mother, now seen as an organizer in her own right . . . ; then the death of the Mother, again at the hands of the state; finally, in the act of narrating the testimonio itself, the emergence of Menchú as a full speaking subject, an organizer and leader in her own right."[6]

Without recurring to Freud, it can be said that Rigoberta was responding to the loss of her family by taking refuge in a new system of coherence.[7] Having escaped to Mexico in fear for her life, out of touch with family and friends, she would have been in need not just of a new community, but of a structure of credibility that could encompass far more violence and contradiction than her previous frames of reference in Chimel, Uspantán, and boarding school. Evidence for this appears throughout *I, Rigoberta Menchú,* as she juxtaposes the securities of childhood with the violence consuming her family and community. The bridge from her cloistered school years to a new system of coherence was her new home in Mexico, with Monsignor Ruiz and the Catholic diocese of Chiapas in 1980–1981. Giving consciousness-raising talks in Catholic schools would have been a confidence-building step for Rigoberta. It was a Catholic context but, unlike boarding school in Guatemala, allowed her to express herself politically by turning her life into a story of oppression, education, and awareness.

Once Rigoberta was in the political apparatus of the Guerrilla Army of the Poor, there could be a pragmatic reason for denying her education: to protect the clergy who smuggled her to safety. However divided her feelings about the Catholic Church, she had been saved by an almost defenseless order of nuns, who were struggling to protect their students from persecution that could turn into a holocaust. To acknowledge the nuns, while on tour for the revolutionary movement, could encourage reprisals or expose their methods for helping people like herself. Perhaps it was advice to be discreet about this part of her life that blossomed into denial of her entire school career. But that does not explain the vigor of Rigoberta's denials, her insistence that she was a monolingual, illiterate peasant until joining the revolutionary movement. Nor why the Chimel of her story ended up looking so different from the village recalled by other survivors.

The consciousness-raising that looms so large in *I, Rigoberta Menchú* provides part of the answer. The very idea of "raising" consciousness is wielded by a movement dissatisfied with the prevailing level of insight. Scholars have long debated whether peasants are ideologically committed to the insurgencies that sweep them up. They might instead be opportunistic, coerced, or desperate—with some in each of the four camps. In Guatemala the most obvious feature of survivor testimony is not ideological conversion. Instead it is terror, especially but not exclusively of the army. Although some peasants acknowledge being attracted to the revolutionary vision, their moment of decision usually follows the onset of army retaliation. They face a grim choice between surrendering to army killers, escaping to coastal plantations, or casting their lot with the insurgency, if only by staying in a village over which the guerrillas are asserting control.

That numerous peasants did not join the guerrillas, and that many who did soon repented, suggests that revolutionary consciousness was usually only a passing phenomenon. If so, had their consciousness been "raised"? For anyone who thinks armed struggle was a mistake—including most peasants and, recently, Rigoberta herself—this is open to question. Instead, what peasants usually say is that they were *engañado* (deceived) by false promises of liberation. Of those who did adopt revolutionary ideology, it would be more accurate to say that they converted to a movement that subsequently disillusioned them.[8]

In Rigoberta's case, the relative safety of exile allowed her to cultivate a revolutionary consciousness into the next decade. She had converted to a movement within which the world looked rather different than before. This included her past life in Chimel, which she now had to reinterpret in order to account for the sudden eruption of violence. But there was a problem. Once she and her mentors decided that her assignment would be to tell the story of her people, Rigoberta faced the disadvantage of coming from an area that (like many others) did not fit the EGP's analysis of the problems facing peasants.

What would her testimony have looked like without a significant amount of reinvention? It would go something like this: Government death squads are on the rampage in some parts of Guatemala, but not in others. One day, a guerrilla column shows up in a village whose most serious conflict is with other peasants. Shortly thereafter, the guerrillas introduce political assassination to the area, which prompts the army to start kidnapping peasants. When relatives go to Guatemala City to protest, fifteen die in the conflagration at the Spanish embassy. Back home, the army kidnaps more villagers. One young woman, who has lost three members of her family while away at boarding school, flees to Mexico. There she joins the revolutionary movement, returns to Guatemala as an organizer, and starts telling her story to the world.

This would have been a fascinating story, but not a very useful one for the Guerrilla Army of the Poor. A frank account of Chimel would have presented an uninspiring picture of peasants feuding with each other. The worst conflicts would have been between K'iche' villagers, not between K'iche's and ladino planters. Finca owners could not have been scapegoated for land conflicts as dramatically as Rigoberta did. Although occasionally a nuisance, they would not have been a threat until two of them were murdered by the EGP.

Rigoberta's mentors probably advised her to broaden her story, to make it more typical of the oppression of Guatemalan peasants. Even without instructions, however, the discrepancies between EGP teachings and her own circumstances could encourage a neophyte to omit inconvenient features of her life and add others. According to the sociolinguist Charlotte Linde, anyone put to the task of telling a life story struggles to maintain coherence principles of causality and continuity. That is, tellers of life stories tend to downplay the incoherence, accident, discontinuity, and doubt that characterize actual lived experience, because these detract from the sense of purpose and agency that audiences expect narrators to demonstrate.[9] In Rigoberta's case, she achieved coherence by omitting features of the situation that contradicted the ideology of her new organization, then substituting appropriate revolutionary themes. Since she was very new to the movement, during a period in which it seemed to offer a solution to Guatemala's crisis, there is no need to question her good intentions. All she had to believe was that revolutionary portrayals of the oppression of campesinos were more typical than the experience of her own land-wealthy village, a lesson that would have been underlined by the sudden, shocking manhunt of her family.

Let us go through a few of Rigoberta's substitutions and the ideological issues behind them. To include the conflict with the Tums would bring up the internecine disputes that absorb so much of the political energy of subordinate groups. It would contradict the vision of virtuous peasants rising up against their true class enemies. How more appropriate, then, to attribute all the boundary problems to ladino planters.[10] Although not to blame around Chimel, they were in other places.

The North Americans who worked with Chimel on development projects were another problem. Not without reason, the EGP viewed Peace Corps volunteers as part of a U.S. strategy to forestall rural protest. It dismissed their efforts as palliatives that could never improve the lives of peasants and diverted their attention from the social roots of oppression. If Rigoberta had included the Peace Corps volunteers in her story, she would have faced an unpalatable choice between (1) acknowledging her father's interest in development projects and (2) belittling esteemed foreigners with whom her father and brothers had worked closely. It was easiest not to mention them at all. What she substituted for the farm projects so appreciated by her father and brothers were the insurrectionary plans of a political-military organization. Once her parents had been murdered, armed struggle would have seemed more to the point than growing bigger vegetables.

The EGP's role in setting off political violence was the central problem, as it had been for her father. If Rigoberta acknowledged the execution of the two ladinos, it would become apparent that the bloodshed had been precipitated by the EGP's decision to turn her area into a battleground. Since a strategy to spread the war into peaceful areas could not be acknowledged, it was more convenient to attribute the persecution of her village to its struggle for land, the inevitable conflict that the guerrilla movement adduced as its raison d'être. Once again, for a traumatized survivor like Rigoberta, the appeal of revolutionary payback would tend to suppress doubts about the EGP.

Finally, there was the problem of boarding school. If Rigoberta had acknowledged this fact about her life, she could not claim to be an eyewitness to the revolutionary movement's version of history. It would detract from her claim to authority. It would be harder to dramatize experiences such as plantation labor that, according to the revolutionary movement, were more typical of her people than her own slightly privileged existence as a scholarship girl. Away at boarding school, she could not have provided irrefutable testimony of how her family and village became peasant revolutionaries of the kind envisioned by the EGP.

The Claim to Be Authentic

> *The stage in which superior virtue is attributed to the oppressed is transient and unstable. It begins only when the oppressors come to have a bad conscience, and this only happens when their power is no longer secure. . . . Sooner or later the oppressed class will argue that its superior virtue is a reason in favor of its having power, and the oppressors will find their own weapons turned against them. When at last power has been equalized, it becomes apparent to everybody that all the talk about superior virtue was nonsense, and that it was quite unnecessary as a basis for the claim to equality.*
>
> **—Bertrand Russell, "The Superior Virtue of the Oppressed"[11]**

Let us review why, under the influence of revolutionary thinking, Rigoberta would reinvent herself so dramatically. To acknowledge the role of the Catholic clergy in smuggling her to safety could have endangered them. As for the vivid imagining of the deaths of her mother and brother, this is an understandable response to having your loved ones dragged away by torturers, never to be seen again. Chimel had to be reinvented to make it fit the ideological needs of the EGP. Ladinos had to be blamed for setting off the violence locally so that it would not be the fault of her new organization. A frank account of how the violence had begun would contradict the revolutionary maxim that the insurgency developed inevitably out of the oppression of her people—a maxim in which a revolutionary convert undoubtedly believed.

The constraints under which Rigoberta told her story are underlined by the fact that, two years before, her father was resorting to some of the same narrative strategies. As we saw in Chapter 8, just before Vicente died, he omitted any reference to the EGP's assassination of two neighbors and blamed ladinos for trying to expropriate Chimel. This left responsibility for the violence exclusively at the door of finca owners and the Guatemalan army. How Rigoberta came to echo her father's narrative is not a question I can answer at present: Perhaps it came from a final encounter with him. Perhaps she listened to a tape of one of his last declarations. Perhaps they received the same orientation from the revolutionary apparatus. Or perhaps they echoed each other because indígenas are tempted to blame ladinos for their problems, just like ladinos are tempted to blame indígenas.

Until Rigoberta addresses the subject, we can only guess to what extent she was censoring inconvenient information as opposed to being caught up in the misinformation in which revolutionary movements envelop themselves. She was quite aware of her father's long struggle with her mother's family. She also must have known that the EGP had executed Honorio García and Eliu Martínez. But once her father blamed ladino interlopers for the kidnapping of Petrocinio, it would be hard not to believe him. The fact that her father had been on friendly terms with Honorio García would seem only a small detail.

None of this explains why Rigoberta was so determined to present herself as monolingual and illiterate before she joined the revolutionary movement. It was not required by the ghost of her father, who valued education sufficiently to commit a daughter to it. Nor was it necessarily required by the EGP, which subjected its recruits to literacy training. Another possibility, suggested by her heavily romanticized portrait of indigenous life, is that she was playing to Western images of the noble savage. It is not true that solidarity activists require their Indians to be barefoot and illiterate. But it is not hard to find people in the left and on the fringes of anthropology who disparage Indians wearing a tie as inauthentic. A decade later, Rigoberta still complained about this kind of racism. Doubtless it cut deeply for a peasant girl who was away at school when her family was hunted down, who had learned that indígenas were deprecated on many levels, and who by 1982 had learned that indígenas could be deprecated in the revolutionary movement, too.

If Rigoberta's denial of Spanish and literacy was a preemptive defense of her authenticity, brought on by racist assumptions she was encountering, then the obsessive quality of these denials suggests that she was not just doing it for her listeners. She also could have been doing it for herself. The noble savage was invented by Europeans, but it has been taken to heart by many an indigenous intellectual seeking to join the wider world on equal terms. Rigoberta would be far from the first Indian who went off to school and the city, who collided with discrimination, and who responded by idealizing her origin as a Rousseauian idyll. It takes time to learn that claims to innocence only encourage paternalism.

Rigoberta Becomes a Symbolic Substitute

It is EGP's ideology and EGP's version of Guatemala's recent history . . . which lie at the bottom of what Rigoberta recounts. When Rigoberta's life and the Menchú's social mobility don't fit with the "correct" image of what it's like to be an Indian in Guatemala, Rigoberta takes it upon herself to rectify her own life. . . . The terrain is continually adjusted so it fits the map.

—Henrik Hovland, 1995[12]

When Rigoberta told her story to Elisabeth Burgos in January 1982, the revolutionary movement had yet to be defeated. That the Lucas García regime was slaughtering peasants was clear enough. But foreign sympathizers presumed that the bloodshed would stir greater uprisings in the future. Within the Guerrilla Army of the Poor, any comprehension of the steady destruction of its support networks was submerged in the confident rhetoric that it maintained into the mid-1980s. Until this point, the war had been prosecuted separately by the EGP, the Organization of the People in Arms (ORPA), the Rebel Armed Forces (FAR), and the Guatemalan Labor Party (PGT). Having broken away from each other in the 1960s, they were too competitive to work together and suffered from their own internal splits, particularly in the case of the EGP. By the end of 1981, the situation was sufficiently desperate to bring the four groups together in the Guatemalan National Revolutionary Union (URNG).

Meanwhile, the EGP's January 31st Popular Front (FP-31), to which Rigoberta belonged, overcame its differences with the more moderate Democratic Front Against Repression (FDCR), to form a new coalition called the Guatemalan Committee for Patriotic Unity (CGUP). Headed by national figures like writer Luis Cardoza y Aragón, it was supposed to appeal to a broader constituency. "Through this bridge," an activist explained, "[the revolutionary movement] can better capture the support of the Guatemalan masses, which at the moment are stirred by the motivations of their own social sector more than for revolutionary reasons. Through this bridge, it can also find more solidarity outside Guatemala."[13] Among the persons whom the URNG invited to join CGUP in February 1982 was Rigoberta. If she had not been a public figure before her trip to Europe and the epic interview, she was now. At a conference of revolutionary Christians in Nicaragua, including the organization named after her father, Rigoberta was considered an important participant even though she had to absent herself from the sessions.[14]

In May 1982 she went to the United States for the first time. The people she impressed were not from the general public (to whom she had little access) but much smaller audiences, who were already preoccupied with

Guatemala and struggling to communicate a horrendous situation to the North American public. "I remember being stunned with her personal poise and precise description of what it meant to be a Mayan woman in Guatemala," wrote a Protestant missionary. "Not in thirteen years had I heard anyone talk like this inside Guatemala. She spoke less like a victim and more like a prophet, less like an ideologue and more like an eye witness."[15] Besides conducting workshops for solidarity committees, Rigoberta lobbied the U.S. Congress and State Department.[16]

Over the next few years, all but one of the organizations and networks that Rigoberta had joined during her first two years in the movement lapsed into silence. The Democratic Front Against Repression and the January 31st Popular Front were unable to work together, with the social democratic FDCR accusing the insurgency-oriented FP-31 of trying to "monopolize the shaping of a future unified mass front."[17] As military regimes suppressed what remained of the left, both networks disappeared without announcement, as did the CGUP and the organization named after Rigoberta's father, the Vicente Menchú Revolutionary Christians.

Of Rigoberta's first revolutionary affiliations, the only one to survive was the Committee for Campesino Unity, and only in exile. With the few surviving founders either quitting the movement or retreating into anonymity, Rigoberta became its most widely known leader. This was particularly so after a split from the Guerrilla Army of the Poor in 1984 led by Mario Payeras, who called for a less authoritarian and militaristic approach, including acknowledgment of the defeat two years before. He and the exiles in Mexico who joined him, in a new group called Revolutionary October, abandoned armed struggle.[18] Among the indigenous militants who left with Payeras was Domingo Hernández Ixcoy, the CUC founder whom we met in Chapters 6 and 7. But not Rigoberta.

One reason she stayed with the EGP was surely that, during this same period, she became crucial to its survival. Because of the tremendous reception for her story, it acquired a function that would not have been apparent when she first told it, before the revolutionary movement was shattered. Aside from Rigoberta's ability to transfix foreigners, she was the daughter of one of the protesters who died at the Spanish embassy. She could speak in the name of her father and the other martyrs, articulately and heartrendingly. As a survivor capable of projecting herself to audiences, she could make her father a powerful symbol to idealize the dead and demonstrate that the struggle continued. Now that guerrilla miscalculations and army repression had destroyed the popular movement, now that most peasants had been alienated from the left, Rigoberta could become a symbolic substitute for them. She could help guerrilla leaders survive the harsh reality that, at home in Guatemala, all they had left were isolated pockets of fighters and refugees.

Here was moral authority, in astonishing amount, which guerrilla leaders needed badly on two fronts. One was to face their own ranks, to keep hope alive and show that tens of thousands of people had not died in vain. The other was abroad, to keep their shrunken columns from being dismissed as irrelevant. Internationally as well as within the revolutionary movement, Rigoberta could substitute for its broken connection to Mayan peasants. Her story could rhetorically erase the difference between a revolutionary leadership in exile and peasants struggling to keep their families alive in wrecked villages. She could speak for a mythologized version of her father, who himself was supposed to represent a revolutionized peasantry, and provide a symbolic substitute for the many indígenas who no longer supported the guerrilla movement, if they ever did. A young woman's claim to have experienced what she had not experienced became the guerrilla movement's claim to speak for Indians.

That Rigoberta reinvented her family to personify EGP ideology will, for some readers, be a damning indictment. To conservatives this was instantly apparent, enabling them to dismiss *I, Rigoberta Menchú* as a tall tale by a gullible young woman being manipulated by Marxist ideologues. However, even the scornful must acknowledge that in the face of an army on the rampage, Rigoberta did not have many choices. She could not, for example, return to Guatemala to seek justice through the legal system. If she wanted to avenge her family, the revolutionary movement was the only option.

In hindsight, Rigoberta could have given her testimony in other ways, such as splicing the stories of other people into her own without eliding their separate identities. She could have recurred to how campesinos customarily report stories they have heard: *dicen que*, or "they say that." But as I discovered in my own attempts to describe the violence, the narrative load of chronologizing what the army did, the numbing repetition of one murder after another, quickly becomes demoralizing. As Sheldon Annis remarked in his chronicle of what befell a Kaqchikel Maya town: "A friend who is a novelist read this account and commented: 'It could not be fiction; there are too many deaths. The plot is too thin to support that many people dying.'"[19]

Among those pondering why Rigoberta told her story the way she did is Elisabeth Burgos. Recently she has edited a second oral testimony, of a survivor of Che Guevara's last guerrilla column named Benigno. Of both experiences, Elisabeth writes, "The person feels carried away by her voice, her memory, and above all her capacity to improvise. She imagines, but in a true manner, on the basis of events that have happened, such that what is imagined has a real dimension. In both [Rigoberta and Benigno], I have become aware that they relate, as their own experiences, what they could not have witnessed directly, what instead happened in proximity to their own histories. It is not that they act in bad faith, nor that they lie. Instead, they are moved by a feeling of belonging. This feeling of belonging, of identifying with peoples, occurs when they feel empowered to elaborate their own version of history. . . . It is not the same as reflecting on the basis of writing. The act of telling a story orally requires recreating what happened through images, it requires setting a stage, like a theater director would, and requires what theater does—to demonstrate. Rigoberta's objective with her testimony was to demonstrate, to shake public opinion to the maximum to win support, and that she has accomplished."[20]

One way to hold an audience is to develop an epic structure around a few exemplary figures—heroes, victims, and villains—who concentrate the experiences of an entire people. Another way to hold an audience is to be an eyewitness. Far more credibility accrues to a person who can claim firsthand experience than one who cannot. The testimonial genre derives its moral authority from this, and it is a lesson Rigoberta may have learned from her first exchanges with the Chiapas diocese and the EGP. Perhaps another exile pointed out that life in boarding school and hearsay about her family would not entrance an audience. Even without that kind of advice, the very situation in which Rigoberta found herself—as a powerless refugee who had to ask for help, answer questions, impress benefactors, and compete against other refugees for attention—could have encouraged her to escalate her claims on listeners.

Suggestive in this regard is the earliest interview with Rigoberta that I have been able to find, perhaps the first ever recorded, by the journalist Alaíde Foppa in Mexico City in December 1980. Just weeks before, Rigoberta had been reunited with the younger sisters who may have been her introduction to revolutionary activism. Alaíde was the mother of three EGP combatants and, like Elisabeth Burgos, an EGP collaborator herself; this was her last radio interview before she returned to Guatemala and was kidnapped. What is most striking about the available transcript is the amount of prompting she does. After introducing "Guadalupe" and two younger girls aged fifteen and thirteen as members of "the organization that brings together the mass of the *pueblo campesino*, the CUC," she refers to the labor strikes on the Pacific coast and asks, "How much did you [the plural "you all"] earn before, Guadalupe?" To which Guadalupe replies in the first-person plural: "We were earning a quetzal, or seventy centavos." From the first question, in other words, Rigoberta is being asked to describe experiences that she never had herself.[21]

In her stories for Elisabeth a year later, Rigoberta sometimes acknowledges the strategy of incorporating the experiences of others into her own. She recounts an action by comrades starting out with "they," showing that she was not physically present, then switches to "we," because of her affinity to those on hand.[22] This is the "we" of a popular organizer encouraging her audience to think of themselves as a group with a shared history of oppression. It is just as legitimate as immigrants adopting U.S. history as their own and identifying themselves as Americans. On other occasions, by concealing the distinction between herself and other indígenas, Rigoberta claims personal experiences that she never had. The result is to inflate herself into a hyperrepresentative figure or everywoman—that is, the completely unrealistic figure of a representative Indian.

Rigoberta's approach is easy to criticize, but a detached account on the order of this one could never be expected. A critical theorist can write a book about epistemic murk and the ambiguity of terror. An investigator like myself can try to reconstruct what probably happened by weighing different sources. Rigoberta filled the void by putting the stories she had heard into the first person. In her defense, it can be said that she felt the responsibility to represent as many of her people as she could, and that she chose to do so in the most convincing manner she knew how. This is what Mayan readers have told me, despite their awareness of the book's shortcomings. "There are many things that she took as her own that happened to the people," an old friend in Uspantán explained. "What happened to the people she wrote as if it was personal, as if it happened to her. . . . She speaks of the reality. She speaks of real things, of the massacres, of the tortures. I suppose that if they give her the [Nobel] prize, she will not take it for herself, as if she were the great queen, but for her people."

Even before publication, in early 1983 *I, Rigoberta Menchú* won a literary award from the Casa de las Américas in Havana. If the book had not served the needs of the Guerrilla Army of the Poor, it never would have received the promotion. But if we credit Elisabeth Burgos's account of how the book came to be, as the unplanned outcome of a magazine interview, it was not conceived by the organization that controlled Rigoberta's movements. The representatives that the EGP sent on solidarity tours were usually better at hewing to the party line than engaging their audiences. The orientation that Rigoberta received from her organization cannot explain a narrative performance that none of its other representatives have ever come near. Even if Rigoberta took to revolutionary ideology with the fervor of a new disciple and learned to tell her story within certain parameters, no one could have programmed the story that she told. Instead, it came out of the encounter between a young woman determined to narrate the suffering of her people and an anthropologist trained to listen. What resulted was an explosion of memory and imagination, in a young woman who had lost most of her family, who had found a new home in the revolutionary movement, and who was determined to fight back.

PART FOUR

The Laureate Goes Home

15

The Campaign for the Nobel

The fact that she lives in exile and denounces abuses has given her a symbolic role in the country's democratization, which has been reflected every time she comes back.

—Santiago Bastos and Manuela Camus, 1993[1]

Following the debacle of the early 1980s, what remained of the revolutionary leadership was in exile. Aside from a few politically isolated guerrilla columns, the Guatemalan National Revolutionary Union (URNG) had little with which to fight except the imagery of the dead, who achieved more immediate results with foreign audiences than at home. Army massacres might have destroyed the guerrilla movement's credibility with peasants, but the same massacres had the paradoxical effect of building its credibility abroad. For whoever could step into the role of denouncing the army, there was moral authority, including moral authority for an insurgency that claimed to represent the victims. When the situation was viewed from a distance, their blood exculpated the guerrilla organizations that had done so much to cause it to be shed.

The URNG comandantes were not about to admit that they had been defeated. But after Guatemala's return to civilian rule in 1986, they realized their only hope lay in negotiation, and the battle for that would have to be waged in the international arena. Since the army saw no reason to bargain with such a weak opponent, the URNG needed support from abroad to make up for the lack of it at home. There lay the importance of Rigoberta's story, which could be used to translate a dead revolution into a peasant movement, guerrilla warfare into agitation for human rights, and defeat at home into diplomatic backing abroad.

Over the next decade, these translations also required the future Nobel laureate to transform herself from a revolutionary into an indigenous human rights activist. She distanced herself from the insurgency and dismissed challenges that she was connected to it as red-baiting.[2] But she never repudiated the affiliations declared in her book, and her international work developed in tandem with the guerrilla movement's needs. In early 1983, according to an indigenous publication, she was "one of the 4-person delegation of Guatemala from the URNG . . . attending the six-week session of the United Nations Commission on Human Rights in Geneva."[3] A Nebaj ex-combatant remembered her speaking to an EGP training camp in 1984, in the Ixcán near the Mexican border. "Don't lose heart in the struggle against the army," he recalled her saying. "For my part, I'm working internationally, doing what can be done to obtain resources for all the fighters and refugees."

The international arena was indeed where Rigoberta's work lay, but raising funds for armed struggle was probably not her assignment, or at least the main one. Instead, it was to appeal to indigenous organizations and their white supporters. The indigenous movement might seem a natural constituency for the guerrillas, but it was anything but that. Back home, relations with Mayan associations had never been warm. Ideologically, two of the four organizations in the Guatemalan National Revolutionary Union—the Rebel Armed Forces (FAR) and the Guatemalan Labor Party (PGT)—had little room for ethnic demands. The EGP and the Organization of the People in Arms (ORPA) did. But although a large majority of their fighters came to be indígenas, their leadership continued to be completely ladino above the level of the columns. Specifically Mayan organizations they distrusted, and the feelings were reciprocated. Mayan activists were usually not enthusiastic about guerrilla warfare.[4] When EGP and ORPA dissidents articulated Mayan nationalism and organized their own guerrilla group, called Ixim, they were put down with bloodshed.[5]

But after 1982 a defeated leadership was desperate for international connections, including indigenous ones. Fortunately for Rigoberta, beyond Guatemala the history of conflict with Mayan activists was unknown. With *I, Rigoberta Menchú* depicting Mayan culture as a basis for revolutionary struggle, she became a professional balancer of ethnic and class perspectives. Indigenous rights complemented her main issue of human rights, always targeted against the plentiful abuses of the Guatemalan army. Though not explicitly promoting the guerrilla movement, she never criticized it.

As the Vicente Menchú Revolutionary Christians and FP-31 faded away, Rigoberta presented herself as a member of the Committee for Campesino Unity (CUC) and the United Representation of the Guatemalan Opposition (RUOG). The new group was started by exiles supporting the URNG, including Rigoberta, in September 1982 to denounce human rights violations and lobby for international sanctions.[6] For Rigoberta's indigenous work, one of the warmest receptions was at the International Indian Treaty Council, a diplomatic offshoot of the American Indian Movement that led the 1973 occupation of Wounded

Knee. The Treaty Council helped Rigoberta lobby the United Nations, and in 1986 she joined its board of directors. Under its auspices as well as RUOG, she became a figure at the UN's conferences for nongovernmental organizations (NGOs).

The NGO conferences are held in Geneva for a rainbow of groups—indigenous, feminist, ecological, human rights—that do not feel represented by governments. The resolutions they obtain usually cannot be enforced. But they return every year with commendable determination, to press issues that the United Nations would otherwise ignore. If the annual distress expressed by the Guatemalan government over UN resolutions is any indication, there is a point to all the lobbying, report writing, and speech making. Via the innumerable conferences worked by Rigoberta and her confederates, international pressure eventually obliged the Guatemalan army to negotiate with the guerrillas and accept UN observers throughout the country.

Four years after Rigoberta told her story in Paris, Guatemala returned to constitutional government. But the first three civilian administrations—of Vinicio Cerezo (1986–1991), Jorge Serrano Elías (1991–1993), and Ramiro De Leon Carpio (1993–1996)—were clearly dominated by the army. Each was plagued by dissension in the officer corps. Although army politics is byzantine, it would appear that institutionalists, who wished to maintain constitutional rule, were periodically confronted by ultramontanists who resented any curb on their license to kill and plotted coups to prove it. The atmosphere was so conspiratorial that the differences between the two tendencies sometimes seemed more imagined than real. In the view of many observers, institutionalists could be using the ultras and their seditious activities to extract concessions from the presidential palace, in coup attempts that were staged by both.

This was the threatening milieu in which Rigoberta returned to Guatemala in April 1988, aboveground for the first time since her escape eight years before. On arrival at the airport, as part of a RUOG delegation trying to set up peace talks, she was arrested. According to the government, her leadership role in CUC made her part of the EGP, which meant that she would have to apply for amnesty. She and a companion were held for eight hours, until street protests and diplomatic intervention (to the level of the president of France) obtained her release.

A year later, in February 1989, Rigoberta and her colleagues returned, this time to join a national dialogue sponsored by the Catholic Church. With the URNG barred, all the weight of representing the revolutionary movement fell on the RUOG delegates, who were soon receiving death threats, including a bouquet with an invitation to their funerals and a car bomb left outside their house. Just before the car bomb, Rigoberta left for Italy to speak to the Socialist Party there. The Italians knew how to deal with the problem. First, they gave Rigoberta a diplomatic seat in the Italian parliament, until such time as she could take her place safely in the Guatemalan one. Second, they started a campaign to give her the Nobel Peace Prize.[7]

Soon Rigoberta was nominated by Adolfo Pérez Esquivel, the Argentine peace laureate. Over the next few years, the winners were the Dalai Lama of Tibet, Mikhail Gorbachev of the Soviet Union, and Aung San Suu Kyi of Burma. Since there is quite a waiting list for the prize—more than a hundred candidates are put forward every year—many are nominated more than once. In Rigoberta's case, the South African laureate Bishop Desmond Tutu joined Pérez Esquivel in nominating her for the 1992 prize. Her candidacy began to pick up momentum for its resonance with the five hundredth anniversary of the colonization of the Americas.

The Popular Organizations Versus the Pan-Mayan Movement

The Nobel campaign began abroad for foreign audiences, but its ultimate target was Guatemalan society. For years, Rigoberta had been presented internationally as an Indian leader, but at home she was largely unknown to the people she was supposed to represent. Now the Nobel campaign would present indígenas with a new kind of hero, giving Rigoberta and the URNG a chance to build up their constituency. An aboveground left had started to reemerge in the mid-1980s, but it was more cautious than the movement destroyed at the start of the decade. Of the five organizations in the January 31st Popular Front, only the Committee for Campesino Unity still existed. No longer did it call itself a "revolutionary mass organization." Now it was a "popular organization" that did not acknowledge its ties with the EGP and was able to open an office in Guatemala City.

During CUC's brief apogee, it had become enshrined in revolutionary mythology, but a new generation of organizations was surpassing it. The leaders tended to be survivors of the earlier popular movement. How independent they were of the URNG was a subject of endless debate. The first to make waves was the Mutual Support Group (GAM), of relatives of people who had been kidnapped by the security forces. "Alive they took them, alive we want them back!" chanted GAM demonstrators, echoing the Mothers of the Plaza de Mayo in Argentina. In 1985 two of the group's founders were themselves tortured to death; ten years later the surviving founder, Nineth Montenegro, the widow of a union leader and guerrilla cadre kidnapped by the security forces, was elected to congress.[8]

Another new organization that earned a heroic reputation was the Runujel Junam Council of Ethnic Communities (CERJ). It used the new constitution to fight the army's conscription of peasants into the civil patrols. Over two years, twenty-six members were murdered or disappeared.[9] Although an indigenous organization, CERJ was founded by a ladino schoolteacher named Amilcar Méndez, who seemed to hold the national record for receiving death threats but also survived to be elected to congress in 1995.

A third new organization was the National Coordinator of Guatemalan Widows (CONAVIGUA). Like CERJ, it started in southern Quiché in 1988 and organized local chapters in municipios that were still under the army's thumb. Widows were not easy to organize. Many were dependent on handouts, therefore vulnerable to the crudest forms of coercion. Many were also under the eye of neighbors who blamed their dead husbands for being guerrillas. But CONAVIGUA was able to use relief projects to organize widows for various objectives, including a successful campaign against the army's roundups of indigenous boys for the barracks. When the government revealed that CONAVIGUA leader Rosalina Tuyuc had a brother who was an EGP commander, it did not prevent her from being elected to congress as well.

Except for Amilcar Méndez, the best-known leaders of the popular movement—Nineth, Rosalina, and Rigoberta—were women whose husband or father died in the violence. If CERJ was predominantly male, GAM and CONAVIGUA consisted mainly of women, and women often played the leading role in rural organizing, one reason being that they were less likely to be killed. Instead of propagandizing directly for the URNG, which would have frightened away many of their constituents, the new organizations focused on the army's human rights violations. Although they had little presence in many municipios, in others they obviously did, despite the army's warnings against them.

Pan-Mayan organizations were also undergoing a renaissance. Before the war, they had been strongest in the central belt of the highlands running along the Pan-American Highway from Chimaltenango to Quezaltenango. There an indigenous-controlled regional economy of petty commerce, artisan production, and small manufacture had produced an indigenous bourgeoisie. Cultural and political equality were the next items on the agenda. Prewar Mayan organizations had not been repressed as severely as CUC and the class-oriented left, but most disbanded during a period in which any activity could attract government killers. By the early 1990s, enough confidence had returned to launch new efforts, and international funders were eager to sponsor them. Hundreds of new Mayan organizations popped up, with a critical attitude toward the guerrilla movement as well as the state.

To underline the novelty of this development, I should reiterate that the term "Maya" is almost missing from the published text of *I, Rigoberta*

Menchú: My computer search came up with just three references, two of which are in the editor's introduction. Rigoberta's only use of the term is in reference to old musical instruments.[10] For her Ixil neighbors, until recently Mayas were an ancient, magical race who lived in caves and could be distinguished from ordinary humans by their six fingers and six toes. The majority of indígenas still identify themselves in terms of their village or municipio, or as speakers of a particular language, and only then as Mayas if at all. In the media only since the early 1990s has reference to indígenas as Mayas become politically mandatory. Out in the villages, the response of campesinos to an impassioned speech on Mayan consciousness can still be embarrassed head-scratching.

Yet this was the new source of legitimacy that would pull Rigoberta away from the movement that launched her career. What the Pan-Mayan movement wanted, at minimum, was an end to discrimination and a new level of recognition for the culture. However, linguistic equality in state institutions implied an unsettling handicap for ladinos, few of whom spoke a Mayan language. Even more unsettling were proposals for political and territorial autonomy that would be difficult, if not impossible, to incorporate into a republican form of government. These were issues capable of raising the temperature in any gathering. As one Uspantano predicted gloomily, "The new enemy will be the indígena, not for planning another uprising, but just for asking for our rights."

Nationally and internationally, the left was going through another of its periodic eclipses, in step with the disintegration of the Soviet Union and its client states. Even the venerable Cuban revolution seemed on the point of collapse. New sources of mystique were needed. If one place to look was human rights, another was Indians. Rigoberta was uniquely situated at a three-way intersection of the left, the indigenous movement, and human rights. It is a tribute to her improving diplomatic skills that she was not run over. She might seem to derive credentials as a Mayan leader from the ethnic fervor expressed in her 1982 story, but it becomes a parable about learning to trust the left. Since the URNG was never capable of promoting indígenas to the highest level, Rigoberta exemplified subordination to ladino leadership until she could prove otherwise.

The Guatemalan revolutionaries of the early 1980s were some of the first Latin American Marxists to recruit significant numbers of indígenas. Unprecedented figures like Rigoberta and Rosalina Tuyuc are not the only sign that empowerment has taken place. Judging from the cadres and ex-combatants I meet in northern Quiché, thousands of young Mayas schooled in the guerrilla movement will provide a new kind of leadership well into the next century. Still, the failure of the revolution had undermined its claim to represent indígenas. However many cadres it produced, their credibility for Mayas was limited until they reinvented themselves. The larger question was whether ethnic organizing should be subsumed within a broader, class-based movement or whether it should stand apart, aligned with the left on many issues but insisting on its own perspective.

Thanks to Rigoberta's progression from an indigenous village to the ladino-led class struggle, her life already incarnated the debate when she met the anthropologist who recorded her story. For Marxists moving into ethnic studies, the Menchú-Burgos collaboration became a classic text because its description of a young woman's political awakening turned indigenous tradition into a platform for class organizing. For precisely the same reason, Pan-Mayan leaders were of two minds about her.[11] If Rigoberta's accounts of army brutality resonated with their own experiences, the confidence she placed in the guerrillas of the early 1980s did not. Because she was still standing by her story from a decade before, many Mayan activists were not convinced that she represented them.

The Quincentenary Conference at Quezaltenango

With the Nobel nomination in the air, Rigoberta finally became a national figure in October 1991, at the awkwardly but precisely titled Second Continental Conference on Five Hundred Years of Indigenous and Popular Resistance. The meeting was held in Guatemala's second largest city. One hundred and fifty years before, the ladino burghers of Quezaltenango had proclaimed an independent Republic of the Highlands, only to be put against a wall and shot. Now a new kind of independence was afoot, in the heart of the Mayan region. The "500 Years" meeting attracted delegates from all over the hemisphere, to plan for the quincentenary and support the country's indigenous movement. Popular organizations marched through the city, and Rigoberta was their hero.

"Rigoberta is like a saint, a huge indigenous symbol who is gaining power like you wouldn't believe," a North American told me. "When she showed up at the conference, people screamed out her name. She's a lot bigger than the government would like to admit. Someone was talking about running her for president; lots of Indians would vote for her. At Quezaltenango, there were twenty to twenty-five thousand people mainly from Sololá, Totonicapán, and so forth. I watched them go by for an hour and a half, with banners and signs, and every group had CUC in it. That's Rigoberta's group. She's the head of a very powerful, fast-growing indigenous movement. Everyone seems to support her."

There were many foreign well-wishers, as is often the case at indigenous gatherings unless they are prohibited. "The meeting was swarming with gringos," another North American said. "And more popular sector [Guatemalans] than Indians, whose representation was weak. The march was very big, with the popular sector, CONAVIGUA, and other organizations bringing out their people. . . . Rigoberta was a center of attention. Hundreds of foreign journalists were there, drooling to interview her. Foreigners were just fawning over this pretty little peasant woman. They were so adulatory and uncritical it was kind of annoying. I was about to barf. No one asked her a tough question. They were too mystified or too reluctant to ask a question like, What's the relation between CUC and the URNG?"

Even if Rigoberta was a symbol of unity, she could not mend the fault line running through the conference. An event of this magnitude is supposed to represent entire populations, but who exactly should be invited as delegates? Now that repression had slackened, Guatemala was bubbling with initiatives of every description. Nowhere was this more evident than among indígenas, which a burgeoning number of groups were trying to represent in one way or another.

Organizing the conference had fallen to the most capable network available, the URNG-aligned popular organizations. The honor of convening it was bestowed upon the Committee for Campesino Unity, hence the prominent display of its name. But this was to invoke continuity with the past, not a practical choice for organizing the event, because CUC was not large or capable enough. Actually, the conference was pulled together by a coalition of activists from CUC and other URNG allies. Since these organizations believe that they represent the Guatemalan people, they chose most of the national delegation from their own ranks. As they were not exclusively Mayan in ethnic composition, they decided that the appropriate ethnic balance for the conference on five hundred years of indigenous and popular resistance was a delegation half of whose members were ladinos.

The half that were Mayas came mainly from the new coalition, Majawil Q'ij (New Dawn). Excluded were independent leaders, who by this time had formed their own network, the Coordinator of Mayan Organizations of Guatemala (COMG). As far as they were concerned, ethnic oppression was more fundamental than the class variety, as demonstrated by how the URNG's ladino leadership had set up Indians to be slaughtered. After a long history of ethnic discrimination, Mayas deserved special treatment. The left would have to accept indigenous demands even if these did not fit with the larger, class-oriented program. For URNG-aligned organizations, that kind of thinking was trouble. They viewed assertive Mayanism as a threat to popular unity. Few independent delegates were chosen, and they were excluded from the conference leadership. To the embarrassment of anthropologists from the United States who had been seated as delegates, well-known Mayan intellectuals ended up as spectators without the right to speak. They fumed that the conference organizers were guerrillas in disguise, only to be dismissed as disruptive, chauvinistic, and backward.[12]

Rigoberta was clearly aligned with the URNG side of the dispute, not the exclusively Mayan organizations. That set her up to be criticized as another indígena colonized by the guerrilla movement. But even the Mayan independents were impressed by her international stature. They were not about to confront her, at least in public. Although the conference widened the split between the two sectors, Rigoberta's reputation as a builder of unity between Mayas and ladinos remained more or less intact. Her refrain that the honors being heaped upon her were for indigenous people in general, not just for herself, was one reason why.

The quincentenary conference became the platform to campaign for the Nobel inside Guatemala. Strictly speaking, a nominee does not campaign for the honor, because the laureate is chosen by a secretive committee in Norway, which can be lobbied only through well-chosen contacts. But it is not unusual for candidates and backers to pump their cause. In Rigoberta's case, she took the nomination very seriously, as a way to protest the army's human rights record under its nose. Inside Guatemala, the nomination could be used as a badge of legitimacy to organize an intimidated population. It was a sign of international recognition that might encourage ordinary Guatemalans to express themselves, like a wedge cracking open a wall of silence. This was the reward for her long years of presenting herself as a representative of her people: the chance to prove that she was. Whatever domestic constituency she could attract would provide a firmer foundation for her international standing.

Over the next year, Rigoberta's name was spread like the gospel by the popular organizations of the left.[13] In Rigoberta's life story was a Mayan odyssey, of a girl born into an oppressed but cohesive village who joined the militancy of the late 1970s, survived the counterinsurgency of the early 1980s, escaped into exile, and was returning home in triumph. Here was the story that Rigoberta had said was the story of all poor Guatemalans. Now it was being repatriated: Would Guatemalans accept it as their own? Flanked by the foreign escorts in her entourage, Rigoberta stepped up her visits, and the popular organizations turned out crowds to greet her. The Nobel campaign opened new ground for the popular movement, in places where peasants still lived in fear. Doubtless there were army officers who wanted to put a stop to the spectacle, but the high command was not so rash as to blow up a Nobel candidate. Thanks to international support, Rigoberta was able to campaign through the central highlands along the Pan-American Highway. However, she never set foot in the department where she was born.

Why Rigoberta?

The Norwegian Nobel Committee has decided to award the Nobel Peace Prize for 1992 to Rigoberta Menchú from Guatemala, in recognition of her work for social justice and ethno-cultural reconciliation based on respect for the rights of indigenous peoples. Like many other countries in South and Central America, Guatemala has experienced great tension between the descendants of European immigrants and the native Indian population. In the 1970s and 1980s, that tension came to a head in the large-scale repression of Indian peoples. Menchú has come to play an increasingly prominent part as an advocate of native rights.

Rigoberta Menchú grew up in poverty, in a family that has undergone the most brutal suppression and persecution. In her social and political work, she has always borne in mind that the long-term objective of the struggle is peace.

Today, Rigoberta Menchú stands out as a vivid symbol of peace and reconciliation across ethnic, cultural and social dividing lines, in her own country, on the American continent and in the world.

—Oslo, October 16, 1992[14]

The peace prize is named after the Swedish inventor of dynamite, Alfred Bernhard Nobel (1833–1896), who wanted to create a weapon so destructive that it would make warfare unthinkable. Some of the awards that his troubled conscience endowed have proven to be just as contradictory as his hopes for the new explosive. Every year a medal and a purse (U.S.$1.2 million to Rigoberta) go to the person who has "done the most or the best work for fraternity between nations, for the abolition or reduction of standing armies and for the holding and promotion of peace congresses."[15] Were the Nobel committee to choose only saintly individuals fitting this description, prizes would go to utopian cranks. The actual range of laureates is wider than Alfred Nobel could have imagined when he wrote his will in 1895, if only because threats to peace have outgrown those familiar to the top-hatted statesmen of his day.

Recent winners include diplomats like Costa Rican president Oscar Arias (1987), for brokering negotiations in three Central American civil wars; human rights advocates such as Adolfo Pérez Esquivel (1980), for exposing the abuses of the Argentine military; and paragons of charity like Mother Teresa (1979).[16] The prize has also gone to opposition leaders, including the Dalai Lama of Chinese-occupied Tibet (1989), the long-imprisoned Aung San Suu Kyi of military-ruled Burma (1991), and José Ramos-Horta and Carlos Ximenes Belo of East Timor (1996), despite ties to armed resistance against illegitimate regimes. Then there are war-making statesmen who might change their ways, as in the 1973 award to Henry Kissinger of the United States and Le Duc Tho of North Vietnam (two Nobel committee members resigned in protest). Even a personal background in terrorism is no disqualification: Sharing the 1978 prize with President Anwar Sadat of Egypt was Prime Minister Menachem Begin of Israel, despite his attacks on British authorities in Palestine thirty years before.

In one important sense, Rigoberta was on higher ground than a number of other peace laureates. Because she never had been in charge of a state or quasi-state organization, she could not be held administratively responsible for human rights violations.[17] Still, her selection revived the debate over the parameters of acceptability, because her 1982 testament clearly advocates violence. Invoking the Bible for precedents, Rigoberta makes Molotov cocktails, endorses bomb threats as a tactic, and debates whether to execute an old woman suspected of being an informer (fortunately for the future peace laureate, the suspect is judged innocent).[18] A related objection was that Rigoberta still belonged to the guerrilla movement. The Nobel committee sidestepped this issue by deciding that it was unknowable. With such problems in mind, it made no explicit reference to the two belligerents in its announcement. Instead the committee attributed political violence in Guatemala to ethnic tension. The committee also avoided any explicit reference to the book that made Rigoberta famous, as if to evade any doubts on that score.

But why the prize to a Native American? The deliberations of the Norwegian committee are secret, by custom as well as statute, but the reasons are not difficult to infer. The 113 candidates for 1992 included Nelson Mandela of South Africa, Václav Havel of Czechoslovakia, and Javier Pérez de Cuellar, the former UN secretary-general. In such distinguished company, the most obvious reason for choosing a Native American was the quincentenary. According to the Norwegian journalist Henrik Hovland, there was also a local subtext in the decision—guilt over the Saami, the indigenous reindeer-herders who live in northern Norway.

Norwegians awoke to their history of colonialism when the Saami put up fierce resistance to the Alta-Kautokeino Dam, which would flood part of their homeland. The Saami lost, but the conflict taught them how to organize, and it also led to obvious divisions in Norway's social democratic government. During the Alta-Kautokeino fight, in 1981, the Labor Party shook up its leadership and replaced Prime Minister Odvar Nordli. Nordli went on to become one of the five Nobel committee members who gave the prize to Rigoberta. "For Nordli and other social democrats" Hovland believes, "awarding the prize to Rigoberta could also have been a way of making amends. Whether or not this was the case, I believe it was felt collectively by a great number of Norwegians."[19]

After the award, there was some muttering in the international indigenous movement that Rigoberta's first loyalty was not to native rights. The ill will grew out of a collision between indigenous activists in the 1980s, over the Miskito rebellion against the Sandinista government in Nicaragua. Because the Miskitos were funded by the Central Intelligence Agency, the international left rallied to the Sandinistas. In the indigenous movement, Miskito and Sandinista supporters polemicized against each other.[20] Eventually the Sandinistas persuaded the rebels to negotiate, but not before the bush war had exposed Rigoberta's loyalties. She was firmly on the side of the Sandinistas. At international forums she sang their praises, contradicted Miskito leaders denouncing human rights violations, and lectured them on their obligations to the antiimperialist cause. For the enemies Rigoberta made, it was all too obvious that her first loyalty was to the Marxist international. When she received the Nobel, however, they held their peace. Accusations would only detract from a rare moment of recognition for indigenous rights.

The Nobel committee could have honored an organization, as it has with Amnesty International (1977) and the United Nations Peacekeeping Forces (1988). For the quincentenary, bodies like the UN Working Group on Indigenous Peoples come to mind, as do well-organized tribes like the Kayapós of Brazil and the Kunas of Panama. The procedure for nominations is not very restrictive, but no such candidates were put forward. As for individuals with international name recognition, there were few from which to choose. Rigoberta's powerful story and the political forces promoting her eclipsed any other possibility.[21] Nor could anyone else have done double duty for honoring indigenous rights and addressing one of Latin America's lengthiest civil wars.

The Guatemalan angle was crucial because Rigoberta's nomination was not promoted by the native rights movement. Instead, it came out of the solidarity networks supporting the Central American revolutionary movements. Playing the indigenous card made sense for guerrilla groups struggling to survive the collapse of the Soviet bloc, the bankruptcy of Cuba, and the exhaustion of the organizing strategies of the late 1970s and early 1980s. Here was a new social movement to which the left could hitch its star. Over in Europe, the social democrats whose sentiments define the acceptable in Nobel awards were also receptive. Romantic views of guerrillas are not hard to find in this milieu, nor the mystique of the noble, oppressed Indian. Such assumptions are rarely contradicted by the Scandinavian media, which in Central America rely on young, idealistic freelancers rather than more experienced, cynical correspondents. The resulting haze has allowed European social democrats, who fought tooth and nail to shut down revolutionary Marxists in their own countries, to be smitten by revolutionary Marxists from Latin America.

In the case of Guatemala, social democrats in several countries—including Norway, Sweden, and the Netherlands—were already investing in URNG-aligned organizations such as CONAVIGUA, GAM, CUC, and the CPRs. Social democrats may also have been contributing directly to the guerrillas, through political parties rather than the governments they controlled, especially after Cuba dried up as a financial source. Hence the 1994 rumors that European supporters, weary of the URNG's part in stalling the peace talks, were threatening to cut off funding. This was the eventual implication of a Nobel award that, at the time, was targeted against the army. However much European social democrats sympathized with the guerrillas, they also wanted to see the last civil war in Central America come to an end. Honoring a figure like Rigoberta not only sent a message to the Guatemalan army. It also implied that, sooner or later, European support for the URNG would be contingent on its willingness to stop fighting.

Peace with Justice or a Nobel for More War?

Question:
What's Rigoberta's blood type?
Answer:
URNG-positive.

—Joke circulating in Guatemala, 1993[22]

After the level of terror in northern Quiché, I never expected that members of Rigoberta's family would still be on the scene, let alone willing to talk about their experiences. Yet when I visited Uspantán for the first time, in June 1989, the town hall was quick to refer me to a man who could address the subject with authority. Despite many narrow escapes, most of the Menchús had survived the violence. They knew that Rigoberta was alive and famous but were only vaguely aware of her book. Of the contrast between their recollections and hers, they seemed to have no idea. After hearing one breathtakingly different version of events, in 1991, I felt obliged to inform my interlocutor of the discrepancy. Even then, he wanted to have his story tape-recorded as Rigoberta had. After a brief attempt, frustrated by forces beyond our control, the project was abandoned. Among other things, I did not want to be responsible for a different version of events from within the family.

My 1989 reconnaissance coincided with the first talk of nominating Rigoberta for the peace prize. My next visits coincided with her Nobel campaign and the opening of peace talks between the government and the URNG. By the time Rigoberta became Nobel laureate, unfortunately, the hopes aroused by the start of peace talks were withering. Both comandantes and generals viewed the negotiations as a way to refurbish the legitimacy they needed to continue the war. The army saw no reason to give up what it had won. What better excuse to keep the country militarized than a few guerrilla columns who posed no serious threat? As for the URNG, it still claimed to speak for the masses. If most Guatemalans said they were tired of the war and wanted the guerrillas to stop fighting, that was because they were too terrorized to express their support. Therefore the URNG would fight until it achieved "peace with justice," that is, major concessions at the bargaining table.

Since Rigoberta's 1982 story vouched for the guerrilla rationale for the war, I wondered if the ever higher honors bestowed upon her would justify the URNG's strategy of prolonging the war until it received improbable concessions. "The subject of this project," my first research proposal began, "is whether a Nobel Peace Prize could have the paradoxical effect of encouraging continued violence." Among foreign supporters, the 1982 defeat of the guerrillas had gradually been digested, with the result that everyone hoped for a negotiated end to the fighting. Yet most activists, and more than a few scholars, still accepted the URNG's version of the war. They believed that the guerrilla movement sprang from local needs, that it was an inevitable response to oppression, and that it represented popular aspirations. If so, then foreigners who wished to be in solidarity with the Guatemalan people should support the URNG's holdout approach to peace talks.

The prestige of *I, Rigoberta Menchú* was so great that when I began to talk about my findings in 1990–1991, some of my colleagues regarded them as sacrilegious. I had put myself beyond the pale of decency. Those still willing to talk to me pointed out that contradicting Rigoberta's story could harm not just the soon-to-be Nobel laureate but the indigenous movement, the Guatemalan left, their ability to work together, even the peace talks. On the last point, I shared their unease. Rigoberta's 1982 story had focused international attention on a conflict that could easily be ignored. At a time when the army's commitment to peace talks was less than certain, undermining the credibility of its best-known scourge did not seem like a good idea.

Some colleagues also warned that a white anthropologist did not have the right to undermine a Native American's right to tell her own story. Embarrassed by their association with Western power, anthropologists are increasingly leery of imposing their own interpretive framework on the narratives of others, especially when they are victims of colonialism. One implication is increasing reluctance to judge the truth of what we are told. Yet failing to subject Rigoberta's account to critical judgment had definite costs. The most serious was to allow her internationally amplified voice to drown out the voices of peasants she was presumed to represent, who did not view the guerrillas as a contribution to their needs, who instead viewed them as another tribulation, and who wanted the war to end far sooner than it did.

One suggestion from colleagues was to bring in these other voices without confronting Rigoberta's 1982 story. Instead of using contradictory stories to construct my own version of events, in relation to which Rigoberta's would become false or distorted, I should base my research entirely on the comparison of narratives. Instead of indicting her for distorting what "really" happened, instead of privileging my own version of events, the result would be a comparison of perspectives, in which I would note the differences between versions, suggest the circumstances that generated each one, and ponder why hers gained such credibility.

This would have been a more diplomatic procedure than the one I followed. But was it practical? What was I supposed to do with written records, mainly human rights reports and land petitions? Scholars know that documents are not a court of final appeal; they can tell more lies than statistics. But they do set up parameters, through dates and official actions, for evaluating oral testimony. Composed in the heat of conflict, documents may also speak more frankly than their authors will decades later. I could not ignore documents just because they indicated that Rigoberta's version of events was impossible. Either their authority had to be incorporated into my account, or I had to ignore what they revealed.

The main reason I decided against confining myself to the comparison of narratives is that I did not want to give up the frank exercise of judgment, as an outside observer, on the reliability of what I was hearing. The cost would have been too high. Consider all the contradictory stories I heard on a trinity of subjects: conflict over land, membership in clandestine organizations, and responsibility for murders. Mainly what I was hearing were narratives of victimization—often, the reciprocal claims to victimization that enemies make against each other. Refusing to judge whose story was more reliable would, in a place like Uspantán, mean giving equal credibility to an army collaborator and the widow of the man he killed. If outsiders have any constructive function to perform in a place like northern Quiché, we can decide how to position ourselves only by stepping back from victimization narratives and weighing their reliability.

16

The Lonely Life of a Nobel Laureate

In order to exist in the social world with a comfortable sense of being a good, socially proper, and stable person, an individual needs to have a coherent, acceptable, and constantly revised life story.

—Charlotte Linde, 1993[1]

For maximum impact, Rigoberta was in Guatemala when the peace prize was announced. Instead of the unpredictable Quiché, she and her organizers chose places where the left could mobilize union members, teachers, and students to bring out crowds. The night before the announcement, she received accolades in San Pedro Sacatepéquez, a prosperous Mayan commercial town in the Department of San Marcos. The morning after, on October 16, she led a march through the coastal town of Retalhuleu and told a crowd of campesinos that, years before, she had harvested cotton and coffee there. The day after, fifteen thousand people greeted her in the capital, at the pre-Columbian ruins of Kaminaljuyú.

President Jorge Serrano Elías (1991–1993) did not join in the celebrations. Eventually the presidential palace issued a terse congratulation and Serrano received her in a cold encounter. The government's feelings were expressed by the foreign minister and an army spokesman, who said her ties to Guatemala's enemies should have disqualified her as a Nobel peace laureate. It was true that the guerrillas had turned down the government's cease-fire proposals. At the official level, enthusiasm was confined to other governments. Following the award, Rigoberta was received by Carlos Salinas of Mexico, François Mitterrand of France, Oscar Luigi Scalfaro of Italy, and Felipe González of Spain, as well as Boutros Boutros-Ghali of the United Nations and Pope John Paul II.[2]

In Guatemala it was easy to hear hostile reactions from ladinos. There were so many sex and race jokes that my colleague Diane Nelson collected them. One day Rigoberta goes to heaven and knocks on the gate.

"Hey, Jesus," Saint Peter calls out, "the tortillas are here!" Related by women and indígenas as well as ladino men, the jokes play off the challenge of Rigoberta's stature to the gender and ethnic norms in Guatemalan society, where women are to be seen rather than heard.[3] "That an indígena is today the Guatemalan personality with the highest profile on the international level," Elisabeth Burgos wrote of the upper classes, "they consider intolerable."[4]

Still, among society ladies there were professions of conversion by Rigoberta's book. "This can't go on anymore," they told my colleague Helen Rivas. "We've changed." Disregarding the glum expressions in the Serrano administration, the Christian Democrats who controlled congress welcomed her, if only to lean on a new pillar of legitimacy. Despite some hate mail, the media were generally favorable, not least because journalists had their own grievances against the security forces. That Rigoberta had escaped her persecutors and disgraced them around the world gave her broad appeal. In Nebaj and Uspantán, I was impressed by the number of ladinos who expressed sympathy for her.

Following the ceremonies, Rigoberta found herself in a predicament that was all the more challenging because it could barely be acknowledged. The journey home required a larger transition than most of her supporters realized. Until this point she had been a revolutionary exile who represented the Indians and poor of Guatemala internationally. Although billed as an Indian leader, she was not well known to her constituents. During the campaign for the Nobel, the very fact that the army felt obliged to let her organize rallies and be hailed by opposition crowds, subject only to threats and petty sabotage, was more important than what she was saying. Now she would have to learn how to be an opposition figure inside Guatemala. She would have to show that she actually represented the people whom international audiences assumed she did. Having as yet brought peace to no one, this was a Nobel laureate who would have to prove herself.

Rigoberta's most serious test was the peace process itself. Formal negotiations between the government and the guerrillas had finally started in April 1991. But the talks were going nowhere; neither side was willing to give ground. This left the peace laureate dangling, between her old sponsors in the Guatemalan National Revolutionary Union (URNG), which she was unable to criticize, and a war-weary population, whose hopes for peace she was supposed to represent. Unable to embrace the guerrillas or break with them, not fully accepted by the independent Mayan organizations, and lionized mainly by pro-URNG popular organizations, she occupied her own lonely symbolic eminence. She still had to find her way out of the smoke and mirrors of a defeated guerrilla movement. She was trapped between her past as a revolutionary militant and the representative role she was now expected to play in a peace process, between who she had been a decade before and who she was now, between the story she told in 1982 and how it stood in need of revision.

Indígenas React to the Prize

> *I never had thought that someone like ourselves could reach such a high honor. She is an indígena and a woman. The times must have changed a great deal for something like this to happen in Guatemala. But how does one know the intentions of the people behind her?*
>
> **—A K'iche' market woman, October 1992[5]**

By 1992 the left could, in some areas, bring together thousands of people who were very conscious of what Rigoberta represented. Here was a person who had suffered what they had suffered, who had made known the army's kidnappings and massacres around the world. A large majority of the indigenous population was still beyond the left's reach, however. If anyone in the popular organizations was aware of how skewed *I, Rigoberta Menchú* was, how contrary some of its claims were to the devastating experiences of her village and many like it, they must have wondered how she would be received.

At least her name was now recognizable. Indígenas were impressed that a member of their race should achieve such a high honor. But being skeptical of anyone involved with the army or the guerrillas, they had questions. A colleague doing fieldwork in Huehuetenango put the new laureate into his structured interview, only to find that the most common response was, "Can you tell me about her?" "She came out of nowhere for a lot of people," Paul Kobrak told me. "They are uninformed but truly interested." "Is it true that she is involved with the guerrillas?" they asked. Confirming that Rigoberta was did not necessarily alienate Huehuetecos: One ex-soldier said that it did not matter to him, because if the army had killed his family, he would have joined the guerrillas, too.

In Nebaj, for the next town fiesta, the schoolteachers organized a march of history in which their pupils appeared as ancient Mayas, Spanish conquistadors, and so forth. At the end of the procession was a girl dressed as a K'iche', under a banner that read "1992/Year of the Indigenous Peoples/Nobel Peace Laureate Rigoberta Menchú." Putting Rigoberta into the parade might seem unremarkable, except that this was the obligatory "civic-military parade," which included the army garrison. Although many Ixils were proud of Rigoberta, that was not the only reaction. "The Nobel is a much debated issue here," a development promoter apologized. "There's a lot of manipulation. This is why people don't trust either what's said for or against her. They're not clear who to believe."

At an army-organized rally, civil patrollers shouted, "Rigoberta is a guerrilla!" "If she comes, we have to kick her out!" "We want peace!" and "If the guerrillas don't lay down their arms, we want more arms!" A Nebaj cultural activist said, "The more aware people don't think Rigoberta Menchú should be honored because they think she's tied to the subversion." "I'm not sure she really deserved it, because she hasn't done anything concrete for peace," an evangelical told me. "Someone who deserved it was Ríos Montt, because he brought peace"—a reference to the widespread belief that he can be credited for ending army massacres. "She went with them here and there," an ex–civil patrol leader said, pretending to pull a trigger with his finger. "She has to ask for pardon." A pardon? I asked, not quite believing what I was hearing. "From her family and her people, for having fallen into *engaño* [the false promises of the guerrillas]. Everyone is back together again, all the families, but she has to ask for pardon."

That distrust of Rigoberta ran deeper than fear of the army is suggested by reactions in Santiago Atitlán, a Tz'utujil Maya town that, after hundreds of murders and disappearances, stood up to the army like no other in Guatemala. On the night of December 1, 1990, drunk soldiers shot a man protecting his daughter from them. Neighbors ran to the Catholic church, rang the bells, and raised the town. Several thousand men and boys poured into the plaza and marched on the garrison carrying machetes and sticks. The army opened fire, killing thirteen and wounding more than forty others. The resulting outcry forced the army to withdraw its garrison. The Atitecos were now a national symbol of resistance, but they also asked the guerrillas to stay away. When Rigoberta planned a conference at Santiago in 1993, the town council refused, on grounds it had not been properly consulted. "Who is she?" "Why is she coming here?" Atitecos asked. "We don't know what she'll bring." Their understanding of themselves had yet to include a Mayan hero constructed on the national and international levels.

Surviving the Peace Process

I think that, for signing the peace, a date ought not to be set.

—Rigoberta Menchú, 1993[6]

Two political crises in 1993 ended Rigoberta's Nobel honeymoon by making her look like she was still working for the guerrillas. The first was President Serrano's suspension of the constitution, to prevent opponents from exposing his appetite for corruption. Trust in the political system was already low after his Christian Democratic predecessor, Vinicio Cerezo, turned the widely hailed restoration of democracy into a sinkhole of graft. Disillusion with the next president was even sharper because Serrano had been elected by voters hungry for morality in government, on the strength of his credentials as an evangelical church leader. At first the army seemed to support Serrano's power grab, in what looked like a military coup. But part of the officer corps opposed the move, as did part of the upper classes, and the international community was quick to condemn it. A few days later the army forced Serrano into exile, leaving behind a constitutional crisis, which ended when the congress elected human rights ombudsman Ramiro De Leon Carpio as the next president (1993–1996).

On the day in May that Serrano suspended the constitution, Rigoberta was chairing a meeting of indigenous leaders from other countries. Since roundups and killings were a possibility, she spent the first day of the coup running to embassies to obtain diplomatic escorts for her guests. Then she joined other leaders of the popular organizations in a street protest. Living up to the expectations created by her book, she was putting herself on the line for democracy. According to the country's main newsweekly, her courage made her "the leader that she had not yet become."[7]

Then something went wrong. Along with the URNG-aligned popular organizations, Rigoberta went off in a direction that seemed laid down by the comandantes in Mexico. At issue was whether to support the Instancia Nacional de Consenso (INC), a committee of civic elites who sprang to the defense of the constitution and prevented Serrano's vice president from succeeding him. Making a mistake, Rigoberta decided that the INC was too compromising to join. Instead, she echoed the URNG position, that suspension of the constitution was a military coup, despite growing evidence that dissident army officers were swinging the army against it.[8] By opposing what became a successful negotiated settlement, she ended up looking like a minion of revolutionary exiles rather than a political actor in her own right.

At the start of 1994, another crisis took the luster off Rigoberta's reputation as a champion of human rights. Being consistent toward governments and their lapses, regardless of one's own political needs, is difficult for any such figure. Some months before, Rigoberta had aroused comment by accepting a decoration from Fidel Castro despite his long history of repressing dissidents. But it was fellow Mayas, across the border in Mexico, who put her in a predicament. Upon accepting the Nobel, Rigoberta had announced that she would not bring the medallion home to Guatemala until the return of peace. Instead, she entrusted it to the Museum of the Sun, on the site of an Aztec temple in Mexico City, in honor of her long-standing support from the government and people of Mexico, who had also provided asylum to the URNG leadership and thousands of Guatemalan refugees.

Little more than a year later, an uprising in the state of Chiapas forced Rigoberta to take a position on the domestic policies of her benefactor. Mayan rebels belonging to a newly proclaimed Zapatista National Liberation Army suddenly occupied towns and attacked the Mexican army. Hundreds of human rights observers rushed to the scene, obliging the army to accept a cease-fire rather than lash back with all the force at its command. The rebellion followed a history of government abuses with which Rigoberta was familiar owing to her friendship with the bishop who had long denounced them, Samuel Ruiz. Instead of joining the chorus of condemnation, Rigoberta decided to refrain from comment until the Mexican government issued a report.[9] It was quite a contrast to her habitual lashing of the Guatemalan authorities, and the Zapatistas withdrew an invitation for her to serve as mediator.[10]

At bottom, Rigoberta's dilemma was the peace process she was supposed to represent. Her Nobel prize told the government and army that their international reputation hinged on opening political space for a democratic opposition. But Rigoberta herself was only a bystander in the peace talks. She envisioned herself as a mediator, but this would have required somehow acknowledging and transcending her own URNG history. Alternatively, she could have become a valuable member of the rebel delegation, but this never surfaced as a possibility either, for equally significant reasons. Her evolution toward the Nobel had required denying her connection to the URNG. She also resented how it was controlled by ladinos. Although these feelings were not yet public, they probably made her untrustworthy in the eyes of the comandantes. By 1994 Rigoberta was joining the Mayan movement's demand for inclusion in the talks as a third party, but neither the government nor the URNG nor the UN mediators brokering the talks considered this feasible. Instead, Mayan organizations were channeled into an Assembly of Civil Sectors at a lower level of the peace process. Rigoberta refused to participate.

Unable to clarify an association that she habitually denied, Rigoberta was left in uneasy proximity to the URNG's demand for "peace with justice"—the strategy of prolonging the war until it won unlikely concessions. As negotiations failed to make headway in 1993–1994, for reasons that were increasingly obscure, Rigoberta's lack of urgency suggested that the war had become a way of life for her as it had for the two sides. She became an easy target for commentators who distrusted her revolutionary background. Was she trying to dampen expectations because, contrary to the wishes of most Guatemalans, she supported the URNG's long-march attitude toward negotiations? When the guerrillas rejected the army's cease-fire proposals, the peace laureate's hermetic reactions suggested that she was in agreement, or at least afraid to criticize them.

"I think it is an error to put a date [deadline] on the process because there are many complications," Rigoberta explained in July 1994. One reason was that the process was secret, another that it was still excluding Mayas. "It has been difficult for any citizen to have influence at the negotiating table," she added. The war is "a profit and a business that has given a large number of frustrated people something to do." The official mediator had invited her to participate more in the dialogue, but "I have wanted to play a more discreet role" because the parties involved have decided the agenda "very secretly and I respect it because I am a common citizen of Guatemala." She also noted that the Group of Friends—the United States, Norway, Spain, Mexico, and Venezuela—have "had great difficulty" in following the negotiations.[11]

Aside from her own divided feelings, there was a compelling reason to deny her ties to the guerrillas, even if these were all too clear from her curriculum vitae. The association was a mark against her for much of the Guatemalan public, including many of the indígenas whom she most wanted to represent. This is not to deny that many of the same Guatemalans also had favorable feelings toward her. But many who sympathized with her as a victim of the violence were also weary of the guerrillas, the disruption they caused, and the excuses they provided for the army's security measures. As the peace talks dragged on year after year, it was hard for Guatemalans to know whom to blame, as both sides had inexhaustible explanations for why the other was responsible for the latest breakdown. The safest conclusion was that both sides shared an interest in prolonging the hostilities. Rigoberta's image suffered from the impasse. By refraining from defending the URNG, instead reiterating simple messages about human rights, she tried to distance herself from it.

Rigoberta on Anthropologists

> *There's a challenge for those who studied the* indios *and made of this their profession, their career, their money and their life. Now at a moment that indígenas are speaking for themselves, this affects their career. I know that there are a lot of people who are never going to like us, who are never going to accept that indígenas speak, because to the extent that they speak, comes Spanish and they're no longer indios, so they say. This is a bit of what many who lack respect have said about me too lately. The racist expressions of many people when I came out at the beginning were incredible. I know many anthropologists or sociologists, and I am not against their profession,*

> *[but] they said that I was manipulated by the left because I'd been indoctrinated and was carrying around a left-wing cassette.*
>
> **—Rigoberta Menchú, September 26, 1992**[12]

Rigoberta no longer suffered anthropologists gladly. If her differences with Elisabeth Burgos were one reason, my own investigation into the historical background of her story was doubtless another. She became acquainted with my work in April 1991, after my initial findings on the death of her brother Petrocinio found their way into the meetings of the Latin American Studies Association (LASA). How this happened is worth a brief digression. Rigoberta's 1982 story is not court testimony, but it is testimonio, an "as told to" genre that gives nonwriters, ordinarily excluded from producing literature, the chance to tell their lives in their own words. Literary scholars debate the extent to which the results should be regarded as truthful, but this is a sensitive issue. Like other such works, Rigoberta's testimonio presents itself as an eyewitness account, therefore asks to be interpreted literally, which makes any suggestion to the contrary sound like an ad hominem attack.[13]

Worried about what to do with my findings, I consulted with an authority on testimonio named John Beverley. Beverley was an advocate for the genre, but he also seemed to be arguing against interpreting it like a fundamentalist interprets the Bible. Perhaps he could help me frame my doubts about *I, Rigoberta Menchú* in a more sympathetic way. After an exchange of drafts, he called up and asked if he could quote me, for a presentation he was giving at the upcoming meetings of the Latin American Studies Association. At this point I had presented my argument just once, at a conference in Berkeley the previous fall, and had no interest in publishing. But not wanting to censor the flow of information, after only a moment's hesitation I said, Why not?

The room at a conference hotel near Washington, D.C., was crowded with professors of literature. I slipped into the back just as Beverley began to speak. This was not my neck of the academic woods; the level of abstraction was beyond me. Suddenly Beverley swooped down from the clouds and dropped his bomb—my unfortunate findings about the death of Petrocinio. Gasps and "no's" escaped from some of the audience. Meanwhile, who should be holding forth in an auditorium below but the cult hero herself, who was often an honored guest at these occasions. Not having intended to make a declaration, suddenly I was in a fix. Since Rigoberta would hear that an anthropologist was bad-mouthing her upstairs, I had no choice but to present her with a copy of the twelve-page talk Beverley had quoted. When I caught up with Rigoberta in a corridor, it was hard to exchange more than a few sentences without being interrupted by the next well-wisher. But I was able to give her a copy, along with a verbal explanation that people in Chajul were giving me another version of how her brother died. Rigoberta was cordial, but I remember her saying that just as I had my work, she had hers, which I took as a polite suggestion to avoid interfering with it. If the people of Chajul were collaborating with the army, she added, why should I believe what they say?

After LASA, my next contact with Rigoberta came at a press conference in Guatemala City in July 1992, a few months before she received the Nobel. When I identified myself and asked a question, she recognized me from the year before. Afterward, she was out on a balcony joking with a crowd of supporters below. Spotting me again, she told the crowd: "Many people, many anthropologists have studied us a lot, and they have made lots of money off of us. But they don't like it when we speak out. Some are honorable, but we're going to see which ones." About the same time, a colleague had the chance to ask her what she thought about my paper on the murder of her brother. She said that it was racist. "Whites have been writing our history for five hundred years, and no white anthropologist is going to tell me what I experienced in my own flesh."

Like many political figures who must steer between telling the truth and telling lies, Rigoberta has long been chary of interviewers with tough questions. But now I heard that she was becoming defensive about her 1982 testimony, to the point of not wanting to talk about it. I also learned that she was suspicious of anyone on her staff taking notes, as if they might be used against her. In June 1994 a Swedish scholar was surprised by the hostile reception she gave him. Jan Lundius is a historian, specializing in the popular religion of the Caribbean, who wanted to interview Rigoberta about the relation between Mayan tradition and Catholicism. He met her at the Vicente Menchú Foundation in Guatemala City, through an introduction by a Guatemalan social scientist.

"What do you want from us?" were Rigoberta's first words. Taken aback, Lundius launched into an explanation of how much he appreciated her testimony, its religious dimensions and ability to reach a wide audience. He added that he was not an anthropologist and wanted to have a dialogue with her. "What's most sacred is a way of thinking," Rigoberta replied. "A people's manner of being. Our people have their manner of being, and it is my conviction that people should not study other people. Least of all the indígenas, they cannot be objects of study, because this doesn't contribute anything." Lundius repeated his wish to have a dialogue with her. "The world is deteriorating," Rigoberta responded. "These are times of much change. Things that are sacred have to be put apart, to struggle for a new ethics, not just law and power. . . . It's going to be very difficult to study our religion. You [plural] are never going to understand the Mayan religion. All that kind of work requires a new relationship. Our people live with more caution than before. Before we were more open. The reason is . . . unilateral imposition. Our people have more and more consciousness of this, and this is why we are demanding a new ethics. We have always been defined by other people. The books define us. Politics defines us. . . . We cannot change [the fact] that [scholarly?] investigation has done a great deal of damage to us."

From here, Rigoberta moved on to the need for practical support for her people, through the projects of the Vicente Menchú Foundation she had started with her Nobel purse. "She's not interested in any dialogue with scientists," Lundius told me five months later. "That's unilateral and like rape. She doesn't want to be studied. What they want is political and economic support. She treated me as if I were an academic vampire. It was upsetting." He tried to rescue himself by praising Rigoberta as a spokeswoman for the Mayan population, as exemplified in her acceptance speech for the Nobel.

"I am a person who learned to be whole *[integral],*" she repeated several times. "It's necessary that a relationship be respectful. One has to understand that the faith of a person, her religion, is the same thing as her struggle for life. Trust costs a great deal to win. One has to understand that many people lost their ability to speak. I believe very much in the capacity [of indigenous people?]. Those who study us have to regain [the ability to?] respect; there exist little-understood age-old values. Integrity is essential in our struggle; it is part of the rights of the indigenous peoples; it is a part of the universal declaration [of rights] of all the peoples of the world. Every dialogue has its limits. It is not right to interpret the people. I arrive as a sister; I have more right than an anthropologist. There is no conflict more painful than our suffering, not even a conflict as modern, as big as the fall of the [Berlin] Wall in Europe. A conflict like that is not as big as the Guatemalan process. I believe that the rights of an individual include respect from others. . . .

"Another kind of comprehension has to begin by [taking] another road. We need completely different relationships. You can say that the religion of Rigoberta Menchú is that one has to dream of the future, and not talk about religion. You [plural] have a moral debt with our people. And we can coexist but, specifically in Guatemala, what remains very clear is our inability to participate in a dialogue of this nature. About investigations I have lots of doubts. You have to understand that I, Rigoberta, I am the object of studies. The politics [of studies?] cannot be as irresponsible as they have been before. We want peace, and we need a quota of tolerance. Now as the war ends, it remains for us to create something new. And I want to say that religion is not our problem, because for me faith is an act of modesty before the world. Many times it is abused. You can write that down. For me, for Rigoberta Menchú, faith is my modesty before the world."[14]

Since Lundius was a UN consultant at the time, Rigoberta may have felt compelled to receive him. But he was not aware of my research (we met later in New York), and the validity of her life story never came up as an issue, at least in his mind. "My impression is that she's a very hurt person," Lundius told me. "Particularly when she said that 'I, Rigoberta Menchú, am an object of studies.' She's reacting against that; she's on the defensive. She speaks as if in defense of her people, but it's easy to suppose that it's a very personal hurt that she's expressing. This 'we' that she assumes is misleading. It's so different from the people I meet out in the countryside, who are full of curiosity about their roots and want to express themselves with foreigners. My impression is that she did *I, Rigoberta Menchú* when she was too young. They got her very young, and now she's growing up. But now she is a huge public symbol who can no longer be herself because she can no longer get out from behind the 'we' that she was forced to assume and which still keeps her trapped. I suspect that Rigoberta reacts not as a person but as a symbol for a movement, that she's afraid of revealing herself as a person."

17

Rigoberta and Redemption

The oppressor-victim dyad seems to be the basis of global morality at the moment. It is as if media and internationalists need the prism of these Manichean dichotomies to make a context meaningful to them. Without Good and Evil, then it's not worth knowing about—a rather operatic approach to life.

—Richard Wilson, 1995[1]

I was not about to stop investigating the historical background of Rigoberta's 1982 testimony, even if she was tired of being the object of studies and regarded mine as racist. Showing how her story was contradicted by other Mayas was not racist. Nor was pointing out how it mobilized international support for a defeated insurgency long after most peasants wanted peace. Yet many readers will recognize the point Rigoberta is making, about the power of representations and who gets to make them. Isn't it about time that anthropologists let Indians speak for themselves? Yes it is. But who decided that Rigoberta was especially worth listening to? Who decided that other Mayas were sellouts?

By claiming to be an eyewitness, Rigoberta validated the idea that her neighbors were pressed to the wall by insatiable landlords and collectively welcomed the guerrillas. This was not what I heard from survivors, but it was what many outsiders wanted to hear. The result was to encourage human rights imagery that met the needs of the revolutionary movement but discouraged reporting what many peasants had to say. What I was forced to question was whom *I, Rigoberta Menchú* represents: the Mayan peasantry from whom its narrator came, the foreign audiences who made her an international figure, or the guerrilla movement that sent her out to appeal to those audiences?

When I presented my doubts about *I, Rigoberta Menchú* to small academic gatherings in 1990–1991, the reactions were very divided. Some colleagues were fascinated, others horrified. Rigoberta had become an icon, a quasi-sacred figure who could not be questioned without arousing bitter controversy. How a human being can achieve godlike status in an American research university where questions are supposed to be welcome is the subject of this chapter. First I look at the intellectual quandaries behind Rigoberta's charge of racism, then at the requirements of solidarity imagery—that is, the symbolism needed to persuade North Americans and Europeans to support opposition movements in distant places. Finally, I suggest why the same kind of logic has penetrated deeply into scholarship and is discouraging certain kinds of questions that need to be asked. The reason some scholars have been so offended by questions about Rigoberta's story, I argue, is that they have unwittingly fallen into the old game of idealizing native people to serve their own moral needs.

Identity, Authenticity, and the Anthropological Attic

> *Inventions are precisely the stuff that cultural reality is made of. . . . The analytic task is not to strip away the invented portion of culture as inauthentic, but to understand the process by which they acquire authenticity.*
>
> **—Allan Hanson, 1989[2]**

I, Rigoberta Menchú is one of many works to win a mass audience by appealing to Western expectations about native people. Unlike most such works, it is in the words of a native person herself. Since indígenas and peasants tend to be viewed as rustic innocents, they may have to charm their audience just to get a hearing. That alone helps explain the kind of mythic inflation Rigoberta committed. Anthropologists are not completely innocent in this regard: Although we refute the crudest expectations, our studies of culture and tradition have encouraged new forms of paternalism, such as expectations about what is typical or authentic. The result is a patronizing attitude toward indígenas who fulfill expectations as well as those who do not. The expectations are also internalized by native people themselves, especially those moving back and forth between village and urban life. Under pressure to live up to notions of authenticity, they deprecate themselves for doing so and deprecate themselves for failing to. But they can play the authenticity game, too. However weary Rigoberta has become of stereotypes, her 1982 story was quite a contribution to them, by appealing to a notion of authenticity revolving around monolingualism, illiteracy, and rejection of Western technology. This hardly describes the K'iche's I meet, but it has encouraged Rigoberta's readers to define her people in ways to which she now objects.

The pull of expectations about native people puts both them and scholars in a difficult position. On the one hand, stereotypes distort debates about indigenous issues, therefore should be questioned. On the other, scholars should respect the right of indigenous people to represent themselves as they see fit. If they feel the need to spin myths about themselves, as does the rest of humanity, should anthropologists avoid confronting imagery that they would not hesitate to demolish if it was propounded by outsiders? What if indigenous mythmakers have been caught up in an external agenda that needs to be questioned?

Conundrums like this have spread over the anthropological landscape. As more native people move to cities, go to school, experience discrimination, and assert their rights, they have been defining ethnic and nationalist identities like other subordinate populations before them. Like the first modern national identities constructed by the English, French, and North Americans, the latest wave of ethnonationalism requires mythic charters that must be constructed out of the materials at hand. These include anthropology. Not only have anthropologists recorded knowledge that otherwise died with elders, but their typologies justify distinctions that activists can use to claim legal rights. Anthropology has become an attic from which indigenous people can choose stories and classifications to demonstrate their validity as distinct groups.

Anthropologists should feel gratified that their research is useful to the people they study. But many are uncomfortable because they have been going in the opposite direction. As the human race commingles, anthropologists have moved away from "essentializing" (or pigeonholing) individuals in terms of particular cultures in particular places. Mayas who move to the United States do not stop being indigenous or Guatemalan just because they and their children become North Americans. Their identity is partly a matter of choice and partly what society imposes on them. But it is constructed, not given, and constantly changing.

Portrayals of tradition-bound cultures are no longer very convincing in anthropology. Instead, scholars have become fascinated by the "invention of tradition," such as the ancestral plaids of Scottish clans (invented by a textile manufacturer in the early 1800s) or the rituals surrounding the British monarchy (many of which were also invented recently).[3] The invention of tradition includes the very concepts we use to apprehend ethnicity, such as the contrast between whites and blacks. There have also been unsettling discoveries about indigenous traditions: Some originated in the parlors of nineteenth-century scholars. Just as indigenous activists and intellectuals were confiding in categories bequeathed by an earlier era of anthropology, contemporary anthropologists began tearing them down. What was "authentic" turns out to be "invented," or so an unwelcome anthropologist claims, and indigenous people feel they are being subjected to a new form of colonialism.[4]

What if the very distinctions I am drawing—between what was mythologized and what verifiably happened, or between opposed local versions of what happened—reflect a Western standard of judgment that I am imposing upon people who would not make the distinction themselves? "The rationale for separating spheres, be they myth, history, politics, geography, or whatever," Alcida Ramos has argued, "is not in the indigenous discourses themselves but in our need to organize ethnographic material into familiar categories in order to make sense of it in our own terms and in those of our readers. . . . The indigenous way of thinking as revealed in what we, not they, call myths, narratives, and so on, challenges the habits of compartmentalization that anthropology has inherited along with the scientific premise of Western rationalism and empiricism."[5]

Jonathan Friedman has objected to the "vast literature debunking the past" produced by Western objectivism. If even history as understood by Westerners is based on a cultural model that guides how it is constructed, then it can be argued that "our own academicized discourse is just as mythical as is theirs. . . . When the Western anthropologist or historian attacks the Hawaiian view of their own past, this must be understood as a struggle for the monopoly of identity. Who is to be able to render an adequate version of History?. . . . When the 'object' begins to define itself, anthropologists are likely to find themselves in an identity crunch."[6]

In the kind of case Friedman describes, anthropologists may find themselves facing a solid phalanx of indigenous opinion. They have trespassed onto sacred ground; they are indicted as an enemy of the culture they swore to respect. But what if anthropologists find themselves in the middle of a debate between indigenous people? In the case of Rigoberta, what Mayas told me raised the issue of how her account compares with theirs, how well it speaks for them, and how well it represents the circumstances that led to so many deaths. Although most Mayas I talked to expressed respect for Rigoberta's story, their feelings about its political corollaries were far from undivided. Until now, Rigoberta's unquestionability has been most obvious among foreign audiences. To their needs I turn next.

Solidarity and the Need for Simplicity

> [I, Rigoberta Menchú] *is one of the most moving books I have ever read. It is the kind of a book that I feel I must pass on, that I must urge fellow teachers to use in their classes. . . . My students were immediately sympathetic to Menchú's story and were anxious to know more, to involve themselves. They asked questions about culture and history, about their own position in the world, and about the purposes and methods of education. Many saw in the society of the Guatemalan Indian attractive features they found lacking in their*

own lives, strong family relationships, community solidarity, an intimate relationship with nature, commitment to others and to one's beliefs.

—A North American literature instructor, 1990[7]

Human rights is a legal discourse, but what propels its application around the world is solidarity—political identification with victims, dissidents, and opposition movements. In the struggles against apartheid in South Africa, for a Palestinian homeland, and for democracy in eastern Europe, North American and European activists have pressured their governments to intervene diplomatically. Other solidarity movements, for Tibet and East Timor, have achieved more visibility than impact. Latin America has inspired a number of solidarity campaigns in the United States and Europe—for the Chilean left after the 1973 coup, for Amazonian Indians, for revolutionary movements in Central America and the Zapatista rebels in Mexico. Thanks to cheap airfares, solidarity can translate very quickly into new forms of foreign intervention. Anyone can go, and everyone is. Under the aegis of nongovernmental organizations, on whom international bodies and national governments are off-loading more of their responsibilities, foreign aid is being privatized. In the name of human rights, ecology, and other important causes, well-off foreigners are stepping into complex local conflicts.

Building support for a movement usually requires simplifying it. The very term "solidarity" implies that certain problems are going to be overlooked in order to build a common front against a greater evil. Unless a distant situation is presented as a melodrama, North Americans and Europeans are not likely to make an emotional investment in it. If they perceive much ambiguity, such as a contest between equally sordid factions, the only response is a check to a relief agency, if that. What they are most likely to embrace is a well-defined cause with moral credibility, whose contradictions have been shoved under the table. In the case of Guatemala, the army was obviously doing most of the killing, but the guerrillas also did their share, and how ordinary people felt was far from clear. By making a firm identification between peasants and insurgents, firmer than what many peasants felt, *I, Rigoberta Menchú* turned a nightmarish experience into a morality play.

Solidarity imagery is a desperate bid for the attention of foreigners who have little at stake but whose governments can have an impact. Successful organizing is achieved in the face of considerable disinterest, and it can melt away quickly. Consider Witness for Peace, the ecumenical Christian network that sent North Americans to Nicaragua in the 1980s to serve as human shields for Sandinista cooperatives being attacked by U.S.-financed counterrevolutionaries. When formal hostilities ended, Witness lost its most spectacular issue. It was much harder to keep North Americans interested when the U.S. government reneged on its aid pledges, the International Monetary Fund imposed austerity policies, and Nicaraguans were left in destitution and under siege from common crime.

In Guatemala's case, the invisibility of U.S. military aid kept the solidarity movement smaller than for Nicaragua and El Salvador. Only when North Americans could be identified as victims did Guatemala make the headlines. That made a figure like Rigoberta all the more important. Yet even she had rather little cachet. The Nobel is the most prestigious award in the world, but not all laureates are created equal. Although media coverage of her selection was better in Europe, in the United States it was rather light. The *New York Times* printed nary a word when Rigoberta spent a week in Gotham soon after the prize.

One of the simplifying functions of solidarity imagery is that it offers a single platform to support. This the Guatemalan guerrilla organizations worked hard to achieve in the form of the Guatemalan National Revolutionary Union. Validated by sources of information like Rigoberta, foreigners could have some confidence that they were supporting a coherent, morally defensible program. What happens without the illusion of a single platform is illustrated by Peru and Colombia. In Peru the Shining Path guerrillas made no effort to conceal their terrorism against noncombatants. A promising electoral coalition called the United Left disintegrated over which was the lesser evil, the Shining Path or the government. In Colombia the guerrillas split into murderous factions, undermining the claim to be a representative political force.[8] As a result, North Americans who care about these countries have not had a single, plausible movement like the Sandinistas or the URNG to support. Instead, they face many-sided conflicts between elected governments, social democratic oppositions, left-wing terrorists, right-wing terrorists, and drug mafias. Even though death tolls in these countries have approached Central American levels, little has developed in the way of solidarity organizing to change U.S. policy.

Campaigns to support indigenous rights pose problems of their own. To stand out from competing causes, they play up the exotic side of indigenous life. The drawback is that international support becomes conditioned on images that have little to do with the actual lives of native people. Mayan Indians have been at the heart of Guatemala's appeal for foreigners. With the women still dressing in traditional garb, it is easy to imagine that Mayan culture is unitary, or would be if it were not for the ravages of colonialism. Then there is the corollary that Mayan Indians are more moral and noble than nonindigenous Guatemalans and ourselves. This might seem an innocent illusion, and some readers will probably deny that it is an illusion at all. Yet it means that support for indigenous rights can become contingent on native people's living up to our rather lofty expectations.[9]

To illustrate this issue, let us compare Rigoberta's story with another remarkable work that has not been as popular, the three-volume diary of Ignacio Bizarro Ujpán, the nom de plume of a Tz'utujil Maya elder on Lake Atitlán. With the encouragement of anthropologist James Sexton, for whom Ignacio worked, he began recording his daily life in 1972. His fifteen-year record of his thoughts and activities provides a very different picture of indigenous life than Rigoberta's. Ignacio is a small labor contractor and precinct captain for the army's political party, although not an enthusiastic one. He is also troubled by the guerrillas, the murders committed by the two sides, supernatural events, and the envy of his neighbors. A chronic worrier under his polite persona, Ignacio is (like many Mayan men) constantly battling his vulnerability to alcohol. Unlike Rigoberta, who eulogizes her community, Ignacio usually presents his in terms of conflict.[10]

In 1986 one reviewer was sufficiently under the sway of solidarity imagery to refer to Ignacio as "a somewhat bizarre manifestation of a Guatemalan Indian. It's a pity [that James Sexton] couldn't find a more interesting—and perhaps a more typical—Guatemalan Indian to write his life story during this critical period."[11] Some years later a literary scholar detailed his dissatisfaction with Ignacio's politics but conceded that the contrast with Rigoberta might represent the "real consciousness" of Indians as opposed to their "potential consciousness."[12] If foreigners attracted to Rigoberta grasped that most peasants do not share her advanced consciousness, would they be as interested in supporting their rights?

If the Central American solidarity movement comes out of any particular sector of North American society, it is the Christian left. Imagery of sacrifice and social redemption is much in evidence. My impression is that Guatemala activists in the United States are almost entirely middle-class Anglos, more often female than male, and usually well educated. They became exposed to Guatemala in college (in which case they tend to be in their twenties and thirties) or in a Catholic or liberal Protestant church (in which case they tend to be in their fifties or sixties). If activists have not already visited Guatemala, often to study Spanish, they are planning to do so soon, and many become regular visitors supporting a panoply of humanitarian projects.

This is a commendable slice of North American society. By the 1990s few Guatemala activists expressed support for guerrilla warfare, even if more did under the military dictatorships of the previous decade. Instead, they were likely to regard themselves as pacifists. When I began to question solidarity assumptions in my book *Between Two Armies,* in particular the idea that the guerrilla movement had been a deeply rooted popular cause, I did not collide with enthusiasm for revolutionary violence.

Rather, I was contradicting assumptions that became enshrined under the counterinsurgency regimes of earlier decades, when North Americans and Europeans built solidarity networks for the Central American left.

During this period, army killing became so massive, and so obviously required an emergency response, that it was difficult not to accept other claims made by the guerrilla movement. If peasants did not support the guerrillas, why would the army kill so many? It also seemed logical that the guerrilla movement grew out of basic peasant needs. All those dead civilians began to certify not just that the Guatemalan army was committing mass murder but other propositions advanced by the guerrilla movement. If most of the combatants were indigenous, then the insurgency must have been a popular uprising. It must also have been an inevitable product of oppression triggered exclusively by Guatemala's power structure.

Polarized thinking was encouraged by U.S. foreign policy under Ronald Reagan (1981–1989), who revived the cold war at the expense of no one more than Central Americans. Under the bane of Reaganism, scholarship on the region became so politicized that there was no need for opponents of U.S. policy to apologize for being "committed." What required apology, and lengthy soul-searching beforehand, was publicly contradicting the Central American left and its North American supporters. To publish unflattering information about the struggle was perceived as aid and comfort to enemies of humanity on a par with the Nazis.[13] This reinforced one of the legacies of the Vietnam War for North American scholars: fear of being associated with counterinsurgency research, that is, findings that could be used against popular movements.

Now that political killing has diminished, Guatemala scholars have been thinking about the problem of what we know but are not supposed to say. Todd Little-Siebold has raised the issue of to whom we listen and to whom we do not, of our fear of betraying the cause, being perceived as selling out, and being shunned by our colleagues. The strength and weakness of solidarity thinking is the insistence on moral simplicity. Speaking of her own case (and mine for that matter), Diane Nelson has described the utopian fantasies about Mayas, peasants, and revolutionaries that bring foreigners to Guatemala. It is as if we were going abroad to find a space of innocence in which to align ourselves on the side of good against evil, without having to acknowledge the moral complexities with which we are all too familiar in our own society.[14]

The search for healing leads to a colonialism of images, in which foreign activists firm up our sense of moral worth by identifying with poor people but fail to be pragmatic about the obstacles to be overcome. That would be too compromising. Instead, a polarized view of Guatemala enables us to magnify the evils of colonialism and the status quo, the redemptive potential of political protest, and our own importance in an unfolding utopian drama. This is how a sense of responsibility for the U.S. record in Guatemala can degenerate into an odd new expression of Manifest Destiny.

Literary Scholars Come to Rigoberta's Defense

The desire for moral validation reaches well into the scholarly community. The first time I presented my doubts about enshrining Rigoberta's story was at Berkeley in October 1990. The Western Humanities Conference was addressing the issue of political correctness. This was a meeting of left-liberal scholars, not the conservatives who would soon be using the "p.c." label to polemicize against them, so most of the proceedings were conducted at a high level of abstraction, to the disappointment of Richard Bernstein, the *New York Times* reporter in attendance. Bernstein was about to set off the media fireworks over political correctness, but he was not finding the concrete examples that journalists require. Since most of the presenters were experienced academics, they were too cautious to be very specific about the disputes they were adjudicating.

I was one of the few who was not. As fate would have it, the speaker before me had never been to Guatemala, took at face value Rigoberta's portrait of Indians living in harmony, and extolled her book as the most meaningful one he had ever read. When my exposition ensued—of the problem of how Petrocinio died, followed by the main point that many of us wished to privilege a voice that met our own needs at the cost of understanding the situation—the implications were unavoidably personal. His reaction was that I was falling into the army's propaganda line. Two anthropologists who had their own problems with political correctness, Smadar Lavie and Susan Harding, spoke up. They had various suggestions for me, but they also cautioned my adversary against ideological policing. Since most conference-goers were off listening to more prominent speakers, only a dozen or so people were present. As word spread that there finally had been a confrontation, Richard Bernstein wanted to talk to me, but I begged off.

Wondering what to do, I sent a copy of my twelve-page talk to the literary scholar John Beverley, who asked to quote it at the upcoming meetings of the Latin American Studies Association, with the results described in the last chapter. A few weeks later, at the end of April 1991, I presented a revised version to my department at Stanford University. I also submitted the paper to Fred Myers, the editor of a journal called *Cultural Anthropology*. Six months later, in March 1992, Myers called up, expressed interest, and urged me to apply for a one-year visiting professorship at the department he chaired, at New York University. The next fall I was at NYU. Asked to give a lecture, I decided to talk about my experiences with

Rigoberta's story. Fortuitously, the department scheduled it for the day before the 1992 peace prize was announced. Knowing that Rigoberta was a strong candidate, I chose a stealth title for the announcement, then told the audience that what they would hear was off the record. Two days later, journalists looking for background on the new laureate were calling up. Once again I fended off the press, and soon I also withdrew my submission to *Cultural Anthropology*.

I wondered whether refusing to talk to journalists was the right decision. Was it not schizophrenic, perhaps even malicious and cowardly, to talk to small groups about the problems I faced but not in a public forum? My options were essentially three. First, I could submit to the self-censorship that is pervasive in graduate schools and junior faculties, bow to Rigoberta's authority, approach the problems I had discovered only in the most abstract terms, or find something else to study. This is what some of my colleagues thought best, for my career as well as Rigoberta's. Second, I could speak up. A few colleagues thought I had the obligation to do so, especially now that a person who had fictionalized part of her autobiography was receiving a Nobel prize. Yet that would undermine an important symbol for the Guatemalan left, the peace talks, and the indigenous movement. I also knew that in such a polarized atmosphere, any criticism of the historical accuracy of *I, Rigoberta Menchú* would be interpreted as sabotage by an agent of the CIA or the Guatemalan army. Third, I could pursue the problem quietly. That would require discussing my findings with peers but refraining from publication.

By the time Rigoberta received the Nobel, I knew the outline of what I have presented here. But I still assumed that Vicente Menchú had been a founder of CUC, and I had yet to hear the stories about how he welcomed the guerrillas to Chimel. Since I had not interviewed extensively in Uspantán, there was a strong argument for lying low until I could. In hindsight, this was a good decision, and not just because I did not want to detract from whatever pressure the Nobel placed on the Guatemalan army. Setting off a scandal would probably have made it harder to gather the competing versions of events that I did. But there was a cost to taking the middle road. Having already addressed the subject on three occasions to perhaps seventy-five people, I had raised issues and now was declining to go on record. Worse, I had unwisely mailed out several copies of my first talk in 1990, without stipulating that they were not for quotation without permission. Since then, the Xerox machines had been at work.

At issue was the reliability of Rigoberta's 1982 story as testimonio, the Latin American genre that has brought the life stories of market women, tin miners, and the like into literature and scholarship, in their own eloquent words. Rigoberta's—like others, the result of taping, transcribing, and editing by a sympathizer—is the most famous example. Everyone concedes that such stories reflect personal viewpoints; for anthropologists the problem is usually not whether they are true or false. More important is what they tell us about the narrator's perspective. But advocates of testimonios would like to believe that they are testimony, that is, a more or less reliable source of information. They hope that *I, Rigoberta Menchú* is not, as one of my colleagues struggled to define it, "a documentary novel posing as a real-life document, manufactured for a certain use."

Of the various responses to the 1990 talk that have reached me, the first was by John Beverley. To warn colleagues against assuming that testimonio is unassailably truthful, he published my findings on the death of Petrocinio, in which I termed Rigoberta's account a "literary invention" but not a "fabrication" since the army indeed killed her brother. Unfortunately, Beverley underestimated the evidence against Rigoberta's version, quoting me incorrectly to the effect that a human rights report coincided with hers, when actually none did. He concluded that even if I was disenchanted with Rigoberta's testimony, I had to admit that there was no alternative source of authority but "other testimonios."[15] (My feeling is that the 1980 denunciations quoted in Chapter 5 should be taken more seriously than a story told in Paris two years later.)

Beverley's coauthor on the subject of testimonio, Marc Zimmerman, went on to accuse me of making malicious, unsubstantiated charges against Rigoberta. To understand Zimmerman's position, we have to go back to the 1991 LASA meetings where Beverley first quoted my findings. Zimmerman was there, too. Against the main reaction in the room—that my findings were an outrage and irrelevant, the truth of Rigoberta's story being a nonissue in the postmodern era—he rose to the occasion and insisted that they were important to discuss.

Later he would accuse me of cowering in the back of the room, leaving him to take the heat from postmodernists who, in apparent violation of their principles, were determined to interpret *I, Rigoberta Menchú* literally, or at least did not want to hear a contradictory account. This was indeed a confrontation I decided to avoid. After all the warnings at the conference on political correctness, it was not my idea to challenge Rigoberta's veracity before the Latin American Studies Association. Not only had LASA invited her as a distinguished guest, but it had also invited an ex–Guatemalan defense minister, General Alejandro Gramajo, and the meeting was swarming with journalists. If there had been an important reason to challenge her 1982 account, I would have done so myself, not through a third party quoting me for a minute or two. What I viewed as the main issue—how outsiders were using Rigoberta's story to justify continuing a war at the expense of peasants who did not support it—was entirely missing from Beverley's presentation.

This was the central question of my 1990 talk—not the precise details of how Petrocinio died, which I identified as secondary. It was not a question in which the scholars responding to my paper were very interested. For them, the most important issue was that an anthropologist would dare challenge Rigoberta's authority, and this they found offensive.[16] The reason is suggested by Beverley's definition of testimonio as a story "by a narrator who is also a real protagonist or witness of the event he or she recounts." Similarly, Beverley's colleague George Yúdice defines testimonio as "an authentic narrative, told by a witness who . . . portrays his or her own experience as an agent (rather than a representative) of a collective memory and identity."

Judging by such definitions, *I, Rigoberta Menchú* does not belong in the genre of which it is the most famous example, because it is not the eyewitness account it purports to be. In contrast to Elisabeth Burgos, who understands the creative nature of oral storytelling and does not interpret my questions about *I, Rigoberta Menchú* as hostile, Beverley and his colleagues have been promoting testimonio in a way that does not allow questioning its reliability. Although they are willing to entertain certain issues, on close examination their conception of peasants and political violence is so bound up with romantic notions of authenticity, collectivity, resistance, and revolution that they have no patience with contradictory evidence.[17] The reactions corroborate the final point of my 1990 talk: that we have an unfortunate tendency to idolize native voices that serve our own political and moral needs, as opposed to others that do not. Despite the fashion for deconstruction, there was something that was hands-off, don't-touch about Rigoberta.

Identities and Icons

> *Indians are nothing if not versatile. . . . The unadmirable qualities of Indians can make whites feel good about themselves. The admirable qualities of Indians can make whites feel bad about themselves. And so, culturally speaking, Indians are useful to have around.*
>
> **—Richard White, 1996[18]**

How could sophisticated literary scholars, who like to think they question all assumptions, be so offended by my questions about *I, Rigoberta Menchú*? In the 1960s many North American academics began to justify their careers by identifying with the oppressed. Instead of studying "down" in the social order as before, for example, we were going to study "up" by investigating power structures. By the 1980s the academic left was marginalized from national politics by conservative backlash. Around the world, socialist alternatives to capitalism were disintegrating.

One place where academics like myself could take refuge was the critique of capitalist hegemony. But as we deconstructed Western forms of knowledge, many of us continued to embrace our preferred causes with more fervor than the reigning cult of skepticism might seem to allow.

The resulting mix of hyperrelativism and doctrinaire thinking came to public attention in the North American debate over political correctness. Until 1990, "p.c." was merely an ironic expression about how easy it was to offend leftist sensibilities. Rarely was it heard outside the ivy walls. Then critics of liberal academics realized that the jokes were about ideological policing, as demonstrated by the occasional persecution of a campus conservative, and began to denounce political correctness as a threat to free speech. Rigoberta was one of many delicate subjects because of the closely related debate over multiculturalism, the curricular battleground over what should be taught in the humanities and social sciences. For those who think multiculturalism is a good idea, it represents a long overdue effort to bring previously excluded voices—particularly those of women, subordinate ethnic groups, gays, and lesbians—into the curriculum. For those who think multiculturalism is a bad idea, it threatens to fragment the educational system and U.S. society into identity blocs that can no longer conceive of what they have in common.

It was in the name of multiculturalism that *I, Rigoberta Menchú* entered university reading lists. Because the book has the useful attribute of being about peasants, indigenous people, and women, it is a readable way to illustrate the intersection of class, ethnicity, and gender, accompanied by fluent discussions of religious syncretism, identity, consciousness, and protest. This is not to say that *I, Rigoberta Menchú* is a good assignment for teaching students about the mundane problems facing Guatemalan peasants. As an anthropologist who dropped it from his reading list told me, "What's left unsaid in that book ends up overshadowing what she does say."

Still, *I, Rigoberta Menchú* can be taught critically at the same time that it is taught sympathetically, as suggested by the following story from a graduate student: "We read it at Macalester College in St. Paul, which makes a point of recruiting children of Third World elites, including police colonels, dictators, etcetera. Her book was on feminist and anthropology and multicultural reading lists, like the Bible. So when Rigoberta showed up at our women's studies class, she seemed larger than life. The three Guatemalans in the class started crying. Even people who hadn't read the book felt her presence. She was so small, smaller than we had expected. Since the class project was to write our own life stories, what came out was how easy it was to cover up. I lied when it came to describing a traumatic episode in my childhood."

Evidently the instructor was encouraging a critical attitude toward a powerful narrative, one of the grand old goals of liberal education. Like any intellectual movement, however, multiculturalism not only makes it easier to ask new questions; it also makes it harder to ask others. For critics, multiculturalism becomes problematical at the difficult-to-define point where old-fashioned pluralism (to which no one seems to object) turns into identity politics. This is the belief that the best way to participate in political life is as a member of a group that identifies itself in terms of a history of grievances, that makes group demands for redress, and that tries to preempt disagreement by accusing critics of racism, colonialism, or some other form of prejudice.

Political correctness, multiculturalism, and identity politics raise many issues that cannot be gone into here. For our purposes, what matters most is the underlying preoccupation with victimhood, claims to which are proliferating and being used to make an array of demands. Since any individual has multiple identities and can be viewed as privileged in regard to others who are less fortunate, dilemmas arise. Exactly who is a victim, and who is not? Who deserves redress? Who is left to play the oppressor, or at least pay the bill? Once one group coalesces in terms of victimhood, others do, too, in sympathy or reaction, until even white males view themselves as an oppressed minority and act accordingly.

Whether victims deserve support is not the issue; instead, it is how we define who they are, why they are victims, and what should be done next. If everyone claims victimhood, who deserves sympathy and who does not? While some cases are clear-cut, others are not. It is hardly rare for people to be both victims and victimizers, including in Guatemalan villages, which human rights activists learn when they find themselves in the middle of land feuds.[19] What if victims contradict each other's testimony and fall into mutual accusations? What if victims misrepresent why they became victims, by omitting how they victimized others who are now lashing back? If a victim claims to represent others, should this be assumed to be true?

Under the influence of postmodernism (which has undermined confidence in a single set of facts) and identity politics (which demands acceptance of claims to victimhood), scholars are increasingly hesitant to challenge certain kinds of rhetoric. They do not want to be accused of "blaming the victim"—an all-purpose, preemptive indictment, like "racism," which has been very effective in suppressing unwelcome information and replacing it with defensive theorizing.[20] In the case of Guatemala, I was to avoid focusing on how peasants contribute to their poverty by having large families, or how guerrillas triggered political killing in some locales, or how the left is out of touch with the people it wants to represent. At bottom, I was to avoid challenging the left's claim to speak for victims.

Obviously, I do not see how scholars can avoid using whatever evidence is available to evaluate the conflicting claims that sooner or later emerge from any serious study. Given all the competing claims to victimhood, solidarity with the oppressed does not provide a refuge from the need to justify judgments and choices. Debate over claims to victimhood is inevitable, yet it seems to be discouraged by the discourse of identity, at least as propounded by critics of Western knowledge. If the kind of empirical study that you hold in your hands is inherently a form of domination, then representatives of the oppressed can dismiss it out of hand as racist or otherwise prejudiced. Absent actual members of the oppressed, which is usually the case in academia, the task of defining the limits of decency in scholarly debate falls to their middle-class allies, such as professors of literature. Authority to speak is reduced to membership in an oppressed group, or to solidarity with it, restricting what can be said to what will be inoffensive.[21]

Getting back to Rigoberta, how does a figure like her become sacrosanct, then spread the mantle of unquestionability to surrounding claims? One clue is how Rigoberta's narrative sets itself against Western civilization but reaches out to Western audiences in their own terms. Although she makes references to Mayan cosmology, Rigoberta seeks religious justification in the Bible. After condemning Euro-Americans for their centuries-old mistreatment of indígenas, she joins a revolutionary movement led by them. Here was a radically "other" indigenous woman who had opened up to the Western left, translating the exotic into the comprehensible and the authentic into radical politics.

Many observers have been struck by the religious overtones of Rigoberta's appearances in the United States, especially when they occur in large churches packed with supporters. Obviously, these are political meetings with a goal that everyone understands—bringing out support for the Guatemalan left. For an audience uncomfortable with its middle-class privileges and the U.S. record in Guatemala, Rigoberta's story of oppression is analogous to a preacher reminding listeners that they are sinners. Then her story of joining the left and learning that not all outsiders are evil makes it possible for the audience to be on her side, providing a sense of absolution.

What occurs is a reconciliation of opposites. That is the function of an icon as I am defining it: a symbol that resolves painful contradictions by transcending them with a healing image. The contradiction resolved depends on the needs of the beholder. For example, icons of the Virgin Mary might help women reconcile themselves to the difference between how they are honored as mothers and abused as wives. Rigoberta's image reconciles contradictions between her people and outsiders, indigenous tradition and revolution, what they want and what we want. For white, middle-class audiences, icons such as Rigoberta, Martin Luther King Jr., and Nelson Mandela bridge the gap between privilege and its opposite. They create identity by pointing to a common enemy—the Guatemalan army, segregation, apartheid—against whom privileged and unprivileged can be on the same side.

Such images, almost sacred in their unquestionability, are probably necessary to pull together any movement. The foibles of the particular human beings who turned into these images may be irrelevant, at least up to a point. That Martin Luther King Jr. plagiarized part of his doctoral dissertation does not detract from his vision of racial equality. Although Rigoberta made up part of her story, many Guatemalans will continue to regard it as a truthful portrayal of their country. Whether an icon is good or bad depends on your opinion of how it is used, that is, the practical results of its aura of unchallengeability. That Rigoberta's story makes readers care about Guatemala is good; that her image has the effect of setting up an exclusion zone around issues that need to be debated is not. The aura of unchallengeability around an icon plays both ways: Although it brings together people in a common cause, it can also discourage questions that need to be asked, prevent lessons from being learned, and redound against the movement it represents.

Unlike other Nobel laureates representing disenfranchised peoples, such as Nelson Mandela and Aung San Suu Kyi, Rigoberta did not become a leader at home before she became an international figure. Hence her particularly ambiguous position, as a representative of peasants who by and large had turned against the revolution for which she spoke, if they ever had supported it at all. Not just for skeptics like myself but for Mayas becoming acquainted with her story, this raised the central question: To what extent did she represent her people and to what extent an agenda for them that was not of their making?

Certainly Rigoberta was a representative of her people, but hiding behind that was a more partisan role, as a representative of the revolutionary movement, and hiding behind that was an even more unsettling possibility: that she represented the audiences whose assumptions about indígenas she mirrored so effectively. I believe this is why it was so indecent of me to question her claims. Exposing problems in Rigoberta's story was to expose how supporters have subliminally used it to clothe their own contradictions, in a Durkheimian case of society worshiping itself. Here was an indígena who represented the unknowable other, yet she talked a language of protest with which the Western left could identify. She protected revolutionary sympathizers from the knowledge that the revolutionary movement was a bloody failure. Her iconic status concealed a costly political agenda that by the time her story was becoming known, had more appeal in universities than among the people she was supposed to represent.

I suspect that Rigoberta has carried iconic authority for the same reason that many of my fellow graduate students said they were studying "resistance." As I heard this term again and again, I came to think of Prometheus chained to a rock—eternally bound, eternally defiant. The preoccupation with resistance assumed the same kind of Prometheus figure, the undying Western individual fighting for rights against oppression. Rigoberta was a Prometheus figure who justified the projection of Western identity drives into the situations we study.[22]

At this point, the identity needs of Rigoberta's academic constituency play into the weakness of rules of evidence in postmodern scholarship. Following the thinking of literary theorists such as Edward Said and Gayatri Spivak, anthropologists have become very interested in problems of narrative, voice, and representation, especially the problem of how we misrepresent voices other than our own. In reaction, some anthropologists argue that the resulting fascination with texts threatens the claim of anthropology to be a science, by replacing hypothesis, evidence, and generalization with stylish forms of introspection. If we focus on text, narrative, or voice, it is not hard to find someone to say what we want to hear—just what we need to firm up our sense of moral worth or our identity as intellectual rebels.

This is how critiques of Western forms of knowledge can degenerate into the worship of symbols of rebellion like *I, Rigoberta Menchú*. By dismissing empirical research as a form of Western domination, critical theorists can end up interpreting texts in terms of simplistic stereotypes of collectivity, authenticity, and resistance that, because they are authorized by identity with victimhood, are not to be questioned. Even though Uspantán and Chimel are places that you can visit, where some of the inhabitants may be willing to talk about their experiences, according to this conception of scholarship they are to be reserved as a land of myth, wrapped in clouds of mystique as well as mist.

Obviously, Rigoberta is a legitimate Mayan voice. So are all the young Mayas who want to move to Los Angeles or Houston. So is the man with a large family who owns three worn-out acres and wants me to buy him a chain saw so he can cut down the last forest more quickly. Any of these people can be picked out to make misleading generalizations about Mayas. But I doubt that the man who wants the chain saw will be invited to multicultural universities anytime soon. Until he does, books like *I, Rigoberta Menchú* will be exalted because they tell many academics what they want to hear. Such works provide rebels in far-off places, into whom careerists can project their fantasies of rebellion. The simplistic images of innocence, oppression, and defiance can be used to construct mythologies of purity for academic factions claiming moral authority on the grounds that they identify with the oppressed. But icons have their cost. What makes *I, Rigoberta Menchú* so attractive in universities is what makes it misleading about the struggle for survival in Guatemala. We think we are getting closer to understanding Guatemalan peasants when actually we are being borne away by the mystifications wrapped up in an iconic figure.

The New Chimel

"You're supporting the guerrillas!"
"I don't know anything about them!"
"Yes you do! You're a pure guerrilla, and you're going to be hunted down like deer. We're going to cut your throat!"

—Threat by a military commissioner against one of Rigoberta's relatives, 1992

The rain was pouring as I squatted under the eaves of a hut with two of the men resettling Chimel. Even though EGP columns were increasingly rare, the fear came up again and again, of being labeled as guerrillas. "Really we have no relation with those who roam around in the montaña, nor with the army, but the rumor continues that we're guerrillas," one said. "The guerrillas come through, information reaches the army, and maybe they come to grab you." The other kept repeating that he wanted to replace his house of wooden slats and thatch with one of cement block. Why? "Block is more secure because it can't catch fire."

When I visited Chimel for the first time in July 1991, it was a tiny hamlet on the edge of the montaña, with just five families. To roof their huts, the families scavenged the tin sheets they found in the underbrush, scorched by fire and punctured by machetes. Supposedly my companion and I were the first foreigners to visit them. Without a civil patrol, which was neither desired nor feasible for so few families, they were especially vulnerable to rumors. One occurred in 1990, after guerrillas passed through and appropriated a bull, some chickens, and a duck. Although they paid for the animals and cuffed a youth who resisted them, another version of events reached the Uspantán civil patrol—that Chimel had gone back to collaborating with the enemy.

In the town of Uspantán, only the most confident put much faith in the apparent return to tranquillity. A Spanish embassy widow told Barbara Bocek and me that her new husband was discouraging her from joining the CONAVIGUA widow's organization, to avoid losing him the same way she lost her last one. "They hardly want to join," a member said. "Because they saw how their men were taken away and dumped with their throats cut. They're afraid to participate, because it can happen again. We already suffered a lot in 1982–1983. I myself almost did not join. . . . 'Why was our father killed?' my children ask. 'Why are you involved in this organization?' they ask. 'What happens if you get killed?' they ask. Even now I'm afraid to go to meetings of the organization. Sometimes I have the desire to go; other times I don't. . . . Maybe when we're all inside for the meeting, if the soldiers come, maybe we'll all get killed. What about our children? We all have children, lots of children. The children ask us not to go. They say, 'If our fathers were killed, then what about our mothers?'"

The Uspantán town council, run by Christian Democrats who had been catechists with Vicente Menchú, was courageous enough to join the ceremonies for the Nobel prize. The mayor journeyed to Oslo for the presentation. Then the entire council went to the capital for a reception at CONAVIGUA headquarters. Despite the presence of many dignitaries, Rigoberta spent three hours with them. The Uspantán delegation presented her with gifts, including two hundred photos of old neighbors who also survived, and came away impressed by the champagne as well as their town's most famous citizen. But when they invited her to come home, she declined. Were she to visit Uspantán, she explained, it would be used against her and her image. That is, the warm reception would enable the government to claim that all was well in terms of human rights. As my source observed, she would "lose internationally," which he considered a good reason to stay away. In the meantime, some of Rigoberta's family and their neighbors were recovering Chimel and helping to start Uspantán's human rights movement. In this chapter, we will look at how that happened and how her story is regarded by Uspantanos and other Guatemalans.

The Resettlement of Vicente Menchú's Land

I'm not going to abandon this. It doesn't matter what they tell me. . . . I'm going to keep faith with those who died.

—Nicolás Menchú, 1989

As if under a curse, Chimel continued to suffer from disagreements over ownership. A few families began to settle there in 1987, only one of them from before the war. Living up to its portrayal in *I, Rigoberta Menchú*, the National Institute for Agrarian Transformation no longer recognized the prewar owners. This was despite the provisional titles that had arrived just before Vicente Menchú's death. Even though Chimel had been abandoned only after repeated raids and many deaths, INTA ruled that the failure to keep up payments (which inflation had reduced to a few hundred dollars a year) invalidated the deeds. Only the intervention of one of the few Mayas in the national congress, Claudio Coxaj, persuaded INTA to recognize the rights of those survivors bold enough to step forward.

Two groups were vying for recognition. Although one had a few of the prewar owners, the other consisted entirely of newcomers, including ladinos, two K'iche' bilingual teachers, and two Christian Democrats who were soon elected to the town council. Because INTA wanted a settler for each of the sixty-one caballerías (the local measure for the 2,753 hectares), it ordered the two factions to merge. Many of the ladino claimants dropped out; more prewar survivors joined. Eventually the fifty-seven families in the new, consolidated group included fifteen households from the 1978 census. Eighteen others from the prewar settlement decided not to return. But the majority of newcomers were not complete outsiders. Instead, they were K'iche's from nearby villages, many related by blood or marriage to the old Chimel.

Performing a heroic role in the petitions was Vicente Menchú's only surviving son, Nicolás, now in his late thirties. Since surrendering with his family in 1983 and surviving several months of army custody, he had settled near town, joined the obligatory civil patrol, led an irrigation project, and served as village mayor. But his deepest commitment was to recovering Chimel, a subject that he addressed passionately from our first meeting in 1989. Clearly his father's son, Nicolás had the air of a man accustomed to asserting his rights, even though paranoia was still rampant and a false step could get him killed. By 1991 he claimed to have made forty trips to the capital to get back his father's land, and these were not the last.

Obtaining new provisional titles was arduous, but it was not the only obstacle to reclaiming Chimel. Because of opposition from the Tums of Laguna Danta, INTA had never recognized Chimel's right to the 151 hectares on which the new as well as old hamlet sat. Now this crucial tract was being disputed with a new rival. During the years that Chimel vanished from the landscape, the Tums made the most intelligent move for anyone in Guatemala with a land problem. They sold it, to a small cattle rancher in Chicamán named Reginaldo Gamarro. INTA had never recognized the Tum title because it lacked boundaries. The new owner was more successful in validating it. Now that the Chimel claimants had died or scattered, he apparently paid for an uncontested survey, went to a court in Santa Cruz del Quiché, and won an uncontested decision. True to the spirit of *I, Rigoberta Menchú*, the entire valley of Chimel was now owned by a ladino.

Soon Gamarro complained that his property was being invaded. The invaders were the first families resettling Chimel, who spent most of the next decade in deep anxiety over this and other land problems. INTA inspectors pointed out that, judging from prewar foundations on Gamarro's property, he never should have been given title in the first place. Eventually the agency brokered a deal in which forty-four percent of the land in dispute went to the rancher and fifty-six percent to Chimel—eighty-five of the 151 hectares for which Vicente had fought for so many years. In 1991 Gamarro sold the rest of his holding to six members of the new Chimel. This might seem a good outcome, but the six did so as individual proprietors, not as representatives of the larger group. The main purchaser was the K'iche' vice mayor of Uspantán, a Christian Democrat who (1) had repeatedly risked his life to stop the vigilantes and (2) would be convicted of embezzling town funds. For homesteaders from the old Chimel, the loss of almost half their village site to better-off associates was a bitter pill. The vice mayor and his copurchasers immediately fenced off their new property, on which they grazed a herd of cattle.

The Catholic parish did what it could by paying off INTA for the 2,753 hectares. Conveniently, inflation had reduced the debt to US$3,000, or about $50 per family, which each would reimburse to the parish over the next five years. Now Chimel could solicit the permanent titles that Vicente Menchú had never received. Predictably, obtaining the precious documents for each family became yet another trial. I myself was party to one journey to Nebaj, for which the new Chimel rented a truck, to receive the titles from the hand of President Serrano. The expedition ended in bitterness when he stood them up, along with thousands of other campesinos. Only after more years of anxiety, of seemingly fruitless meetings and bureaucratic pilgrimages, did President Ramiro De Leon Carpio come to Uspantán to give each family its papers in September 1993.

That was not the end of Chimel's problems. Soon the deal with Reginaldo Gamarro broke down, jeopardizing the village's right to the land on which it sat. INTA had talked the rancher into giving Chimel eighty-five hectares by offering him property elsewhere, but he was not impressed by what he was shown and began asking the villagers for payment. Like every other crisis, this one required more journeys to the capital. "The people are going to get demoralized over spending so much money on trips," Nicolás Menchú predicted. With their hats in their hands, they persuaded Gamarro to reduce his price from Q25,000 to Q11,000 (about US$2,000), which they eventually paid with the help of the Catholic parish and Rigoberta.

An even more alarming conflict broke out with the García family, who still blamed the Menchús for the assassination of their patriarch, just as Chimel still blamed them for the destruction of the prewar village. Whatever the factual limitations of *I, Rigoberta Menchú,* it was prophetic about what would happen after it was published. The principal aggressor against Chimel was one of the late Honorio's sons-in-law, a man from the

Zona Reina whose violent behavior had made him persona non grata there. According to local custom, the first victims he chose in Soch were his own in-laws, by seizing the holdings of two Martínezes on the ever disputed Finca El Rosario. He also moved north of the line that INTA had established between Rosario and Chimel, invaded fifteen hectares, and fenced them off. To ratify the acquisition, he threatened to shoot anyone who crossed the new fence. When Chimel complained to the justice system, he refused to obey a summons. That meant the villagers would have to hire a lawyer, obtain an order from a distant court, and coax the national police to arrest him. Following the inevitable appeal to INTA, it arrived for an inspection and suggested a new survey, several years hence owing to its backlog of three hundred cases.[1]

Fortunately, Honorio's son-in-law retreated for reasons unknown. By 1995 the Garcías were merely blocking access to a path and a water supply. When I showed up one morning to see the disputed hillside, two old men from Chimel were cultivating it in obvious contentment. Down in the valley, not far away, was the stone house where Honorio used to live and his widow still does. The night before, while enjoying the García family's hospitality as I would Chimel's the following night, I acquired another perspective on the conflict. Honorio's widow and sons do not have a large estate in Soch, but the 113 hectares they own is good land along the valley bottom. It is also the last stretch of the valley where you can walk through the sweetly scented, humid shade of cloud forest. To east and west the trees that used to fill the valley have been chopped out, leaving hot, dry pasture. Much of the two steep ridges that wall the valley are still in forest, but that is changing.

Honorio's son Julio talked about his land with the same passion that Vicente's son Nicolás did. "Now the streams are drying up because the people of Chimel, San Pablo, and Jumuc are deforesting," he complained. "They come to cut two hundred trees this year, and they come to cut two hundred trees the next year, and it's a disaster. Where there is montaña, they cut it down." There is still considerable forest up there, therefore much that could be saved, but when I asked Julio why he didn't talk with the offending parties, he dismissed the suggestion as hopeless. No, that would just set off more accusations that he was threatening them. As for appealing to government forestry authorities, Julio said, they would simply extract bribes and go away. As for taking the problem to the mayor, he would simply decide in favor of the larger group with more votes—Julio's adversaries. He recriminated people who had been given so much land that they did not feel the need to conserve it.

A few days later, when I raised Julio's fears with a Chimel leader, he laughed bitterly. "It's just that he doesn't want poor people to get ahead. The poor have their families, their needs, and there are lands new and good in San Pablo. He doesn't want poor people to get ahead." Aside from everything else involved in this conflict, it is also about forest cover, rainfall, and water flow.

Community in Conflict

Chimel had finally regained the 2,753 hectares for which Vicente Menchú had struggled for so many years. But the new owners did little celebrating. Aside from continuing problems over the 151 hectares on which the hamlet sat, and with the García family over the southeast corner, the owners of the new Chimel had serious disagreements among themselves. In Chapter 3 we saw how the prewar village was afflicted by discord between Vicente and other homesteaders weary of his land feud. First the Q'eqchi's departed, then most of the K'iche' families from Parraxtut, leaving mainly K'iche' farmers from Uspantán. The new Chimel was more heterogeneous than Vicente's village in two ways. Ethnically, the fifty-seven households now included six or so ladino families. Three of the ladino households were among the first to resettle Chimel, perhaps because they feared the army less than the K'iche's did or perhaps because they were especially poor. By withstanding the Garcías at the southeast corner when only a handful of men were on hand, they were among the group's stoutest defenders.

Ethnicity seemed to be a less significant divider than social class. In 1986–1987, when most of the prewar homesteaders were afraid to assert their rights, the few who did were joined not just by farmers from nearby villages but bilingual teachers, truck owners, and Christian Democrat politicians living in town—seven in total. All seven were K'iche's who contributed professional skills, financial resources, political connections, and badly needed confidence to the struggle for the new titles. While none was wealthy by urban standards, they were better-off than all but a few of the farmers in the new Chimel. According to INTA regulations, each homesteading family was to live on the property and use only its own labor. That hardly described men who had houses in town, obtained most of their income from nonagricultural activities, and were not about to raise their children in a hamlet without a school. The issue surfaced when one of the group's first organizers was expelled for misappropriating funds. He retaliated by telling INTA that some of the claimants did not meet its criteria. When a delegate arrived to investigate, everyone rallied to the defense of the town influentials, insisting that they had prewar ties to Chimel and worked the land themselves.

One reason for the solidarity was that the majority had not moved to Chimel either. Although indisputably campesinos, they were not landless or homeless elsewhere, and they, too, were finding reasons to put off the move. With only eleven houses by 1994, some of them occupied only intermittently, the new Chimel was not a community in the residential sense of the old one, most of whose members had lived there. Instead, it was a group of fifty-seven coproprietors with divergent interests. Rebuilding at the old site was paramount for some of the prewar homesteaders, as well as the poorest families who had nowhere else to call home. But for other owners, probably a majority, the preferred site for the new village was a long walk to the north. Cuatro Chorros (Four Streams) was in the montaña at the northeast corner of the 2,753 hectares, where the topography dropped toward the Zona Reina and the climate was warm enough to grow coffee. This was the perennial crop Vicente had dreamed of planting, and the only one that could make Chimel prosper.

Upon the location of the new village hinged infrastructural decisions such as where to put the potable water system. It was crucial to maintain a facade of unity because evidence to the contrary warned away aid groups, who wished to avoid feuds. On at least one occasion, the heterogeneity of the new Chimel subverted a project when various agencies reacted against the prosperity of some members and received mixed signals as to where the new village would be. The poorer families living in Chimel felt they had been betrayed by prosperous townfolk.

Another issue was whether to recognize the prewar boundaries of old members as their current property. Acknowledging the prewar holdings of old members might seem the best solution, but these had not necessarily been equitable in the first place. The ideal was a fair distribution of house lots in the village, marginal ridge land, and the more fertile limestone sinks or bowls. One family, among the first to brave the uncertainties of resettling Chimel, was subject to unnerving forms of intimidation by other families who returned later and wanted their old land back. There were also painful accusations over the management of group finances, a common problem in peasant organizations.

Figuring in most disputes was Vicente's son Nicolás. For several years, he was president of the Chimel committee, until the escalating disagreements led him to stop attending meetings. By the early 1990s, Nicolás was a survivor who counted many scars and enemies. Determined to recover the land of his father, he was perceived by many in the group, particularly the town influentials, as overbearing. One example was his last-minute demand for three of his sisters—the three who had ended up in Mexico—to be recognized as co-owners. Except for Nicolás and a sister living nearby, the Menchús had been slow to rejoin the resettlement. An uncle and his sons never did, for fear of reviving the accusation that they were guerrillas.

"The parents paid for this with their blood," Nicolás told me, "and isn't it right that the children receive it?" When other members failed to support the inscription of his sisters and INTA said that it was too late, Nicolás quit the committee.[2] Even though he was an important symbol of legitimacy in the new Chimel, feelings about his family's history were complex. More than a few blamed the Menchús for having brought the guerrillas. But anxiety over being identified with Rigoberta was mixed with anxiety over being ignored by her new charity, the Vicente Menchú Foundation.

Fortunately, mutual accusations did not prevent the reconciliations needed for the next petition. In 1994 Nicolás rejoined the committee, which now wanted to make proposals to his sister. Two years later, as she put up half the US$2,000 to buy the village site from the ladino rancher, Rigoberta suddenly insisted on taking personal title to half the eighty-five hectares being purchased. It was her father's old land, she said, and for members of the Menchú family who had been unable to obtain titles from INTA. There was quite a row, but her demand was accepted. One reason was that her foundation had promised Chimel an ambitious development package. She would help the community climb out of poverty without destroying the cloud forest, a problem obvious to any development worker if not to all the homesteaders. Of most importance to the new Chimel, she would help them build their dream of progress, a road through the forest primeval to their prosperous future as coffee growers at Cuatro Chorros. In exchange, they would set aside part of their land as an ecological reserve. This was a story in which there was no last chapter.

Human Rights Organizing Comes to Uspantán

Except when jammed with campesinos on market day, Uspantán is a sleepy country town. Like most Guatemalans, its inhabitants pride themselves on good manners. But when I returned in 1993, the town was astir with confrontation. At issue was the local administration of the Christian Democrats (DC), a party that had given hundreds of lives in the national struggle for democracy. There had just been a municipal election, in May, and it had not gone well for anyone. Once again the Christian Democrats had won, for the fourth time in a row, but by a much slimmer margin than before, and only because their many opponents had run six competing lists of candidates. Now the departing mayor and the newly elected one, both K'iche' Christian Democrats who owned land in Chimel, faced indictment for graft.

On election night, their heretofore divided challengers found enough in common to stage a riot, for which they were also being indicted. The mob burned two trucks that belonged to the mayor-elect, attacked his victory party, and chased DC activist Nicolás Menchú through the streets, inflicting enough damage to send him to the hospital. In July the opposition seized the town hall to prevent inauguration of the new administration. Instead, they wanted a new election. Only after several weeks without a town council did national authorities show up to mediate. In return for the mayor-elect's resignation, the anti-DC coalition allowed the rest of the winning candidates to take office. Eventually, four members of the previous council and their municipal secretary wound up in jail in Santa Cruz del Quiché. As in other towns, the Christian Democrats of Uspantán were led by K'iche' catechists. They were the only party in living memory to elect indígenas to the mayor's office. When Rigoberta won the peace prize, they braved threats to honor her. And they were my friends—four of the five were among the first to welcome me to Uspantán.

According to the Christian Democrats, the accusations and rioting were racist reactions by the town's ladinos. The hostile coalition was indeed led by ladinos, some of whom had the ugly habit of distributing anonymous, threatening fliers. Their handiwork appeared on the streets after Rigoberta received the peace prize, after the riot on election night, and after two men went to jail for burning the mayor-elect's trucks. But the anti-DC coalition did not consist simply of ladinos. It also included a significant number of indígenas, particularly evangelicals and Uspantekos, and their complaints against the Christian Democrats were all too common in other towns. After the party captured the presidency and a majority of municipal governments in the 1985 election, many of its new indigenous mayors succumbed to temptation. Suddenly they were buying houses and motor vehicles, and soon mobs were chasing them out of town.

"Aren't we Mayas?" an anti-DC activist asked indignantly. A delegation from the Communities of Population in Resistance had just passed through, to join a human rights rally, and this was much on his mind, not least because he used to be a civil patrol leader. "They say there aren't guerrillas anymore, but here are the guerrillas!" he railed against the CPR delegation, whom he accused of stockpiling guns in the montaña. "The town is divided," he ranted against the Christian Democrats, "for the robberies they've committed and for the people they've deceived. They know that [the CPR visitors] are the armed people who come to screw us. They come to start the thing again. And there right beside them is [the new mayor who was forced to resign]; there is [the former mayor] who stole so much money. They ate up so much cash. When they go to jail, we're going to shoot off skyrockets [to celebrate]. Look at the streets. With four million [quetzals] the entire town could be fixed up, but they ate it. They bought their trucks and their fincas. When they entered [office], they didn't have anything. They entered in sandals and left in shoes. The cash that the government sent, the cash that we paid [in taxes], all of it they ate up. These are the town thieves. They took what we paid in taxes and they ate it all.

Go down there to look at the school that they assessed at 72,000 quetzals, there in their fiscal report, and it doesn't exist! They took it all! Up there is a land parcel that they bought for 3,500 quetzals, and they assessed it at 8,000 quetzals. They took the difference!"

This was an unusually vehement reaction to human rights rallies that most of the population seemed to be watching in silence. One example was the Catholic procession that Barbara Bocek and I joined on February 14, 1994, up the road that climbs the steep ridge behind town. As we neared our destination—a pleasant little valley where a wooden cross marks the site of the Calanté massacre—the hundred or so people from town were met by another 150 living nearby—an impressive turnout, but far from the number who had family members to mourn. Included was a delegation from CONAVIGUA, the national widow's organization, and its local chapter. As is customary at these events, a dozen women carried simple wooden crosses bearing the names of relatives, the dates of their deaths, and who had killed them—the army, vigilantes, or the civil patrol. Periodically, we stopped to do a station of the cross, at which the priest or catechist taking the microphone would compare the victims to Jesus Christ. Like Jesus, they had died for the forgiveness of sins.

If human rights activism grows out of any one practice in Uspantán, it is the parish commemorations of the dead. The equation with the crucifixion is one that the Catholic Church has made widely. It corresponds with feelings that Barbara and I heard expressed by widow after widow: that victims had done nothing to deserve their fate. Encouraged by a parish committee, organizing went public in Uspantán in 1993. Suddenly there were local chapters of CONAVIGUA and other popular organizations. The new activists drew inspiration from Rigoberta, as a symbol of their right to say what they wanted without being punished, but the more immediate impetus was the conflict with the ladino-led coalition for control of the town hall. Arguing that the real issue was ladino racism, one of the DC councilmen persuaded various organizations to sign a petition supporting him and the other leaders accused of graft.

An index of the political space in Uspantán was our ability to interview a wide range of people on subjects that they were still afraid to discuss in public. No one tried to stop us, nor did anyone warn me that I was causing trouble, although I sometimes heard that my visits had provoked much discussion. When an adolescent shouted at me, "Rubber boots, guerrilla, *canche*[3]—shoot him!" it was a joke. But the stories of loss that we heard were usually in private, with no one but a friend or family member present. An important reason that Barbara and I were able to hear the stories that we did was that we were citizens of a foreign power, enjoying immunity from the intimidation that Guatemalans still faced. "With this fear my generation will go to its grave," an Uspantán ladino admonished me.

"It's easy for you to do your interviews, write your report, and head for the airplane, but the people here have to stay."

At human rights meetings, speakers would make passionate references to the violence, but without naming the army and its collaborators. Instead, their most pointed complaint was the government's failure to build a new road, the most widely held grievance in Uspantán. The funding that was to connect Chimel and Cuatro Chorros had been diverted to another route in the rival municipio of Chicamán. "The people of the Zona Reina are fenced in like animals!" the president of the human rights committee told me. "For the coast we hear of so many projects, because only finca owners, millionaires are there. But in the northern zone, abandonment. At times the people are on their knees, begging the pilots to take them to Cobán."

Among the new groups invited by the human rights committee was Majawil Q'ij (New Dawn), organized by a coalition of the left's popular organizations to broaden their appeal. "It's an uprising of the Mayan culture," one of the soon-to-be-jailed councilmen told me. "We're not going to fight with weapons or gunpowder, but with intelligence, to demand respect for our Mayan culture." Actually, the most active on the cultural front were Uspantekos who lived in town, had been to school, and for obvious demographic reasons, felt most in danger of losing their heritage. They organized a local chapter of the Academy of Mayan Languages, which teaches Mayas to read and write in the vernacular. Some activists talked about recovering Uspanteko land, particularly from ladinos, but others denied this was an objective, in view of the enormous practical difficulties.

The human rights committee also affiliated itself with the Procurator for Human Rights, a government agency that had acquired a reputation for standing up to the army. However, the Uspantán activists were disillusioned by the tepid responses of the nearest procurator, in Nebaj. "They don't want to make denunciations; they don't want to get involved," one activist told me, of an accusation that civil patrollers had staged a shootout to terrorize travelers.[4] "The lawyer said there aren't proofs. 'Why not leave it alone?' he told us. 'Otherwise, it could get worse.' From them there's no support. This is why we're not going to work with them anymore."

Instead, the committee began taking its cases to a new group called the Defensoría Maya. Associated with Majawil Q'ij, it, too, had been set up by the popular organizations to broaden their appeal, in areas where peasants were too distrustful or intimidated to respond to more militant forms of organizing. To respond to the growing interest in constitutional rights, the Defensoría stressed that it pursued its denunciations and appeals through the law. A small Uspantán office opened in January 1995 but received few complaints. In the absence of killings and kidnappings, what it reported to human rights networks and the media were alleged threats. The category was defined broadly to include any occasion on which the army warned people that the popular organizations were connected to the guerrillas.

"Really there has been little, not as much as last year," an activist told me in 1995. But distrust was rife: If die-hard civil patrollers interpreted anyone from the popular organizations as a guerrilla sympathizer, human rights activists regarded any unrepentant patroller as an "ear" for the army. Yet the sight of an educated youth behind a typewriter made a salutary impression on the army's local allies. "Many in my family chastise me for being involved with human rights," an activist told me. "My father says that it could return to like it was before. But I've never been threatened. Now the ears are afraid because they have debts, that is, [they are guilty of] crimes. They're afraid of the law and also of the insurgents."

Across the country, small offices like this were being financed by international donors to serve as trip wires against a resurgence of violence. Once they were in place, the next step might be exhuming the victims of the 1980s. Locally, two clandestine burials had been excavated at early dates for criminal prosecutions, but thanks only to the raw courage of family members and their supporters. For those accustomed to Anglo-American jurisprudence, the Guatemalan judicial system places astonishing burdens on seekers of justice for murder victims. Relatives must step forward as plaintiffs because the state takes little responsibility for the indictment; they face a high risk of reprisal from the accused, as well as responsibility for gathering evidence and pressing the prosecution. The targets of the first exhumations in Uspantán were local vigilantes, the Aarones brothers and Eugenio Juarez, not the army that had given them license to kill. Nor were the two exhumations politicized on the national level, as others would be in the 1990s.

In 1994 the Catholic parish sponsored a procession to the Peñaflor body dump, but there were no immediate plans to look for remains. Reactions from vigilantes were likely, and just two exhumation teams were available for the entire country. "It's our duty to dig up the bones from the clandestine cemeteries and take them to sanctified ground," a CONAVIGUA leader told me emphatically. "It's a big job; it takes money to excavate and remove bones. Nobody has an idea how they're going to pay for all this. They [CONAVIGUA] are in agreement that this is the job that must be done, but they don't know how to pay for it. CONAVIGUA doesn't have funds, and the clandestine cemeteries are many." What are you going to do with the information you're gathering? I asked a widow leader. "Who knows?" she responded. "But it's going to be given to Rosalina Tuyuc. Perhaps if there's a threat we will talk on the telephone the same day. By means of the nationals and internationals of human rights, I hope that God sends us his blessings."

Rigoberta and Remembered History

> *We both came from small villages. She never went to school as a child; neither did I. When she was 8, she migrated to coastal plantations to pick coffee and cotton; so did I. Like her, I did not learn Spanish until I was in my late teens. She is an exile; so am I.*
>
> **—Kaqchikel training to be a Catholic priest, 1993[5]**

Aside from the international ramifications, another reason Rigoberta did not visit Uspantán was that it might not be safe. "There are lots of people who don't like her, for being a guerrilla," a family member told me in 1993, "and they say that we are guerrillas." Rigoberta had always denied serving as a combatant, and I was not aware of any evidence that she had, but stories to that effect could be heard. "She says that she never carried weapons, that she didn't wear a uniform," an old neighbor told me, "but my brother-in-law saw her in Caracol dressed in an olive green uniform and carrying a gun around 1977–78" (when she was in boarding school).

Many were still perplexed that a person they remembered only as a girl, on the losing side of the violence, could become so famous. The praise heaped on her was quite a contrast to the punishment meted out to her family. "On the one hand, they think it's a great honor," a ladino teacher explained. "Many people approved of her getting the prize as recognition for the Indian people. But on the other hand, they hate the guerrillas, and she passed through the guerrilla movement. So there are a number of different reactions. Also hope that because of her international connections, she could attract donations for Uspantán. Look at the standard of living here. Uspantán is poor. But of action, nothing. People want action."

Interest in the help Rigoberta might provide was keen. A somewhat distant cousin was preoccupied with the need to "organize ourselves as a family." In his early twenties, struggling unhappily through primary school, he was hunting for basic information about his famous relative. What did she do? Where did she live? Did I have her address? Like many other youth, he also wanted to know if I could get him a job in the United States. "I hope she remembers us" was a refrain. When a town councilman opened Uspantán's first *maquiladora,* a small handwork factory to export Christmas decorations to the United States, the rumor was that it belonged to the Nobel laureate and only Christian Democrats would get the sought-after jobs.

As cornucopian fantasies went unrequited, Rigoberta came in for the predictable battering. "She has isolated herself from the people who were closest to her, with whom she passed very profound, very happy, very sad moments," said an old friend. "She knows certain people to whom she could send a book, a magazine, a letter, but never. She's forgotten her people. I have heard some very strong commentaries, that she's really gotten ahead socially and economically, too much so, but that she doesn't come back to struggle on her native soil. That now she's Doña Menchú, that she makes lots of trips, that her expenses are paid, that she's not with her people who still go barefoot, lack food and medicine. That she's a big fat cat . . . that they set her up with quite a line."

The more sympathetic tended to assume that Rigoberta never really had been involved with the guerrillas. "I was working for the parish when Rigoberta Menchú was around fifteen," a human rights activist recalled. "There was a land problem in the village from which she came, when the guerrillas showed up. That's how the conflict between two groups of campesinos began, and there was her father, Vicente Menchú. . . . It's said that it was the guerrillas who began to encourage the parents of Rigoberta Menchú to protest, to criticize the government, because there was a group supporting them. At that time she was studying in Chiantla. Some of her sisters joined the guerrillas, and her father burned to death in the embassy of Spain. Her mother, Juana, was kidnapped while leaving town. Some say that [Juana] was going around in uniform under her dress, others say that she had wrapped in her clothes a pistol that had been given to her in the church. That's what the army said. But during the six years that I worked in the church, I never saw a weapon there.

"With her father burned to death, her mother kidnapped, her brother dead, she left; through the Catholic Church it is known. People say she went to Cuba, they say she joined the guerrillas, but from what I know it's a lie. She went into exile. The people against Rigoberta are confidants of the army. They say that she was a guerrilla. 'If Rigoberta Menchú took a course in Cuba to become a combatant, what do we want with her?' But I'm confident she was not involved. Some forty percent [of the people around here] believe she was a guerrilla, and some sixty percent are confident she was not involved. . . . The people now know that the guerrillas operated outside the law, and there's not even one madman around here who says he supports the guerrillas." Among Rigoberta's own people, this was the credibility issue she faced. Was she a guerrilla? The association with the guerrilla movement was clear enough to anyone who had read *I, Rigoberta Menchú*, but few indígenas had done so, and she did not feel she could acknowledge it even after she won the peace prize. That would stigmatize her for supporters who wanted nothing to do with the insurrectionary left.

Discrepancies between Rigoberta's version of events and local ones have been the subject of this book. In deciding to excavate them, I assumed that they would make it difficult for her to go home. Yet Rigoberta did not face widespread incredulity over her story, even in Uspantán. Most indígenas had heard only an outline—over the radio, in speeches, or from friends—and the central theme of persecution was close enough to their own experience. Her story of victimization had broad appeal to the many Guatemalans, ladinos as well as indígenas, who had learned to expect the worst from the Guatemalan army. From a factual point of view, that was the least problematic part of her story anyway.

Only in Uspantán, where old neighbors could compare her story with their own memories, did I hear Guatemalans object to the factuality of *I, Rigoberta Menchú*. These included a few indígenas as well as the García and Martínez families. "She didn't see the violence here because she was studying in Huehuetenango," said an Uspanteko grandmother who knew her as a child. "We listen on the radio and she lies, she says a pile of things. She didn't see how her mother died; she didn't see how her father died. If she's free to come and go, why doesn't she visit her pueblo? Why doesn't she want to come?" Why not? I asked. "She realizes what she's gotten herself into." A K'iche' critic noted, "There's a mix. It is false that she has gone to the coast. . . . It is false that she has worked as a maid in Guatemala City . . . as is her saying that she belonged to CUC. It could be the Peasant League, but that is something else. . . . It is true what she says of the Garcías and Martínezes, because she went with the guerrillas and the Garcías and Martínezes went with the army."

However, the book's accuracy was not as significant an issue as I expected even in Uspantán. One reason was that most of the population could not read it, either because they lacked the necessary skills or had no access to a copy. Except for learning manuals and Bibles, books are rare in this milieu. Of those who had read *I, Rigoberta Menchú,* my impression was that most had only perused passages of a borrowed copy, not worked their way through the entire text. In any case, Uspantanos tended to regard the book as a monument that possessed its own authority. No, several told me, they had never heard of CUC in Uspantán, but if Rigoberta said so, it must have been there behind the scenes.

When I discussed the issue of factuality with one capable ladino reader, his reaction was, What else to expect from someone who had suffered so much? What mattered to sympathetic Uspantanos like himself was that Rigoberta's story was poetically true. To an unsympathetic reader from the García family, meanwhile, the book demonstrated that the Menchús had cast their lot with subversion. If in Rigoberta's telling Chimel went over to the guerrillas in the late 1970s, her polarized view of the situation met the ideological needs of counterinsurgents as well as of the EGP. Requiring no interrogation, *I, Rigoberta Menchú* provided sufficient material for the polemics of Guatemalan society. It could be interpreted as a cry against injustice or as evidence of how much Indians hated ladinos.

On the national level, I assumed that journalists interviewing the Menchú family and their neighbors would soon report some of the discrepancies I was discovering. But no. Maybe journalists failed to ask the kind of historical questions that I did. Or if they heard about details like Rigoberta's education (which would be hard not to), perhaps these did not seem significant. Or perhaps they thought it indecent to contradict a Nobel laureate. Perhaps any journalist who took the trouble to bump up the long road to Uspantán was, by definition, a political sympathizer. Perhaps the newspaper pundits who liked to pillory Rigoberta were too well padded to have any desire to make the trip. Or perhaps they felt no need to probe an account confirming their belief that indígenas cling to their backward ways and are easy to stir into rebellion. Still, I found it odd that in a country that runs on rumors, including the one that Rigoberta's 1982 story is a *mentira* (lie), no critic bothered to spend the few days needed to make the case.

As I talked to Guatemalans about Rigoberta, it became apparent that her story was acquiring the status of legend, a story that meets certain needs so well that the question of whether it is true or not is almost beside the point. Was this the same spell she cast over her admirers in the United States and Europe? Even among scholars who might have known better, Rigoberta's portrait of deeply traditional Indians becoming revolutionaries was so gratifying that it disarmed our critical faculties. One particular life had been reworked into a life that met the expectations of sympathetic foreigners, making it famous. With prestige conferred by international accolades, the legend had been transmitted back to Guatemala, through the media and into folklore. Where it would go now was up to Guatemalans.

My impulse to investigate the historical background of *I, Rigoberta Menchú* and ferret out what really happened is one step. But only that. What will count in the future is what Zygmunt Baumann calls "remembered history"—what Guatemalans care to remember their history has been, not what a foreign scholar thinks it is.[6] Some of Rigoberta's compatriots may feel that I have tried to take away their history. I believe that is impossible. They will remember their history the way they want, long after my efforts have been relegated to a footnote. If they wish, Vicente Menchú will always be a founder of the Committee for Campesino Unity, and he will always go to the Spanish embassy to defend his land from finca owners. The history that Guatemalans will remember is hardly settled. They are not in agreement about what the violence meant; they may never be. Still, if they can agree that *I, Rigoberta Menchú* is a national work, however skeptical or convinced they are of its merits, that is a step on the way to becoming the nation that so many of them want to be.

Rigoberta Leaves the Guerrilla Movement

The path to reconciliation will face many difficult challenges. It will be hard to forget those who have died and those who committed the murders. But we must do it. Menchú was careful in discussing the reconciliation process because there are so many truths—the families of the soldiers who have been slain, the families of those who fought with the guerrilla forces, all have strong feelings. Menchú emphasized that it is important . . . that neither side manipulate these feelings to inspire revenge and prolong the struggle.

—Solidarity publication quoting Rigoberta on a U.S. visit, 1995[1]

After her parents died, Rigoberta renounced marriage and motherhood.[2] But after three years of turmoil as a Nobel laureate, she started showing up at public occasions with a bundle in her arms. Peeking out of the wraps was little Mash Nawalja', an adopted infant whose name means Tomás Water Spirit. Shortly thereafter, Rigoberta married a member of her staff named Angel Francisco Canil Grave, a fellow K'iche' who, like herself, had sought refuge in Mexico.[3] Then, amid another family occasion, what had long been dreaded finally came to pass. On November 4, 1995, one of Rigoberta's nieces, the only surviving child of Victor Menchú, was getting married in Guatemala City. Suddenly the festivities were interrupted by terrible news. Another of Rigoberta's nieces had been descending from a bus when her infant son was snatched out of her arms. Men with guns sped away with the child in a car with polarized windows.

Since Rigoberta had been investigating an army massacre, it was logical to suppose that this was a reaction, if not from the high command, then from officers whom it was strangely unable to constrain. "The purpose was to kidnap my son," Rigoberta declared.[4] "If it was not the State, show me the contrary."[5] As personages up to the UN secretary-general condemned the kidnapping, the security forces set up roadblocks to find little Juan Carlos Velásquez Menchú.

Three days later, Rigoberta asked the authorities to investigate the boy's father. Miguel Velásquez Lobos was not among her favorite in-laws. Known for his drinking and prolonged absences, he was now refusing to answer telephone calls from a kidnapper, who was demanding half a million dollars in a Mayan accent. "If the child doesn't appear," Miguel responded to Rigoberta's interrogations, "you will be to blame." On the sixth excruciating day, he arranged the reappearance of his son. With the complicity of his wife, Rigoberta's niece, he had parked the baby with his parents near Santa Cruz del Quiché. The laureate had refused to loan him US$6,000 to expand his business selling watches, boom boxes, and bootleg cassette tapes.

The child's return was followed by mutual finger-pointing. Vindicated for once, the army confined itself to asking Rigoberta for an apology. President Ramiro De Leon Carpio accused her of irresponsibility.[6] A government editorialist accused her of planning the hoax. Fortunately, Rigoberta had been the first to identify the boy's father as a suspect. Embarrassed and irritated, she demanded an investigation of whether army agents had lured her relatives into their inept plot.[7]

Meanwhile, the Nobel laureate was finally demonstrating some independence from the Guatemalan National Revolutionary Union. In Mexico Rigoberta never had been completely welcome in the community of revolutionary exiles. She was a latecomer, as well the movement's most famous member internationally, so she was perceived as an upstart. She was also a woman and an Indian in a leadership dominated by ladinos and males. But she and the URNG leadership were too useful to each other for a parting of the ways. Even after the Nobel gave her a basis for independence, she and the comandantes knew too much about each other for public airing of their differences. In the early 1990s, Rigoberta was said to be distancing herself from the URNG, but to skeptics that sounded like the latest positioning. Never had she publicly criticized the movement that launched her career. This is why I was impressed when she joined the Mayan movement in accusing both sides, the URNG as well as the government, of marginalizing her people from the peace negotiations. "How is it possible," she asked in October 1994, "that the guerrillas and the government are discussing the theme of the identity and rights of the indigenous peoples without taking into account those afflicted, leaving us marginalized by the armies that have repressed the same indigenous peoples?"[8]

In January 1995, when the guerrilla movement's most prominent dissident, Mario Payeras, died in Mexico, the URNG remained silent. It was still offended by his conclusion that the guerrilla movement in the highlands emerged "out of phase with the struggle and real movement of the masses."[9] But Rigoberta joined the homages to the foremost Guatemalan writer of his generation.[10] She also removed her father's name from her organization and renamed it the Rigoberta Menchú Foundation. Many supporters had asked that she name it after herself, she said. Another explanation was that she wanted to distance herself from the Committee for Campesino Unity and the Guerrilla Army of the Poor.[11]

No longer was Rigoberta a member of CUC. After winning the Nobel, she had little time for the organization that credentialed her as an indigenous leader. Even before, Rigoberta's busy schedule and broadening horizons were difficult to coordinate with a collective leadership that was still wedded to the URNG and whose options were rather limited. After the prize, her absence became so conspicuous that the issue was raised at CUC's 1993 assembly, whereupon she agreed to leave the directorate and join a less demanding honorary board. Even then she failed to show up for meetings, remain accessible, or respond to funding proposals, so her old organization decided to get along without her. "She ended up totally disconnected," CUC director Rosario Pu told me. "She never showed up; there was no invitation from her. Since then there has been no connection."[12]

The Laureate Repositions Herself in the Peace Process

> *Through these meetings [with civic committees in Mayan towns], we were understanding that, in reality, there is a different face to Guatemala: not the ruined Guatemala, not the subjected Guatemala, not just a repressed and deprived country, but a country with many initiatives expressing indigenous leadership at the local level, at the regional level, [with] much desire on the part of communities to rebuild trust . . . and define their political participation in these elections.*
>
> **—Rigoberta Menchú, 1995[13]**

International honors continued to be heaped on Rigoberta. By 1996 she had received her fourteenth honorary doctorate, been given the Legion of Honor by President Jacques Chirac of France, and been appointed a United Nations Educational, Scientific, and Cultural Organization (UNESCO) goodwill ambassador for the next decade. She was even on an advisory board for the Council on Foreign Relations in New York. But the most critical sphere for her future was no longer international. As she moved away from the guerrillas, an important shift in the left's attitude toward elections gave her the chance to take a more active role in political life. Until this point, the URNG and popular organizations following its line had urged Guatemalans to abstain from voting. After decades of intimidation, many supporters were not registered. Of those who were, many would be afraid to vote for the left, whose candidates lacked an electoral vehicle. The disappointing results would undermine the revolutionary movement's claim to represent the Guatemalan people.

Now several advances in the peace process opened up a new panorama. In 1994 the URNG had virtually shut down the peace talks, after its acceptance of a weak truth commission alienated the popular organizations. The following year the onus of holding up the peace process shifted to the army because of its recalcitrance on human rights cases. Under international pressure, the government accepted a sweeping agreement on indigenous rights, which finally gave the revolutionary movement something to show Mayan voters. Meanwhile, the arrival of hundreds of UN observers offered as much protection as it could hope for.

Still more decisive in changing the left's attitude toward elections was the specter of Efraín Ríos Montt. The "born-again butcher" of 1982–1983, infamous for preaching the gospel while his army massacred villagers, was on the verge of returning to power. Even worse, he would do so legitimately, because his law-and-order reputation made him the most popular candidate for president. In the 1994 by-election, Ríos Montt's party won control of the national congress. For much of the next year, he looked like the winner of the next presidential campaign. Even after opponents managed to disqualify him on constitutional grounds, his stand-in came within two percentage points of winning the January 1996 runoff.

Facing the nightmare of another Ríos Montt administration, the guerrillas and their allies decided they could no longer afford to abstain from elections. With UN observers in place, it was time to organize an electoral campaign. It was time for supporters to overcome their fears. The resulting New Guatemala Democratic Front (FDNG) was not as broad as hoped; many social democrats dropped out after realizing that it was being steered by the URNG. The departures included Rigoberta's. Among other things, she objected to the presidential candidate, who had been chosen by the comandantes in Mexico.[14] Yet now that electioneering was legitimate on the left, it opened up a new mission for the laureate: registering her people to vote. Hostile pundits accused her of stumping for the subversive FDNG, which in turn accused her of backing the front-runner for president, Alvaro Arzú, and his Party for National Advancement. The left was also appalled that she refused to denounce the Riosmonttistas.

As far as Rigoberta was concerned, she was running a nonpartisan drive for indigenous candidates, regardless of political affiliation. It included unannounced visits to Mayan towns, pointedly not arranged through the URNG-aligned popular organizations, to meet a broader spectrum of people. The campaign was also conducted over the radio, in four Mayan languages as well as Spanish. Instead of making speeches about human rights, which had come to sound like a litany of complaints about everything, she stressed the need for Guatemalans to take responsibility for government by exercising their political rights. "Vote against fear" was her theme.

If the voter registration drive put Rigoberta back on moral high ground, so did a new army massacre. Xamán was a well-organized settlement of refugees who had returned from Mexico. One day an army patrol appeared, violating an agreement that Xamán was off-limits to both sides. The soldiers were surrounded by hundreds of villagers, some of whom demanded that the troops lay down their weapons. Hysteria mounted: An old woman may have wrestled a gun from a soldier. Some of his comrades machine-gunned the crowd, leaving eleven dead and thirty wounded. Since Rigoberta had helped finance Xamán, she rushed to the scene and started a campaign to indict the soldiers.

One slip was to demand the *pena capital* (death penalty), which many were surprised to hear from a peace laureate, especially against Mayan soldiers who had panicked. What she meant, according to the retraction, was the maximum prison sentence. Leaving a deeper impression was the ability of Rigoberta and her lawyers to take advantage of the new judicial code. Over the army's opposition, they established the precedent of trying the soldiers in a civilian court. Like the other women around whom the Guatemalan human rights community has organized itself, Rigoberta was focusing political energy on a test case in the struggle against impunity—the army's de facto immunity from accountability for human rights violations.

Rigoberta continued to distance herself from the popular organizations that had been her staunchest supporters. This was despite the FDNG's success in the November 1995 balloting, in which it elected six congressional representatives, three of them Mayas. Although not a spectacular showing, it was a credible one in view of the FDNG's hasty formation and the still widespread intimidation. In Quiché supporters concealed their preference from pollsters, then elected CERJ leader Amilcar Méndez. But Rigoberta pointedly declined to join a new indigenous coalition supporting the FDNG called Nukuj Ajpop. She was also quick to oppose an FDNG proposal for a new indigenous affairs ministry. It would segregate Mayas in one small corner of the state apparatus, she argued, when they should be spreading throughout it.

"In the past, I have worked in concert with other opposition groups, the most militant compañeros, but there comes a time when the population is so fragmented that it's wisest to play a unifying role," she told a North American solidarity publication in early 1996. "Nobody represents all the people." When asked if she no longer considered herself part of the left, her answer was: "It's that I don't know what is meant by 'left.' For me, for a long time now, those old labels have been problematic."[15]

After so many years of being criticized as a guerrilla apologist, Rigoberta was making clear that she would work with anyone she pleased. Before the election, she was obviously cultivating a relationship with the leading candidate for president, Alvaro Arzú. After he was elected, they engaged in regular consultations. The new president led a neoliberal businessman's party. Although from one of the wealthiest families in Guatemala, he had credibility as a good-government reformer. That included improving the collection of taxes from the rich and privatizing dysfunctional state enterprises. Arzu was also committed to signing a peace agreement with the URNG by the end of 1996. It required quite a balancing act: He needed to convince the rebels and their supporters that they were getting important concessions, and at the same time he had to convince the business lobbies and the army that he was not betraying them.

Rigoberta's ecumenical approach to the ladino-indígena issue was very helpful. For several years, ladino commentators had been expressing anxiety over the Mayan movement in the belief that it would lead to awkward new demands on ladinos and racial separatism. They were gratified by the laureate's invocation of a Guatemalan nationality in which both ladinos and Mayas would feel at home.[16] For Rigoberta, the association with a credible new administration conferred legitimacy with the media and the upper classes that had been lacking since her Nobel honeymoon. The Arzú government was also giving her the chance to become seriously involved with the peace process. Complex agreements were being signed that the state would have to implement, among them an accord on indigenous rights. Like other Mayan leaders, Rigoberta was tired of agitation; now she could help institutionalize a new level of participation in the Guatemalan state.

To that end she joined K'amal B'e (The Road), a discussion group of Mayan influentials from left, indigenist, and neoliberal perspectives who were seeing eye to eye.[17] The Menchú Foundation was also participating in other new groups, such as the Council for Mayan Education, to make sure that the state carried out its many new commitments to indigenous rights. The foundation also subsidized Fundamaya, a new organization to support the growing number of town halls run by Mayan-controlled civic committees.

This is not to say that everything was coming up roses for Rigoberta. Joining the establishment for the peace process meant disappointing her most loyal Guatemalan constituency, the leaders of the URNG-aligned popular organizations. Paradoxically, this put her back in the same boat with the comandantes, whose compromises in peace negotiations were also disappointing the popular organizations. The signing of the socioeconomic accord in 1996, preparatory to the final peace agreement at the end of the year, was not the first time that URNG supporters felt abandoned by the leadership, but now the stigma extended to Rigoberta. The URNG had given up land reform because the powerful agribusiness lobbies would never agree to it. At the ceremonial signing of surrender on one of the left's most basic demands, Rigoberta did a dance with a beaming comandante. The performance did not go over well with the popular organizations. "She's alienated herself from her indigenous being," was one comment I heard. What the political establishment perceived as maturity much of the left perceived as betrayal.

As Rigoberta edged away from the URNG and became involved with the Arzú administration, her foundation became locked in patronage battles with URNG loyalists. In the Ixcán, Huehuetenango, and Sololá, Rigoberta's representatives and their opponents tried to shut each other out of committees administering foreign donations for the peace process. Fractures are inevitable when a guerrilla movement surfaces into legality. Highly centralized, clandestine organizations that view dissenters as traitors and are a law unto themselves must learn how to act as if they were run democratically. Since the Menchú Foundation was staffed by ex-EGP members, it could be considered a breakaway from that organization. The most embarrassing issue was whom to blame for the killing uncovered by exhumations and truth commissions. In 1998 Rigoberta's foundation director, Gustavo Meoño, who had left the EGP five years before in opposition to how it was manipulating grassroots organizations in the Ixcán, was among the figures accused of responsibility for the murder of three EGP members in 1982.[18]

Rigoberta has often been told that she can be elected president of Guatemala and views herself in that light. As a Nobel laureate, national symbol, and woman, she is supposed to be a paragon of virtue. However, public life in Guatemala offers many opportunities for losing your friends and going to bed with your enemies. As of early 1998, the latest example was her surprising decision to side with large landowners and Riosmonttistas against the Arzú administration and the left, to defeat a new property tax required by the peace agreements. The tax was supposed to make the upper classes shoulder a reasonable share of the fiscal burden, but some peasants feared that it would increase theirs as well.[19]

"It's not easy to stop being a victim," Rigoberta told an audience in the United States two years before. "Somehow or other we have to take our historical memory and bring it into line with the future." The Xamán episode showed that conflicts must be resolved via the courts and the political process, she said. Military conflict brings nothing but woe, she reiterated. Asked about the U.S. role in the massacres of the early 1980s, she answered that although the CIA deserved further investigation, she appreciated the ballistics analysis that the U.S. embassy provided for her Xamán investigation. On the subject of the Zapatista rebels in Chiapas, she denied any affiliation, affirmed their right to organize for a better life, explained the parallels to Guatemala, and concluded: "I don't believe that armed struggle solves anything, I believe that negotiated solution is the only one. How destructive of communities armed conflict is. It causes conflict and division among the people."[20] At the end, members of the audience came up and asked her to sign copies of *I, Rigoberta Menchú*.

Epitaph for an Eyewitness Account

The book may not be true about her, but it is true about Guatemala.

—Ladino to gringo, 1998

That Rigoberta turned herself into a composite Maya, with a wider range of experiences than she actually had, is not a very serious problem. Certainly, it should be known that her 1982 testimony is not a literal account of her life. Yet she was explicit that this was the story of all poor Guatemalans. On reflection, that could never be the story of one poor Guatemalan. Her narrative strategy is easy to defend because her most important claims, about the Guatemalan army's killings, are true. Rigoberta was dramatizing her life like a Hollywood scriptwriter might, in order to have an impact. Still, factuality is a legitimate issue for any narrative claiming to be an eyewitness account, especially one that has been taken as seriously as Rigoberta's. Even if she should not be held to the same standard as a UN observer, this book has suggested the importance of comparison with other forms of evidence. Where Rigoberta's account is seriously misleading is in its depiction of the social background of the killing, in particular, why it started around her home. Uspantán is not a microcosm for the entire war, but through Rigoberta's story it has been widely construed as archetypal. Moreover, what happened there illustrates the fate of tens of thousands of victims. Clarifying how the killing started in Uspantán is therefore germane on a broader scale.

Perhaps causality was a secondary issue in 1982 when the killing was at its height, but it was still an important one. It is even more so now that truth commissions are publishing reports and Guatemalans are trying to put the violence behind them. If identifying crimes and breaking through regimes of denial has become a public imperative in peacemaking, if there is a public demand for establishing "historical memory," then *I, Rigoberta Menchú* cannot be enshrined as true in a way that it is not. If you take

Rigoberta's story at anything like face value—if you argue, sure, some points are exaggerated but it is basically accurate—you have been led astray about the conditions facing her people, what they wanted, and how political killing started in her area.

The need to respond to carnage by establishing facts is hardly rare. If anything, it is becoming more common, as civil wars become a way of life and the world responds by setting up human rights networks, truth commissions, and tribunals. Cutting through competing versions of events to approximate what happened will continue to be crucial on many levels: for understanding all manner of conflicts, for grasping the contradictions at work inside what have been assumed to be homogeneous groups, and for judging the various armed groups who claim to represent a wider population. Only by establishing chronologies, vantage points, and probabilities can we have any hope of evaluating the reciprocal stories of victimization that are used to justify violence, or how these claims become rationales for larger political interests, or how human beings can be induced into committing mayhem.

That it is legitimate to question Rigoberta's 1982 story requires emphasis because, with postmodern critiques of representation and authority, many scholars are tempted to abandon the task of verification, especially when they construe the narrator as a victim worthy of their support. At a time when rumor, myth, representation, and the construction of what we consider "real" pose fascinating issues, it has become all too easy to deprecate the task of separating truth from falsehood, deferring instead to the authority of fashionable forms of victimhood. This is the juncture at which *I, Rigoberta Menchú* became a book with a cult following and wide influence on international perceptions of Guatemala. That leaves us with three reasons for reassessing the laureate's 1982 story. Doing so can tell us about (1) how the Guatemalan violence was misconstrued, (2) how myths about guerrilla warfare continue to misguide the urban left, and (3) how legitimacy in social sciences and the humanities is being redefined to discourage investigation and debate.

Guatemalan Scapegoat, Gringo Saint

I, Rigoberta Menchú was an echo in Paris of the Guerrilla Army of the Poor. It was also the story of a young woman who "tried to turn my own experience into something which was common to a whole people."[1] For foreigners responding to a human rights emergency, a single story came to personify a nation in crisis, giving it an aura of representivity and significance that it otherwise would not have had. The result was mythic in two senses. In a narrow sense, part of her story was untrue. In a wider sense, her story became a mythic charter, a way for different groups of people to understand who they are and what they should do next. But a charter for whom and for what? Foreigners and Guatemalans have brought different needs to Rigoberta's odyssey, as becomes evident when we look at differences in how they perceive it.

What staggers Rigoberta's old neighbors is that a schoolgirl could become an international celebrity. Most Uspantanos hear her story through oral transmission, which washes out details to which they might object, leaving a sequence of persecution, survival, and denunciation with which many can identify. The same holds for a much wider Guatemalan public. Rigoberta was not known to most indígenas until the left began to publicize her as a Nobel candidate in 1991. Many warmed to the idea that a Maya was being honored internationally for what her people had suffered. Her story also appealed to the many ladinos who have had similar experiences. If poetic truth is good enough for you, this is the part of her story that is all too true.

Paradoxically, although Rigoberta has not faced much incredulity over her version of events, she is the butt of criticism from almost every corner of Guatemalan society, including her own disappointed supporters. This should not be a surprise: Contradictory feelings toward celebrities are integral to their power in the public imagination. As living symbols of the good, the bad, and the inevitable; of the tremendous role of luck in human affairs; and of the unfairness of it all, they exist to be adored one moment and envied the next, damned today and forgiven tomorrow. The same is true of Rigoberta, whose story has become a way for an entire country to reflect on its contradictions. By presenting herself as an everywoman, she has tried to be all things to all people in a way no individual could be. As Nobel laureate, she has bestowed her symbolic authority on the building of bridges between indígenas and ladinos, indígenas in the guerrilla movement and those opposed to it, and the political establishment and the majority of Guatemalans who are disillusioned with it. The peace process has implicated her in compromises that are bound to offend her supporters but are probably not going to convince her adversaries.

International adulation for Rigoberta has brought out the Guatemalan penchant for backbiting.[2] But there has been little interest in challenging the factuality of her narrative. For many Guatemalans, the simple thread of persecution, exile, and vindication is enough to validate her for the purpose intended by the Nobel committee, as a symbol for all who have suffered. Factual issues could seem insignificant because the atrocities she was trying to dramatize are so unquestionable. As Nobel laureate she has come to occupy a position similar to American presidents and British royals, whose symbolic importance is larger than any individual's ability to play the part. Ridicule of such figures can even protect an underlying respect for the office by preserving it from the shortcomings of the occupant. Scorned one moment, they can become a national rallying point the next.

Sometimes Rigoberta's last supporters seem to be the Europeans and North Americans who first responded to her story and set her on the path to fame. This reflects the outsize role that international opinion has played in the Guatemalan civil war—in the 1980s to help the guerrillas prolong a war they had lost, and in the 1990s to end a war that they and the army would otherwise have continued. Abroad it is the published version of Rigoberta's story that prevails, not the oral one, so foreign admirers have put their faith in a more detailed, problematic version of Rigoberta's story. Moreover, they have a different set of needs than Guatemalans do. For most Guatemalans, their moral solidarity with victims of the violence is not at issue—they are the victims. Guatemalans are also less likely to feel the need to vindicate the left's tradition of armed struggle, just as few of them wish to justify the Guatemalan right's history of repression. Instead, they tend to view the two sides as partners in a dance of destruction.

Rigoberta's foreign supporters are in a different position. Some continue using her story to prove that the guerrilla movement had deep popular roots and was an inevitable response to oppression. They want to defend the Latin American left's history of armed struggle, or at least show that it was not a complete disaster. For a wider circle of human rights activists, who regard themselves as pacifists but unknowingly have absorbed a guerrillaphile perspective, respect for Rigoberta's story is a test of solidarity with the oppressed. By believing in her story, they demonstrate their commitment. For scholars, meanwhile, believing in Rigoberta's story has helped us deal with a professional but very personal moral dilemma, over our legitimacy as observers of people who are so much less fortunate than we.

Since the 1980s a theoretical literature indicting Western knowledge as inherently colonialist has acquired considerable prestige in North American universities.[3] In parts of the humanities and the social sciences, its exponents look like the new establishment. Under various headings, such as cultural studies and postmodernism, much of this literature carries on the self-critical, empirical tradition in Western thought. But the new theories can also be used to shut down investigation and debate, by reducing intellectual discourse to relations of power and dismissing opposed points of view as reactionary.[4]

Here is how what purports to be critical thinking degenerates into dogmatism: If any empirical portrait of a sensitive subject reflects ethnocentric or bourgeois assumptions (e.g., my wish to approximate the facts), there is not much sense in debating the fine points, such as whether Vicente Menchú belonged to the Committee for Campesino Unity or even whether Rigoberta gave us a reliable account of her village before the war. Instead, what matters is the "metanarrative"—the discourse of power lurking behind a text. In the case of the book you hold in your hands, a white male anthropologist is accusing an indigenous woman of making up part of her story. The important issue is not whether she did or not. Instead, it is Western domination, which I am obviously perpetrating. Reasoning like this enables Rigoberta's story to be removed from the field of testable propositions, to instead become a proof-text that foreigners can use to validate themselves.

But how do we decide to which victims to listen? When I began to question Rigoberta's 1982 story, I learned that the testimony of victims can be used to discourage unwelcome questions. Not all victims are enshrined in this manner—just the ones who serve our purposes, because enshrining certain claims to victimhood involves rejecting others. What results are stereotypes reducing the complexities of history, inequality, and ambition to melodramas populated by stock characters, who will always meet our expectations because we disqualify evidence that they do not. The intellectual climate that results has consequences for the kind of work that young scholars do, for what is encouraged and discouraged, for what does and does not get published.

For scholars insecure about their moral right to depict "the Other," testimonio and related appeals to the native voice have been a godsend. By incorporating native voice into the syllabus and deferring to it on occasion, we validate our authority by claiming to abdicate it. This is not necessarily a bad thing—anthropology and Latin American studies are hard to imagine without it. But in an era of truth commissions, when there is a public demand to establish facts, privileging one version of a history of land conflict and homicide will not do. What if, on comparing the most hallowed testimonio with others, we find that it is not reliable in certain important ways? Then we would have to acknowledge that there is no substitute for our capacity to judge competing versions of events, to exercise our authority as scholars. That would unravel a generation of efforts to revalidate ourselves through idealized reimaginings of the Other.

Romancing the Revolution

Arguing for the need to exercise judgment is not to claim that mine are necessarily definitive. Even on the mundane level of who did what to whom, the end of the army-guerrilla confrontation means that more survivors will tell their stories. I can only speculate as to what Vicente Menchú hoped to accomplish by cooperating with the guerrillas, exactly when and how his daughter joined the insurgency, and why Rigoberta broke away from the Guatemalan National Revolutionary Union in 1994. Yet other points can be established. Vicente Menchú's most serious conflicts were with other K'iche's, not ladino plantation owners. He worked with the Behrhorst Clinic and the U.S. Peace Corps, but probably not with the CUC until the last days of his life. The army began kidnapping peasants after the Guerrilla Army of the Poor assassinated Eliu Martínez and Honorio García, not because peasants were defending their land from ladinos. Rigoberta was away in boarding school when her village was sucked into the violence. If anyone doubts my findings, they can be checked through further research.

What might seem narrow factual questions, about one corner of a big slaughter, lead to a more significant one. This is the use to which Rigoberta's story was put, to prop up at the international level a guerrilla movement that had lost its credibility at home. Knowing what I did about the contrast between Rigoberta and other violence survivors, her politics and theirs, I faced a disturbing possibility: that a Nobel peace prize could be used to prolong an unpopular war. Because of the circumstances under which Rigoberta told her story in 1982, it was tailored to the propaganda needs of a guerrilla movement that may never have had the popular support it claimed and soon lost most of what it did have. For another fourteen years, the guerrilla movement continued a war it had lost in the hope of generating enough international pressure to extract concessions. Enshrining Rigoberta's 1982 story helped guerrilla leaders (1) use the international human rights movement to keep up pressure on the Guatemalan army, (2) maintain international legitimacy after they lost the support of most peasants, and (3) finally obtain the December 1996 peace agreement.

Even as I write, the Guatemalan left is debating whether the comandantes obtained enough at the bargaining table, whether they should have continued the war, or whether they should have given up sooner. The underlying question, whether it was good or bad to use international imagery to bolster a defeated insurgency, is for history to decide. By manipulating human rights symbolism to stave off defeat and eventually win a peace agreement, the URNG has conceivably initiated the gradual dislodgment of the army from its dominant position. If that occurs, it will be quite an achievement, in which the imagery of the dead accomplishes what the dead themselves never could in life. In the meantime, a paradox calls for attention. Rigoberta's story may have given voice to the dead in the early 1980s, but by the late 1980s it had become so sacrosanct that it was drowning out the voices of other Guatemalans who, every time I visited, told me they wanted the war to end.

Rigoberta's politics have evolved considerably since 1982. Yet her rather naive views from that time, after little more than a year in the revolutionary movement, continue to be viewed as evidence for a dubious proposition with profound consequences. This is the idea that guerrilla warfare is an inevitable response by the poor, their way of defending themselves from exploitation. In the 1960s, insurgents and counterinsurgents shared the belief that Latin America was a tinderbox of revolution. Assuming that the masses were awaiting their leadership, middle-class intellectuals started dozens of guerrilla groups, often over the objections of the aboveground left, which was soon decimated along with any civilians in the vicinity. Most guerrilla organizations were exterminated, and none captured power, but the same hopes led to a new wave of armed struggle in Central America in the late 1970s. This time one movement took power, in Nicaragua for a decade, but two others that seemed close to victory, in El Salvador and Guatemala, ultimately failed.

Some Central Americans believe that only armed struggle could have dislodged the dictatorships ruling their countries. In their view, guerrilla warfare was a tragic but necessary step in democratization, if only because of the international pressure that it generated against unyielding oligarchies. They could be right, but it also has to be asked: What gave rise to such ferocious regimes in the first place? Consider the evolution of the Guatemalan army—from bourgeois progressivism in the 1940s, to its divided response to the 1954 CIA invasion, to resistance to the U.S. agenda in the early 1960s, to the killing machine that it became in the late 1960s. Evidently the officer corps included a broader ideological spectrum than it is usually credited with. What reduced it to the fanatical anticommunism that allowed it to slaughter so many men, women, and children? The United States bears much of the responsibility for this tragedy, but it could not have happened without the specter of foreign communism, as provided by the revolutionary theatrics from Cuba. Insurgency would seem to be a remedy that prolonged the illness, by bolstering the rationales of the most homicidal wing of the officer corps in one country after another.

Some scholars feel that the romance of the guerrilla is no longer in need of demystification. Support for armed struggle has indeed gone into eclipse in the Southern Cone and much of the Andes as well as in El Salvador, Nicaragua, and Guatemala.[5] Now that the Cuban revolution seems to be in its death throes, the Marxist-Leninist ideology that sought to reproduce it through armed struggle seems anachronistic. But the romance of the Latin American guerrilla is not dead, as can be seen in the periodic revivals of nostalgia for Che Guevara.[6] Nor will it die as long as many on the left presume that guerrilla warfare grows out of the needs of the poor. The most obvious example of how the myth continues to be reborn is the Zapatista uprising in Mexico.

When Mayan rebels seized the town of San Cristobal de las Casas on January 1, 1994, solidarity poured forth from the rest of Mexico, the United States, and Europe. Going to Chiapas became the new pilgrimage, surpassing even Guatemala's appeal. Under other circumstances, the Zapatista assault on the Mexican army would have been suicidal. Fortunately, the government's hands were tied by a new trade agreement with the United States and the arrival, virtually overnight, of hundreds of journalists and activists armed with video cameras. Suddenly, the media became the pivot of Zapatista strategy, protecting the rebels from reprisals that would otherwise have been overwhelming.

In some respects the uprising was a tremendous success. It galvanized the Mexican left, set off a chain of protests that rocked the Mexican government, and forced it to negotiate. Still, after hearing what Guatemalan peasants had to say about the cost of guerrilla strategy, I was uneasy about this latest demonstration of the appetite for indígenas as symbols of rebellion. The Zapatistas met the urban left's fondest dreams: They were indigenous and radical, Mayan yet Marxist, armed but relatively nonviolent. Foreigners were especially smitten by Subcomandante Marcos, the urbane, pipe-smoking intellectual in the face mask.

The picture was a bit too perfect. The Zapatistas were indisputably a peasant movement, but they were led by Subcomandante Marcos and other outsiders, a faction of the urban left resurrecting the guerrilla strategies of the 1970s. Even in their own corner of Chiapas, the Zapatistas were just one of several factions and used strong-arm tactics against peasants who failed to support them. Soon they were also confronting fellow peasants over land, which is in short supply because of rapid population growth as well as large landholdings. If that were not enough, the Mexican army was prevented from strangling the Zapatistas only by media attention. As novelty dwindled, the army tightened the noose and prevented foreign supporters from reaching the area. The government also funneled aid to opposed peasant factions, who began to burn the Zapatistas out of their houses and turn them into refugees. Rebels who once had something—like the cow they sold to buy a rifle—were left with nothing.

Back to the old question—was the 1994 uprising an inevitable reaction to oppression? Or were Marxists once again sacrificing peasants to a doomed strategy? The Mayas of Chiapas were headed for confrontation with the state long before Subcomandante Marcos and his comrades appeared. Development programs, colonization schemes, liberation theology, evangelical churches, peasant leagues, electoral opposition—Mayas have tried them all. A one-party state has kept a tight grip on power; its neoliberal economic policies have made it harder for peasants to make a living. When the explosion finally came, it took the form of the Zapatista uprising and not some other only because a handful of dedicated revolutionaries managed to find peasants who saw nothing anachronistic in their doctrines. Although confrontation may have been inevitable, there was nothing inevitable about this particular form of it. As usual, a guerrilla strategy and the predictable backlash from the state had profound consequences for the political climate. These included higher levels of violence, more open conflict among peasants themselves, and occupation by the Mexican army.[7] Could another strategy have lessened some of these consequences? The question is worth asking.

The importance of looking at guerrilla claims with a cold eye is underlined by the tragic history of foco theory, the strategy of armed struggle that has inspired so many disasters. The model consisted of the rural insurgency that Fidel Castro led against the dictator Fulgencio Batista from the Sierra Maestra of Cuba. Once Fidel was in power, Che Guevara and Régis Debray theorized that, operating from the countryside, professional revolutionaries could overthrow other regimes more or less regardless of national conditions. As the Cuban revolution became the trendsetter for the rest of the Latin American left, the theory achieved ever more grandiose formulations, culminating in Che's 1967 debacle in Bolivia. The irony at the heart of foco theory is that it never worked even in Cuba. According to a fascinating analysis by the historian Matt Childs, foco theory's claims for rural guerrillas grew out of factional struggles in the revolutionary coalition that brought Fidel to power. As he purged his rivals, Che's writings on guerrilla war monopolized the credit for overthrowing Batista, to the point of producing a false model of how the victory was achieved.

After Che's death in Bolivia, Régis Debray recognized the error of overestimating the role of the Sierra Maestra guerrillas, to the point that he disavowed foco theory.[8] But that hardly ended the adulation of Che, who has become a Christ figure redeeming middle-class leftists from their inability to deal with the poor on their own terms. Nor has it ended the urban left's dream of finding the revolution in the countryside, as illustrated by adulation of the Zapatista rebels. Illusions about this high-risk form of politics are far from dead. They survive in false assumptions about the past that will continue to encourage revivals. Despite all the evidence that armed struggle is a disaster, its romantic cachet continues to attract new cohorts of believers, who rework the paradigm and repeat the experience. If they have any sense of public relations, they will be hailed by foreigners attracted by the same imagery. Thirty years after the myth of the guerrilla should have died in Bolivia, there is no shortage of intellectuals who continue to fall prey to it. They are attracted by the premise that middle-class intellectuals can set off a revolution and by the moral simplicity of the just war. The bill will be paid by the peasants who are turned into military targets.

Well before the romance of the guerrilla, there was a long history of projecting fantasies of rebellion into Indians. Obviously, some indígenas have made the decision to take up arms, and they are worthy of attention—but so is the eagerness of outsiders to identify native people as an insurrectionary subject, even though the majority have never been very interested in the assignment. Indigenous imagery has not always had a central place in the guerrilla romance, but it is usually in the background, if only as a symbol of resistance and Rousseauian innocence. In Guatemala indígenas occupied center stage around 1980, and imagery about them has been crucial to the guerrilla movement's legitimacy ever since. This is why it is so important to understand the illusions at work in Rigoberta's 1982 story, even if she has moved on politically. If we take what purports to be an eyewitness account at face value, as many readers will continue to do unless warned otherwise, indígenas are depicted facing hopeless conditions, when in fact families like the Menchús were doing rather better than that; an insurgency is attributed to indígenas that instead originated in the plans of nonindigenous revolutionaries; and the lack of land is attributed exclusively to expropriation by landlords, when a burgeoning population is making the situation worse for each new generation.

Facing the limitations of *I, Rigoberta Menchú* will, I hope, help the Latin American left and its foreign supporters escape from the captivity of Guevarismo. At bottom rural guerrilla strategies are an urban romance, a myth propounded by middle-class radicals who dream of finding true solidarity in the countryside. The injustices that induce some peasants to join guerrilla organizations are all too real; physical confrontation may be inevitable; but the kind of armed struggle envisioned by guerrilla organizations is not. For the better part of four decades, a misguided belief in the moral purity of total rejection, of refusing to compromise with the system and seeking to overthrow it by force, has had profound consequences for the entire political scene. It has strengthened rationales for repression, poisoned other political possibilities that might have been more successful, and repeatedly been fatal for the left itself, by dismaying lower-class constituents and guaranteeing a crushing response from the state. It is time to face the fact that guerrilla strategies are far more likely to kill off the left than build it.

Rigoberta Comes Home

> *In no country of America today can we have a nation just of indígenas. . . . We would have to sweep away borders and sustain a racist struggle to separate indígenas and ladinos. In reality, no one can appropriate the right to say who is an indígena and who is not. . . . What we need is a country in which we can live with mutual respect.*
>
> **—Rigoberta Menchú, December 1992**

In 1982 a young woman told a story that focused international attention on one of the most repressive regimes in Latin America. Her success took everyone by surprise, and it is quite an accomplishment. On the left, the story she created in 1982 with the help of Elisabeth Burgos has become a classic text for debating the relation between indigenous peoples and social transformation. Even if it is not the eyewitness account it claims to be, that does not detract from its significance. Her story has helped shift perceptions of indigenous people from hapless victims to men and women fighting for their rights. The recognition she has won is helping Mayas become conscious of themselves as historical actors.

To many ladinos as well as Mayas, Rigoberta is a national symbol and will continue to be one, however many vicissitudes she suffers because she is a living one. In Guatemalan intellectual life, she is a Mayan voice attempting to transcend the ladino-indígena dichotomy at the root of struggles over national identity. By pointing toward a more equitable relation between the two great ethnic groups in Guatemalan history, her book is a national epic. The key passage in *I, Rigoberta Menchú* is the first one: that "my story is the story of all poor Guatemalans." Even if the life told is not particularly her own, even if it is a heavily fictionalized heroic life, she achieved what she intended in a way that one person's actual life never could.

For several years after returning from exile, Rigoberta conspicuously refrained from visiting Uspantán. During the voter registration campaign, in July 1995, she finally did. Arriving without announcement, she was greeted warmly as she walked through the streets. Then she and her entourage took the road that climbs the ridge north of town. It is hard to imagine the expectation and dread she must have felt as she descended from Laguna Danta. For the first time in fifteen years, she beheld Chimel.

The village where she spent her earliest years no longer existed. At the sight of how much had changed—the houses that were gone, the slopes fenced into cattle pasture—and how much had remained the same—the contours of the mountains, the clouds boiling up from lower elevations—she cried for her parents. The few families there tried to console her. They also asked her to meet with them. Composing herself, she listened to their litany of needs. Then she promised to fight for the new road to their promised land, Cuatro Chorros, at the far corner of her father's domain.

A few months later, for her next visit to Uspantán, supporters were able to organize a reception. There in the town where two members of her family were kidnapped, another was shot down, and her father left for the Spanish embassy, they received her with skyrockets and a band. She said she wanted to exhume the remains of her mother. Many indigenous groups tell stories about culture heroes, ancestors who gave them fire, maize, or manioc. Some are tricksters; others are tragic figures. They make mistakes, and they have lots of enemies. They make choices that turn out badly; their people turn against them. They get chopped to pieces, then they grow back together again. The story Rigoberta gave her people can be chopped to pieces, like some of her neighbors were during the violence, but it will grow back together again, and maybe Guatemala will, too.

Notes

Preface

1. "Menchú reniega de Así me nació la conciencia," *El Periódico* (Guatemala City), December 10, 1997. All translations into English are my own unless indicated otherwise.

Chapter 1

1. Following the Academy of Mayan Languages of Guatemala, I will spell the names of Mayan language groups as follows: "Quiché" becomes "K'iche'," "Uspanteco" becomes "Uspanteko," "Kekchi'" becomes "Q'eqchi'," "Pocomchi" becomes "Poqomchi'," "Aguacateco" becomes "Awakateko," "Cakchiquel" becomes "Kaqchikel," "Kanjobal" becomes "Q'anjob'al," and "Tzutujil" becomes "Tz'utujil."

2. Burgos-Debray 1984:174–179.

3. For estimates of the cost of the violence in Ixil country, see Stoll 1993:227–233, 341.

4. Burgos-Debray 1984:102–115.

5. Burgos-Debray 1984:92.

6. As heard by my colleague Stephen Elliott. Guatemala's first Nobel laureate was Miguel Angel Asturias, who won the literature prize in 1967 for *Men of Corn, Señor Presidente,* and other novels. His son Rodrigo became the founder of the Organization of the People in Arms (ORPA).

7. Blanck 1992 and "Una chica superpopular," *Crónica* (Guatemala City), June 7, 1994, p. 8.

8. The conservative critic who brought Rigoberta into this debate was Dinesh D'Souza (1991:59–93). For a response, see Bell-Villada 1993.

9. Duncan Earle, personal communication, November 1992.

10. Stoll 1993.

11. The need for distinguishing between human rights and solidarity activism becomes apparent when human rights activists prove to have little interest in the abuses committed by the movement or government with which they are in solidarity. In practice the two spheres can be very difficult to distinguish.

12. Burgos-Debray 1984:1. This phrase on the first page of the English edition owes something to the eloquence of Ann Wright's translation. In the original Spanish (Burgos-Debray n.d.:21), Rigoberta says, "Quiero hacer un enfoque que no soy la única, pues ha vivido mucha gente y [este testimonio] es la vida de todos. La vida de todos los guatemaltecos pobres y trataré de dar un poco mi historia. Mi situación personal engloba toda la realidad de un pueblo." Translated more literally: "I want to emphasize that I am not the only one, since many people have lived, and [this testimony] is the life of all. The life of all the poor Guatemalans, and I will try to give a bit of my story. My personal situation encompasses all the reality of a people." Two years later, for the documentary *When the Mountains Tremble* (Yates et al. 1985), Rigoberta began her narration with the words: "Les voy a contar mi historia, que es la historia de todo el pueblo de Guatemala" (I am going to tell you my story, which is the story of all the people of Guatemala).

Chapter 2

1. For a map showing the complexity of language distribution, see Diócesis del Quiché 1994:25.
2. Arias de Blois 1987:8.
3. Piel 1989:213, 253–261, 309, 320–322, 340–342.
4. Wealthy ladino families like the Brols (see Chapter 4) and Botráns still have substantial holdings near Uspantán, but even before the violence most of the heirs lived in Guatemala City, removing them from the local social scene. Since most fincas in northern Quiché are of marginal profitability, the violence of the early 1980s accelerated a preexisting trend to divest them. Typically, the properties are subdivided for the peasants already living on them.
5. If indígenas welcomed ladinos as brokers, the reason could be that they were accustomed to mediation by parish priests, who became increasingly rare under the anticlerical Liberal regime.
6. Burgos-Debray 1984:4–5, 43, 109.
7. According to another member of the family, Vicente's father was named Pio Pérez and failed to "recognize" his son, which explains why the latter preferred his mother's to his father's surname. Ordinarily, a Spanish surname consists of the father's followed by the mother's. Hence Vicente would have been Vicente Pérez Menchú. In documents submitted to INTA, he sometimes appears as Vicente Menchú Pérez, perhaps because a clerk asked him to supply a second surname.
8. Burgos-Debray 1984:2–3. Although the English translation of *I, Rigoberta Menchú* identifies the patrón as a ladino, the original Spanish refers to him both as a ladino and "de los *Uspantanos*" (Burgos n.d.:23). In this book I use the term "Uspantano" to refer to any person born in Uspantán, including K'iche's and ladinos, while reserving "Uspanteko" for speakers of this language.
9. Based on surveys from the early 1970s, Carol Smith (1984:212–215) has reported declining migration to plantations in much of the western highlands.
10. In her 1982 story, Rigoberta mentions seeing her two eldest brothers die from lack of food on plantations, but later she says that she never knew the eldest

who died and describes the other she saw perish as the youngest of her siblings (Burgos-Debray 1984:4, 38–41, 88). According to a family source, the two died long before Rigoberta was born.

11. Burgos-Debray 1984:4. Menchú and Comité de Unidad Campesina 1992: first unnumbered section.

12. Certification of land title for Finca Rústica 2,864, folio 244, libro 15, del Departamento del Quiché, "Segundo Registro de la Propiedad," November 14, 1966 (INTA archive, paquete 3650, pp. 51–54).

13. The figure of 151 hectares appears in an undated draft resolution, apparently based on a 1972 survey (INTA archive, nuevo paquete 139, pp. 37–38).

Chapter 3

1. Burgos-Debray 1984:105–114.

2. The one reference to the Tums occurs on p. 172, in another context.

3. Compare Kobrak 1997.

4. Dated November 22, 1961, the petition is referred to in informe no. 35, Departamento Legal y Asesoría Jurídica, May 26, 1978 (INTA archive, paquete 3650, pp. 549–550).

5. The Martínez name does not appear on the title to finca no. 3305, which the Tums purchased in 1965 (INTA archive, paquete 3650, pp. 212–214), but Martínez heirs affirm that Angel was the seller, as corroborated by at least one other reference in the INTA documents (paquete 3650, p. 138).

6. This date appears on a February 3, 1975, affidavit signed by Edwyn Edmundo Domínguez, Juez de Primera Instancia, Santa Cruz del Quiché (INTA archive, paquete 3650, p. 504).

7. Registro de Procesos, Primer Juez de Primera Instancia, Santa Cruz del Quiché, entry no. 757 for 1970. Complaint initiated by Francisco Hernández against Vicente Menchú Pérez on September 21, 1970.

8. Local accounts plus memo from Victor A. Ortiz M., Encargado Control de Títulos, to Señor Jefe de la Sección de Beneficiarios INTA, November 13, 1978 (INTA archive, paquete 3650, pp. 583–584).

9. The two men were Juan Us Imul, who became the leader of the dissidents, and Juan Us Mejía, according to a petition to the president of INTA by twenty men from Chimel dated February 20, 1974 (INTA archive, paquete 3650, pp. 460–461). The arrest date is from Registro de Procesos, Primer Juez de Primera Instancia, Santa Cruz del Quiché, entry no. 111 for 1974, for a complaint initiated by Vicente Menchú against Juan Us Imul for *lesiones*.

10. *See Table 3.1 on page 288.*

11. Petition from Francisco Us Imul and Juan Us Imul to INTA director, January 25, 1972 (INTA archive, paquete 3650, p. 376).

12. Petition from Juan Us Imul et al. to President of INTA, December 17, 1973 (INTA archive, paquete 3650, pp. 446–447).

13. Petition from Vicente Menchú to President of INTA, October 18, 1976 (INTA archive, paquete 3650, pp. 89–92).

TABLE 3.1 Household Attrition in Chimel, 1962–1991

	Total Household Heads	*Household Heads Remaining from Previous Census*	*Household Heads Lost from Previous Census*	*Attrition from Previous Census*
1962	30	–	–	–
1965	66	10	20	67%
1969	53	23	43	65%
1978	45	28	25	47%
1991	57	16	29	64%

SOURCE: INTA archive, paquete 3650, "Lista los que están viviendo en el terreno valdía Chimel," January 29, 1962; "Nómina de los peticionarios del baldio 'Chimel' todos con residencia en el mismo terreno," June 1965, pp. 14–15; INTA census form, September 1969, p. 65; INTA census form, November 1978, p. 584. INTA archive, nuevo paquete 139, INTA census form, June 1991.

14. Petition from Francisco Tum Tiu et al. to President of INTA, February 20, 1974 (INTA archive, paquete 3650, pp. 460–461). The dissidents wanted INTA to recognize Juan Us Imul, one of the two men jailed for assaulting Vicente in 1974, as their representative.

15. Henrik Hovland, personal communication, October 22, 1994.

16. Petition to President of INTA, November 18, 1978 (INTA archive, paquete nuevo 139, pp. 40–41).

17. Petition to President of INTA, December 8, 1978 (INTA archive, paquete nuevo 139, pp. 47–48).

18. This was not Vicente's father-in-law but a nephew who bore the same name.

19. Burgos-Debray 1984:17, 106.

20. Burgos-Debray 1984:3, 26, 181–184.

21. Compare Kobrak 1997:206.

Chapter 4

1. Debray 1974:307, quoted in Le Bot 1995:279.

2. Smith 1992. For the best scholarship on the evolution of land tenure, see McCreery 1994 and Davis 1997.

3. Gleijeses 1991; Schlesinger and Kinzer 1982.

4. The officers were offended that President Miguel Ydígoras had given the CIA a training base for its 1961 invasion of Cuba. Since the Guatemalan army was not allowed into the CIA installation, the rebel officers felt that their honor as defenders of national sovereignty had been compromised. For accounts of the first decade of guerrilla initiatives and defeats, see Debray 1974 and Jonas and Tobis 1974.

5. Compare Wickham-Crowley 1991:5.

6. Perales 1990:61–66.

7. Albertani and Molina 1994:19–20 and the special memorial issue of the magazine Payeras founded, *Jaguar-Venado* 1995.

8. According to Debray (1974:298), "Guatemala was the first Latin American country where revolutionaries carried out an 'economic kidnapping'—i.e., for ransom. . . . The Guatemalan revolutionaries were also the first in the history of Latin America—well before the Brazilians, Uruguayans or Argentinians—to introduce political kidnapping for purposes of exchange."

9. Harnecker 1984:295.

10. Asociación de Investigación y Estudios Sociales 1995:649.

11. Amnesty International 1981:141 and Clerc 1980a. For an account of the urban left during this period, see Levenson-Estrada 1994:148ff.

12. Compare Kobrak 1997.

13. Diócesis del Quiché 1994:228.

14. Burgos-Debray 1984:103, 105, 109.

15. Payeras 1983:61–63 and Stoll 1993:35, 68–71.

16. Burgos-Debray 1984:103–107. Except for the Chimel land claim, the figures for other landholders are based on local estimates and therefore approximate.

17. Burgos-Debray 1984:150–152.

18. I was able to confirm the name and date of death at the civil registrar's office in Uspantán.

19. Petition from Juan Gamarro González to Señor Director General de Asuntos Agrarios, September 21, 1964 (INTA archive, paquete 1963, p. 220).

20. Petition from Miguel Martínez López to President of INTA, August 22, 1972 (INTA archive, paquete 3650, p. 403).

21. Letter from Uspantán justice of the peace Salvador Figueroa Montúfar to President of INTA, accompanied by sketch map locating damages, November 16, 1976 (INTA archive, paquete 3650, pp. 94–95). According to a Martínez, Vicente was denouncing him for cutting a few pine trees from both properties to build a public bridge between them. When a forestry inspector arrived, according to this source, he instead fined Vicente's brother for cutting down a larger number of trees. For Rigoberta's denunciation of forestry regulations, see Burgos-Debray 1984:158–159.

22. For example, Rarihokwats 1982:42. I do not have the original material, but other sources to this effect are cited in Paige 1983:732 and Paul Yamauchi's Geo-Violence Information System data base, entries for August 14 and 19, 1979, under "Uspantán." Solidarity sources also rationalized the murder of Honorio and Eliu by dating it to after the kidnapping of the nine peasants, as if the two were killed for collaborating in those crimes ("Report on Violence in Northern Quiché, Guatemala, by a Parish Priest, August 1979 to January 1980" and Committee of Solidarity with the People of Guatemala 1980). Still, the sequence of events described by local sources (the murder of the two ladinos, followed by the nine kidnappings) is echoed by various solidarity-influenced sources, including Paige 1983, Yamauchi's data base, Rarihokwats 1982, and Diócesis del Quiché 1994:282.

23. Democratic Front Against Repression, "Report on the Spanish Embassy Massacre in Guatemala," February 1980, p. 3. Judging from an interview distrib-

uted by Amnesty International (1980), the soldier guarding them may have been murdered or committed suicide the next morning.

Chapter 5

1. In the scholarly literature, these are known as the moral economy model (Scott 1976), the rational peasant model (Popkin 1979), and the "coercion conquest" model (Leites and Wolf 1970).

2. "Report on Violence in Northern Quiché, Guatemala, by a Parish Priest, August 1979 to January 1980" and *Polémica* 1982.

3. Compare Kobrak 1997:76–77.

4. I am indebted to Kobrak (1997:9–10, 132) for illustrating this approach in his study of the violence in the Awakateko and K'iche' Maya municipio of Aguacatán, Huehuetenango.

5. Burgos-Debray 1984:172–181.

6. Untitled transcription of tape-recorded interview with peasant delegation, 13 pp., January 26, 1980.

7. Comité Pro Justicia y Paz 1980.

8. Transcription of interview with peasant delegation, January 26, 1980. Earlier in the same interview, Vicente dated the kidnapping to September 9, as corroborated by other sources.

9. "Copia Integra del Discurso Pronunciado en el Congreso de la República," typescript, 1 p., September 1979.

10. "Dice el Ejército: Campesinos de Uspantán Están Siendo Utilizados," *Impacto,* September 28, 1979, p. 5.

11. Soon after Guatemala's constitutional court approved Ochoa's extradition to the United States, the chief justice was murdered. The crime was made to look like a car robbery, but the court reversed the extradition eleven days later, with the result that Ochoa could be arrested only if he set foot on U.S. soil. In 1997 the Guatemalan authorities arrested him for another cocaine deal, this time at a shopping mall.

12. "Cien campesinos irrumpieron en el Congreso," *Prensa Libre,* September 27, 1979, p. 4, and "Campesinos pidieron a diputados cese de la represión en Uspantán," *Impacto,* September 27, 1979, p. 2.

13. "Copia Integra del Discurso."

14. "Campesinos de Quiché Procuran Liberación de Secuestrados," *Noticias de Guatemala* 27, October 8, 1979, pp. 388–391. At an interview the day after the congress was occupied, the group's explanation—that the kidnappings were reprisals for refusing to accept the mistreatment of Honorio's sons and a son-in-law—was interrupted by a thirteen-year-old boy. Unlike the others in the delegation, he mentioned the August 12 assassination of the two ladinos and how San Pablo was being blamed for it. Following his statement, another spokesman returned to the theme that the finqueros had complained to the army because peasants would not accept their low pay. In the same interview, a taciturn woman identifies Petrocinio Menchú as her son and says the army took him from her house, contrary to an-

other person in the delegation who says he was kidnapped from town (Amnesty International 1980).

15. Victor Perera (1993:106) cites my Chajul interviews as his source for a version of the massacre that I never heard from anyone. No Chajules ever told me that the victims were shot in the plaza, or that they showed few outward signs of torture, or that they had seen Vicente Menchú at the scene, or that they had not seen Rigoberta. What I did tell Victor, in comments on a draft of his book, is that he should not interpret Rigoberta's version literally.

16. Chicamán is a small town with a ladino majority that used to be part of the municipio of Uspantán. As the violence started, it was becoming an independent municipio that includes the outlying settlements of Soch and San Pablo. The new municipio also seems to include much of Chimel, but the latter's owners regard themselves and their property as part of Uspantán, as does San Pablo, and the boundary has yet to be defined.

17. "Carta abierta," dated January 31, 1980, signed "Comunidades campesinas de Chajul, Nebaj, Cotzal y San Miguel Uspantán del Departamento de El Quiché," distributed by the Democratic Front Against Repression on February 1, 1980.

18. Transcription of interview with peasant delegation, January 26, 1980.

19. The version of events that Chajules gave in 1980 and repeated to me in the late 1980s also appears in Davis and Hodson 1982:48–49 and Payeras 1987:49. Only *I, Rigoberta Menchú* dates the incident to September 24, with most other sources dating it to December 6. Rigoberta also describes herself as an eyewitness in her testimony for the Iglesia Guatemalteca en el Exilio (1982:30–40), the Comité Guatemalteco de Unidad Patriotica (n.d.:27–31), and the Russell Tribunal (Jonas et al. 1984:120–125).

20. One more feature of Rigoberta's account calls for comment. After the army murders its captives, according to her version of events, the infuriated onlookers rush the soldiers with machetes and force them to retire. That a mob could confront soldiers without being slaughtered might seem the height of improbability, yet such an incident occurred at an earlier date, and stories about it may have contributed to Rigoberta's. Two months before Petrocinio's death, on October 18, 1979, the Guerrilla Army of the Poor occupied Chajul and held a meeting in the plaza. The next day it killed three soldiers and brought their bloodstained weapons to town. Like the army laying out seven bodies to dramatize its warnings against collaborating with the guerrillas, the guerrillas used the bloody weapons to dramatize the message that the people must organize to defend themselves against the army.

On the third day, according to a Catholic priest, "an Army patrol occupied Chajul and began a systematic search, beating and abusing the people. When the traditional shout of the Chajules began, men, women, youths, children and old people came out of their homes armed with stones, sticks and machetes and the whole town confronted the army in the central plaza. Between the two groups were the bodies of the three soldiers killed by the Guerrillas. An Army helicopter began to fly over the group as they talked. The people demanded that the Army leave and if they didn't do so, they were prepared to attack them. They said that they would kill more than the Army could. One citizen demonstrated he had been beaten by the soldiers. The lieutenant in command asked for a stick and began to beat the responsible soldier leaving him almost dead. The people again demanded that the Army leave and began to push the soldiers until they left the town. Indignant over the situation they had endured . . . , they decided to lynch Pedro Pacheco and Melchor Xinic [as] Army collaborators and informers" ("Report on Violence in Northern Quiché, Guatemala, by a Parish Priest, August 1979 to January 1980").

Chapter 6

1. My translation, Payeras 1987:9.
2. Burgos-Debray 1984:108–111.
3. INTA archive, nuevo paquete 139, pp. 75–78. The titles are referred to in both the singular and plural because although each household receives a separate document, these are to shared rights in the same land.
4. "Campesinos Denuncian Masacre de Chajul," *Noticias de Guatemala* 34, January 21, 1980, pp. 505–507, 512.
5. "Embajador de España acusado de facilitar toma de la embajada," *Prensa Libre,* February 5, 1980, p. 2, and Alvaro Contreras Velez, "Apuntes para la historia: Toma de la Embajada de España," *Prensa Libre,* February 5, 6, 7, 8, and 9, 1996.
6. The law students coordinating the protest could have learned through the San Carlos law school that the two men had an appointment with the ambassador. Molina Orantes was on the faculty there. Moreover, he and Cáceres were accompanied by a law professor named Mario Aguirre Godoy, who escaped as the hostages were being herded into the ambassador's office (Aguirre Godoy 1982). The occupiers' plan (see note 26 below) specifies that they will take down the names of hostages "to ascertain if there is not among them a better prisoner, a hostage who could be a better guarantee."
7. Author's interview with municipal firefighter, July 5, 1996. According to an official at the city morgue, there were no autopsies because the bodies were in such bad condition.
8. Danilo Rodríguez, "La masacre de la embajada de España y la necesidad de la Comisión de la Verdad," *Tinamit* (Guatemala), February 10, 1994, pp. 8–10.
9. "Semblanza de los Caídos el 31 de Enero," *Noticias de Guatemala* 37, March 8, 1980, pp. 609–612.
10. Burgos-Debray 1984:195.
11. "Comunicado oficial sobre sucesos en Embajada de España," *Prensa Libre,* February 1, 1980, p. 11. The escapee was the lawyer Mario Aguirre Godoy. According to his 1982 memoir, the protesters overlooked him just as they were herding the other eleven prisoners into the ambassador's office.
12. For obituaries of the martyrs, see "Semblanza de los Caídos el 31 de Enero," *Noticias de Guatemala* 36, February 18, 1980, pp. 579–582; 37, March 8, 1980, pp. 609–612; and 39, April 1, 1980, pp. 658–659. There may be others in issue number 38, which I was unable to obtain. CUC published obituaries for its five members in Comité de Unidad Campesina 1980.
13. Menchú and Comité de Unidad Campesina 1992:59.

14. "Los sucesos de la embajada española, un duro golpe para el régimen," *El País* (EFE), February 5, 1980, p. 3.

15. Burgos-Debray 1984:186–187, Menchú and Comité de Unidad Campesina 1992:59.

16. Foreign Broadcast Information Service, February 5, 1982, as quoted by Nancy Peckenham in Fried et al. 1983:205–206.

17. "Ataque Injustificado: El Embajador Español," *Ultimas Noticias* (Agence France Presse), February 1, 1980, pp. 1ff.

18. Quoted in "Spain Cuts Relations with Guatemala, Blames Police for 39 Embassy Deaths," *Miami Herald*, February 2, 1980.

19. "Treinta y siete muertos en el asalto e incendio a la sede de la embajada de España en Guatemala," *El País*, February 1, 1980, pp. 1–3.

20. "La Comisión de Exteriores del Congreso apoyó la actuación del embajador Cajal en Guatemala," *El País*, February 8, 1980, p. 13. See also the statement by Ambassador Jesús Elías of Venezuela, whom the Spanish government placed in charge of its affairs ("Incidentes en Incendio de la Embajada a Luz, Revelados por el Embajador Cajal y López," *El Imparcial* (Guatemala City), February 7, 1980, pp. 1–2).

21. Telephone interviews with Máximo Cajal y López, October 17, 1995, and January 18, 1996, supplemented by a letter, January 31, 1996. The ambassador also clarified that:

- an occupier put a machete rather than a pistol to his neck;
- the occupiers threw only one Molotov cocktail within his field of vision. The bomb was not directed against the door, and it was thrown some minutes before the fire broke out. It was at this point that he stamped out a lit match with his foot, not later when an explosion and fire propelled him through the doorway;
- he saw the police carrying hatchets, revolvers, and machine guns but no other devices;
- he does not remember the room having a skylight, contrary to reports that the police broke through one and introduced the fire through it.

22. The gas fumes could have been ignited in various ways, according to the two investigators: a match or lighter from either side, a spark from a firearm or an electrical device, or the detonation of an antiriot grenade. The kind of tear-gas or smoke grenade that the police would have carried—called a burning-discharge device—is falling into disuse in the United States because the triggering mechanism can produce enough heat to start an unintended fire. Although the police may have been carrying such devices, journalists on the scene did not detect their use.

23. "Comunicado oficial sobre sucesos en Embajada de España," *Prensa Libre*, February 1, 1980, pp. 11, 59.

24. "Grupo supuestamente de campesinos de El Quiché ocupó radio Rumbos y radio Favorita para transmitir mensaje," *Diario El Grafico*, January 29, 1980; Rarihokwats 1982:46.

25. Lartigue 1984:330–333.

26. "Plan de Subida," reproduced in *La Nación*, February 1, 1980, pp. 6–7.

27. Asociación de Investigación y Estudios Sociales 1995:582–583.

28. "Pavoroso genocidio, ayer," *La Nación,* February 1, 1980, pp. 4–5. "Ataque Injustificado," *Ultimas Noticias,* February 1, 1980, quotes the ambassador to the same effect: "The campesinos had specified that they were ready to die with us in the office."

29. Aguirre Godoy 1982: June 19. The same expression is found in the occupation plan: "Si el enemigo quiere reprimir, todos los que van a estar adentro, correrán la misma suerte" (If the enemy wants to repress, all those inside will face the same fate). The implication is a fate imposed by the protesters rather than the police, who would presumably treat the hostages they liberated better than the protesters they captured.

30. Black et al. 1984:98.

31. Burgos-Debray 1984:136–137, 231.

32. "Plan de Subida," February 1, 1980.

33. "Here no one talked about a fiesta [for a wedding]," another delegation member told us. "Vicente said that lots of people were going to gather in the church, but not for a wedding, just that they were going to meet there. Those who went with them were going to defend their rights and those who didn't, they wouldn't be able to—this is what Vicente told people."

Chapter 7

1. My analysis of CUC's origins is indebted to the work of José Manuel Fernández Fernández (1988), Robert Carmack (1988), Arturo Arias (1990), and Yvon Le Bot (1995).

2. Burgos-Debray 1984:136–137, 146–147.

3. Burgos-Debray 1984:114–115, 123–140, 196.

4. Burgos-Debray 1984:114.

5. Burgos-Debray 1984:115.

6. *Noticias de Guatemala* 1981.

7. Comité de Unidad Campesina 1980:4. When the Catholic-based Committee for Justice and Peace memorialized Vicente as a "hero and martyr of the Christian people," it made no reference to CUC. Instead, it identified him as a sixty-three-year-old agriculturalist and catechist struggling for a land title and village school (Comité Pro Justicia y Paz 1980). The founding manifesto of the organization named after him ("Manifiesto de Cristianos Revolucionarios Vicente Menchú") also failed to refer to him as a CUC member, as did its January 1981 narrative of his life (Centro de Estudios y Publicaciones 1981:147–148).

8. Founding member: McConahay 1993:4. Not a founder: Blanck 1992:31; Menchú and Comité de Unidad Campesina 1992.

9. Lartigue 1984:342, 298–303.

10. Le Bot 1995:160–179.

11. For parallel testimony from a man in southern Quiché, see Simon 1987:106–107.

12. Diócesis del Quiché 1994:192–193. For the Catholic antecedents of CUC, see also Fernández Fernández 1988:6–8.

13. Iglesia Guatemalteca en el Exilio 1982:44. For the Jesuit relation to CUC, see also Iglesia Guatemalteca en el Exilio 1983:10; Diócesis del Quiché 1994:104–107; and Le Bot 1995:146–152.

14. Fernández Fernández 1988:14–15.

15. U.S. Senate Judiciary Committee 1984:233–234.

16. Chea 1988:249.

17. Frente Popular 31 de Enero 1982:17.

18. Hoyos de Asig 1997:141, 191. According to an intellectual who used to belong to the EGP, it failed to recruit many people around Santa Cruz del Quiché until after the 1976 earthquake, when it was joined by some of the same activists who started CUC. "Catholic Action totally penetrated the lower and middle levels of the [EGP] organization, to the point that it had to be recognized."

19. Harnecker (1984:297–303) was married to Cuban spymaster Manuel Piñeiro, whose duties included training, supplying, and bringing together guerrilla leaders throughout Latin America.

20. Le Bot 1995:272.

21. Harnecker 1984:299.

22. Carmack 1988:56–59.

23. For example, Castañeda 1993:93 and Le Bot 1995.

24. So far, the best description of peasants clamoring to take up arms comes from Rabinal, in the Department of Baja Verapaz, through a team of forensic anthropologists exhuming massacre victims. Rabinal is an Achí Maya municipio with an unusually long history of involvement with the left. Achís were to be found in peasant organizations before the 1954 CIA invasion, then in the mainly ladino guerrilla organizations of the 1960s, and by 1976 were welcoming delegates from the EGP and the proto-CUC. By that time there was a clear threat to livelihood in the rising waters of the Chixoy Dam, which would displace some thirty-five hundred people. The story recovered by the forensic team begins with a small confrontation, between one of the villages threatened by the dam and three members of the security forces. CUC's Rabinal members decide they need guns to protect themselves, but CUC leaders discourage them, on the grounds that carrying weapons will only trigger ferocious reprisals. Local army collaborators start to attack the villagers anyway, so next they go to the EGP for weapons—which the EGP refuses to provide. Finally, after the fire at the Spanish embassy, an EGP commander meets with local CUC leaders and authorizes them to form a military column if they can find weapons on their own. The important point for us is that, in Rabinal, CUC was a grassroots movement that grew out of a long history of peasant discontent. It also appears to have been pushing for incorporation into armed struggle, not being pushed into it by guerrilla strategists (Equipo de Antropología Forense de Guatemala 1995:82–103).

25. Equipo de Antropología Forense de Guatemala 1995:206.

26. Author's interview with Gustavo Porras, Guatemala City, July 20, 1994.

27. Fernández Fernández 1988:35, 38.

28. Frank and Wheaton 1984:50, who quote an interview with Petrona Zapon plus Ricardo Falla's "Martirio y Lucha" (Iglesia Guatemalteca en el Exilio

1982:46). Frank and Wheaton date Vicente's arrival in La Estancia to 1977, whereas Falla dates the same story to two years later.

29. Author's interview with Sebastian Morales, Guatemala City, July 5, 1996.

30. Equipo de Antropología Forense de Guatemala 1995:89, 92–93.

31. Victoria Bricker (1981:4) quoting Claude Lévi-Strauss (1966:22).

Chapter 8

1. Letter to editor, *Crónica,* September 17, 1993, p. 11.

2. Untitled transcription of tape-recorded interview with peasant delegation, 13 pp., January 26, 1980.

3. Shaw 1980.

4. Transcription of interview with peasant delegation, January 26, 1980.

5. This includes the issues of *Noticias de Guatemala* I have been able to inspect; Committee of Solidarity with the People of Guatemala 1980; and various typewritten documents distributed by the solidarity movement. The latter include two open letters in the name of the peasant delegation from Quiché, dated January 31 and February 1, 1980; an undated media communiqué in the name of the peasant delegation; an undated, four-page "Interview with the peasants of Quiché prior to their death in the Spanish embassy"; a three-page "Massacre in the Spanish embassy in Guatemala," February 1, 1980; a five-page "The truth about the massacre that took place inside the Spanish embassy. . . ," February 1980; an eleven-page "Report on the Spanish Embassy Massacre in Guatemala" by the Democratic Front Against Repression, February 1980; and an undated "Statement by the Democratic Front Against Repression to national and international public opinion."

6. For example, Rarihokwats 1982:42. Although I don't have the original material, sources to this effect are cited in Paige 1983:732 and Paul Yamauchi, Geo-Violence Information System data base, entries for August 14 and 19, 1979, under "Uspantán."

7. These include declarations by the Comité Pro Justicia y Paz, the Diocese of Quiché, and the magazine *Diálogo,* republished in Diócesis del Quiché 1994:234–243. An interesting exception is an Amnesty International interview with the September 1979 delegation to the capital, already quoted in the notes to Chapter 5, in which a thirteen-year-old mentions how the kidnappings followed the murder of the two ladinos (Amnesty International 1980:5–6). When Amnesty took the case, it organized a letter-writing appeal to Honorio's sons without reference to the fate of their father. Because Honorio and Eliu were not murdered by agents of the state, they may have fallen outside the domain of human rights reporting as practiced at the time. In the 1990s Amnesty and Americas Watch gave more attention to violence by opposition groups.

8. Wolf 1969:289–292.

9. Mary Jo McConahay, "Interview: Rigoberta Menchú," October 1992, typescript, 9 pp., p. 6.

10. See Chapter 5, note 20.

11. Transcription of interview with peasant delegation, January 26, 1980. I presume this was Vicente because he was known for his good Spanish and the delegation probably did not include another army veteran from the Ubico era.

12. Wickham-Crowley 1990 and Stoll 1993:18–21. As a survivor from San Pablo El Baldío told me: "If the soldiers had not killed, the people would have gone to town [as refugees under army protection]. If they went with the guerrillas, they were killed by the soldiers. If they went with the soldiers, they were killed by the guerrillas."

13. For a portrait of the mutual incomprehension and adjustment required by an alliance between culturally distinct groups, see White 1991. Brown and Fernández 1991 suggests how indigenous people can become engaged with Marxist guerrillas, but on their own terms, and not without considerable disagreement.

Chapter 9

1. Burgos-Debray 1984:242.
2. Burgos-Debray 1984:185, 195–196.
3. Guerrilla Army of the Poor, "Las luchas guerrilleras golpean sin cesar al criminal gobierno luquista," 2 pp., May 15, 1980.
4. Burgos-Debray 1984:198–200.
5. Beverley 1989:21.
6. Montejo 1987:82.
7. Burgos-Debray 1984:126–127.
8. The chronologies I reviewed include the EGP's publication *Informador Guerrillero,* its press communiqués, and Paul Yamauchi's Geo-Violence Information System data base.
9. Burgos-Debray 1984:243.
10. Following her story for Elisabeth Burgos, Rigoberta told a Mexican journalist that her two little sisters went with the guerrillas for protection after being left alone at the age of ten and eleven (Calloni 1982).
11. Payeras 1991:91–92, 109.
12. See John Watanabe's ethnography of the Mam town of Santiago Chimaltenango (1992:179–183); Shelton Davis's report on Kanjobals in the *Harvest of Violence* collection (Carmack 1988:24–26); and Paul Kobrak's (1997) dissertation on Aguacatán.
13. Le Bot 1995:118–119, 258, 288–292.

Chapter 10

1. Huggins 1991.
2. Burgos-Debray 1984:121, 133–134.
3. For a fascinating account of this pastoral project into the 1990s, see Falla 1995.
4. OSM-CONFREGUA and Jornados por la Vida y la Paz 1992:89–95.
5. According to a man who was about to pass before the encapuchados, the shooting began when a youth who had just been identified as a subversive bolted

and ran. According to a woman in the marketplace, the soldiers shouted, "Everyone on the ground!" before firing and only shot at those who were fleeing. She thinks the army took away seventeen people in the truck and that another sixty were killed when they tried to escape. According to a human rights report (Davis and Hodson 1982:50), some sixty people were killed.

6. "Masacre de Macalajau, Uspantán, 14 de febrero de 1982–14 de febrero de 1992," sheet handed out at memorial mass. See also "Masacre en el Quiché matan a 53 campesinos," *Noticias de Guatemala,* March 5, 1982, pp. 11–15.

7. "El pueblo se hace guerrilla: Huehuetenango," *Noticias de Guatemala,* October 20, 1981, pp. 4–7.

8. Other people living nearby would bring the total figure close to the 370 estimated by my first acquaintance from Chimel.

9. Of the twenty-five who reportedly died in the violence, twenty were men and five were women. Four died at the embassy (the two other dead from Chimel were not named on the census). Ten others were shot by the army or its auxiliaries or disappeared in their hands. Another, found dead, is presumed to have been killed by vigilantes. Still another is said to have been killed by the guerrillas. One more was either killed by the army or died of hunger (my sources disagreed), along with eight others who starved to death—for a total of thirty-two percent of the household heads. As for the children, in the absence of names my sources found their fate much harder to recall, but they did remember that at least a few died violently and many more from hunger. Aside from the ten widows who survived, there were also sixty-five orphans who had been young enough to live with their parents at the 1978 census. Of these, thirty-seven lost one of their parents, eleven lost their only parent, and seventeen lost both parents. Of the children who lost both parents, at least seven of the seventeen died.

10. Wickham-Crowley 1991:82–89.

11. Actually, the countryside did not have to be emptied of peasants to destroy support for the guerrillas, since peasants do not support an insurgency just because they are attracted to its political program. Peasants are also very sensitive to shifts in power balances, that is, to whom they must submit to ward off harm. To the degree that Mayan peasants were cooperating with the guerrillas because they were afraid of them, the army would give them even more reason to be afraid of it. By killing more peasants than the guerrillas did, the army would make peasants realize they had less to lose by collaborating with the stronger and more homicidal of the two sides.

12. For a cross-cultural example corroborating this point, see Fellman 1989, which describes the consequences of irregular warfare in an egalitarian, ethnically homogenous evangelical Protestant milieu in nineteenth-century North America. Van Creveld 1991 explains how the mobilization of civilians for "popular" forms of warfare has contributed to making them the majority of casualties since World War I.

Chapter 11

1. Burgos-Debray 1984:89, 114, 120, 162, 190, 205. Rigoberta's new life story, *Crossing Borders,* expresses gratitude to the nuns of the Sacred Family, especially

the Chiantla school director, Gertrudis, for supporting her after her parents' death. However, the boarding school remains a "convent" (Menchú et al. 1998:231–235; although my citations are to the Spanish edition, Verso published an English edition in New York in 1998).

2. Another schoolmate recalled Vicente coming to visit Rigoberta at the Colegio Belga the day before he died—a fascinating memory that I do not interpret literally, as other schoolmates and Rigoberta herself place her away from the capital at this decisive moment.

3. Menchú et al. 1998:109–111.

4. A brief, terrified visit would explain another story I heard, about Rigoberta hiding with a friend's family in town. According to a corroborating account from a Chiantla schoolmate, Rigoberta was allowed to leave the boarding school to search for her little sisters but came back without them after eight days.

5. "Semblanza de los Caídos el 31 de Enero," *Noticias de Guatemala* 39, April 1, 1980, p. 658. One of Rigoberta's Uspantán peers told me that his cohort of indigenous students included two who finished primary, four who finished middle school, and three who finished high school. Except for himself, they were all dead. None was involved with the guerrillas, he said, and all had been kidnapped or arrested in 1980–1982.

6. The Spanish relayed to me was: "Yo no lo voy a dejar así. . . . Tengo que ver que voy a hacer."

7. A member of the Sacred Family helped me establish the post-Rigoberta date. She arrived at Chiantla after Rigoberta's departure, then experienced the raid, which she dated to a June or July 14 under Ríos Montt. A fellow Uspantano told me how she was taken to the Huehuetenango army base (but soon released) because of her association with Rigoberta.

Chapter 12

1. Burgos-Debray 1984:120, 161.

2. In the words of a parish priest, "The people behind the [revolutionary] movement are young Indians, who have received an education, often thanks to [scholarships] from the church. They have become very Marxist" (Clerc 1980b).

3. Burgos-Debray 1984:232–242. For other veiled references to her Huehuetenango schooling, see Burgos-Debray 1984:184 and Iglesia Guatemalteca en el Exilio 1982:36.

4. Blanck 1992, as reiterated in Menchú et al. 1998:231–245.

5. For a fascinating portrait of Ruiz, especially his complicated relations with the Zapatistas and their 1994 rebellion, see De la Grange and Rico 1998:259–289.

6. Burgos-Debray 1984:236–237, 242–244. Rigoberta gives a new account of her reunion with her sisters in her 1997 life story. Now they are only young orphans, not guerrilla recruits, who are rescued by relatives and clergy and brought to her by Bishop Ruiz six months after her own arrival. After spending Christmas together in Chiapas, the three sisters go to Mexico City for two weeks. There they meet Alaíde Foppa, who interviews them, and Bertha Navarro, who films them (cf. Foppa 1982). Only later, after returning to their CUC comrades in Guatemala,

do her two sisters go on to join the guerrillas (Menchú et al. 1998:210–211, 231–245).

7. Frente Popular 31 de Enero 1982:16–18.

8. Black et al. 1984:114–115 and Le Bot 1995:157, 194.

9. *Latin America Regional Report: Mexico and Central America*, February 12, 1982, as quoted in Black et al. 1984:115.

10. Two-page letter on FP-31 letterhead, dated February 29, 1982, addressed to "estimados compañeros" and hailing formation of the URNG. Interview with Fernando González of the Revolutionary Workers Nuclei, by Harry Fried, "Popular Front Grows in Guatemala," *Guardian* (New York), August 19, 1981, p. 13. Frente Popular 31 de Enero, "Proclama Internacional," 2 pp., apparently January 1981. "Manifiesto de Cristianos Revolucionarios 'Vicente Menchú,'" 2 pp., January 1981.

11. For example, "The Guatemalan Reality: Interview with Rigoberta Menchú," *Eagle Wing Press* (Naugatuck, Conn.), October 1982, pp. 1ff.

12. Burgos-Debray 1984:228–229.

13. In practice, the cadres running these groups reported to "the organization," that is, the EGP. The Revolutionary Christians and FP-31 never appear in Rigoberta's 1997 life story, *Crossing Borders*. Instead, she describes herself working for CUC.

14. Burgos-Debray 1984:130–135, 234, 245–246.

15. Menchú et al. 1998:243–245.

16. *Noticias de Guatemala* 1981. Under the pseudonym "Guadalupe," Rigoberta did refer to herself as a member of CUC in a radio interview with Alaíde Foppa in Mexico City in December 1980. Judging from a partial transcript, Rigoberta did so in response to much prompting from the interviewer (Foppa 1982 and Menchú et al. 1998:240–241). For more on the interview, see Chapter 14.

17. Harnecker 1982:11.

18. For the destruction of the urban labor movement and the guerrilla contribution to it, see Levenson-Estrada 1994:165–171; Asociación de Investigación y Estudios Sociales 1995:617–658; and Le Bot 1995:153–160.

19. Since the height of repression, according to research by Liz Oglesby (1997), plantation managers have kept labor unions outside the gates with the help of human relations techniques such as focus groups. Meanwhile, mechanization has enabled plantations to increase the productivity of workers and trim their number.

20. Draft version (1991) of Berryman 1994:114–115.

21. Castañeda 1993:92.

22. Menchú and Comité de Unidad Campesina 1992, translated in Sinclair 1995:63.

23. Le Bot 1995:178.

Chapter 13

1. "La conciencia de Rigoberta," *El Periódico* (Guatemala City), December 14, 1997. An earlier report appeared in the December 9 *Periódico,* followed by a horri-

fied reaction from her ally and indigenous leader Rosalina Tuyuc ("May God pardon her!") on December 10, and a letter of clarification on December 12, in which Rigoberta reiterated that Elisabeth despoiled her testimony, edited it without consulting her, and never paid her royalties.

2. Menchú et al. 1998:253.

3. Whom she subsequently divorced.

4. Castañeda 1993:129–132.

5. Canteo 1998. When Régis published an assessment of the prospects for armed struggle in various countries in 1974, the chapter on Guatemala was a joint effort with Ramírez (Debray 1974), who died of a heart condition as this book went to press.

6. Burgos-Debray 1984:xiv, xix.

7. Juana Ponce de Léon, "Mission of Peace: Winner of 1992 Nobel Peace Prize Speaks for Native People Everywhere," *Vista* (New York), December 1992, pp. 6ff. Compare Brittin and Dworkin 1993:216–218.

8. In her 1997 life story, the laureate describes Arturo Taracena as one of her most important advisers and gives him, as well as herself, a significant role in editing *I, Rigoberta Menchú*. "The taping of my testimony lasted around twelve days. Afterward, there was a Guatemala solidarity collective in Paris that helped with the transcription. There I met Juan Mendoza, a close friend to the present. Dr. Taracena participated greatly in ordering the book, together with Elisabeth Burgos. At the end, they also selected the chapters together. With this, I would like to say that Arturo Taracena has a significant role in the book. . . . Afterward came the text already arranged. For two months or more, I took time to understand it. What one feels speaking is very different than when it is on paper. I realize that in those years I was very timid . . . innocent and ingenuous. I simply was not aware of the commercial rules when I wrote that reminiscence. I was just giving thanks to the Creator that I was alive, and I did not have any idea of my author's rights. I had to go to my compañeros, in Mexico City where I was living, to try to understand the text. It was very painful to relive the content of the book. I censored various parts that appeared imprudent to me. I took out the parts that referred to the village, much detail about my younger siblings, many name details" (Menchú et al. 1998:252–255).

Some months later, Rigoberta accused Elisabeth of preventing Arturo and herself from performing the above-described functions: "All those tapes were transcribed by persons who wanted to help. . . . Arturo Taracena, with his wisdom and patience reviewed and corrected the errors that I committed in the use of Spanish. . . . Elisabeth Burgos took those manuscripts, arranged them according to her own criteria, and added and suppressed what suited her. She put in subtitles and included brief quotations from other books at the start of each chapter. . . . Never did she permit that I or Dr. Taracena know the final version, much less make observations or corrections to the text. We learned that Ms. Burgos had taken my testimony from me when the first edition appeared in French, with her name as the only author ("Carta de Rigoberta Menchú," *El Periódico*, December 12, 1997).

9. This means that Rigoberta's aspiration to testimonio—in the sense of wanting to speak for an entire class of people—predates her meeting with Elisabeth. A ref-

erence to her upcoming tour suggests that this was the task assigned by her organization. The detailed description of her brother's immolation in Chajul suggests that she was conscious of the need to dramatize her story in a way that would attract attention. The seven-hundred word item does not include any reference to her working on plantations, to her father and herself as CUC members, or to having witnessed the massacre of her brother at Chajul. But it does emphasize how peasants have been thrown off their land, suggesting how poorly revolutionary appeals matched the actual needs of peasants (*Noticias de Guatemala* 1981).

10. Burgos 1982.

11. Author's interviews and Canteo 1998.

12. The documentary, which depicts Rigoberta and Elisabeth in Paris, reiterates the key points of the January 1982 testimony (Burgos and Romero 1983). In an earlier version of this chapter, I stated that no comments were ever received from Rigoberta, that she never displayed interest in the manuscript, and that she never gave Elisabeth her permission to publish it (Stoll 1997:36). Now that I have a copy of the two-page typed letter, dated August 8 (not the 9th, as incorrectly stated), addressed to "Compañera Elizabeth," and signed "HASTA LA VICTORIA SIEMPRE, Vicente," it is apparent that, at the very least, Rigoberta served as a courier in the editorial process.

13. Second thoughts and recriminations by the subjects of books like *I, Rigoberta Menchú* are not rare. Another example is Phoolan Devi, a child bride who escaped an abusive husband to become an outlaw and ultimately India's "bandit queen" (Shears and Gidley 1984). From prison, Devi smuggled out a diary that became the basis of writer Mala Sen's book *Bandit Queen,* Shekhar Kapur's rape-filled film about her life, and a successful campaign to free her. Although Devi had signed a contract agreeing to the use of her story, she went to court to prevent the film from being screened, arguing that it violated her right to privacy, distorted facts about her life, jeopardized her legal defense against murder charges, and would inflame hatred between castes (Hamish McDonald, "Queen's Gambit," *Far Eastern Economic Review,* November 3, 1994, p. 29; "Hands Up," *Economist,* November 12, 1994, pp. 116–117). Sometimes Devi took responsibility for the massacre of twenty-two members of a caste that had abused her; other times she denied it. In 1996 the Socialist Party elected her to the Indian parliament, where she became part of a coalition keeping the government out of the hands of Hindu nationalists.

14. The Cuban revolution still interprets criticism as betrayal, as illustrated by the reaction to Régis's unflattering recollections of his old comrade Che Guevara. The countercharge has been led by Che's daughter Aleida Guevara, who accuses Régis of betraying information to his Bolivian captors and therefore sharing responsibility for her father's death (Vilas 1996). Meanwhile, Elisabeth has edited a second life story, by one of the three survivors of Che's Bolivian expedition. Corroborating earlier accounts, Benigno describes how Che's column was betrayed by distrustful peasants and a carelessly recruited Bolivian member who turned out to be an ex-policeman (Alarcón Ramírez 1997:138–143).

15. Brittin and Dworkin 1993:218, as translated in Brittin 1995:110–111, except for the phrase *derecho del autor*. In the plural (*derechos del autor*), this would refer to royalties, but the context suggests that here the singular form is better translated literally as "the right of the author," even if royalties also became an issue.

16. In May 1998 Elisabeth sent me photocopies of correspondence including:

- a typed note on CUC letterhead stating, "A quien interese: La que firma abajo, Rigoberta menchú, miembro del Comité de Unidad Campesina—CUC—, por este medio hace constar que acepta la suma que le corresponde a Elizabeth BURGOS por derechos de autor. Atentamente, [signed] Rigoberta Menchú. Guatemala, Junio de 1982."
- a typed note addressed to Elisabeth in Paris, dated September 24, 1986, stating, "Estimada señora, Me dirijo a usted con un saludo fraternal y respetuoso. De acuerdo con nuestra última conversación, del 22 de Septiembre de 1986, usted me cede los derechos económicos del Libro '*Me llamo Rigoberta Menchú*,' los que, por el momento, ascienden a la suma de 74,335.98 francos, conforme al cheque extendido por las ediciones Gallimard, el 7 de Marzo del año en curso. Por medio de la presente quiero dejar constancia que el beneficiario de dichos derechos económicos será el Collectif Guatemala (Asociación 1901), con sede en el 67 rue du Theatre, París 75015. Me despido de usted agradeciendo su fina atención y espero volver a verla pronto. Atentamente, [signed] Rigoberta Menchú Tum."
- a handwritten note, datelined Paris, September 25, 1986, in which Rigoberta and Juan Mendóza acknowledge receipt of the aforementioned 74,335.98 francs on behalf of the Collectif Guatemala.
- four typed notes on Editions Gallimard letterhead, dating from May 26, 1989, to December 18, 1992, reporting the remittance of a total of 221,466.80 francs to the Fondation France-Libertés, which was associated with the Fondation Danielle Mitterrand.

17. Burgos-Debray 1984:35. Of this oft-cited phrase, a finca owner comments: "It's complete bullshit that a coffee picker has to treat a coffee bean like a wounded person. It's got a thick hull on it, so the point is to strip a branch of mature beans, leaving the green ones and not breaking the branch."

18. In May 1999 I was able to listen to another sixteen hours of tape at Elisabeth's apartment in Paris. They bear out my earlier conclusion, as well as Rigoberta's own statements, that she is the sole narrator of *I, Rigoberta Menchú*.

Chapter 14

1. Burgos-Debray 1984:9–13, 67–69, 188–189, 201–203.

2. Sommer 1991 and Gugelberger 1996.

3. For an example of this argument, see the introduction by Arturo Arias to Thorn 1996. Trouillot 1995:7–8.

4. Compare Beverley 1989:21 on their hallucinatory intensity, or "magical realism."

5. Compare Zur 1993:218 on "the loss of the body as an object to be mourned." For references to the Argentine case and the difficulties of mourning without remains, see Suárez-Orozco 1992:241–242.

6. Beverley 1996:268.

7. See Linde 1993:176 on "coherence systems."

8. This part of my argument is indebted to Timothy Wickham-Crowley (1991: 107, 124–125) for his discussion of terror, consciousness-raising, and ideological conversion in El Salvador.

9. Frank 1995:146, quoting Linde 1993:3.

10. Oddly, blaming the problems of peasants on outsiders is also very appealing to foreigners. As Norma Kriger (1992) points out, nationalist movements, the left, and Western sympathizers all tend to underestimate the conflicts dividing peasants and exaggerate their grievances against outsiders. The few references that *I, Rigoberta Menchú* makes to internal conflicts are chiefly to informers betraying the community to the army (Burgos-Debray 1984:146, 173).

11. Russell 1950:58–64.

12. Hovland 1995:9. Hovland was the first person to challenge the factuality of *I, Rigoberta Menchú,* based on interviewing in Uspantán, in a book about his experiences as a war correspondent titled (in Norwegian) "On secret trails in Guatemala and Central America" (Hovland 1996).

13. "Elections Amid Gunfire," *Latin American Weekly Report,* March 5, 1982, pp. 6–7, and Iglesia Guatemalteca en el Exilio 1982:76–84, which includes a list of CGUP members, who were to function like a similar group, "The Twelve," had for the Sandinista insurrection in Nicaragua.

14. Iglesia Guatemalteca en el Exilio 1982:31.

15. David Scotchmer, "Blood or Water? Mayan Images of Church and Mission from the Underside," paper, n.d., pp. 15–16.

16. "Guatemala: Just an Old-Fashioned Indian War," *Akwesasne Notes* (Rooseveltown, N.Y.), Late Fall 1982, pp. 11–13.

17. Black et al. 1984:115–116.

18. Castañeda 1993:92; Payeras 1991; and *Opinión Política,* a publication of Octubre Revolucionario. See also Arias 1984.

19. In Carmack 1988:172.

20. Personal communication, January 28, 1997. Rigoberta does not make references to theater in her 1982 testimony, but she does make several to movies, for example, "Everything in our life is like a film" (Burgos-Debray 1984:116, 181, 188). For Benigno's testimony, see Alarcón Ramírez 1997.

21. Foppa 1982. In her 1997 life story, Rigoberta refers to the interview with Alaíde and mentions that she was called "Lupita," a diminutive for "Guadalupe" (Menchú et al. 1998:240–241).

22. Burgos-Debray 1984:186, 197.

Chapter 15

1. Bastos and Camus 1993:69.

2. "Determined to fight for social justice but unwilling to join the guerrillas, she chose the more peaceful path of community activism" (Kasey Vannett, "Activist Fights to Preserve Indigenous Culture," *Times of the Americas,* January 22, 1992, p. 7). The same transformation is also very evident in Rigoberta's 1997 life story (Menchú et al. 1998).

3. "Organization of the People in Arms: Indians in Guatemala," *Indigenous World* (San Francisco) 2(2)(1983):4–5.

4. Falla 1978 and Arias 1985.

5. This is such a taboo subject that I have yet to see it properly documented. However, Mario Roberto Morales (1994:87–88) describes such killings in his docu-novel *Señores bajo los arboles.*

6. The other members were Raúl Molina, Rolando Castillo Montalvo, Frank LaRue, and Marta Gloria Torres (Menchú et al. 1998:299–302).

7. "Hostigamiento a la RUOG," *Diario El Gráfico,* May 13, 1989, p. 7. "Rigoberta Menchú, una persona que no merece el Premio Nobel," *Prensa Libre,* May 22, 1989, p. 4; and "A Nobel Peace Prize for an Indigenous Woman," *Noticias de Guatemala* 165, June 1989, pp. 1–3.

8. Amnesty International 1987:136–148 and Simon 1987:209, 212.

9. Bastos and Camus 1993:86.

10. Burgos-Debray 1984:xvi, xix, 154.

11. For a rare published reference to the divided feelings, omitting the issue of Rigoberta's URNG ties, see Bastos and Camus 1993:181–184 and 1995:32–36. Bastos and Camus detail the organizational development of the *clasista* (URNG) and *etnicista* (Pan-Mayan) wings of the Mayan movement, including the periodic attempts to bring them together, but Stener Ekern (1997) provides a more candid analysis of the contradictions involved. For the many forms of linguistic and cultural activism that Mayas are pursuing, see the collection by Edward Fischer and McKenna Brown (1996).

12. This account of the conference is indebted to Smith 1992; Bastos and Camus 1993:95–97, 169–175; and Hale 1994.

13. According to Rigoberta's 1997 life story, the coordinating team for the campaign was Rosalina Tuyuc of CONAVIGUA, the union leader Byron Morales of the Union of Labor and Popular Action (UASP), the Kaqchikel pastor Vitalino Similox of the Evangelical Indigenous Council of Guatemala (CIEDEG), Arlena and Rolando Cabrera, and the journalist Luz Méndez de la Vega (Menchú et al. 1998:320, 327).

14. Golden 1992.

15. Nobel Foundation, "Nobelstiftelsen: Statutes of the Nobel Foundation," Stockholm, 1988, p. 1. For a biography of Nobel, see Fant 1993.

16. For a different perspective on Mother Teresa, see Hitchens 1995.

17. The year after Rigoberta's award, the peace prize went to F. W. de Klerk and Nelson Mandela of South Africa, despite the fact that ten thousand people had died in political violence since de Klerk's release of Mandela from prison. Even after the prize, the two co-laureates accused each other of not doing enough to control the various security forces and street gangs under their command. The 1994 award was even more controversial. It went to Yitzhak Rabin, prime minister of Israel, and Yasir Arafat, chairman of the Palestine Liberation Organization. A member of the Nobel committee resigned on grounds that Arafat was still advocating terrorism. As for Rabin, he could be held responsible for the actions of the Israeli Defense Forces. Unlike the South African peace agreement, which took

hold and reduced political violence, the Israeli-Palestinian agreement disintegrated in further attacks and reprisals. Under different circumstances, it is easy to imagine more than a few peace laureates being put on trial for the actions of their subordinates.

18. Burgos-Debray 1984:136–137, 146–147, 232–233.

19. Henrik Hovland, personal communications, January 6 and June 11, 1995.

20. The newspaper of the Mohawk Nation, *Akwesasne Notes* (Rooseveltown, N.Y.), covered this debate extensively.

21. One wing of the fractured American Indian Movement wanted to nominate Leonard Peltier, a militant sentenced to life in prison for murdering two federal agents despite anomalies in the evidence against him. A campaign to free him had been going on for years, with Amnesty International adopting him as a prisoner of conscience. In return for Rigoberta's support, the Peltier people agreed to call off their own Nobel campaign.

22. Diane Nelson, personal communication, August 1993.

Chapter 16

1. Linde 1993:3 as quoted in Frank 1995.

2. Juan Luis Font, "El galardón se va al exilio," *Crónica,* October 23, 1982, pp. 23–24; Golden 1992; "Support of the International Community for the Nobel Prize," *Noticias de Guatemala,* December 1992, pp. 9–11; and David Loeb, "Rigoberta Menchú Wins Nobel Peace Prize," *Report on Guatemala* (Oakland, Calif.), Winter 1992, pp. 2–3, 14.

3. Nelson 1993. Tortilla joke in Tobar 1994:29.

4. Burgos 1992.

5. Font, "El galardón se va al exilio," p. 23.

6. Gregorio De Broi, "Nuevo sol" (interview with Rigoberta Menchú), *Pensamiento Propio,* March 1993, pp. 21–22.

7. Evelyn Blanck, "Entrevista con Rigoberta Menchú: 'Con la crisis, todos aprendimos algo,'" *Crónica,* June 11, 1993, p. 30.

8. Lionel Toriello, an INC founder, published a scathing description of meeting with Rigoberta and her advisers as they apparently received instructions over the telephone from Mexico ("La noche que 'enloquecí,'" *Siglo Veintiuno,* June 13, 1993, pp. 1–4, *Opinión* insert). Menchú and the popular organizations wanted the congress to resign and be replaced by a national constituent assembly to write a new constitution (Haroldo Shetemul et al., "La caída de un dictador de papel," *Crónica,* June 4, 1993, pp. 16–22).

9. "La Nobel no ve, a veces," *Siglo Veintiuno,* January 13, 1994, p. 10.

10. In Rigoberta's defense, criticizing the Mexican government might have affected the many Guatemalan refugees who depended on its good will. The Zapatista rebellion put the entire URNG in a difficult position since the Mexican government had long tolerated its use of Chiapas as a logistical base ("Obispo y Nobel de la Paz mediarán en enfrentamiento armado mexicano," *Prensa Libre,* January 10, 1994, p. 4, and "Guerra a muerte piden contra EZLN!" *El Regional,* January 21, 1994, p. 18).

11. Oscar René Oliva, "Menchú duda de firma de la paz en diciembre," *La República*, July 5, 1994, p. 6.
12. Menchú and CUC 1992: interview with Bernardo Atxaga, n.p.
13. MacFarquhar 1996:46.
14. My translation of the notes of Jan Lundius, of an interview on June 13, 1994. Ellipses mark gaps in his notes.

Chapter 17

1. Personal communication, September 29, 1995.
2. Hanson 1989:898.
3. Hobsbawm and Ranger 1983.
4. See James Clifton's 1990 collection on "the invented Indian," with a response from Ward Churchill (1991), along with Hanson 1989, Linnekin 1991, Webster 1995, and Jackson 1995. For collisions in Guatemala, see Allen 1992, Watanabe 1994, and Fischer and Brown 1996.
5. Ramos 1988:229.
6. Friedman 1992:194, 197, 202–203.
7. Allen Carey-Webb, "Teaching Third World Auto-Biography: Testimonial Narrative in the Canon and Classroom," *Oregon English*, Fall 1990, quoted in Beverley 1993b:147.
8. Poole and Rénique 1992; Pizarro Leongómez 1996.
9. For the dangers of such imagery in the Amazon case, see Ramos 1991 and 1994 as well as Conklin and Graham 1995.
10. Sexton 1981, 1985, and 1992.
11. *Survival International News*, 1986, p. 8.
12. Zimmerman 1991:40 and 1995:vol 2, 72–90. Obviously, setting up either Rigoberta or Ignacio as typical is a mistake because Mayan society embraces many social types. Another interesting comparison is with life stories by other female activists, including two that were published in English. Elvia Alvarado, the Honduran organizer who narrates *Gringo, Don't Be Afraid!*, is a gritty realist who includes frank descriptions of machismo and conflict among the poor ("There are lots of Judases among us") (Benjamin 1987). The Bolivian miner's wife who narrates *Let Me Speak!*, Domitilia Barrios, is also frank about domestic abuse, strife among the poor, and conflict within the left (Barrios de Chungara 1978). Rigoberta provides her own critique of machismo (Burgos-Debray 1984:216–226), but it seems far more diplomatic than Elvia's and Domitilia's, perhaps because of the need to tread lightly in a movement that she had joined so recently. Both Elvia and Domitilia were mature women when they told their stories, with far longer histories of political leadership than Rigoberta's in 1982. Unlike Rigoberta, they had not just lost three members of their immediate family, nor were they part of a revolutionary movement that seemed close to overthrowing the old regime. They do not hold out the hope of an imminent revolutionary transformation, nor do they romanticize the poor, nor do they claim identity as Indians. There is also a difference in how they portray repression: The nightmarish experiences they suffer in their own flesh are less spectacular than the calvaries through which

Rigoberta puts her mother and brother. Elvia's and Domitilia's testimonies are well known to Latin Americanists, but neither has evoked as wide a response as Rigoberta's.

13. For a description of how the requirements of political capital relayed through the mass media encourage dichotomous thinking, see Mark Pedelty's (1995) ethnography of war correspondents in El Salvador. Orin Starn (1995) has shown how the Shining Path rebellion in Peru confounds the quest for the "insurrectionary other" and other fashionable dichotomies in recent scholarship.

14. Todd Little-Siebold, "Introduction," and Diane Nelson, "Gringa Positioning, Vulnerable Bodies and Fluidarity," for the panel "Kaxlan Construction: Transnational Research in 1990s Guatemala," meeting of the Latin American Studies Association, Washington, D.C., September 28, 1995.

15. Beverley 1991 and 1993a:491–492.

16. See Zimmerman 1995:vol. 2, 63–68; Brittin 1995; Handley 1995; Thorn 1996:63–69; and Beverley 1996:278, 285.

17. Beverley and Yúdice are quoted in Gugelberger 1996:8–9. Unwillingness to compare a testimonio with other forms of evidence turns it into a reductive anecdote, that is, truth as summarized by a certain story. When empirical evidence and testable generalizations are replaced by an appealing story, Roy D'Andrade (1995:405) reminds us, readers are still likely to assume that it is representative, that is, a valid generalization about an entire social class.

18. Richard White, "The Return of the Natives," *New Republic*, July 8, 1996, pp. 37–41.

19. Stoll 1996 and 1998.

20. The phrase comes from William Ryan's *Blaming the Victim*, a critique of the 1965 Moynihan report, which identified the disintegration of families as a critical factor in U.S. inner-city poverty. For Ryan (1971), the fundamental problem was racism. For critiques of "victimism" and the "culture of complaint" in differing veins, see Sykes 1992 and Hughes 1993. For a critique of identity politics, see Gitlin 1995.

21. Compare MacFarquhar 1996:46. Claims to identity, and for the superiority of autobiography over more detached approaches, discourage the expression of skepticism by their very nature. To refute this book, all you have to do is figure out where I lack evidence or have misinterpreted it; I do not have to be guilty of anything but making mistakes. But if Rigoberta tells us that she saw her brother die in Chajul, to argue that she did not is to verge on calling her a liar.

22. As "the icon of testimonio writing," according to Georg Gugelberger (1996: 1), *I, Rigoberta Menchú* has been assimilated into the canon of university-assigned literature and become "merely another commodity" or "fetish," that is, a symbol covering up something that cannot be acknowledged. What is being covered up, according to Gareth Williams (1996) in the same collection, are "fantasies of cultural exchange"—the wish to resolve one's contradictions by identifying with the oppressed. Although Gugelberger and Beverley distinguish between icons and fetishes, I assume that any icon functions as a fetish. For a definition of icons in the mass media, see Roger Horrocks (1995:17) and Amelia Simpson (1993:47–48), who (following Stewart Ewen and Rosemary Coombe) defines the iconography of a blonde Brazilian pop star as a "symbolic pathway, connecting each aspiring individual to a universal image of fulfillment."

Chapter 18

1. For a press account of the conflict with the Garcías, see "Temen nuevas masacres en Chimel," *Tinamit* (Guatemala), August 5, 1993, pp. 30–31.

2. Also excluded were the Chimel survivors residing in the Communities of Population in Resistance. "We're suffering here while rich people are putting cattle in pastures that didn't cost them anything," an orphan grown to manhood in the CPRs told me. "The people from before cut down the trees and cultivated, and now these are eating from what didn't cost them anything."

3. A *canche* is a person with light hair. The term is also used to refer to guerrillas, apparently because the army used to claim that the mainly Mayan guerrillas were led by foreigners.

4. Campesinos returning from a human rights rally lost the trail during a torrential downpour at dusk. As they bushwhacked their way down into Soch, civil patrollers responded with gunfire, either because they were alarmed or were expressing their feelings about human rights. No one was hit.

5. Frank Maurovich, "Nobel Prize for Noble Lady," *Maryknoll*, February 1993, pp. 35–38.

6. Baumann 1982:1.

Chapter 19

1. Account of an interview with Steve Scher on KUOW-Seattle, in "Rigoberta Menchú in Seattle," *Guatemala Update* (Seattle: Guatemala Solidarity Committee), Winter 1995, pp. 1, 4–5.

2. Burgos-Debray 1984:88, 220–226.

3. "Rigoberta Contrae Matrimonio," *Prensa Libre*, March 27, 1995, p. 4.

4. "Menchú: 'El propósito era secuestrar a mi hijo,'" *Diario El Gráfico*, November 6, 1995, p. 3.

5. Fernández García 1995:9.

6. "Irresponsable la versión sobre el secuestro de sobrino de Menchú," *Diario El Gráfico*, November 13, 1995, p. 10.

7. "No es con calumnias y campañas negras como se construirá la paz, la reconciliación, y el estado de derecho en Guatemala," press release, Rigoberta Menchú Foundation, November 24, 1995.

8. *Noticias de Guatemala*, October 24, 1994, in "Guatemalan News Update: Indigenous Demand to Be Taken into Account in Peace Talks," *Anthropology Newsletter*, January 1995, p. 24. When the two sides finished negotiating the indigenous rights agreement, Rigoberta refused to endorse it (Bastos and Camus 1995:75).

9. Payeras 1991:109.

10. Rigoberta Menchú Tum, "Recordatorio de Mario Payeras," in *Jaguar-Venado* 1995:19.

11. Paul Jeffrey, "Menchú's Grassroots Battle," *Latinamerica Press*, October 5, 1995, p. 15.

12. Author's interview with Rosario Pu, Guatemala City, July 5, 1996.

13. Sally Burch, "Rigoberta Menchú Promueve Participación Ciudadana," Agencia Latinoamericana de Información, Quito, Ecuador, 1995.

14. "Cambio de rumbo," *Crónica,* September 15, 1995, p. 11.

15. NACLA Report on the Americas 1996:7–8.

16. She went so far as to deny the indigenous resentment of ladinos that was such a marked feature of her 1982 story: "Objectively, in Guatemala an anti-ladino attitude does not exist like I have encountered in other countries"—such as among the Sioux (Gustavo Berganza, "Rigoberta Menchú Tum: 'Nos guste o no, Guatemala es un país multiétnico,'" *Crónica,* April 19, 1996, pp. 31–32).

17. For analysis of how the Maya movement is trying to change the Guatemalan state, see Ekern 1997 and Nelson 1996.

18. "Dos crímenes en la agenda del EGP," *Crónica,* March 27, 1998, p. 28. The worst such case was the EGP's massacre of more than a hundred villagers in Chacalté, Chajul, on June 13, 1982, for joining the army's civil patrol. The incident has been verified by an exhumation carried out by the Archbishop's Human Rights Office (Ana Lucía González, "La venganza del EGP," *Revista* [*Prensa Libre*], August 31, 1997, pp. 8–10).

19. Pablo Rodas Martini, "Rigoberta Menchú: miembro honorario del CACIF," *El Periódico,* February 27, 1998, p. 10.

20. From the notes of a colleague who attended the speech, at Columbia University in New York City, on February 28, 1996.

Chapter 20

1. Burgos Debray 1984:118.

2. For example, Trejo 1996.

3. As Carolyn Nordstrom and Antonius Robben (1995:11) put it, anthropologists "depart for the field bowing under the weight of our own culture, propped up and propelled by Western assumptions we seldom question, shielded from the blaze of complex cultural diversity by a carefully crafted lens of cultural belief that determines as much as clarifies what we see. When we purport to speak for others, we carry the Western enterprise into the mouths of other people."

4. Ellis 1997.

5. Castañeda 1993. For analysis of why guerrilla strategy became self-defeating in Colombia, see Eduardo Pizarro Leongómez (1996) on "insurgency without revolution."

6. Doreen Carvajal, "From Rebel to Pop Icon: 30 Years After His Death, Che Guevara Has New Charisma," *New York Times*, April 30, 1997.

7. I do not have space to give the Zapatistas the attention they deserve. That the movement was started by urban Marxists does not invalidate them as an indigenous movement. To the contrary, as Gary Gossen (1996) has pointed out, Mayas have a long history of choosing outsiders as their leaders. For analysis of why some peasants supported the Zapatistas and others did not, see Collier 1994 and 1997. For an ecological analysis of the Zapatista context, see Simon 1997:91–125. For skeptical portraits of Subcomandante Marcos, see Tello Díaz 1995 and De la Grange and Rico 1998. For a more sympathetic view, see Le Bot 1997.

8. Childs 1995:622–623.

Bibliography

Adams, Richard N. 1991. "Las masacres de Patzicía de 1944: Una reflexión." *Winak: Boletín Intercultural* (Guatemala: Universidad Mariano Galvez). 7(14):3–40.

Aguirre Godoy, Mario. 1982. "La Tragedia de Guatemala en la Embajada de España." *Prensa Libre*, June 17, 18, 19, 21, 22.

Alarcón Ramírez, Dariel. 1997. *Memorias de un Soldado Cubano: Vida y Muerte de la Revolución*. Barcelona: Tusquets Editores.

Albertani, Claudio, and Francisco Molina. 1994. "Mario Payeras: Literatura y Revolución." *Jaguar-Venado*. 1(1):19-24.

Alecio, Ronaldo. 1995. "Uncovering the Truth: Political Violence and Indigenous Organizations." In Minor Sinclair, ed., *The New Politics of Survival: Grassroots Movements in Central America*, pp. 25–45. New York: Monthly Review Press and Washington, D.C.: Ecumenical Program on Central America and the Caribbean.

Allen, Arthur. 1992. "Unriddling the Glyphs." *Lingua Franca*, November/December, pp. 52–58.

Amnesty International. 1980. "Guatemala Campaign: English Translation of Interview with Peasants of San Miguel Uspantán." AI Index: AMR 34/08/80, February 8.

______. 1981. "Guatemala: A Government Program of Political Murder." In Jonathan L. Fried, Marvin E. Gettleman, Deborah T. Levenson, and Nancy Peckenham, eds., *Guatemala in Rebellion: Unfinished History*, pp. 139–145. New York: Grove Press.

______. 1987. *Guatemala: The Human Rights Record*. London: Amnesty International.

Arias, Arturo. 1984 "The Guatemalan Revolution: A Reassessment." *Guardian* (New York), May 23.

______. 1985. "El Movimiento Indígena en Guatemala, 1970–83." In Daniel Camacho, ed., *Movimientos Populares en Centroamerica*, pp. 63-119. Costa Rica: Ciudad Universitario Rodrigo Facio.

______. 1990. "Changing Indian Identity: Guatemala's Violent Transition to Modernity." In Carol A. Smith, *Guatemalan Indians and the State: 1540 to 1988*, pp. 230–257. Austin: University of Texas Press.

Arias de Blois, Jorge. 1987. *El Crecimiento de la Población de Guatemala y sus Implicaciones*. Guatemala City: Asociación Pro-Bienestar de la Familia de Guatemala.

Asociación de Investigación y Estudios Sociales (ASIES). 1995. *Reorganización, Auge y Desarticulación del Movimiento Sindical.* Vol. 3 of *Más de 100 Años del Movimiento Obrero Urbano en Guatemala.* Guatemala City: ASIES.

Barrios de Chungara, Domitilia, with Moema Viezzer. 1978. *Let Me Speak! Testimony of Domitilia, a Woman of the Bolivian Mines.* New York: Monthly Review Press.

Bastos, Santiago, and Manuela Camus. 1993. *Quebrando el Silencio: Organizaciones del Pueblo Maya y sus Demandas (1986–92).* Guatemala City: Facultad Latinoamericano de Ciencias Sociales.

______. 1994. *Sombras de una Batalla: Los Desplazados por la Violencia en la Ciudad de Guatemala.* Guatemala City: Facultad Latinoamericano de Ciencias Sociales.

______. 1995. *Abriendo Caminos: Las organizaciones mayas desde el Nobel hasta el Acuerdo de derechos indígenas.* Guatemala City: Facultad Latinoamericano de Ciencias Sociales.

Baumann, Zygmunt. 1982. *Memories of Class.* London: Routledge & Kegan Paul.

Bell-Villada, Gene H. 1993. "Why Dinesh D'Souza Has It in for Rigoberta Menchú." *Monthly Review* 43(1):36–45.

Benjamin, Medea, ed. 1987. *Don't Be Afraid, Gringo: A Honduran Woman Speaks from the Heart, the Story of Elvia Alvarado.* San Francisco: Institute for Food and Development Policy.

Berryman, Phillip. 1984. *The Religious Roots of Rebellion: Christians in Central American Revolutions.* Maryknoll, N.Y.: Orbis Books.

______. 1994. *Stubborn Hope: Religion, Politics, and Revolution in Central America.* Maryknoll, N.Y.: Orbis Books.

Beverley, John. 1989. "The Margin at the Center: On Testimonio." *Modern Fiction Studies* 35(1):11–28.

______. 1991. Untitled talk presented to the Latin American Studies Association, Crystal City, Virginia.

______. 1993a. "El Testimonio en la Encrucijada." *Revista Iberoamericana* 59:484–495.

______. 1993b. "'Through All Things Modern': Second Thoughts on Testimonio." In Steven M. Bell, Albert H. Le May, and Leonard Orr, eds., *Critical Theory, Cultural Politics, and Latin American Narrative,* pp. 125–51. Notre Dame, Ind.: Notre Dame University Press.

______. 1996. "The Real Thing." In Georg M. Gugelberger, ed., *The Real Thing: Testimonial Discourse and Latin America,* pp. 266–286. Durham, N.C.: Duke University Press.

Binford, Leigh. 1996. *The El Mozote Massacre: Anthropology and Human Rights.* Tucson: University of Arizona Press.

Black, George, with Milton Jamail and Norma Stoltz Chinchilla. 1984. *Garrison Guatemala.* London: Zed Press.

Blanck, Evelyn. 1992. "Rigoberta Menchú Tum: Lider del Comité de Unidad Campesina." *Crónica,* July 17, pp. 31–32.

Bocek, Barbara. 1998. "Guatemalan Indigenous Views of Politics and the Peace Process" and "Land Rights and Population Pressures in a Mayan Village." *Active Voices, the Online Journal,* no. 4, March. Available: http://www.cs.org.

Bouvard, Marguerite Guzman. 1994. *Revolutionizing Motherhood: The Mothers of the Plaza de Mayo.* Wilmington, Del.: Scholarly Resources.

Bricker, Victoria Reifler. 1981. *The Indian Christ, the Indian King: The Historical Substrate of Maya Myth and Ritual*. Austin: University of Texas Press.
Brittin, Alice A. 1995. "Close Encounters of the Third World Kind: Rigoberta Menchú and Elisabeth Burgos's *Me llamo Rigoberta Menchú*." *Latin American Perspectives* 22(4):100–114.
Brittin, Alice A., and Kenya C. Dworkin. 1993. "Rigoberta Menchú: 'Hemos sido protagonistas de la historia.'" *Nuevo Texto Crítico* 6(11):207–222.
Brown, Michael, and Eduardo Fernández. 1991. *War of Shadows: The Struggle for Utopia in the Peruvian Amazon*. Berkeley: University of California Press.
Burgos, Elisabeth. N.d. (original edition 1983). *Me llamo Rigoberta Menchú y así me nació la conciencia*. Guatemala City: Arcoiris.
______. 1982. "Guatemala: Voyage au bout de l'horreur." *Le Nouvel Observateur*, April 24, pp. 130ff. (Spanish translation published by *Uno Más Uno* [Mexico City], May 29, 1982.)
______. 1992. "Rigoberta Menchú: El Triunfo de los Vencidos." *El Nacional* (Caracas), December 13, p. 8.
Burgos, Elisabeth, and Isidro Romero. 1983. *Pourquoi ils nous tent*. 54 min. Documentary videocassette.
Burgos-Debray, Elisabeth. 1984. *I, Rigoberta Menchú: An Indian Woman in Guatemala*. Trans. Ann Wright. London: Verso.
Calloni, Stella. 1982. "'¿Hasta cuándo morirá la semilla de los hombres?,' pregunta víctima guatemalteca." *Uno Más Uno* (Mexico City). May 31, p. 15.
Canteo, Carlos. 1998. "Yo soy la autora, yo tengo los derechos y punto." *Siglo Veintiuno*, April 5.
Carlsen, Robert S. 1997. *The War for the Heart and Soul of a Highland Maya Town*. Austin: University of Texas Press.
Carmack, Robert M., ed. 1988. *Harvest of Violence: Guatemala's Indians in the Counterinsurgency War*. Norman: University of Oklahoma Press.
Castañeda, Jorge G. 1993. *Utopia Unarmed: The Latin American Left After the Cold War*. New York: Knopf.
Centro Ak'kutan Bartolomé de Las Casas. 1994. *Evangelio y Culturas en Verapaz*. Cobán, Guatemala: Centro Ak'kutan Bartolomé de Las Casas.
Centro de Estudios y Publicaciones. 1981. *Morir y Despertar en Guatemala*. Lima, Peru: Centro de Estudios y Publicaciones.
Chea, José Luis. 1988. *Guatemala: La Cruz Fragmentada*. San José, Costa Rica: Editorial DEI.
Childs, Matt D. 1995. "An Historical Critique of the Emergence and Evolution of Ernesto Che Guevara's *Foco* Theory." *Journal of Latin American Studies* 27:593–624.
Churchill, Ward. 1991. *Fantasies of the Master Race: Literature, Cinema and the Colonization of the American Indian*. Monroe, Maine: Common Courage Press.
Clerc, Jean-Pierre. 1980a. "Bananas and Death Squads." *Manchester Guardian Weekly*. August 10, pp. 12ff.
______. 1980b. "Rumblings of an Indian Awakening." *Manchester Guardian Weekly*. August 3.
Clifton, James A., ed. 1990. *The Invented Indian: Cultural Fictions and Government Policies*. New Brunswick, N.J.: Transaction Publishers.

Colby, Gerard, with Charlotte Dennett. 1995. *Thy Will Be Done: The Conquest of the Amazon: Nelson Rockefeller and Evangelism in the Age of Oil*. New Yorker: HarperCollins.

Collier, George A. 1997. "Reaction and Retrenchment in the Highlands of Chiapas." *Journal of Latin American Anthropology* 3(1):14–31.

Collier, George A., with Elizabeth Lowery Quaratiello. 1994. *Basta! Land and the Zapatista Rebellion in Chiapas*. Oakland, Calif.: Food First.

Comité de Unidad Campesina. 1980. "Homenaje a Nuestros Heroes del 31 de Enero." *Voz del Comité de Unidad Campesina* 2(9), February.

Comité Guatemalteco de Unidad Patriotica. N.d. [1983]. *Alto al Genocidio de un Pueblo en Lucha*. N.p.

Comité Pro Justicia y Paz. 1980. *Seguiremos el ejemplo de los resuscitados!*

Committee of Solidarity with the People of Guatemala. 1980. "Spanish Embassy Massacre." *Guatemala: Vamonos Patria a Caminar* no. 6, January-March.

Conklin, Beth A., and Laura R. Graham. 1995. "The Shifting Middle Ground: Amazonian Indians and Eco-Politics." *American Anthropologist* 97(4):695–710.

D'Andrade, Roy. 1995. "Moral Models in Anthropology." *Current Anthropology* 36(3):399–408.

Davis, Shelton Harold. 1997. *La Tierra de Nuestros Antepasados: Estudio de la herencia y tenencia de la tierra en el altiplano de Guatemala*. Antigua: Centro de Investigaciones Regionales de Mesoamérica.

Davis, Shelton H., and Julie Hodson. 1982. *Witnesses to Political Violence in Guatemala: The Suppression of a Rural Development Movement*. Boston: Oxfam America.

Debray, Régis. 1967. *Revolution in the Revolution? Armed Struggle and Political Struggle in Latin America*. Trans. Bobbye Ortiz. New York: Grove Press.

______. 1974. "Guatemala." In collaboration with Ricardo Ramírez. In Régis Debray, *The Revolution on Trial: A Critique of Arms*, trans. Rosemary Sheed, vol. 2, pp. 269–364. Middlesex, England: Penguin Books.

De la Grange, Bertrand, and Maite Rico. 1998. *Marcos, la Genial Impostura*. Madrid: Aguilar.

Diócesis del Quiché. 1994. *El Quiché: El Pueblo y su Iglesia*. N.p.

D'Souza, Dinesh. 1991. *Illiberal Education: The Politics of Race and Sex on Campus*. New York: Free Press.

Ekern, Stener. 1997. "Institutional Development Among Mayan Organizations in Guatemala." In Norwegian Programme for Indigenous Peoples, *Institutional Development in an Indigenous Context*, pp. 35–47. Oslo: Norwegian Programme for Indigenous Peoples, Fafo Institute for Applied Social Sciences.

Ellis, John M. 1997. *Literature Lost: Social Agendas and the Corruption of the Humanities*. New Haven: Yale University Press.

Equipo de Antropología Forense de Guatemala (EAFG). 1995. *Las Masacres en Rabinal: Estudio Histórico Antropológico de las Masacres de Plan de Sánchez, Chichupac y Río Negro*. Guatemala City: EAFG.

Falla, Ricardo. 1978. "El Movimiento Indígena." *Estudios Centroamericanos* (Universidad Centroamericana José Simeon Canas, San Salvador) 356–357:439-461.

______. 1983. *Masacre de la Finca San Francisco, Huehuetenango, Guatemala*. Copenhagen: International Work Group for Indigenous Affairs.

______. 1992. *Masacres de la selva: Ixcán, Guatemala (1975–1982)*. Guatemala City: Editorial Universitaria.

______. 1995. *Historia de un Gran Amor*. Guatemala City: N.p.

Fant, Kenne. 1993. *Alfred Nobel: A Biography*. New York: Little, Brown.

Fellman, Michael. 1989. *Inside War: The Guerrilla Conflict in Missouri During the American Civil War*. New York: Oxford University Press.

Fernández Fernández, José Manuel. 1988. *El Comité de Unidad Campesina: Origen y Desarrollo*. Cuaderno 2. Guatemala City: Centro de Estudios Rurales Centroamericanos.

Fernández García, Dina. 1995. "Blanco de una conspiración." *Prensa Libre, Actualidad,* December 3, pp. 8–10.

Fischer, Edward F., and R. McKenna Brown, eds. 1996. *Maya Cultural Activism in Guatemala*. Austin: University of Texas Press.

Foppa, Alaíde. 1982. "Ultima entrevista de Alaíde Foppa." In *Guatemala, Las Lineas de Su Mano,* pp. 131–134. Mexico City: Centro de Estudios Económicos y Sociales del Tercer Mundo, Instituto de Investigaciones Estéticas, Universidad Autónoma de México.

Frank, Gelya. 1979. "Finding the Common Denominator: A Phenomenological Critique of Life History Method." *Ethos* 7(1):85.

______. 1995. "Anthropology and Individual Lives: The Story of the Life History and the History of the Life Story." *American Anthropologist* 97(1):145–148.

Frank, Luisa, and Philip Wheaton. 1984. *Indian Guatemala: Path to Liberation*. Washington, D.C.: Ecumenical Program for Interamerican Communication and Action.

Frente Popular 31 de Enero. 1982. "CUC: Los hombres de maíz escriben su historia." *Boletín Internacional* (Mexico), September, pp. 16–23.

Fried, Jonathan L., Marvin E. Gettleman, Deborah T. Levenson, and Nancy Peckenham, eds. 1983. *Guatemala in Rebellion: Unfinished History*. New York: Grove Press.

Friedman, Jonathan. 1992. "Myth, History, and Political Identity." *Cultural Anthropology* 7(2):194–210.

Gitlin, Todd. 1995. *The Twilight of Common Dreams: Why America Is Wracked by Culture Wars*. New York: Metropolitan Books.

Gleijeses, Piero. 1991. *Shattered Hope: The Guatemalan Revolution and the United States*. Princeton, N.J.: Princeton University Press.

Golden, Tim. 1992. "Guatemala Indian Wins the Nobel Peace Prize." *New York Times*, October 17, p. 1.

Gossen, Gary. 1996. "Maya Zapatistas Move to the Ancient Future." *American Anthropologist* 98(3):528–538.

Gugelberger, Georg M., ed. 1996. *The Real Thing: Testimonial Discourse and Latin America*. Durham, N.C.: Duke University Press.

Gugelberger, Georg, and Michael Kearney. 1991. "Voices for the Voiceless: Testimonial Literature in Latin America." *Latin American Perspectives* 18(3):3–13.

Hale, Charles R. 1994. "Between Che Guevara and the Pachamama: Mestizos, Indians and Identity Politics in the Anti-Quincentenary Campaign." *Critique of Anthropology* 14(1):9–39.

Handler, Richard. 1986. "Authenticity." *Anthropology Today* 2(1):2–4.

Handley, George B. 1995. "'It's an Unbelievable Story': Testimony and Truth in the Work of Rosario Ferré and Rigoberta Menchú." In Deirdre Lashgari, ed., *Violence, Silence and Anger: Women's Writing as Transgression*, pp. 62–79. Charlottesville: University of Virginia Press.

Handy, Jim. 1984. *Gift of the Devil: A History of Guatemala*. Boston: South End Press.

Hanson, Allan. 1989. "The Making of the Maori: Cultural Invention and Its Logic." *American Anthropologist* 91(4):890–902.

Harbury, Jennifer. 1994. *Bridge of Courage: Life Stories of the Guatemalan Compañeros and Compañeras*. Monroe, Maine: Common Courage Press.

______. 1997. *Searching for Everardo: A Story of Love, War and the CIA in Guatemala*. New York: Time Warner Books.

Harnecker, Marta. 1982. "Guatemala: EGP Leader Interviewed." *Punto Final*, October 6, p. 11.

______. 1984. *Pueblos en armas*. Mexico City: Ediciones Era.

Hitchens, Christopher. 1995. *The Missionary Position: Mother Teresa in Theory and Practice*. London: Verso Books.

Hobsbawm, Eric, and Terence Ranger, eds. 1983. *The Invention of Tradition*. Cambridge: Cambridge University Press.

Hooks, Margaret. 1991. *Guatemalan Women Speak*. London: Catholic Institute for International Relations.

Horrocks, Roger. 1995. *Male Myths and Icons: Masculinity in Popular Culture*. New York: St. Martin's Press.

Hovland, Henrik. 1995. "Who Is Rigoberta Menchú?" Draft book chapter.

______. 1996. *Paa hemmelige stier i Guatemala og Mellom-Amerika*. Oslo: Cappelen.

Hoyos de Asig, María del Pilar. 1997. *Fernando Hoyos, Donde Estás?* Guatemala City: Fondo de Cultura Editorial.

Huggins, Martha K., ed. 1991. *Vigilantism and the State in Modern Latin America: Essays on Extralegal Violence*. New York: Praeger.

Hughes, Robert. 1993. *Culture of Complaint: The Fraying of America*. New York: Oxford University Press.

Iglesia Guatemalteca en el Exilio. 1982. *Iglesia Guatemalteca en el Exilio: Martirio y Lucha en Guatemala*. December.

______. 1983. *Iglesia Guatemalteca en el Exilio: Fernando Hoyos, Presente!* July.

Jackson, Jean E. 1995. "Culture, Genuine and Spurious: The Politics of Indianness in the Vaupés, Colombia." *American Ethnologist* 22(1):3–27.

Jacoby, Russell. 1994. *Dogmatic Wisdom: How the Culture Wars Divert Education and Distract America*. New York: Doubleday.

______. 1995. "Marginal Returns: The Trouble with Post-Colonial Theory." *Lingua Franca*, September-October, pp. 30–37.

Jaguar-Venado (Mexico City). 1995. "Homenaje a Mario Payeras." *Jaguar-Venado* 1(4), January-March.

Jelin, Elizabeth. 1994. "The Politics of Memory: The Human Rights Movement and the Construction of Democracy in Argentina." *Latin American Perspectives* 21(2):38–58.

Jonas, Susanne. 1991. *The Battle for Guatemala: Rebels, Death Squads, and U.S. Power*. Boulder, Colo.: Westview Press.

Jonas, Susanne, Ed McCaughan, and Elizabeth Sunderland Martinez. 1984. *Guatemala: Tyranny on Trial, Testimony of the Permanent People's Tribunal*. San Francisco: Synthesis Publications.

Jonas, Susanne, and David Tobis. 1974. *Guatemala*. Berkeley: North American Congress on Latin America.

Kobrak, Paul. 1997. "Village Troubles: The Civil Patrols in Aguacatán, Guatemala." Ph.D. dissertation, Department of Sociology, University of Michigan.

Kriger, Norma J. 1992. *Zimbabwe's Guerrilla War: Peasant Voices*. Cambridge: Cambridge University Press.

Kuper, Adam. 1994. "Culture, Identity and the Project of a Cosmopolitan Anthropology." *Man* 29:537–554.

Lartigue, François. 1984. "Guatemala, las raices de una realidad práctica" and "Testimonios de Guatemala." *Civilización* (Mexico) 2(September):291–357.

Le Bot, Yvon. 1995. *La Guerra en Tierras Mayas: Comunidad, Violencia y Modernidad en Guatemala (1970–1992)*. Mexico City: Fondo de Cultura Económica.

______. 1997. *El Sueño Zapatista*. Barcelona: Plaza y Janés.

Leites, Nathan, and Charles Wolf Jr. 1970. *Rebellion and Authority: An Analytic Essay on Insurgent Conflicts*. Chicago: Markham and the Rand Corporation.

Levenson-Estrada, Deborah. 1994. *Trade Unionists Against Terror: Guatemala City, 1954–1985*. Chapel Hill: University of North Carolina Press.

Lévi-Strauss, Claude. 1966. *The Savage Mind*. Chicago: University of Chicago Press.

Linde, Charlotte. 1993. *Life Stories: The Creation of Coherence*. New York: Oxford University Press.

Linnekin, Jocelyn. 1991. "Cultural Invention and the Dilemma of Authenticity." *American Anthropologist* 93:446–449.

MacFarquhar, Larissa. 1996. "The Color of the Law." *Lingua Franca*, July-August, pp. 40–47.

Manz, Beatriz. 1988. *Refugees of a Hidden War: The Aftermath of Counterinsurgency in Guatemala*. Albany: State University of New York Press.

McConahay, Mary Jo. 1993. "Vision of a Multiethnic Nation: An Interview with Rigoberta Menchú." *Report on Guatemala* (Oakland, California), Spring 1993, pp. 2–4ff.

McCreery, David. 1994. *Rural Guatemala, 1760–1940*. Stanford, Calif.: Stanford University Press.

Menchú, Rigoberta. 1992. "The Quincentennial—A Gift of Life: A Message from the Indigenous People of Guatemala. *Social Justice* 19(2):63–72.

Menchú, Rigoberta, and Comité de Unidad Campesina. 1992. *Trenzando el Futuro: Luchas campesinas en la historia reciente de Guatemala*. Donostia, Spain: Tercera Prensa.

Menchú, Rigoberta, with Dante Liano and Gianni Miná. 1998. *Rigoberta: La nieta de los Mayas*. Madrid: Aguilar [English ed., *Crossing Borders*. New York: Verso].

Mondragón, Rafael. 1983. *De Indios y Cristianos en Guatemala*. Mexico City: COPEC/CECOPE.

Montejo, Victor. 1987. *Testimony: Death of a Guatemalan Village*. Willimantic, Conn.: Curbstone Press.

Morales, Mario Roberto. 1994. *Señores bajo los arboles*. Guatemala City: Artemis-Edinter.

NACLA Report on the Americas. 1996. "An Interview with Rigoberta Menchú Tum." *NACLA Report on the Americas* (New York) 29(6):6–9.

Nelson, Diane. 1993. "La formación de las identidades étnico-nacional y de género." *Foro* (Guatemala) 1(10):11–14.

______. 1996. "Maya Hackers and the Cyberspatialized Nation-State: Modernity, Ethnonostalgia, and a Lizard Queen in Guatemala." *Cultural Anthropology* 11(3):287–308.

Nordstrom, Carolyn, and Antonius C.G.M. Robben, eds. 1995. *Fieldwork Under Fire: Contemporary Studies of Violence and Survival*. Berkeley: University of California Press.

Noticias de Guatemala. 1981. "Sección testimonios: Cristianos revolucionarios (CR) 'Vicente Menchú.'" *Noticias de Guatemala* 74, December 16:10–11.

______. 1984. "Semblanza de Gregorio Yujá Xoná." *Noticias de Guatemala* 101, February:10–12.

Oglesby, Liz. 1997. "Labor and the Sugar Industry: Scientific Management on the Plantation." *Report on Guatemala* 18(1):6–7ff.

OSM-CONFREGUA and Jornadas por la Vida y la Paz. 1992. *Y dieron la vida por El Quiché*. Guatemala City: OSM-CONFREGUA and Jornadas por la Vida y la Paz.

Paige, Jeffrey. 1983. "Social Theory and Peasant Revolution in Vietnam and Guatemala." *Theory and Society* 12(6):699–737.

Palencia, Tania. 1996. "Peace in the Making: Civil Groups in Guatemala." Study prepared for the Catholic Institute of International Relations, London.

Payeras, Mario. 1983. *Days of the Jungle: The Testimony of a Guatemalan Guerrillero, 1972–76*. New York: Monthly Review Press.

______. 1987. *El Trueno en la Ciudad: Episodios de la Lucha Armada Urbana de 1981 en Guatemala*. Mexico City: Juan Pablos.

______. 1991. *Los fusiles de octubre: Ensayos y artículos militares sobre la revolución guatemalteca, 1985–88*. Mexico City: Juan Pablos.

Pedelty, Mark. 1995. *War Stories: The Culture of Foreign Correspondents*. New York: Routledge.

Perales, Iosu. 1990. *Guatemala Insurrecta: Entrevista con el Comandante en Jefe del Ejército Guerrillero de los Pobres*. Madrid: Editorial Revolución.

Perera, Victor. 1993. *Unfinished Conquest*. Berkeley: University of California Press.

Piel, Jean. 1989. *Sajcabajá: Muerte y resurreción de un pueblo de Guatemala*. Mexico City: Centre D'Etudes Mexicaines et Centreaméricaines.

Pizarro Leongómez, Eduardo. 1996. *Insurgencia sin Revolución: La guerrilla en Colombia en una perspectiva comparada*. Bogotá: Tercer Mundo Editores.

Polémica. 1982. "La Toma de Nebaj." *Polémica*, January-February, pp. 37–43.

Poole, Deborah, and Gerardo Rénique. 1992. *Peru: Time of Fear*. London: Latin America Bureau.

Popkin, Samuel L. 1979. *The Rational Peasant: The Political Economy of Rural Society in Vietnam*. Berkeley: University of California Press.

Ramos, Alcida Rita. 1988. "Indian Voices: Contact Experienced and Expressed." In Jonathan Hill, ed., *Rethinking History and Myth: Indigenous South American Perspectives on the Past*, pp. 214–234. Urbana: University of Illinois Press.

______. 1991. "A Hall of Mirrors: The Rhetoric of Indigenism in Brazil." *Critique of Anthropology* 11(2):155–169.

______. 1994. "The Hyperreal Indian." *Critique of Anthropology* 14(2):153–171.

Rarihokwats, ed. 1982. *Guatemala! The Horror and the Hope*. York, Pa.: Four Arrows.

"Report on Violence in Northern Quiché, Guatemala, by a Parish Priest, August 1979 to January 1980." 1980. Typescript.

Russell, Bertrand. 1950. *Unpopular Essays*. New York: Simon and Schuster.

Ryan, William. 1971. *Blaming the Victim*. New York: Vintage Press.

Schlesinger, Stephen, and Stephen Kinzer. 1982. *Bitter Fruit: The Untold Story of the American Coup in Guatemala*. New York: Doubleday.

Schwartz, Stephen. 1993. "Phoo, Menchú." *American Spectator*, January, p. 55.

Scott, James C. 1976. *The Moral Economy of the Peasant: Rebellion and Subsistence in Southeast Asia*. New Haven: Yale University Press.

Sexton, James D. 1981. *Son of Tecún Umán: A Mayan Indian Tells His Life Story*. Tucson: University of Arizona Press.

______. 1985. *Campesino: The Diary of a Guatemalan Indian*. Tucson: University of Arizona Press.

______. 1992. *Ignacio: The Diary of a Maya Indian of Guatemala*. Philadelphia: University of Pennsylvania Press.

Shaw, Terri. 1980. "Gap Between Rich and Poor Clouds Guatemala's Future." *Washington Post*, February 3.

Shears, Richard, and Isobelle Gidley. 1984. *Devi: The Bandit Queen*. London: George Allen & Unwin.

Simon, Jean-Marie. 1987. *Guatemala: Eternal Spring, Eternal Tyranny*. New York: Norton.

Simon, Joel. 1997. *Endangered Mexico: An Environment on the Edge*. San Francisco: Sierra Club Books.

Simpson, Amelia. 1993. *Xuxa: The Mega-Marketing of Gender, Race, and Modernity*. Philadelphia: Temple University Press.

Sinclair, Minor, ed. 1995. *The New Politics of Survival: Grassroots Movements in Central America*. New York: Monthly Review Press and Washington, D.C.: Ecumenical Program on Central America and the Caribbean.

Smith, Carol A. 1984. "Local History in Global Context: Social and Economic Transitions in Western Guatemala." *Comparative Studies in Society and History* 26(2):193–228.

______. 1990. *Guatemalan Indians and the State: 1540 to 1988*. Austin: University of Texas Press.

______. 1992. "Maya Nationalism." *Report on the Americas* 25(3):29–33.

Smith-Ayala, Emilie. 1991. *Granddaughters of Ixmucané*. Toronto: Women's Press.

Solórzano, Silvia. 1989. *Mujer Alzada*. Barcelona: Ediciones Sendai.

Sommer, Doris. 1991. "Rigoberta's Secrets." *Latin American Perspectives* 18(3):32–50.

Starn, Orin. 1995. "To Revolt Against the Revolution: War and Resistance in Peru's Andes." *Cultural Anthropology* 10(4):547–580.

Stoll, David. 1983. *Fishers of Men or Founders of Empire? The Wycliffe Bible Translators in Latin America*. London: Zed Press and Cambridge, Mass.: Cultural Survival.

______. 1990. "*I, Rigoberta Menchú* and Human Rights Reporting on Guatemala." Paper presented at the Conference on Political Correctness and Cultural Studies, Western Humanities Institute, University of California, Berkeley, October 19–20.

______. 1993. *Between Two Armies in the Ixil Towns of Guatemala*. New York: Columbia University Press.

______. 1995. "Guatemala: Solidarity Activists Head for Trouble." *Christian Century* 112(1):17–21.

______. 1996. "To Whom Should We Listen? Human Rights Activism in Two Guatemalan Land Disputes." In Richard Wilson, ed., *Human Rights, Culture and Context: Anthropological Perspectives*, pp. 187–215. London: Pluto Press.

______. 1997. "The Construction of *I, Rigoberta Menchú*: Excerpts from a Work in Progress." *Brick, a Literary Journal* (Toronto) 57 (Fall):31–38.

______. 1998. "Human Rights, Land Conflict, and Memories of the Violence in the Ixil Country of Northern Quiché." In Rachel Sieder, ed., *Guatemala After the Peace Accords*. London: Institute for Latin American Studies.

Suárez-Orozco, Marcelo. 1992. "A Grammar of Terror: Psychocultural Responses to State Terrorism in Dirty War and Post-Dirty War Argentina." In Carolyn Nordstrom and JoAnn Martin, eds., *The Paths to Domination, Resistance and Terror*, pp. 219–259. Berkeley: University of California Press.

Sykes, Charles J. 1992. *A Nation of Victims: The Decay of the American Character*. New York: St. Martin's Press.

Taracena Arriola, Arturo. 1997. *Invención criolla, sueño ladino, pesadilla indígena. Los Altos de Guatemala: de región a Estado, 1740–1850*. San José, Costa Rica: Editorial Porvenir and Antigua, Guatemala: Centro de Investigaciones Regionales de Mesoamérica.

Tello Díaz, Carlos. 1995. *La rebelión de las Cañadas*. Mexico City: Cal y Arena.

Thorn, Judith. 1996. *The Lived Horizon of My Being: The Substantiation of the Self and the Discourse of Resistance in Rigoberta Menchú, MM Bakhtin and Victor Montejo*. Tempe: Arizona State University Center for Latin American Studies Press.

Tobar, Hector. 1994. "Rigoberta Menchú's Mayan Vision." *Los Angeles Times Magazine*, January 23, p. 16ff.

Trejo, Alba. 1996. "A cuatro años del Nobel, quién es la verdadera Rigoberta?" *Magazine 21* (*Siglo Veintiuno*), September 8, pp. 8–9.

Trouillot, Michel-Rolph. 1995. *Silencing the Past*. Boston: Beacon Press.

U.S. Senate Judiciary Committee. Subcommittee on Security and Terrorism. 1984. *Marxism and Christianity in Revolutionary Central America: Hearings Before the Subcommittee on Security and Terrorism, October 18–19, 1983*. Washington, D.C.: Government Printing Office.

Van Creveld, Martin. 1991. *The Transformation of War*. New York: Free Press.

Vilas, Carlos. 1996. "Fancy Footwork: Regis Debray on Che Guevara." *NACLA Report on the Americas*, November-December, pp. 9–13.

Watanabe, John M. 1992. *Maya Saints and Souls in a Changing World*. Austin: University of Texas Press.

______. 1994. "Unimagining the Maya: Anthropologists, Others, and the Inescapable Hubris of Authorship," *Bulletin of Latin American Research* 14(1):25–45.

Webster, Steven. 1995. "Escaping Post-cultural Tribes." *Critique of Anthropology* 15(4):381–413.

White, Richard. 1991. *The Middle Ground: Indians, Empires, and Republics in the Great Lakes Region, 1650–1815*. New York: Cambridge University Press.

Wickham-Crowley, Timothy P. 1991. *Exploring Revolution: Essays on Latin American Insurgency and Revolutionary Theory*. Armonk, N.Y.: M. E. Sharpe.

______. 1992. *Guerrillas and Revolution in Latin America*. Princeton, N.J.: Princeton University Press.

Williams, Gareth. 1996. "The Fantasies of Cultural Exchange in Latin American Subaltern Studies." In Georg M. Gugelberger, ed., *The Real Thing: Testimonial Discourse and Latin America*, pp. 225–253. Durham, N.C.: Duke University Press.

Wilson, Richard. 1996. "Introduction" and "Representing Human Rights Violations: Social Contexts and Subjectivities." In Richard Wilson, ed., *Human Rights, Culture and Context: Anthropological Perspectives*, pp. 1–27, 134–160. London: Pluto Press.

Wolf, Eric R. 1969. *Peasant Wars of the Twentieth Century*. New York: Harper.

Yates, Pamela, Thomas Siegel, and Peter Kinoy. 1985. *When the Mountains Tremble*. Documentary video shown on Public Broadcasting System.

Yoldi, Pilar. 1996. *Don Juan Coc: Principe Q'eqchi' (1945–1995)*. Guatemala City: Fundación Rigoberta Menchú Tum.

Zimmerman, Mark. 1991. "Testimonio in Guatemala: Payeras, Rigoberta, and Beyond." *Latin American Perspectives* 18(4):22–47.

______. 1995. *Literature and Resistance in Guatemala: Textual Modes and Cultural Politics from El Señor Presidente to Rigoberta Menchú*. 2 vols. Athens: Ohio University.

Zur, Judith. 1993. "Violent Memories: Quiché War Widows in Northwest Highland Guatemala." Ph.D. dissertation, London School of Economics.

______. 1994. "The Psychological Impact of Impunity." *Anthropology Today* 10(3):12–17.

Index

Aarones, 142, 150
Academy of Mayan Languages, 259
Activism, 237–238
  community, 304(n2)
  human rights, 256–261
  proto-CUC, 95–96
Aguirre Godoy, Mario, 292(n6), 294(n29)
AIM. *See* American Indian movement
Alcalde indígena, 21
Allende, Salvador, 179
Alta Verapaz department, 19–20, 51, 56
American Indian Movement (AIM), 204–205, 306(n21)
Annis, Sheldon, 198
Anthropologists, 11–12, 216–217, 231, 239
  defining identity, 232–234, 247
  historical role, 11–12
  representation of indígenas, 181–182
  Rigoberta's view of, 226–229
Arana Osorio, Carlos, 46
Arbenz, Jacobo, 45–46
Arévalo, Juan José, 45, 45–46
Armed resistance, xiii, 179
  defense of, 278–281
  versus negotiation, 272
  origins of, 9–10
Army, Guatemalan, ix
  appointing vigilantes, 141
  attacks on villages, 92, 128–130, 132–134, 152–153
  civil patrols, 133, 148–149, 150, 151–152
  finca massacres, 145–146, 298(nn 6, 7)
  governmental role, 46, 205
  guerrilla movement and, 44–46, 48
  immolations, 69–70
  land disputes, 73
  obstruction of peace process, 268
  persecution of peasants, 117–118, 222
  Petrocinio Menchú's death and, 65–67
Arriola, Aura Marina, 180, 186
Arzú, Alvaro, 268, 269
Asturias, Miguel Angel, 186, 285(n6)
Asturias, Rodrigo, 186, 285(n6)
Autonomy, indígenas, 208

Baja Verapaz department, 101, 295(n24)
Bandit Queen (Sen), 302(n13)

Barahona y Barahona, Elias, 80
Baumann, Zygmunt, 264
Behrhorst, Carroll, 93–95
Behrhorst Clinic, 109
Belgian Order of the Sacred Family, 144, 160, 298–299(n1)
Bernstein, Richard, 239
Berryman, Phillip, 175
Between Two Armies (Stoll), 237–238
Beverley, John, 127, 190–191, 226, 239, 241, 242
Bizarro Ujpán, Ignacio, 237
Black, George, 86
Body dumps, 67, 127–128
Botrán family, 286(n4)
Brazilian embassy, 83
Brol, Jorgé, 53
Brol, Pedro, 52
Brol family, 30, 145, 286(n4)
Burgos, Elisabeth, xi, xiii, 177, 220
  contact with Rigoberta, 180, 186–188, 301(n8)
  contact with the author, 184–186
  correspondence with Rigoberta, 303(n16)
  personal history, 178–180
  testimonio, 3, 198–199, 242
Burgos-Debray, Elisabeth. *See* Burgos, Elisabeth

Cáceres Lehnhoff, Eduardo, 74, 80, 292(n6)
Cajal y López, Máximo, 74, 75, 79–82, 88, 293(n21)
Calanté, 146
Campesinos. *See* Indígenas; Mayas; Peasants
Cano, Oralio, 150–151
Caracol, Quiché, 126–127
Cardoza y Aragon, Luis, 196
Cargos, 21
Casa de las Americas, 187
Castellanos, Rubén, 113
Castillo, Otto René, 180
Castillo Armas, Carlos, 46
Castro, Fidel, 47–48, 187, 281
Catechists, 21–22, 95, 109, 109–110, 131, 144
Catholic Action, 90, 97, 109–110, 117
Catholic Church, 19, 50
  Belgian Order of the Sacred Family, 160, 298–299(n1)
  clergy, 143–144
  cooperatives, 131
  Dominicans, 19
  education of Rigoberta, 159–163
  human rights activism and, 258
  INTA and, 252
  Jesuits, 97
  persecution of, 143–144, 164
  protecting Rigoberta, 191
  revolutionary involvement, 173
  Rigoberta's flight, 168–169
  See also Committee for Justice and Peace; Guatemalan Church in Exile; Liberation theology
Central Intelligence Agency (CIA), 45–46, 214, 288(n4)
CERJ. *See* Runujel Junam Council of Ethnic Communities
CGUP. *See* Guatemalan Committee for Patriotic Unity
Chajul, 1–3, 65–67, 77, 116–117, 143
Chiantla, Huehuetenango, 161, 164
Chichicastenango, 103, 160
Chile, 179
Chimel, xiii, xx(fig.), 192
  appropriation of land, 30
  Christmas Eve attack, 129
  description of, 29–30
  destruction of, 54, 133–134, 152
  development programs, 93–94
  EGP and, 108–109

factionalization of community, 34–37, 254–255
founding of, 3
household attrition, 288(table)
land disputes, 30–34, 56–57, 72–73
organized defense, 91–92
resettling of, 250–256
Rigoberta's last visit, 163
Rigoberta's return to, 283
Vicente Menchú's community role, 38
Christian Democrats (DC), 22, 250, 256–257
CIA. *See* Central Intelligence Agency
Civilian rule, 6, 203
Civil patrols, 133, 148–149, 150, 151–152
CNUS. *See* National Committee for Labor Unity
Coffee, 53, 255, 303(n17)
Colegio Básico Nuestro Señor de Candelaria, 161
Colegio Belga, 144, 161, 162, 299(n2)
Collaboration, 132, 136, 148
false accusations of, 117–118
García/Martínez families, 113, 289(n22)
motives for, 63–64, 290(n1)
Tum family, 121–122
Collective memory, 189–191, 199
Colonialism, 5, 30, 238–239, 276–277
COMG. *See* Coordinator of Mayan Organizations of Guatemala
Committee for Campesino Unity (CUC), xiii, 197, 204
as voice of peasants, 102
EGP affiliation, 99, 206
embassy massacre, 76–79, 88
Menchú family and, 3–4, 6, 167–169
organizing labor, 145
popular organization, 171, 203
promise of liberation, 51
Rigoberta's disengagement from, 267
Rigoberta's history in, 173–174
rise and fall of, 89–91, 175, 294(n1), 294(n7)
role in quincentenary, 210
strategy of, 99–100
in Uspantán, 92–95
vision and goals, 95–97
Committee for Justice and Peace, 294(n7)
Committee of Solidarity with the People of Guatemala, 296(n5)
Communities of Population in Resistance (CPR), 130, 134, 257, 309(n2)
CONAVIGUA. *See* National Coordinator of Guatemalan Widows
Concientización. See Consciousness–raising
Consciousness-raising, 90, 96–98, 102–104, 191–192, 283
Cooperatives, 131–132
Coordinator of Mayan Organizations of Guatemala, 210
Corruption, 222–223, 256–258
Council for Mayan Education, 270
Counterinsurgency, paradoxes of, 235–239
Coxaj, Claudio, 251
CPR. *See* Communities of Population in Resistance
Critical theory, 242–245, 247
Crossing Borders (Menchú), 170, 182, 298–299(n1)

Cuatro Chorros, Quiché, 134–135, 255
Cuba, xiii, 47–48, 178–180, 187, 281, 288(n4), 302(n14)
CUC. *See* Committee for Campesino Unity
Cultural Anthropology, 239–240

DC. *See* Christian Democrats
Death squads, 49, 141, 192
Debray, Régis, xiv, 43, 178–179, 187, 281, 301(n5), 302(n14)
Defensoría Maya, 259–260
Deforestation, 18, 253–254
De Leon Carpio, Ramiro, 223, 252
Democratic Front Against Repression (FDCR), 69, 171, 196, 197, 289(n23)
El Desengaño, 152
Development programs, 93–94
Devereux, George, 184
Devi, Phoolan, 302(n13)
Dichotomous thinking, 61, 308(n13)
D'souza, Dinesh, 285(n8)

Ecology, 16, 23. *See also* Deforestation
Economy, failure of, 46
Editions Gallimard, 186, 188
Education
  in Chimel, 160–161
  of Rigoberta, 159–163
Education and Promotion of Popular Organization (EFOP), 130
EFOP. *See* Education and Promotion of Popular Organization
EGP. *See* Guerrilla Army of the Poor
Elections, 5–6, 45–46, 256–257, 267–268, 270
Embassy, Spanish. *See* Massacre, Spanish embassy
La Estancia, 103
Ethnic conflict, 21, 52–53, 204–205
Ethnicity
  as political issue, 208–209
  as revolutionary factor, 180
  See also Indígenas; Ladinos; Mayas
Ethnic model, bipolar, 16–17
Ethnic transformation, 22–24
Executions, 58–61. *See also* Immolations
Exhumations, 147, 260, 271, 295(n24)
Exile, of Rigoberta, 203, 205–206, 220
Expropriation of land, 153–154

FAR. *See* Rebel Armed Forces
FDCR. *See* Democratic Front Against Repression
FDNG. *See* New Guatemala Democratic Front
Felipe Antonio García Revolutionary Workers Nuclei, 171
FERG. *See* Robin García Revolutionary Student Front
Fernández, Juan Alonso, 144
FIL. *See* Local Irregular Forces
Fincas, 3, 44, 286(n4)
  CUC uprising, 99–102
  massacres, 144–146, 297(n5), 298(n16)
  quinceneros, 53
  El Rosario, 54, 56, 59, 253
  San Francisco, 44, 52–56, 144–146
  Vicente Menchú, 25
  See also García family; Martínez family; *Quinceneros*

500 Years Meeting. *See* Quincentenary
Foppa, Alaíde, 199, 299(n6)
Foquismo, 138, 281
Forestry regulations, 289(n21)
FP-31. *See* January 31st Popular Front
Freire, Paolo, 96–97
Friedman, Jonathan, 234
FTG. *See* Guatemalan Workers Federation
Fundamaya, 270

Galindo, Otomero, 117
GAM. *See* Mutual Support Group
Gamarro, Reginaldo, 251–252
García, Julio, 253
García, Robin, 84
García family, 30, 53–56, 58–61, 112–113, 142, 252–253
García Fetzer, Carlos, 54
García Samayoa, Honorio, 54–55, 57–60, 108–109, 289(n22), 296(n7)
German settlers, 19–20, 54
Government
  civilian rule, 6, 203
  constitutional, 205
  suspension of constitution, 223, 306(n8)
Gramajo, Alejandro, 241
Las Guacamayas, 52–53, 133–134
Guatemala City, 161
  occupation of embassy, 71–75
  peasant delegations to, 66–70, 73–74
  Rigoberta's revolutionary career, 172–173
  See also Massacre, Spanish embassy
Guatemalan Church in Exile, 143–144, 291
Guatemalan Committee for Patriotic Unity (CGUP), 196, 197, 291(n19), 304(n13)
Guatemalan Labor Party (PGT), 84–85, 196
Guatemalan National Revolutionary Union (URNG), 4, 6, 306(n10)
  international support, 203–204
  member organizations, 196
  peace process and, 220–221, 224–225
  rationale for war, 216
  role in quincentenary, 210
  solidarity and, 236
  See also Guatemalan Labor Party; Guerrilla Army of the Poor; Organization of the People in Arms; Rebel Armed Forces
Guatemalan Workers Federation (FTG), 67
Guerrilla Army of the Poor (EGP), xiii, 2–3, 96, 192, 291(n20), 300(n13)
  in Chimel, 109–111, 126
  clergy involvement, 98
  CUC affiliation, 99, 196
  FIL and, 148
  foquismo, 138
  formation of, 46–48, 50, 53
  igniting political violence, 9–10
  internecine conflict, 175
  massacres, 58–61, 145–146
  Menchús' involvement with, 170, 204, 267
  organization of peasants, 120–121
  Peace Corps and, 193
  promise of liberation, 51
  recruiting support, 52, 63–64, 295(n24)
  El Soch and, 53–55

struggle to survive, 197–198
support for, 101
ties to church, 143–144
Uspantano recollections of, 43–44, 113–116
See also Liberation theology
Guerrilla movement, ix, xiv, 43–44, 48, 171
accountability, 61
bases in Mexico, 169
Catholic church and, 143–144
civil patrols, 133, 148–149, 150, 151–152
credibility, 203–204
CUC and, 91
elections, 268–269
indígena representation, 204
Ixim, 204
organizing peasants, 118–120
origins of, 238
peasants' involvement, 8–9, 126, 192, 250
popular organizations, 206–211
raids on El Soch, 109
retaliation on vigilantes, 142
role in army violence, 153–155
Shining Path, 236, 308(n13)
student protesters, 84
support of Nobel campaign, 214–215
third wave, 50–51
urban warfare, 49
See also Committee for Campesino Unity; Guatemalan National Revolutionary Union; Guerrilla Army of the Poor
Guevara, Aleida, 302(n14)
Guevara, Che, 47, 138, 179, 281, 302(n14)

Hanson, Allan, 232
Harnecker, Marta, 49, 99, 174, 295(n19)
Hernández Ixcoy, Domingo, 83, 95–96, 197
Hostages, 289(n8), 292(n6). *See also under* Massacre, Spanish embassy
Hovland, Henrik, 35, 196, 304(n12)
Hoyos, Fernando, 97–98, 99
Huehuetenango department, 90, 128, 271, 290(n4)
Human rights movement, x, 6, 256–261, 285(n11), 296(n7)
analyzing abuses, 10–11, 61

I, Rigoberta Menchú, viii, 6–7
consciousness-raising, 283
genesis of, 185–186
genre of, 189–190, 198–199, 273–274
multiculturalism and, 243–244
multiple-narrator hypothesis, 182–183
portrayal of indígenas, 232–233
quotes from, 29, 34, 63, 89, 91, 159, 163, 167, 170, 189
symbolism of, 192–193
Uspantán's reaction to, 261–264
Icons, 245–247, 308(n22)
Identity
collective, 199, 199–200
defined, 232–234
indígena, 232–233
insurgents versus army, 235
national, 207–208, 232–233, 270, 283
personal, 244–245
Identity politics, 244–245
Ideology, 63–64, 88, 192
Immigration, 286(n9)
Immolations, 1–2, 4, 65–67, 69–70. *See also* Massacre, Spanish embassy
Indígenas, xiv, 7
autonomy issues, 208–209

disengagement from EGP, 249
ethnic conflict, 16–17, 57–58
expectations of, 232–233
fear of reprisals, 258–260
history of, 44–45
involvement with guerrillas, 43–44, 49–50, 210–212
land disputes, 31–36
massacres, viii
methods of rebellion, 40
political representation, 21–22
population in Uspantán, 20–21
reaction to Nobel award, 221–222
revolutionary movement, 48, 133
segregation in school, 161
"typical," 307(n12)
upward mobility, 25–26
violence against, 16–17, 57–58, 222
voice of, 102, 181–182, 227–229, 237
Indigenous movement
international support for, 235–237
reaction to Nobel Prize, 214–215
representation in guerrilla movement, 204
Rigoberta as symbol for, 227–229
See also Runujel Junam Council of Ethnic Communities
Insurgency
Mexico, 224. *See also* Zapatista National Liberation Army
motives for, 63–64, 153–155
origins of, 9–10
"popular uprising," 238
theory of, 137, 278–279
INTA. *See* National Institute for Agrarian Transformation
International community
intervention in national politics, 235–236
reaction to Nobel award, 214–215, 219–220
support for revolutionaries, 203–206
support for Rigoberta, 276
support for URNG, 216
International Indian Treaty Council, 204–205
Italy, 205–206
Ixcampari, Abraham, 74
Ixcán, 271

January 31st Popular Front (FP–31), 171, 196, 197
Journalists, 239–242, 264
Juarez, Eugenio, 151
Judiciales. See Vigilantes
Judicial system, 269
land conflict, 32

K'amal B'e (The Road), 270
Kidnappings, 60–61, 65–67, 91, 126–127, 166, 174–175, 289(n8), 289(n22), 290(n14), 296(n7), 299(n5)
King, Martin Luther, Jr., 245–246
Kriger, Norma, 304(n10)

Labor disputes, 144–145
Labor movement, 98, 174–175, 300(n18). *See also* Committee for Campesino Unity
Labor strikes, 172
Labor unions, 300(n19)
Ladinos, 3
as scapegoats, 193
defined, 16
hegemony of, 19–22
land conflict and, 31–34

population in Uspantán, 20–21
reaction to Nobel award, 219–220
resettling Chimel, 250–252
Rigoberta's perception of, 54–55
role in quincentenary, 210
Vicente's perception of, 38–39
vigilantes and, 142
violence against, 57–58, 154
versus indígenas, 16–17
wealthy families, 286(n4)
See also Fincas
Laguna (La) Danta, 26–27, 29, 121
Land
acquisition by Brol family, 52–53
control of, 17–18
importance of, 15
Land disputes, 27, 31, 113
factions in Chimel, 34–36, 56–57, 250–253
interfamilial, 54–55, 59–60
internecine, 195
lack of resolution, 36–37, 36–38
role in insurgency, 9, 112–114, 153–154
titles, 22, 23–24, 27, 72–73
Land reform, 46
Language, 22, 259
as political issue, 208
Ixil, 1
K'iche', 34
loss of, 22–24
Language groups, Mayan, 17, 22–24, 285(n1), 286(n8)
LASA. *See* Latin American Studies Association
Latin American Studies Association (LASA), 226, 239–240
Laugerud, Kjell, 50–51
Le Bot, Yvon, 100, 138, 174
Leftists, 89, 278
account of Spanish embassy massacre, 80–82
Achi' Mayas, 295(n24)
Chile, 179
Christian, 237
elections, 267–268, 270
perception of indígenas, 51
response to *I, Rigoberta Menchú*, 5–6
support of Rigoberta, 211
transitions, 208
under Samuel Ruiz, 169–170
See also Catholic Action; Democratic Front Against Repression; Popular movement
Lévi-Strauss, Claude, 104
Liberation theology, 90, 97, 99, 103
Linde, Charlotte, 193, 219
Little-Siebold, Todd, 238
Local Irregular Forces (FIL), 148
López, Francisco, 27
López, Miguel, 126
López Gamarro, Gonzalo, 142–143
Lucas García, Romeo, 51, 67, 196
overthrow of, 147
persecution of church, 143–144
Spanish embassy massacre, 75, 80, 83, 88
Luis Turcios Lima Guerrilla Front, 99
Lundius, Jan, 227–228, 307(n14)

Macalajau, 76–77, 131–132, 166
McMillen, Margot, 58–59
McMillen, Stan, 58–59
Majawil Q'ij (New Dawn), 210, 259
Manifest Destiny, 239
Martínez, Angel, 55, 60
Martínez, Eliu, 57, 59–60, 195, 289(n22), 296(n7)
Martínez, Miguel, 60
Martínez family, 30, 52–56, 58–61, 112–113, 253, 287(n5)

Massacre, Spanish Embassy, 171–172, 292(nn 6, 7, 11)
ambassador's account, 79–82, 293(n21)
Chimel origins, 72–73
CUC and, 76–79, 88
death toll, 76–79
fire origin, 82, 86, 293(n22)
Lucas García and, 80, 83, 88
occupation by peasant delegation, 71–75
survivors' comments, 87
See also January 31st Popular Front
Massacres, 148–149
Calanté, 146
Chajul, 69–70, 291–292(n20)
death tolls, 76–79, 297(n5), 298(nn 8, 9)
Finca San Francisco, 145–146, 297(n5)
indígenas, viii
Panzós, 51
Rabinal, 295(n24)
Xamán, 269
Mayas, xiv–xv
Achí, 295(n24)
Awakateko, 290(n4)
defined, 17
exclusion from peace process, 225
indigenous rights, 270
insurgency in Mexico, 224
Ixil. *See* Mayas, Ixil
Jakalteko, 128
K'iche', 16, 17, 22–24, 34, 35, 43, 53, 56, 290(n4)
Majawil Q'ij, 259
national identity, 207–208, 232–233
nationalism and, 203–205
Pan-Mayanist movement, 7, 207–208
Poqomchi', 54, 56
portrayal of, 231–232
Q'eqchi', 20, 34–35
reaction to *I, Rigoberta Menchú,* 199–200
representation at quincentenary, 210–211
Rigoberta as representative, 246
Tz'utujil, 222, 237
Uspanteko, 16–17, 17, 22, 22–23, 22–24, 286(n8)
voice of, 102, 181–182, 227–229, 237, 247
See also Christian Democrats
Mayas, Ixil, 208, 221–222
army violence and, 116–117
in Chajul, 1–3
land disputes, 23–24, 53, 145
Riosmonttismo, 149–150
support of guerrillas, 63–64
view of guerrillas, 8–11
Media, 68, 74
Menchú, Nicolás, 135–136, 250, 251–257
Menchú, Vicente, xii, 144, 195
as perceived by community, 36–40
as symbol of resistance, 197
consciousness-raising, 102–104
death of, 4, 163–165. *See also* Massacre, Spanish embassy
factionalization of Chimel, 35–37
founding of Chimel, 3
hospitalization/incarceration of, 32–33
land disputes, 27, 30–31, 56–57
military service, 39
peasant delegation to capital, 73–74
protest of son's kidnapping, 67–68
quotes from, 111–112

revolutionary movement and, 64–65, 91–93, 112–114
Rigoberta's recollections of, 39
upward mobility, 24–27
villagers' recollections of, 94–95
See also Massacre, Spanish embassy; Menchú–Tum feud; Tum family
Menchú, Victor, death of, 134–136
Menchú Tum, Ana, 130, 170, 173, 297(n10), 299(n6)
Menchú Tum, Petrocinio, xi, 4, 6, 61, 65–67, 69–70, 290(n14)
Menchú Tum, Rigoberta, 6–7, 197–198, 205
as representative of indígenas, 209–211, 246
as symbol, 188, 274–276
education, viii, 159–166, 177–178, 189, 299(nn 2, 4)
election involvement, 268–269
in exile, 164–165, 168, 261–263
flight to Nicaragua, 173
international lobbying efforts, 203–206
interview with Burgos, 180–181
local popularity, 209–210
Nobel Prize and, 4, 236
peace process and, xiv, 222–225
quotes from, 117, 226, 267
return from exile, 220
Rigoberta Menchú Foundation, 256, 267, 271
views on anthropologists, 226–229
Menchú Tum, Rosa, 25, 130, 170, 173, 297(n10), 299(n6)
Menchú-Tum feud, 30–34, 72, 121
Méndez, Amilcar, 207, 269
Mendoza, Gaspar, 117
Mendoza, Juan, 301(n8)
Meoño, Gustavo, 271
Mestizo, defined, 16
Mexico, 306(n10)
Rigoberta in exile, 168–169, 191, 223–224
uprisings, 279–280
Military. *See* Army
Military rule, Chile, 179
Mitterrand, François, 179–180
Mitterrand, Danielle and Foundation, 188
Molina Orantes, Adolfo, 74, 80, 292(n6)
Molotov cocktails, 79, 80, 81, 82, 83, 85, 86–87
Montejo, Victor, 128
Morán, Felipe, 61
Morán, Paulino, 60
Morán, Rolando (pseud.). *See* Ramírez, Ricardo
Multiculturalism, 243–245
Mutual Support Group (GAM), 206–207

National Committee for Labor Unity (CNUS), 78, 174
National Coordinator of Guatemalan Widows (CONAVIGUA), 207, 249–250, 258, 260
National Institute for Agrarian Transformation (INTA), 30, 113
Brol family and, 52
function of, 3
land disputes, 24, 27, 31–36, 72–73
resettling of Chimel, 250–251
See also Menchú–Tum feud
Navarro, Bertha, 299(n6)
Nebaj, Quiché department, 23
Nelson, Diane, 238
New Dawn. *See* Majawil Q'ij
New Guatemala Democratic Front (FDNG), 268, 268–269

Nicaragua, 6, 50, 214, 235–236
1954 invasion, 39, 47
See also Central Intelligence Agency (CIA)
Nobel Peace Prize, viii–ix, 4
campaign for, 187–188, 206, 211
committee's choice, 214–215
controversy over recipients of, 305(n17)
government reaction to, 219–220
history of, 212–213
laureates, 246
literature, 285(n6)
quotes from award speech, 212
reactions to, 214–215, 219–222
Norway, political tensions, 213–214

Occupations
Brazilian embassy, 83
Swiss Embassy, 84
See also Massacre, Spanish embassy
Ochoa, Arnaldo, 187
Ochoa Ruiz, Carlos Roberto, 67, 290(n11)
Oppression
racial, 5
voices of, 11–12
Orejas, 141, 148. *See also* Vigilantes
Organization of the People in Arms (ORPA), 49–50, 186, 196, 285(n6)
ORPA. *See* Organization of the People in Arms

Pan-Mayan movement, 7, 207–208
Parraxtut, 35
Party for National Advancement, 268
Patronage politics, 53
Payeras, Mario, 47, 70, 137–138, 197
Peace Corps, 93–94, 193
Peace process, xiv, 4, 8, 11, 216, 222–225, 268
government role, 270
Rigoberta's role, 220–221
Peasant League, 92–93
Peasants
armed self-defense, 100–101, 278–281, 291(n20), 295(n24)
as political victims, 279–282
between two fires, 101–102
delegations to capital, 66–70, 73–74
internecine conflict, 304(n10)
lack of organization, 138–139
organization by EGP, 118–121, 129–131
response to guerrillas, 8–9, 63–64, 148–149
See also Committee for Campesino Unity; Indígenas; Mayas
"Pedagogy of the oppressed," 96–97
Pellecer, Luis, 98
Perera, Victor, 291(n15)
PGT. *See* Guatemalan Labor Party
Piñeiro, Manuel, 295(n19)
Plantations. *See* Fincas
Polarization, political, 89–91, 238–239
Political correctness, 239–241, 243–245
Popular movement, 171, 174–175, 206–211
Population growth, 18
Porras, Gustavo, 100, 100–101
Postmodernism, 189–190, 276–277
Procurator for Human Rights, 259

Quezaltenango, 50, 209–210
Quiché department, xxi(fig.)
Catholic Action, 90
described, 2, 15–16

land shortage in, 18
southern, 50, 207
Quiché department, northern, 8–9, 86, 145
first revolutionary theater, 138
massacres, 143
massacre victims, 76–79
political changes, 43–48
Spanish embassy massacre victims, 76
See also San Francisco; Uspantán
Quiché department, southern, 89–91, 103–104
CUC origins, 95
EGP uprising, 101
origin of CUC, 88–89
persecution of clergy, 143
Quinceneros, 53
Quincentenary, 209–211, 213–214, 305(n13)

Racism, xi, xv, 195, 227, 231, 258, 308(n20)
Ramírez, Ricardo, 47, 99, 100, 174, 180, 186, 301(n5)
Ramos, Alcida, 234
Reagan, Ronald, 238
Rebel Armed Forces (FAR), 196
"Remembered history," 264
Resistance, study of, 246
Revolution, 43–44
models for, 47–48, 50–51
See also 1954 invasion
Revolutionary movement, viii, 3–4
catechist members, 173
embassy massacre and, 76–82
massacre victims, 76–79
new "popular" organizations, 206–211
organizational coalition, 196
representation of indígenas, 7–8
Rigoberta's joining of, 168–174
Spanish Embassy massacre, 71–79
student members, 84–85
Revolution in the Revolution? (Debray), 178
Rigoberta Menchú Foundation (formerly Vicente Menchú Foundation), 256, 267, 271
Ríos Montt, Efraín, 128, 147–148, 149, 222, 268
Riosmonttismo, 149, 271
The Road. *See* K'amal B'e
Robin García Revolutionary Student Front (FERG)
formation of FP-31, 171
origins of, 84
peasant protest, 67–68
Spanish embassy massacre, 78–79, 88
El Rosario, 54, 56, 59, 253
Ruiz, Samuel, 168, 169, 224
Runujel Junam Council of Ethnic Communities (CERJ), 206–207
RUOG. *See* United Representation of the Guatemalan Opposition
Russell, Bertrand, 194

El Salvador, 6, 180, 304(n8)
San Carlos University, 74
San Cristobal de las Casas, 169
Sandinistas, 6, 50–51, 71, 214, 304(n13)
San Francisco, 44, 52–56, 144–146, 145–146
San José El Soch, 44, 52–56, 59, 109, 113–114, 129, 150
San Marcos department, 219
San Pablo El Baldío, 56–58, 73, 76–79, 108–109, 132, 152
San Pedro La Esperanza, 129–130, 132–133, 152
Santa Cruz del Quiché, 89–90

Santa Rosa Chucuyub, Quiché department, 25
Scholars, literary, 189, 239–245
Security police, 173
kidnappings, 174–175
role in land conflict, 33
Spanish embassy massacre, 71, 79–82
Serrano Elías, Jorge, 219, 222–223, 252
Settlements. *See* Chimel; San José El Soch; San Pablo El Baldío
Sexton, James, 237
Shaw, Terri, 112–113
Shining Path, 236, 308(n13)
SIL. *See* Summer Institute of Linguistics
Slash-and-burn agriculture, 17–18. *See also* Deforestation; Land disputes
Social class, 180, 254–255
La Soledad, 54
Solidarity, 196–197, 234–239, 285(n11), 289(n22)
Sololá, 271
Sometidos, 56
Somoza Debayle, Anastasio, 50–51, 71
South coast, 49–50, 90
Strikes, labor, 90–91
Students
as activists, 74
protests, 76–79, 88
revolutionary movement, 84–85
See also Massacre, Spanish embassy; Robin García Revolutionary Student Front
Summer Institute of Linguistics (SIL), 58–59
Symbolism
of human rights, x–xi
of *I, Rigoberta Menchú*, xiv, 274–276, 308(n22)
of Menchú family, 105, 197–198, 203–204, 229, 245–246
of resistance, 7–8, 222
See also Icons

Taracena, Arturo, 182, 184, 185–186, 301(n8)
Testimonio, 181–182, 277
as collective voice, 301–302(n9), 308(n17)
as documentary, 11–12, 226, 240–242
of survivors, 191–192
other examples of, 302(n13)
Titling laws, 45
Toj Medrano, Emeterio, 98
Tomás Lux, María, 134
Tradition, invention of, 233
Tremblay, Marie, 184
Trinidad Gómez Hernández Barrio-Dwellers Committee, 171
Trouillot, Michel-Rolph, 189
Tum, Antonio, 27, 32, 36
Tum Castro, Nicolás, 37, 121
Tum Cotojá, Juana, 26, 32
kidnapping/death of, 4, 126–128
Tum family, 251, 287(n5)
incarceration of Vicente Menchú, 32–33
land disputes, 27, 30, 30–34, 56–57, 112–113, 121
See also Menchú–Tum feud
Tum Gómez, Marcelo, 60
Tum Gómez, Ramon, 60
Tum Tiu, Francisco, 287(n14), 288(n14)
Turcios Lima, Luis, 180
Tuyuc, Rosalina, 300(n1), 305(n13). *See also* National Coordinator of Guatemalan Widows

Ubico, Jorge, 45
Unions, labor, 45, 50, 98, 175
United Fruit Company, 46–47
United Nations, 205
United Representation of the Guatemalan Opposition (RUOG), 205–206
United States, 271–272
  democratic reform and, 48
  1954 invasion, 39, 45–47
  Rigoberta's first visit, 196–197
  suppression of revolutionaries, 179
  See also Central Intelligence Agency
URNG. *See* Guatemalan National Revolutionary Union
Us Hernández, Bernardina, 166
Us Hernández, Reyes, 166
Us Imul, Juan, 287(n9)
Us Mejia, Juan, 287(n9)
Uspantán, xx(fig.), 3
  CUC in, 92–95
  described, 15–16, 19–20
  human rights organizations, 256–261
  indígena/ladino population in, 20–21
  reaction to *I, Rigoberta Menchú,* 261–264
  recollections of EGP, 113–116
  revolution, 43–44

Venezuela, 178–179
Vi, Baltazar, 117–118
Vi, Gaspar, 117–118
Vicente Menchú Foundation. *See* Rigoberta Menchú Foundation
Vicente Menchú Revolutionary Christians, 6, 170, 171, 197, 204
Victimhood, 244–245, 308(n20)
Vigilantes, 131, 141, 142–144, 148, 151
Violence
  accountability, 61
  against indígenas, 222
  Menchú-Tum feud, 32–33
  personal, 55–56
  "reconstructions of," 65–70
  Rigoberta's reaction to, 190–192
  study of, 273–274
  symbolic value, x–xi

Western highlands, 49–50, 286(n9)
Western Humanities Conference, 239
White, Richard, 242
Witchcraft, 121–122
Witness for Peace, 235–236
Wolf, Eric, 116
Women
  effect of Nobel award, 220
  reaction to Spanish embassy massacre, 87
  in revolutionary movement, 207

Xamán massacre, 269
Xejul, 67, 127
Xolá, Quiché department, 26, 131
Xoná, Gregorio, 60–61
Xoná Chomo, Pascuala, 55–56

Yat López, Juan, 61
Yúdice, George, 242
Yujá, Gregorio, 76
Yujá Pacay, Domingo, 60
Yujá Suc, Ambrosio, 60

Zapatista National Liberation Army, 169, 224, 272, 279–280,306(n10)
Zimmerman, Marc, 241
Zona Reina, 20, 255